Talking with
ROBERT
PENN
WARREN

Talking with
ROBERT
PENN
WARREN

Edited by
Floyd C. Watkins
John T. Hiers
Mary Louise Weaks

The University of Georgia Press
Athens and London

© 1990 by the University of Georgia Press
Athens, Georgia 30602

The paper in this book meets the guidelines for
permanence and durability of the Committee on
Production Guidelines for Book Longevity of the
Council on Library Resources

Printed in the United States of America

94 93 92 91 90   5 4 3 2 1

Library of Congress Cataloging in Publication Data

Warren, Robert Penn, 1905–89
Talking with Robert Penn Warren /edited by Floyd C.
Watkins, John T. Hiers, Mary Louise Weaks.
p.   cm.
Includes bibliographical references.
ISBN 0–8203–1219–3 (alk. paper.)—
ISBN 0–8203–1220–7 (pbk. : alk. paper)
1. Warren, Robert Penn. 1905–89—Interviews.
2. Authors, American—20th century—Interviews.
I. Watkins, Floyd C. II. Hiers, John T. III. Weaks,
Mary Louise. IV. Title.
PS 3545.A748Z478 1990
813'.52—dc20   89–20570
                              CIP

British Library Cataloging in Publication Data available.

Contents

Acknowledgments

The editors wish to acknowledge the publications in which the selections in this volume first appeared and those who have given permission for their use. Rights in all cases are reserved by the owner of the copyright.

"A Self-Interview" by Robert Penn Warren. From the *New York Herald Tribune Book Review*, October 11, 1953. Copyright I.H.T. Corporation. Reprinted by permission.

"Talk with Mr. Warren" by Harvey Breit. From *The New York Times Book Review*, June 25, 1950. Copyright © 1950 by The New York Times Company. Reprinted by permission.

"Fugitives' Reunion: Conversations at Vanderbilt." From *Fugitives' Reunion: Conversations at Vanderbilt, May 3-5, 1956*, edited by Rob Roy Purdy. Nashville: Vanderbilt University Press, 1959. Reprinted by permission of Vanderbilt University Press.

"Warren on the Art of Fiction" by Ralph Ellison and Eugene Walter. From *Writers at Work, Vol. I*, ed. Malcolm Cowley. Copyright © 1957, 1959, renewed © 1985, 1986 by The Paris Review, Inc. All rights reserved. Reprinted by permission of Viking Penguin, a division of Penguin Books USA, Inc.

"An Interview with Flannery O'Connor and Robert Penn Warren." From *The Vagabond*, 1960. Reprinted by courtesy of Vanderbilt University.

"A Conversation with Robert Penn Warren" by Frank Gado. From *First Person: Conversations on Writers and Writing.* Schenectady, N.Y.: Union College Press, 1973. Reprinted by permission of the author and Union College Press.

"Conversation: Eleanor Clark and Robert Penn Warren" by Roy Newquist. Reprinted by permission of Mr. Newquist.

"The Uses of History in Fiction" by C. Vann Woodward. From *The Southern Literary Journal* (Spring 1969). Copyright © The University of North Carolina Press. Reprinted by permission.

"An Interview in New Haven with Robert Penn Warren" by Richard Sale. From *Studies in the Novel* (1970). Reprinted by permission of the editor.

"Robert Penn Warren: An Interview" by Marshall Walker. From *Journal of American Studies,* vol. 8, no. 2 (1974). Reprinted by permission of Cambridge University Press and Mr. Walker.

"A Conversation with Robert Penn Warren" by Ruth Fisher. From *Four Quarters,* 1972. Copyright © 1972 by La Salle College. Reprinted by permission of *Four Quarters.*

"Speaking Freely" by Edwin Newman. Printed by permission of Mr. Newman.

"A Conversation with Robert Penn Warren" by Bill Moyers. Broadcast on WNET Thirteen, 1976. Copyright © 1976 by Educational Broadcasting Corporation. Printed by permission of Educational Broadcasting Corporation.

"Talk with Robert Penn Warren" by Benjamin DeMott. From *The New York Times Book Review,* January 9, 1977. Copyright © 1977 by The New York Times Company. Reprinted by permission.

"An Interview with Robert Penn Warren" by Peter Stitt. First published in *The Sewanee Review,* vol. 85 (1977). Copyright © 1977 by the University of the South. Reprinted by permission.

"A Conversation with Robert Penn Warren" by John Baker. From *Conversations with Writers*, vol. 1, edited by Richard Layman, Margaret M. Duggan, Glenda G. Fedricci, and Cara L. White. Copyright 1977 by Gale Research Company, Inc. Reprinted by permission of the publisher.

"The South: Distance and Change" by Louis D. Rubin, Jr. Reprinted by permission of Louisiana State University Press from *The American South: Portrait of a Culture*, edited by Louis D. Rubin, Jr. Copyright © 1980 by Louisiana State University Press.

"Reminiscences: A Conversation with Robert Penn Warren" by David Farrell. From *The Southern Review* (1980). Reprinted by permission of Mr. Farrell.

"The Oral Roots of Literature" by William C. Forrest and Cornelius Novelli. From *The Sewanee Review*, vol. 89 (1981). Copyright © 1981 by the University of the South. Reprinted by permission.

"Interview with Eleanor Clark and Robert Penn Warren." From *The New England Review*, vol. 1, no. 1 (1978). Reprinted by permission.

"A Dialogue with Robert Penn Warren on *Brother to Dragons*" by Floyd C. Watkins. From *The Southern Review*, vol. 16, no. 1 n.s. (1980). Reprinted by permission of Professor Watkins.

"Poetry as a Way of Life: An Interview with Robert Penn Warren" by David Farrell. From *The Georgia Review*, vol. 36, no. 2 (1982). By permission of *The Georgia Review* and Mr. Farrell.

"Of Bookish Men and the Fugitives" by Thomas L. Connelly. Reprinted by permission of Louisiana State University Press from *A Southern Renascence Man: Views of Robert Penn Warren*, edited by Walter B. Edgar. Copyright © 1984 by Louisiana State University Press.

"A Conversation with Robert Penn Warren" by Tom Vitale. From *Ontario Review* (Fall 1986/Winter 1987). Reprinted by permission.

Introduction

Perhaps in no literary genre is an author more completely and accurately himself or herself than in an interview. Every attribute of Robert Penn Warren—his folksiness, his wit, his honesty and openness—or, in short, the full man—is peculiarly adapted to the genre. Warren has almost nothing to hide, or he is so open that he does not care whether things are hidden or not.

Many of Warren's literary works are full of carefully crafted talk of his characters and personae. The flow of words is distinctive, often regional or ethnic in nature, variable from work to work, character to character, situation to situation. Talk in Warren's writing is as distinctive as voice is said to be in Faulkner's novels. Talk may be narrative, meditative, lyrical, oratorical, humorous, or whatever seems most appropriate at the moment.

Even before Warren had written much narrative prose, the metaphysical poems of the early period sounded like folk talk and stories. The poem "Original Sin: A Short Story," for example, sounds like the talk of a tale-teller at a bar or even on a whittler's bench: "The nightmare stumbles past, and you have heard / It fumble your door before it whispers and is gone: / It acts like the old hound that used to snuffle your door and is gone." Willie Proudfit's long story about his life, told to Percy Munn in Warren's first novel, *Night Rider*, signifies the major meaning and accomplishment of the work. Jack Burden, Willie Stark, and Cass Mastern fill *All the King's Men* with talk, which varies with the occasion and time as much as it does with the person. Jack Burden is a smart aleck and a journalist; Willie is a Southern political orator who knows how to talk to the people; Cass speaks or writes—whichever—with the rhetoric of a nineteenth-century Southern planter. Robert Penn Warren himself is both the author-mover and a character in that work of diverse genre *Brother to Dragons*, possibly Warren's greatest accomplishment. And *World Enough and Time* is replete with the early nineteenth-century talk of Jeremiah Beaumont. Some critics assume that Warren tells the story; others find an unnamed and little-characterized narrator who tells the story for him. So talk runs on in unusual variation throughout the many volumes of poetry and narrative and discourse in Warren's writings.

Warren has published in as many genres as any American writer of note. The Library of Congress's list of his published work is in fact little short of astonishing. With a few objectors, Warren is regarded as a truly great writer. Many have called him the greatest American poet, although Allen Tate regarded his criticism as his finest achievement.

For those who have read all his works and the criticism and scholarship about him, there are still surprises in his lectures, conversation, and talk. Warren's poetry, for example, is so often provincial and folkish and dialectal that it is surprising to encounter indications of the extent of his technical knowledge of special genres, techniques, and subjects of poetry in the works of great poets and in his own work. Some of the interviews collected for the first time in this volume illustrate the knowledge and care with which he has written for years on a single work, *Brother to Dragons*. William C. Forrest and Cornelius Novelli, furthermore, raise practical down-to-earth questions about literature and writing, to which Warren responds in a display of erudition worthy of Pound or Eliot.

One collector of a modern author's interviews regards that writer's talk as filled with "contradictions, self-promotion, and more than a little misleading information." Similarly, only the erudite Faulknerian can detect (most of the time) whether the reserved and shy Faulkner in *Faulkner in the University* is being purposefully deceitful to protect his privacy or shield his art or whether he is stating a truth about a work which no critic/scholar has ever discovered. Warren, on the other hand, seems so simple that his readers or listeners frequently overlook his complexity.

Warren is ever on the lookout for preciosity and inflation in his questioners. Yet every question by an interviewer in this volume, we believe, meets a polite and honest answer. Warren is modest, unassuming, like sandpaper textured rough enough to do the needed work and fine enough not to leave ugly scratches.

Often the creative mind and the critical mind cannot meet in the same head. Faulkner, for example, is often wonderfully self-explanatory and modest, but seldom if ever self-critical. T. S. Eliot once suggested that his criticism and his poetry came from the same workshop. In Warren's mind, there is very little separation of creation and commentary. Without reticence he can speak simultaneously from the point of view of creator-explainer, creator in the process, creator remembering his intentions (whether with fallacies or not), and critic who seems to be approaching a new work for the first time. From any or all of these perspectives, he seems to speak without reserve, reticence, or deceit. A few authors, perhaps notably Henry James, have attempted to lay their plans and processes completely open to the reader, but none, we believe, achieves the honesty, humor, bluntness, and charm of Robert Penn Warren.

Much of the talk in this book is about writing, but writing is such a comprehensive subject that Warren says as much about himself and his friends and contemporaries as has been said in any other book about Warren and his works. Strangely and paradoxically, the good manners and the gentle view of the world do not contradict—as one would expect—Warren's view of the complexity and imperfectibility, depravity, and evil of the world.

In manner Warren is aphoristic. He states truths that seem to belong to the moment and the point of the talk but at the same time seem to derive from enduring principles: "The past is always a rebuke to the present." "Get drunk prayerfully." What he said long ago seems to apply to the next lecture one is obligated to attend. "Every age had its jargon, every group. When the jargon runs away with the insight, that's no good. Sure, a lot of people think they have the key to the truth if they have a lingo. And a lot of modern criticism has run off into lingo—into academicism—the wrong kind of academicism."

Learned as Warren is about literature, its creation, and the criticism of it, he is still steeped in the technicalities so that it is hard for his listener or reader to believe that so much philosophy and practice of composition can be stated by a person who in the works can seem so folkish, so ordinary. It is as if Huckleberry Finn were proclaiming the critical truths of Aristotle or Derrida. The exactness of the weight and the faceting of a beautiful stone in jewelry seems at first thought not to be characteristic of Warren, but then he asserts, "The change of the weight of one syllable in a line can make a vast difference." Paradoxically, that syllable may be in a line of Warren's metaphysical and philosophical verse or in backwoods and ribald poetry like that in his first frontier and narrative poem, "The Ballad of Billie Potts." The complexity of the mind of the artist is as apparent in the unconscious as it is in careful planning. It is hard to imagine another writer saying so honestly as Warren, "Things exist in you without your knowing it."

The ultimate meanings and philosophies of Warren are also more easily and fully apparent in the interviews than in his artistic works or in his criticism. In a discussion on the perfectibility of man, Warren makes as good a statement as he ever has about ultimate meanings. He *enacts* the imperfectibility of man in *Brother to Dragons*, "Homage to Emerson," "Billie Potts," and *All the King's Men*. The interviews *explain* how man, as Willie Stark says, is born in the stink of the didie and passes to the stench of the shroud.

So Warren may be known personally and more fully in his interviews than in anything else he has presented for the public view. Gradually a full portrait of a whole and kindly man emerges from these conversations. Warren is an asserter of principles, never of himself. He has an abhorrence of the phony, but he lets the false reveal itself, as it nearly always does. He praises the unassuming and the genuine. He remains a Southern personality though he is no longer a citizen of the South. He is an earnest seeker for truth and for God, but he suspects that the search may be greater than the ultimate discovery.

In these interviews Warren talks about the South, about his own works, about ways of writing and reading literature, about history and the past, other writers, philosophical and current issues, the primacy of poetry. He speculates tentatively on who Americans are, what they have been, and where they may be going. A special concern is technological change and the reactions to it in a world bereft of historical continuity. Indeed, he talks about the things one would expect from reading his fiction and poetry and criticism.

The art of talk is in Warren's bones, a legacy of his heritage which not merely preserved but also thrived on an oral tradition. On the casual level, Warren's talk is a mode of neighborliness, but it rises from Melvillean humor to Melvillean or Miltonic profundity to discuss historical continuity and a sense of community or the lack of it. Warren's tone and wisdom indicate much about the fundamental nature and convictions of the critic, the artist, and the person. In a different way from his planned and written works, his talk reveals what a great mind and a good man thinks of our daily world.

F.C.W.
J.T.H.
M.L.W.

A Note on the Texts

We have adopted one format for all interviews. At times we have silently made minor changes, especially in punctuation. Several obvious transcriber's errors called for editing. We have occasionally cut to avoid redundancies. Moreover, in the case of the conversations in which there are several participants, we have cut ruthlessly to eliminate all talkers but Warren and those questions and comments necessary for context. For various reasons we have omitted a few interviews in their entirety.

The chronological arrangement of these pieces is imperfect. The first serves well as Warren's own introduction to the collection. Thereafter, interviews are arranged by date of interview or by date of publication if no interview date was given.

A Self-Interview

This short sketch first appeared in the New York Herald Tribune Book Review *on October 11, 1953, shortly after the publication of* Brother to Dragons. *It resembles an autobiography as much as anything that Warren has written, and for that reason is placed first, out of chronological order.*

To begin at the beginning, I was born at 7 A.M., April 24, 1905, in Guthrie, in southern Kentucky, a town which has had about the same number of inhabitants—1,500, more or less—ever since I can remember.

The country around, part of the Cumberland Valley, is a mixed country, fine rolling farmland breaking here and there into barrens, but with nice woodlands and plenty of water, a country well adapted to the proper pursuits of boyhood. The streams seem somewhat shrunken now and the woodlands denuded of their shadowy romance, but certain spots there and farther west, where I used to spend my summers on my grandfather's farm, are among my most vivid recollections.

I recollect that grandfather [1] very vividly, too—already an old man when I knew him, a Confederate veteran, a captain of cavalry who had ridden with Forrest, given to discussing the campaigns of Napoleon and, as well, of the immortal Nathan Bedford and to quoting bits of Byron and Scott and compositions like "The Turk Lay in the Guarded Tent." His daughters used to say that he was "visionary," by which they meant he was not practical. No doubt, in their sense, they were right. But in quite another sense, he was, I suppose, "visionary" to me, too, looming much larger than life, the living symbol of the wild action and romance of the past. He was, whatever his own small part in great events may have been, "history." And I liked history. That was what my own father usually selected when he read aloud to his children.

I went to school in Guthrie and at Clarksville, Tennessee, and then, by great good fortune, to Vanderbilt University. For this was the time of the Fugitives at Vanderbilt, a group of poets and arguers—including John Crowe Ransom, Donald Davidson, Allen Tate, Merrill Moore—and I imagine that more of my education came from those sessions than from the classroom. But aside from the Fugitives, writing poetry was almost epidemic at the university, and even an all-Southern center on the football team did some very creditable lyrics of a Housmanesque wistfulness.

After Vanderbilt, graduate work at the University of California, Yale and Oxford (Rhodes Scholar). During those years I had been publishing a good deal of poetry in *The New Republic* and similar magazines, and in my last year at Oxford, at the invitation of Paul Rosenfeld, I did a novelette for *The American Caravan*. It is called *Prime Leaf*.

It is now some six and a half novels (two unpublished and one unfinished) and a collection of short stories later. But the poetry has gone along with the fiction, and I suppose that my last book, *Brother to Dragons*, is a kind of hybrid. It even started out to be a novel, and though it is in verse and is a poem, it has a complicated narrative and involves many fictional problems.

I like to write in the morning. I try never to depend on

later revision: don't leave a page until you have it as near what you want as you can make it that day. I like to write in foreign countries, where the language is not your own, and you are forced into yourself in a special way. I like to travel and especially like Italy. I like swimming, walking in the country, arguing, and admiring my six-week-old daughter.

Talk with Mr. Warren

▬▬▬

The New York Times Book Review *published this interview and a review of* World Enough and Time *in its June 25, 1950, issue. Harvey Breit, one of the editors of the* Book Review, *talked with Warren in a bar of a New York hotel. As Warren drank iced tea, Breit opened the conversation with a comment on William Faulkner.*

WARREN: Well, criticism missed him. There was a fashionable liberalism—as opposed to the real thing—and it wrote Faulkner off as politically bad, and a whole generation missed him. And now you meet them—people with no background for him and yet the furious impact he makes on them is a marvel. There's been a whole lag on Faulkner, based on a too-political criticism.

. . . They don't even get the politics in Faulkner, . . . let alone the other—the tonality, the rhythms, the texture. They make an even more horrendous error than that; they insist on a political interpretation and then misunderstand the doctrine!

HARVEY BREIT: *One knew that Mr. Warren would teach Faulkner (and Coleridge and Blake, two of his favored moderns) scrupulously, but what with the success of* All the King's Men *in all its aspects—as novel, play, and film—and of the new novel (a Literary Guild selection), would Mr. Warren teach again?*

WARREN: I intend to teach. . . . I'm on leave this fall. I've been teaching sort of on a two-fourths basis. . . . There are very fundamental compensations in teaching if you're in the right kind of place and have the right kind of students.

I think the academic process, although on one side it has its comic aspects, on the other, produces truly profound and humanistic people who serve as a sort of buffer against the jittery fashionable kind of thing. A university has the failures and defects of institutions, just like government or the family or anything else. But I do think it gives certain perspectives in its better reaches that you'd not get if you were outside. The question doesn't come up in teaching, but it does in writing—whether it is a worthwhile activity: Is it really something to do? Is it a serious thing for a grown-up man to do? That sort of questioning today blanks out a lot of fellows.

BREIT: *Mr. Warren was going to keep on writing?*

WARREN: Yup. . . . I've got my plans. I don't know what's going to come of them. I generally carry a couple of novels around in me. I'm also trying to revise the verse play of *All the King's Men* for publication, and I'm at work on a long poem, based on an episode in American history, which may be a verse play or a poem of voices.[2] I have to carry things around for so long that they're all overlapping.

BREIT: *Would Mr. Warren "unlap" for a moment and talk about the new verse play?*

WARREN: It has to do with two sons of Charles Lewis, who was related to Meriwether and married to Thomas Jefferson's sister. The sons became involved in a perverse, violent, and hideous situation, out west in Kentucky. One Lewis opened up the West, and two Lewises were devoured by it.

Jefferson was a kind of foster father to Lewis; he will be the chorus of the piece. The great libertarian founder of our country will have to face this terrible thing in his own blood. What I've written are just fragments. I haven't solved the basic style for it yet. But I hope to get things assembled and then I will try to make the big push.

Fugitives' Reunion: Conversations at Vanderbilt

In May 1956 many of the Fugitives (Warren, John Crowe Ransom, Allen Tate, and Donald Davidson were the most prominent) met at Vanderbilt University for three days of talk, conferences, and readings. Warren's talk during these days is here extracted from the book Fugitives' Reunion _(1959). A major topic of the first session was the question of why the group had "lost the epic in poetry."_

JOHN CROWE RANSOM: Well, I would think Mr. Warren ought to speak to that question. Now I know that . . . before he published the long poem _Brother to Dragons_ he spoke of why he found that that was not to be represented best in the form of prose fiction, that it would take the poem. I don't think he quite conceived it as an epic, but I would like very much to hear what went through his mind, what he thought of.

WARREN: It never crossed my mind I was trying to write an epic, I'll say that. [_Laughter and murmurs_]

WILLIAM Y. ELLIOTT: And he didn't write one.

WARREN: Well, if I had, it would have been by inadvertence.

.   .   .   .

ELLIOTT: And this is the point I am really trying to make: the poets are really diagnosticians and not creators. And is it possible that our times are so completely out of joint that that's the case?

WARREN: Bill, I don't accept your distinction.

ELLIOTT: Well, let's see why not.

WARREN: I think you're just making it awfully easy for yourself, the way I look at it.

ELLIOTT: Well, I'm making it hard for you. [*Laughter*] It would have been by inadvertence, I believe, your handling—

WARREN: I feel no compulsion. It just doesn't interest me. [*Murmurs*] Definitely, I don't feel any compulsion to try to write a poem. [*Amidst general murmur*] And you don't worry about whether you're going to call it an epic or "X."

ELLIOTT: What we started out—

WARREN: You try to say something in the best way you can.

ELLIOTT: Let me put it this way—

WARREN: Your concern isn't there, I think, with trying to write. And what I was quarreling about was the distinction between diagnostics and creation, because *The Waste Land* as a diagnostic poem is as much a creation to me as, well, say, a poem like—what? *Lycidas?* Is that one of the better creative poems?

ELLIOTT: That's right; it's a creative poem.

ALLEN TATE: You don't think *The Waste Land* is—

ELLIOTT: I don't think *Samson Agonistes* is a creative poem.

WARREN: I don't see the distinction, you see. I think they are both at the same level, not in value, necessarily. Though I would be willing to argue that on another occasion, perhaps. But they belong to the same kind of— *Lycidas* is as much a diagnostic poem, a critical poem, as it is a creative poem.

ELLIOTT: Well, I'm just trying to untangle something—

WARREN: And it's a real wrangle with the world at large. And

more of a wrangle—more explicitly a wrangle than any of
this is.

. . . .

TATE: . . . It was through Baudelaire that I began to investigate
the Symbolists under the suggestion of some of the early
writings of Ezra Pound rather than T. S. Eliot.

WARREN: That was in '23, wasn't it?

TATE: Yes.

WARREN: If I remember correctly, that's when I began to read
them. Because you and Bill started me reading them—

LOUIS D. RUBIN: How did you get on to Pound?

TATE: Well, I don't know. I had seen him in *The Little Review*
and in *Poetry* magazine and various others—the *Dial*, which
began about 1920.

WARREN: I don't remember a time when Pound wasn't read
around here.

TATE: The first time we knew each other, which was in 1921—

WARREN: Yes, fall of '21.

TATE: —well, you'd already read Pound, and so had I.

WARREN: Well, I read Pound as a freshman, didn't I? That's
'21–'22. And I guess it was the next year, it was '22 or '23, I
guess, Baudelaire and some other French poets.

TATE: When we were rooming together, particularly, we used
to talk about him.

WARREN: That was in '22–'23.

TATE: But, Red, I wouldn't think that the Symbolist influence
accounted for very much in anything that this group wrote.
It was somewhere in the background; we were certainly not
Symbolist poets. And I think that some of the critics who
have tried to place us in that historical perspective are wrong
about it.

WARREN: Well, I think you are right about that. I don't think
it counted in that sense—

TATE: No.

WARREN: —I mean I remember—I think in a very indirect way
you'd count it.

TATE: Yes.

WARREN: At least for some people. As far as state of mind was concerned about poetry, it was not in terms of direct use of a method. I mean Baudelaire had a very definite effect on some people, say, the line, anyway—

TATE: Yes, on me, too.

WARREN: Two or three of us, anyway. I think John passed by without—

TATE: John by-passed those, yes. [*Laughter*]

RANSOM: Well, I was two years in France fighting the battle in a rear area, instructing in French matériel, and several nice young ladies introduced me to the poetry of the nineteenth century of France, and I came back—

WARREN: I was saying something quite different from that. [*Laughter*]

RANSOM: —and I came back with a lot of volumes, and I know that the French Symbolists attracted and perplexed me a great deal. I may not have talked about them, but they were in my consciousness after 1919. Very decidedly.

WARREN: Well, I wasn't thinking of your knowledge of them, or awareness of them. I was thinking simply, well, something in relation to your own poetry.

RANSOM: Well, I think the—

WARREN: And your own state of mind, temperament, as I read it.

RANSOM: They had a great gift of phrasing, and they had a great boldness of metaphor. And I felt sure that that belonged some way or other in verse; I don't remember any talk of it, but—

WARREN: I remember your talking about it, not only once but on several occasions. But I wasn't thinking of awareness of it in that sense, but something quite different: just a temperamental affinity which I never detected between your work—

TATE: Same time, Red, you know what Edmund Wilson has called the "conversational ironic" thing—

WARREN: Yes.

TATE: Now, it seems to me that John developed something

of his own which was similar to that but not in the least influenced by it.

WARREN: It was similar, but it's not based on it; it's not influenced by it.

TATE: No, not at all. No.

WARREN: And I remember at that time that John introduced me to Hardy. And I was struck very early with an affinity there—

TATE: Yes.

WARREN: —again no imitation, no modeling, but an affinity of some kind there which I sensed right away. This has no reference to the topic, but I happen to have an anecdote about John's first book of poems. I encountered in California some years ago a man named McClure, who edits the paper at Santa Monica. He owns and edits that paper. Well, he was in France at the same time that John was as a soldier. And when I was living out there, he wrote me a note—I had never met him or knew anything about him— and said, "I am a friend of an old friend of yours. Won't you come to dinner?" So I went to dinner at his house and had a very pleasant evening. And he said that he was walking down the street with John Ransom, who was a good soldierly companion of his during that period, and they went to get the mail at the battery mail distribution. And they got a few letters, and John got a little package. And he opened the little package, and there were two copies of *Poems About God* in it. And he said John hadn't seen the book before, and he opened it and inspected it with composure, and then turned to McClure and said, "I'd like to give you a copy of this." [*Laughter*] And McClure treasured this copy; and over the years, he said, along with other later writings of John's, followed his career with delight.

. . . .

TATE: I remember Curry [3] in those days—well, of course, he was a bachelor and I think perhaps he was the last one of our teachers, you see, to get married—he was enormously hospitable to all the younger people. I remember Red and I used to practically live in his room there and—

WARREN: Borrow his typewriter.

TATE: —we'd borrow his typewriter. And he had infinite patience with us.

RANSOM: A very good talker.

TATE: Excellent talker.

ELLIOTT: Wonderful man, always with his pipe, smoke-curing our learning.

TATE: Yes.

WARREN: There's one factor, I think—I don't know how to assess it, really, but in a small and close provincial college, anybody who's there who has quality on the faculty stands out like a diamond on a piece of black velvet, you see. I mean if you had five able students of philosophy on the faculty, it would sort of cancel out, in a way. It ceases to be something; it just becomes then a convenience for you for passing a course or fulfilling the requirements. And the limitations made a kind of personal focus on individuals and on ideas; I remember this quite distinctly, since some of these people represented the great world of ideas and the great world of geography, of wider horizons, in a very special way which is no longer true in educational institutions, I suppose. So once given, by accident, certain persons on the faculty, their impact is much greater than it would be otherwise.

Now, the other night I was at dinner at Northrop's [4] house in New Haven. An eminent professor of law was there, and he and Northrop were talking about big world universities and certain small colleges. And they both had made surveys and had been around a lot, and this professor of law had actually made trips around looking at small colleges. It started by Northrop saying that when you had very large departments of philosophy, or other large departments where there were a lot of high-powered people, the students didn't learn how to think, because they didn't follow one man closely enough to see how his mind worked, for better or for worse, on a problem. They only took his view and put it down as "that's what he thinks"; they didn't follow the process, because they were never with him enough. If you had five different courses in philosophy with five different people—and all of them splendid, let us say, or not splendid, or something, but they are different— you'd never learn how one of them thought at all. You never followed his thinking.

TATE: Red, you remember—

WARREN: And they had no sense of the process of his mind— Excuse me [to Tate]. Northrop was saying, well, something is lost by the accumulation of a lot of really first-rate people under one academic roof. It becomes a cafeteria of intellects, then, rather than a good square meal where you follow through the way a few people think or feel, and have a model to accept or reject.

TATE: I think there were three men like that at Vanderbilt in our time: John, Tolman,[5] and Sanborn.[6] And we had them right through from the beginning. We weren't shopping around.

ELLIOTT: We took all the courses that they offered—

DONALD DAVIDSON: And I'd like to add, too, that we had very easy personal access to them, at any time—

WARREN: That's right, and all the personal relations. . . . One thing that strikes me in recollection, now: a few years after I left Vanderbilt, and people began to refer to those people as a unit, you see, as if there were a church or an orthodoxy; and I was so shocked by that—

TATE: I was, too; I had no idea—

WARREN: —because I was so aware of the differences of temperament, and the differences of opinions, you see, in conversation—the Fugitive meetings were outside—but the notion of a unity had just never occurred to me, really, except that the unity was just purely a unity of friendship and common background.

.   .   .   .

WARREN: . . . Greatness is not a criterion—a profitable criterion—of poetry; that what you are concerned with is a sense of a contact with reality. And it's maybe a pinpoint touch or a whole palm of a hand laid, or something; but the important thing is the shock of this contact: a lot of current can come through a small wire. And there you are up against, well, big subjects and little subjects. It's just so it's a real subject, and, of course, you've got this word to deal with; you've got to have something that will actually create human heat in that contact. Well, language can in certain ways, because language drags the bottom of somebody into being, in one way or another, directly or indirectly. But if I had to say what I would try to hunt for in a poem—would hunt for in a poem, or would expect from a poem that I would call a poem—it would be some kind of a vital image, a vital and evaluating image, of vitality. That's a different thing from the vitality you observe or experience. It's an image of it, but it has the vital quality—it's a reflection of that vital quality, rather than a passing reflection, but it has its own kind of assurance, own kind of life, by the way it's built. And when you get around to talking about the scale, it's not the most important topic. It is an important topic, but it's something that comes in very late in the game.

Now, I think we started last night with that, and it's really not our province to discuss that, except in the realm of theory—late in the game. That is, I see no difference in the degree of reality between, say, "Janet Waking" and *The Dynasts*. One's a little poem, a short poem, and one's a big side-of-beef of a poem; but the significance of one can be as great as that of the other in the sense of your contact; the stab, the flash, the— I'm not arguing for short poems, now, mind you; I'm not doing a Poe thing about that,[7] and the scale may be necessary in certain things to get the sense of reality. But there's no virtue or defect in the size one way or the other. The question is: Where do you get that image, that speaking image, the walking statue, and how would we interpret that? I would interpret it myself, but it would bring on, of course, a lot of wrangling and hassling about individual poems and a lot of other things. I'm not interested in getting anything said here except that— But when this problem of scale comes in early, I always begin to lose my bearings; I have to go back and start over again and try to see what it's about for myself—I don't mean writing, but I mean reading. It's that stab of some kind, early; that's the important thing for me in the sense of an image that makes that thing available to you indefinitely, so you can go back to it, can always find that peephole on the other world, you see—that moment of contact with the . . . well, with reality, or realness, or something.

. . . .

TATE: . . . The Fugitives' objective was the act of each individual poet trying to write the best poetry possible. I'm afraid we're getting highfalutin again. I just don't— May I speak a little to this point, John, just to something that Red said? It seems to me this test of reality is the test by which we determine whether a given work is poetry or not; and the scale is of importance only after we decide that question, because if we dissolve the poetry into the subject matter, then I think that in the long run—

WARREN: We have a document.

TATE: —we have a document; and what we call the literary tradition is dissolved into its historical flux again. Now take— If I may refer to one of your poems, "Janet Waking" or "Bells for John Whiteside's Daughter"—in both of those poems there is a very intense reality which exists in the language, created in the language. That same thing happens in *The Divine Comedy* throughout, not uniformly, but by and large throughout all the hundred cantos. Now, we've got there not the difference of reality but a difference of scale. The scale is important only after we decide that difference of reality, or discern that reality. Otherwise we lose the whole conception of literature. It's all gone.

WARREN: May I break in here for a moment? Two things. I would string along on what Allen has said about the prior question: it's a question of its existence out of the poem. That's really what I was fumbling at saying. And the other things follow. Another thing: poetry is an exploration; the process of writing is an exploration. You may dimly envisage what a poem will be when you start it, but only as you wrangle through the process do you know your own meanings. In one way, it's a way of knowing what kind of poem you can write. And in finding that you find out yourself—I mean a lot about yourself. I don't mean in the way Merrill's [Moore] talking about: I mean in the sense of what you can make available, poetically, is clearly something that refers to all of your living in very indirect and complicated ways. But you know more about yourself, not in a psychoanalytic way, but in another way of having dealt with yourself in a process. The poem is a way of knowing what kind of a person you can be, getting your reality shaped a little bit better. And it's a way of living, and not a parlor trick even in its most modest reaches; I mean, the most modest kind of effort that we make is a way of living. And I think Bill has something important when he insists that there is such a thing as a poetic condition, which is the willingness to approach a poem in that spirit, rather than in the spirit of a performer, when you get down to the business of writing a poem, or even thinking about poetry.

TATE: In that sense a man is a poet all the time.

WARREN: All the time, insofar as he brings that spirit into his reading or thinking about poetry or about other things as well. It's a tentative spirit, and a kind of—well, I don't know exactly what's the word, except a lack of dogmatism in dealing with your own responses and your own ideas as they come along, a certain kind of freedom and lack of dogmatism under some notion of a shaping process. The other thing I had to say is more along what Merrill said. I believe that what Merrill, quite properly—now this is again not controversial, but just to make distinction—what Merrill has been talking about deals with the psychology of the process of writing and not with a literary question at all, it seems to me; that it's a psychological interest that has no bearing on the good poem or the bad poem as such.

ELLIOTT: Yes, that was what I—

WARREN: The bad poem or the good poem could be equally

interesting in terms of the way the mind works in creating it, or in the stuff that may call the attention of any of us to the poet himself, or to Merrill Moore—what his psychic history has been. But I can see, I can imagine—this is guess-work, of course—no point-to-point equation between the psychological interest such a process would have from one case to another and the quality of the work that came out of it. That is, the clinicism of it, the clinical interest, would have no relation to the poetic value, necessarily; in fact, it might work the other way.

CLEANTH BROOKS: If I may break in for a moment with an illustration: Hulme makes a point that Rider Haggard's *She* is almost as interesting to the psychologist as—

ANDREW NELSON LYTLE: More so.

BROOKS: —Melville's *Moby-Dick*, or perhaps more so.

LYTLE: More so. Yes. May I say something here, in extension to this, or support of it? Red, in this self-exploration, it's both intuitive and deliberate, isn't it? And you may start out with what you think is a subject—say, a subject matter larger than you really end up with, or you can reverse the thing.

WARREN: Yes, you've got to be willing to always shut your eyes and then deal the cards. Just don't look yet.

LYTLE: That's right. And you know Lubbock in *The Craft of Fiction* makes the point that the form, really, uses up all the subject, and the subject all of the form in the ideal situation—

WARREN: In heaven, in heaven.

LYTLE: —in heaven, you see—

TATE: You approach that—

LYTLE: —but you have to approximate that kind of thing. . . . But in this self-exploration there is one danger: if the poet limits it to too close a self-exploration, then it becomes a kind of narcissistic thing, and you digress, you see.

WARREN: Oh, yes—excuse me. You can't think you are interest-ing while you are doing it.

LYTLE: No, that's right.

WARREN: You've got to think of something else.

LYTLE: Don't you really have to raise against the discrete objects the word, you see?

WARREN: Yes, your self is not involved.

LYTLE: No, that's right.

WARREN: But when you get through you find out that you ate that, too.

. . . .

RANSOM: Couldn't we say that he [the poet] creates a new experience—that's empirical—a new happiness. He finds, he compounds experiences, or he takes, he's on the verge, he feels an experience; and he stays with it until he realizes the experience. He does it over and over. Other poets akin to him do the same thing. And presently the philosophers will come along, and they are not creative, and they have no existence until the creative people have refined and perfected types of experience. But evidently there is a universal, in the Aristotelian sense, within those—

TATE: Yes.

RANSOM: —experiences, and the wise philosopher can find them out.

TATE: I would have to agree with that. I think that is right.

RANSOM: But that is distinct from the work that the poet does.

WARREN: But you might say their availability depends on their —let's use this word *depend* a little bit—that their availability depends upon that faculty of the universal; but he is not working in those terms. He's working in quite different terms, and probably even in terms of ideas, ultimately. When Wordsworth was getting along in years, there's a tale I think Crabb Robinson gives, of a clergyman—whose name I think was Miller—calling on him, very reverentially, and telling him while they were taking a walk one morning, "Mr. Wordsworth, I want to tell you how much I admire your poems for their fine morality." And that stumped Wordsworth for a moment; and then he said, "I don't value them for that. I value them for the new view they gave of the world." [8]

RANSOM: Not bad.

WARREN: That's almost the phrasing, not quite. But that's the sense of it—unless I've very badly forgotten the episode—which I think is pretty good. Wordsworth knew what he was up to, I guess.

.   .   .   .

WARREN: May I nag this communication business again, just a little bit? If a thing is made right, it's going to be available to a lot of people—if it's made right. But you can't make it right by thinking of those people.

LYTLE: That's right, that's right.

WARREN: You see what I'm getting at. I think you are trying to find the principles of creating that object somehow, out of what? I mean, you are bound to be in there somehow; but you cannot take it from the side of the communications. It's going to communicate: you create the thing, and there it sits on the mantelpiece, or wherever it is—

LYTLE: Red, that's what I meant when I said—

WARREN: —and then everybody can look at it. And if it's made right, it's going to signify, so that we can all look at it.

ALFRED STARR: Well, Red, you are talking—

WARREN: It'll make us all feel something significant, big or little. But what you have to keep your mind on is making that "thing." And making it significant to me would not make it significant to somebody else. Working at the object is finding the laws of that object that you are working with.

LYTLE: Yes. If you think of anything outside of the thing that you are doing, you are lost. You can't do it; you'll never do it.

WARREN: It's all right to think about whether it's going to be in it or not. [Laughter] But that doesn't matter. You see what you get.

.   .   .   .

WARREN: I can only speak of what it signified for me—what Agrarianism signified for me. And of late years I have tried to give it some thought, and I must confess that my mind tended to shut up on the subject for about ten years. It seemed irrelevant at one stage to what I was thinking and feeling, except in a sentimental way—I mean at the level of what these things signify; I ceased to think about it during the war years. Before we got in the last war, just before it and several years after, there was the period of unmasking of blank power everywhere. And you felt that all your work was irrelevant to this unmasking of this brute force in the world—that the de-humanizing forces had won. And you had no more relevance in such discussions as we used to have, or are having this morning, except a sort of quarreling with people over the third highball.

Well, as I remember the thing as it came to me, there were several appeals in it. It hit me at an age when I was first away from this part of the country for any period of time, having lived in California two years, and a year in New Haven in the Yale Graduate School, and then in Oxford. And I had broken out of the kind of life I was accustomed to in that part of the world I knew. And there was a sentimental appeal for me in this. It happened to coincide with my first attempt, my first story about Southern life—a novelette which I was writing at that time at Oxford. And it had coincided, a little earlier that is, with a book on John Brown. But this book led to fiction—that's what the Brown was: a step toward fiction. It was a sentimental appeal and an attempt to relive something—to recapture, to reassess. This was not thought out; it was just what happened in a sort of an instinctive way. And that tied in with some perfectly explicit speculations, in conversation with friends, such as Cleanth at Oxford—and, I must say, this topic would never appeal very much to anybody in California.

But the question of—well, there are two questions: one, the sense of the disintegration of the notion of the individual in that society we're living in—it's a common notion, we all know—and the relation of that to democracy. It's the machine of power in this so-called democratic state; the machines disintegrate individuals, so you have no individual sense of responsibility and no awareness that the individual has a past and a place. He's simply the voting machine; he's everything you pull the lever on if there's any voting at all. And that notion got fused with your own personal sentiments and sentimentalities and your personal pieties and your images of place and people that belong to your own earlier life. And the Confederate element was a pious element, or a great story—a heroic story—a parade of personalities who are also images for these individual values. They were images for it for me, I'm sure, rather than images for a theory of society which had belonged to the South before the war. They became images for that only because they are lost. There was a pretty tough practical guide involved in that; they were out to make power, and money interested them. They can only become images for this other thing insofar as they could not participate later on in their version of a gilded age, probably. I'm not being simple; I mean this is an overstatement that I'm making. There were some correctives in Southern society as a matter of preventing that—the excesses of the seventies, eighties, and nineties, and so forth, and some that we enjoy now, perhaps. But as to how these elements related in their personal appeal to me? Now, I don't know how much that situation would be shared by others; but I was no economist and didn't fancy myself as one. But for me it was a protest—echoing Frank here—against certain things: against a kind of dehumanizing and disintegrative effect on your notion of what an individual person could be in the sense of a loss of your role in society. You would take it a loss that you had no place in that world.

Well, later on I began to read people like Bertrand Russell, during that time—about their idea of how the individual was affected by the state: in the power state he lost existence, disappeared, was a cipher. All of that was involved. And your simpler world is something I think is always necessary —not a golden age, but the past imaginatively conceived and historically conceived in the strictest readings of the researchers. The past is always a rebuke to the present; it's bound to be, one way or another: it's your great rebuke.

It's a better rebuke than any dream of the future. It's a better rebuke because you can see what some of the costs were, what frail virtues were achieved in the past by frail men. And it's there, and you can see it, and see what it cost them, and how they had to go at it. And that is a much better rebuke than any dream of a golden age to come, because historians will correct, and imagination will correct, any notion of a simplistic and, well, childish notion of a golden age. The drama of the past that corrects us is the drama of our struggles to be human, or our struggles to define the values of our forebears in the face of their difficulties.

DOROTHY BETHURUM: It's also encouragement.

WARREN: It's encouragement.

BETHURUM: But the thing that impresses me is that I can't see that it isn't always possible in any period under any circumstances to live the life of aristocratic humanism. I feel very strongly all these things, but I think that the Agrarian movement was too pessimistic, was too unhappy about the future.

. . . .

WARREN: I thought we were trying to find—insofar as we were being political—a rational basis for a democracy. That, I thought, was what we were up to.

FRANK LAWRENCE OWSLEY: I agree with that.

TATE: Yes, I do too.

WARREN: And not to try to enter into competition of whether it was five slaves or five hundred slaves. In fact, that question was relevant only as an image—which Faulkner has now made available even to Frenchmen—for something else, for the crime against the human that we were expiating in our history. And I think that the word *aristocratic* used in a Jeffersonian sense is fine; but that was my notion—that aspect of it at that time. We were trying to find a notion of democracy which would make it possible for people to be people and not be bosses, or exploiters, or anything else of other people, but to have a community of people, rather than a community of something else. And Bill Elliott years ago, I mean at Oxford, was I think the first person who ever called my attention—when I first met him, our first meeting in a college there; which one it was I forget; Balliol, I guess it was—

ELLIOTT: Balliol.

WARREN: —it was your place; where you were staying that time you were on a visit. Well, anyway, he used to say that the great problem of democracy is a problem of responsible leadership. And he developed that and went on to the question of the role of the individual. I remember the conversation distinctly. And that was in no relation to Agrarianism; but this thing, to me, started something that tied right into that when we began to talk about and write about the Agrarians.

.   .   .   .

WARREN: Last night, Charlie Moss [Executive Editor of the *Nashville Banner;* Vanderbilt '24.] and I were talking, after you all had left his house. He said, talking about Agrarianism, "The question of civilizing and making progress amounts to a moral progress, or civilizing progress, and is a matter always of a fifth column in a society." And the effect is slow; if we had any function, we were a fifth column. We couldn't step out and take over the powers of the state. Poetry is a fifth column—

ELLIOTT: That's right.

WARREN: —in the same way. Universities should be fifth columns, but usually aren't.

WARREN: Randall, may I lower the tone of the conversation? [*Laughter*]

[RANDALL] STEWART: Yes, you certainly may.

WARREN: Not quite to the smoking-car level, but a story occurs to me. It's a little indecorous, but we're among friends and all of that. There was a sociological survey made several years ago I saw a news account of: of juvenile delinquency among young girls, girls in New York City. And they had many thousands interviewed, and asked them why they did it. And there were about seven or eight hundred said, "My mother doesn't like me," and about two thousand of them said, "My father doesn't like me"—Merrill probably can give you the proportion of these things—and another seventeen hundred said, "Well, they quarrel at night, and I have to go outdoors to keep from hearing their quarrels," and "I don't like my baby brother," and one thing and another. This got down to four thousand, nine hundred and ninety-nine of them. And then they had one more little girl to talk to—and they asked her why she did it, and she said, "I likes it." [*Laughter*] Well, I think that's what the Rockefeller Foundation's [9] going to find out— [*Laughter*] We haven't got any alibis.

Warren on the
Art of Fiction

This interview by Ralph Ellison and Eugene Walter first appeared in the Paris Review *in 1957 and was later published in* Writers at Work: The Paris Review Interviews, *edited by Malcolm Cowley (1958). The text here is from the original uncut transcript and is the first to identify the interviewers. The interview took place in Ellison's apartment at the American Academy in Rome—in the fall or winter of 1956, as Walter remembers.*

RALPH ELLISON: First, if you're agreeable, Mr. Warren, a few biographical details just to get you "placed." I believe you were a Rhodes Scholar . . .

WARREN: Yes, from Kentucky.

ELLISON: University of Kentucky?

WARREN: No. I attended Vanderbilt. But I was Rhodes Scholar from Kentucky.

ELLISON: Were you writing then?

WARREN: As I am now, trying to.

ELLISON: Did you start writing in college?

WARREN: I had no interest in writing when I went to college. I was interested in reading . . . oh, poetry and standard novels, you know . . . my ambitions were purely scientific, but I got cured of that fast by bad instruction in freshman chemistry and good instruction in freshman English.

EUGENE WALTER: What were the works that were especially meaningful for you? What books were—well, doors opening?

WARREN: Well, several things come right away to mind. First of all when I was six years old, "Horatius at the Bridge" I thought was pretty grand.

WALTER: And others?

WARREN: Yes, "How They Brought the Good News from Aix to Ghent"[10] (at about the age of nine). I thought it was pretty nearly the height of human achievement. I didn't know whether I was impressed by riding a horse that fast or writing the poem. I couldn't distinguish between the two, but I knew there was something pretty fine going on . . . Then *Lycidas*.

ELLISON: At what age were you then?

WARREN: Oh, thirteen, something like that. By that time I knew it wasn't what was happening in the poem that was important—it was the poem. I had crossed the line.

WALTER: An important frontier, that. What about prose works?

WARREN: Then I discovered Buckle's *History of Civilization*. Did you ever read Buckle?

WALTER: Of course, and Motley's *Rise of the Dutch Republic*. Most Southern bookshelves contain that.

WARREN: . . . And Prescott . . . and *The Oregon Trail* is always hovering around there somewhere. Thing that interested me about Buckle was that he had the one big answer to everything: *geography*. History is all explained by geography. I read Buckle and then I could explain everything. It gave me quite a hold over the other kids, they hadn't read Buckle. I had the answer to everything. Buckle was my Marx. That is, he gave you one answer to everything, and the same dead-sure certainty. After I had had my session with Buckle and the one-answer system at the age of thirteen, or whatever it was, I was somewhat inoculated against Marx and his one-answer system when he and the

Depression hit me when I was about twenty-five. I am not being frivolous about Marx; but when I began to hear some of my friends talk about him in 1930, I thought, "Here we go again, boys." I had previously got hold of one key to the universe. Buckle. And somewhere along the way I had lost the notion that there was ever going to be just one key. But getting back to that shelf of books, the Motley and Prescott and Parkman, and so on, isn't it funny how unreadable most history written now is when you compare it with those writers?

WALTER: Well, there's Samuel Eliot Morison.

WARREN: Yes, a very fine writer. Another is Vann Woodward, he writes very well indeed. And Bruce Catton. But Catton maybe doesn't count, he's not a professional historian. If he wants to write a book on history that happens to be good history and good writing at the same time, there isn't any graduate school to try to stop him.

ELLISON: It's very interesting that you were influenced by historical writing so early in life. It has always caught one's eye how history is used in your work—for instance, *Night Rider*.

WARREN: Well, that isn't a historical novel. The events belonged to my early childhood. I remember the troops coming in when martial law was declared in that part of Kentucky. When I wrote the novel I wasn't thinking of it as history. For one thing, the world it treated still, in a way, survived. You could still talk to the old men who had been involved. In the 1930's I remember going to see a judge down in Kentucky—he was an elderly man then, a man of the highest integrity and reputation—who had lived through that period and who by common repute had been mixed up in it—his father had been a tobacco grower. He got to talking about that period in Kentucky. He said, "Well, I won't say who was and who wasn't mixed up in some of those things, but I will make one observation: I have noticed that the sons of those who were opposed to getting a fair price for tobacco ended up as either bootleggers or brokers." But he was an old-fashioned kind of guy, for whom bootlegging and brokerage looked very much alike. Such a man didn't look "historical" thirty years ago. Now he looks like the thigh bone of a mastodon.

ELLISON: Beyond the question of the historical, from the first your work is very explicitly concerned with moral judgments. This during a period when much American fiction was concerned with moral questions only in the narrow way of the "proletarian" and "social realism" novels of the 1930's.

WARREN: I think I ought to say that behind *Night Rider* and my next novel, *At Heaven's Gate*, there was a good deal of the shadow not only of the events of that period but of the fiction of that period. I am more aware of that fact now than I was then. Of course, only an idiot could have not been aware that he was trying to write a novel about, in one sense, "social justice" in *Night Rider* or, for that matter, *At Heaven's Gate*. But in some kind of a fumbling way I was aware, I guess, of trying to find the dramatic rub of the story at some point a little different from and deeper than the point of dramatic rub in some of the then current novels. But what I want to emphasize is the fact that I was fumbling rather than working according to plan and already arrived-at convictions. When you start any book, you don't know what, ultimately, your issues are. You try to write to find them. You're fiddling with the stuff, hoping to make sense, whatever kind of sense you can make.

ELLISON: At least you could say that as a Southerner you were more conscious of what some of the issues were. You couldn't, I assume, forget the complexity of American social reality, no matter what your aesthetic concerns, or other concerns.

WARREN: It never crossed my mind when I began writing fiction that I could write about anything except life in the South. It never crossed my mind that I knew about anything else; know, that is, at the level you know something to write about it. Nothing else ever nagged you enough to stir the imagination. But I stumbled into fiction rather late. I've got to be autobiographical about this. For years I didn't have much interest in fiction, that is, in college. I was reading my head off in poetry, Elizabethan and the moderns, Yeats, Hardy, Eliot, Hart Crane. I wasn't seeing the world around me—that is, in any way that might be thought of as directly related to fiction. Be it to my everlasting shame that when the Scopes trial was going on a few miles from me, I didn't even bother to go. My head was too full of John Ford and John Webster and William Blake and T. S. Eliot. If I had been thinking about writing novels about the South, I would have been camping in Dayton, Tennessee—and would have gone about it like journalism. At least the Elizabethans saved me from that.

. . . .

ELLISON: It's very striking when you consider writing by Southerners before the 1920's. There were few writers as talented or as competent, or as confident as today, when writers seem to pour out of the South. This strikes me as a very American phenomenon in spite of its specifically regional aspects. Because when the South began to produce writers in great numbers, they emerged highly conscious of craftsmanship, highly aware of what literature was about, how to relate it to society and philosophy, and so on. Would you say that this was a kind of repetition of the cultural phenomenon which occurred in New England, say, during the 1830's?

WARREN: Yes, I do see some parallel between New England before the Civil War and the South after World War I to the present. The old notion of a shock, a cultural shock, to a more or less closed and static society—you know, what happened on a bigger scale in the Italian Renaissance or Elizabethan England. After 1918 the modern industrial world, with its good and bad, hit the South and all sorts of ferments began. As for individual writers, almost all of them of that period had had some important experience outside the South, then returned there—some strange mixture of continuity and discontinuity in their experience—a jagged quality. But more than mere general cultural or personal shocks, there was a moral shock in the South, a tension that grew out of the race situation. That moral tension had always been there, but it took new and more exacerbated forms after 1920. For one thing, through the growing self-consciousness of the Negroes was involved the possibility of expanding economic and cultural horizons. The Southerner's loyalties and pieties—real values, mind you—were sometimes staked against his religious and moral sense, those real values. There isn't much vital imagination, it seems to me, that doesn't come from some sort of shock, imbalance, need to "relive," redefine life.

ELLISON: Would you say that by the time you were editing *The Southern Review*, the between-the-wars period, that this moral shock was making itself felt in writing?

WARREN: Well, the *Review* started in 1935 and went on till '42. So it was late for the first ferment of things. But there were a lot of good young, or younger, writers in it. Not all Southern either.

ELLISON: I remember that some of Algren's first work appeared there.

WARREN: Oh yes, two early stories, for example; and a longish poem about baseball.

ELLISON: And the story "A Bottle of Milk for Mother."

WARREN: And the story "Biceps." And three or four of Eudora's first stories were there—Eudora Welty—and some of Katherine Anne's novelettes—Katherine Anne Porter.

ELLISON: There were a lot of critics in it—young ones, too.

WARREN: Oh yes, younger then, anyway. Kenneth Burke, F. O. Matthiessen, Theodore Spencer, R. P. Blackmur, Delmore Schwartz, L. C. Knights.

ELLISON: Speaking of critics reminds me that you've written criticism as well as poetry, drama, and fiction. It is sometimes said that the practice of criticism is harmful to the rest. Have you found it so?

WARREN: On this matter of criticism, something that appalls me is the idea going around now that the practice of criticism is opposed to the literary impulse. Is *necessarily* opposed to it, in an individual or period. Sure, it *may* be a trap, it may destroy the creative impulse, but so may drink or money or respectability. But criticism is a perfectly nattural human activity, and somehow the dullest, most technical criticism may be associated with full creativity. Elizabethan criticism is all, or nearly all, technical—meter, how to hang a line together—kitchen criticism, how to make the cake. People deeply interested in an art are interested in the "how." Now, I don't mean to say that that is the only kind of valuable criticism. Any kind is good that gives a deeper insight into the nature of the thing—a Marxist analysis, a Freudian study, the relation to a literary or social tradition, the history of a theme. But we have to remember that there is no *one, single, correct* kind of criticism—no *complete* criticism. You only have different kinds of perspectives, giving, when successful, different kinds of insights. And at one historical moment one kind of insight may be more needed than another.

WALTER: But don't you think that in America now a lot of good critical ideas get lost in terminology, in its gobbledygook style?

WARREN: Every age had its jargon, every group. When the jargon runs away with the insight, that's no good. Sure, a lot of people think they have the key to truth if they have a lingo. And a lot of modern criticism has run off into lingo—into academicism—the wrong kind of academicism, that pretends to be unacademic. The real academic job is to absorb an idea, to put it into perspective of other ideas, not to dilute it to lingo. As for lingo, it's true that some very good critics got bit by the bug that you could develop a fixed critical vocabulary. Well, you can't, except within narrow limits. That is a trap of scientism.

WALTER: Do you see some new ideas in criticism now emerging?

WARREN: No, I don't see them now. We've had Mr. Freud and Mr. Marx and—

ELLISON: Mr. Frazer and *The Golden Bough.*

WARREN: Yes, and Mr. Coleridge and Mr. Arnold and Mr. Eliot and Mr. Richards and Mr. Leavis and Mr. Aristotle, and so on. There have been, or are, many competing kinds of criticism with us—but I don't see a new one, or a new development of one of the old kind. It's an age groping for its issue.

WALTER: What about the New Criticism?

WARREN: Let's name some of them—Richards, Eliot, Tate, Blackmur, Winters, Brooks, Leavis (I guess). How in God's name can you get that gang into the same bed? There's no bed big enough and no blanket would stay tucked. When Ransom wrote his book called *The New Criticism* he was pointing out the vindictive variety among the critics and saying that he didn't agree with any of them. The term is, in one sense, a term without any referent, or with too many referents. It is a term that belongs to the conspiracy theory of literary history. A lot of people—chiefly aging, conservative professors scared of losing prestige or young instructors afraid of not getting promoted—middle-brow magazine editors—and the flotsam and jetsam of semi-Marxist social-significance criticism left stranded by history—they all have a communal nightmare called the New Criticism to explain their vague discomfort. I think it was something they ate.

WALTER: What do you mean—conspiracy?

WARREN: Those folks all had the paranoidal nightmare that there was a conspiracy called the New Criticism, just to do them personal wrong. No, it's not quite that simple but there is some truth in this. One thing that a lot of so-called New Critics had in common was a willingness to look long and hard at the literary object. But the ways of looking might be very different. Eliot is a lot closer to Arnold and the Archbishop of Canterbury than he is to Yvor Winters, and Winters is a lot closer to Irving Babbitt than to Richards, and the exegeses of Brooks are a lot closer to Coleridge than to Ransom, and so on. There has been more nonsense talked about this subject than any I can think of (and I don't want to add to the burden of history right now).

ELLISON: Well, getting back to your own work, there is, for us, an exciting spiral from *I'll Take My Stand* through the novels to *Segregation*. It would seem that these works mark stages in a combat with the past. In the first, the point of view seems orthodox and unreconstructed. How can one say it? In recent years your work has become more intense and has taken on an element of personal confession which is so definite that one tends to look, for example, on *Segregation* and *Brother to Dragons* as two facets of a single work.

WARREN: You've thrown several different things at me here. Let me try to sort them out. First you refer to the Southern Agrarian book *I'll Take My Stand*, of 1930, and then to my recent little book *Segregation*. My essay in *I'll Take My Stand* was about the Negro in the South, and it was a defense of segregation. I haven't read that piece, as far as I can remember, since 1930, and I'm not sure exactly how things are put there. But I do recall very distinctly the circumstances of writing it. I wrote it at Oxford at about the same time I began writing fiction, the two things were tied together—the look back home from a long distance. I remember the jangle and wrangle of writing the essay and some kind of discomfort in it, some sense of evasion, I guess, in writing it, in contrast with the free feeling of writing the novelette *Prime Leaf*, the sense of seeing something fresh, the holiday sense plus some stirring up of something inside yourself. In the essay I reckon I was trying to prove something, trying to find out something, see something, feel something—exist.

Don't misunderstand me. On the objective side of things, there wasn't a power under heaven that could have changed segregation in 1929—the South wasn't ready for it, the North was not ready for it, the Negro wasn't. The Court, if I remember correctly, had just reaffirmed segregation, too. No, I'm not talking about the objective fact, but about the subjective fact, yours truly, in relation to the objective fact. Well, it wasn't being outside the South that made me change my mind. It was coming back home. In a little while I realized I simply couldn't have written that essay again. I guess trying to write fiction made me realize that. If you are seriously trying to write fiction, you can't allow yourself as much evasion as in trying to write essays. But some people can't read fiction. One reviewer, a professional critic, said that *Band of Angels* is an apology for the plantation system. Well, the story of *Band* wasn't an apology *or* an attack. It was simply trying to say something about something. But God Almighty, you have to spell it out for some people, especially a certain breed of professional defender-of-the-good, who makes a career of holding the right thoughts and admiring his own moral navel. Well, that's getting off the point. What else was it you threw at me?

ELLISON: Would you say that each book marks a redefinition of reality arrived at through a combat with the past? A development from the traditional to the highly personal of reality?

WARREN: Yes, I see what you mean. But I never thought of a combat with the past. I guess I think more of trying to find what there is valuable to us (the line of continuity to us, and *through* us). The specific Southern past, I'm now talking about. As for combat, I guess the real combat is always with yourself, Southerner or anybody else.

ELLISON: Well, that may bring up another of the four things I threw at you—the increasing element of personal confession in your work which is so serious that one tends to look, for example, on *Segregation, Brother to Dragons,* and *Band of Angels* as parts of one work. Or maybe this is doing violence to them?

WARREN: Not at all. But it wouldn't have occurred to me. You fight your battles one by one and do the best you can. Whatever pattern there is, develops—it isn't projected—really basic patterns, I mean, the kind you live into. As for confession, that wouldn't have occurred to me either, but I do know that in the last ten years, or a little more, the personal relation to my writing changed. I never bothered to define the change. I quit writing poems for several years; that is, I'd start them, get a lot down, then feel that I wasn't connecting somehow. I didn't finish one for several years, they felt false. Then I got back at it, and that is the bulk of what I've done since—*Band of Angels,* and a new book of poems which will be out in the summer. But cutting back to where we started —the confession business. When you try to write a book, even objective fiction, you have to write from the inside, not the outside—the inside of yourself—you have to find what's there—you can't predict it, just dredge for it, and hope you have something to work the dredging. That isn't "confession"—that's just trying to use whatever the Lord lets you lay hand to. And of course you have to have common sense enough and structural sense enough to know what is relevant. You don't choose a story, it chooses you. You get together with that story somehow . . . you're stuck with it. There certainly is some reason it attracted you and you're writing it trying to find out that reason; justify, get at that reason. I can always look back and remember the exact moment when I encountered the germ of any story I wrote—a clear flash . . .

. . . .

ELLISON: Speaking of crafts, how conscious are you of the dramatic structure of your novels when you begin? I ask because in it there is quite a variety of subforms, folklore, set pieces like "The Ballad of Billie Potts" or the Cass Mastern episode in *All the King's Men*. Are these planned as part of the dramatic structure, or do they arise while you are being carried by the flow of invention as it falls into form?

WARREN: I try to think a lot about the craft of other people— that's part of my long years of teaching. When you've been explaining things like how the first scene of *Hamlet* gets off . . . thinking of how things have been done . . . and when it comes to work, you have made some objective decisions, like who is going to tell the story. That's a prime question, a question of control. You have to make a judgment. You find one character is more insistent, he's more sensitive and more pointed than the others. But as for other aspects of structure and craft, I guess, in the actual process of composition or in preliminary thinking, I try to immerse myself in the motive and *feel* toward meanings rather than plan a structure or plan effects. After a thing is done, then I try to get tough and critical with myself. But damn it, it may sometimes be too late then. But that is the fate of man. What I am trying to say is that I try to forget the abstractions when I'm actually composing a thing. I don't understand other approaches that come up when I talk to other writers. For instance, some say their sole interest is experimentation. Well, I think that you learn all you can and try to use it. I don't know what is meant by the word "experiment"; you ought to be playing for keeps.

ELLISON: Yes, but there is still great admiration of the so-called experimental writing of the twenties. What of Joyce and Eliot?

WARREN: What is "experimental" writing? James Joyce didn't do "experimental" writing—he wrote *Ulysses*. Eliot didn't do "experimental" writing—he wrote *The Waste Land*. When you fail at something, you call it an "experiment," an elite word for flop. Just because lines are uneven or capitals missing doesn't mean experiment. Literary magazines devoted to experimental writing are usually filled with works by middle-aged or old people.

WALTER: Or middle-aged young people.

WARREN: Young fogeys. But to come back to the experimental business. In one way, of course, all writing that is any good *is* experimental; that is, it's a way of seeing what is possible —what poem, what novel is possible. Experiment—they define it as putting a question to nature, and that is true of writing undertaken with seriousness. You put the question to human nature—and especially your own nature—and see what comes out. It is unpredictable. If it is predictable—not experimental—then it will be worthless.

ELLISON: What about the use of history in your fiction? Obviously you don't write "historical" novels: they are always concerned with urgent problems, but the awareness of history seems to be central.

WARREN: I'm gonna jump back . . . something is hanging on the edge of my mind . . . about planning . . . I try to, awful hard. At some point, you know, you have to try to get one with God, and *then* take a hard cold look at it— and try again on it afterwards and plan to take it, trusting in your viscera and nervous system and your previous efforts as far as they've gone. The hard thing, the objective thing, has to be done before the book is written. And if anybody dreams of "Kubla Khan," it's going to be Coleridge. If the work is done, the dream will come to the man who's ready for that particular dream; it's not going to come just from dreaming in general. About historical novels; I don't think I write historical novels. I try to find stories that catch my eye, stories that seem to have issues in purer form than they come to one ordinarily.

ELLISON: A kind of unblurred topicality?

WARREN: I wrote two unpublished novels in the thirties. *Night Rider* is the world of my childhood. *At Heaven's Gate* was contemporary. My third published, *All the King's Men*, was worlds I had seen. All the stories were contemporary.

ELLISON: *Brother to Dragons?*

WARREN: This last belonged to a historical setting but I don't see any break myself. A matter of dealing with issues in a more mythical form. The novel I'm writing now, and two I plan, are all contemporary. I hate costume novels, but maybe I've written some and don't know it! I have a romantic kind of interest in the objects of American history: saddles, shoes, figures of speech, rifles, and so on. They're worth a lot. Helps you focus. There *is* a kind of extraordinary romance about American history. That's the only word for it . . . a kind of self-sufficiency. You know, the grandpaws and the great-grandpaws who carried the assumption that somehow their lives and their decisions were important, that as they went up, down, here and there, such a life was important and a man's responsibility to live it.

ELLISON: In this connection, do you feel that there are certain themes which are basic to the American experience, even though a body of writing in a given period might ignore or evade them?

WARREN: First thing, without being systematic, that comes to mind without running off a week and praying about it, would be that America was based on a big promise—a great big one: the Declaration of Independence. . . . When you have to live with that in the house, that's quite a problem—

particularly when you've got to make money and get ahead, open world markets, do all the things you have to, raise your children, and so forth. America is stuck with its self-definition put on paper in 1776, and that was just like putting a burr under the metaphysical saddle of America—you see, that saddle's going to jump now and then and it pricks. There's another thing in the American experience that makes for a curious kind of abstraction. We had to suddenly define ourselves and what we stood for in one night. No other nation ever had to do that. In fact, one man did it. One man in an upstairs room, Thomas Jefferson. Sure, you might say that he was the amanuensis for a million or so people stranded on the edge of the continent and backed by a wilderness, and there's some sense in that notion. But *somebody* had to formulate it—in fact, just overnight, whatever the complicated background of that formulation—and we've been stuck with it ever since. With the very words it used. Do you know the Polish writer Adam Gurowski? [11] Of a high-placed Polish family, he came and worked as a civil servant in Washington, a clerk, a kind of self-appointed spy on democracy. His book *America*—of 1856, I think—begins by saying that America is unique among nations because other nations are accidents of geography or race, but America is based on an idea. Behind the comedy of proclaiming that idea from Fourth of July platforms, there is the solemn notion *Believe and ye shall be saved*. That abstraction sometimes does become concrete, is a part of the American experience.

ELLISON: What about historical time? America has had so much happening in such a short time.

WARREN: Awful lot of foreshortening in it. America lives in two times, chronological time and history. The last widow drawing a pension from the War of 1812 died just a few years ago. My father was old enough to vote when the last full-scale battle against Indians was fought—a couple of regiments of regulars with artillery.

ELLISON: You had a piece in the *New Republic* once where you discuss Faulkner's technique. One of the things you

emphasize is Faulkner's technique of the "still moment."
I've forgotten what you called it exactly: a suspension, in
which time seems to hang.

WARREN: That's the frozen moment. Freeze time. Somewhere,
almost in a kind of pun, Faulkner himself uses the image of
a frieze for such a moment of frozen action. It's an important quality in his work. Some of these moments harden
up an event, give it its meaning by holding it fixed. Time
fluid versus time fixed— In Faulkner's work that's the drama
behind the drama. Take a look at Hemingway; there's no
time in Hemingway, there are only moments in themselves,
moments of action. There are no parents and no children.
If there's a parent, he is a grandparent off in America
somewhere who signs the check, like the grandfather in
A Farewell to Arms. You never see a small child in Hemingway. You get death in childbirth but you never see a
child. Everything is outside of the time process. But in
Faulkner, there are always the very old and the very young.
Time spreads and is the important thing, the terrible thing.
A tremendous flux is there, things flowing away in all
directions. Moments not quite ready to be shaped are already there, waiting, and we feel their presence. What you
most remember about Jason in *The Sound and the Fury*,
say, is the fact that he was the treasurer when the children
made and sold kites, and kept the money in his pocket. Or
you remember Caddy getting her drawers muddy. Everything is already there, just waiting to happen. You have
the sense of the small becoming large in time, the large
becoming small, the sweep of time over things. That, and
the balance of the frozen, abstracted moment against violent
significant action. Those frozen moments are Faulkner's
game. Hemingway has a different game. In Hemingway,
there's no time at all. He's out of history entirely. In one
sense, he tries to deny history, he says history is the bunk,
like Henry Ford.

ELLISON: This intrigues me very much because we reach a
moment in American history where we have a man like
Twain coming along who is highly moral and who is a

humorist. He's master of moral literature, of native folk-lore, and though some people miss his mastery of literary technique, he was highly conscious of technique, and he was certainly conscious of language, of how it operates, what it means.

WARREN: He's a great inventor of language. He made a language.

ELLISON: You have Hemingway taking up that language side of his work and emphasizing it and extending it while he muted down, inverted Twain's moral questioning. And you have Faulkner picking up both that side, the inventiveness, plus the explicit concern with moral continuity. It seems that this comes back to the Southern experience. Due not to anything that comes in the blood, not through any intention either, but to the fact that something shocking, something traumatic had occurred. We were all there, and we had certain beliefs and certain conflicts of belief and certain conflicts between our beliefs and our actions, and history was alive. It wasn't a matter of abandoning a central issue after Reconstruction or after the Hayes-Tilden Compromise, shall we say, and then saying, "Now these issues are no longer important."

WARREN: That was said elsewhere. On Wall Street, to be exact. History didn't stop that day south of the Mason-Dixon line. Of course, the big split in American life is that history *did* stop for certain other people at a certain date. It stopped for the happy children of the gilded age. They settled down to making money and getting those railroads built out West and digging the gold out and speculating in land and watering stock and developing a continent, and on the way sometimes looting it and a fair percentage of their fellow citizens. The heroic effort and the brigandage are both in the brew. But for a variety of reasons, history didn't stop for certain other people. Down South they were stuck with it, sometimes for some very poor reasons, including stupidity. But one good and sufficient reason was that the South was stuck with a lot of unresolved issues, including the question of the relation of the South to the rest of the country—for one thing, the relation of the economy of the South to that of the rest of the country—and including the race question. To sum up, you might say that the South got bogged down in history—in time—and the North got bogged down in nonhistory—non-time—and that split is the tragic fact of American life.

ELLISON: Switching to something which might be related to this—there seems to be in the early Hemingway a conscious effort *not* to have a very high center of consciousness within the form of the novel. His characters may have a highly moral significance, but they don't talk about things. They seldom discuss issues. They prefer to hint. Thus distinctions may be lost in the oversimplification of gesture. In the underplaying of important lines.

WARREN: Sure, Hemingway sneaks it in, but he is an intensely conscious and, even, philosophical writer. When the snuck-in thing or the gesture works, the effect can be mighty powerful. But in general, I was in no sense making an invidious comparison between the two writers—or between their special uses of time. They are both powerfully expressive writers. But it's almost too pat, you know, almost too schematic, the polar differences between those two writers in relation to the question of time. Speaking of pairs of writers, take Proust and Faulkner. There may be a lot written on the subject but I haven't encountered much of it. They'd make a strange but instructive pair to study—in relation to time. I want to go back to something—the question of the center of consciousness. French fiction, it has been said, usually has a hero who deals very consciously with the issues. He is his own chorus to the action, as well as the man who utters the equivalent of the Elizabethan soliloquy. But in our fiction of the twenties, in Hemingway, for instance, you had these matters sneaked in. You had hints or you had the issues left out completely, especially among those writers who didn't know what was going on anyway, who didn't know what Hemingway knew very well. By contrast, nineteenth-century fiction could deal with the issues. Those novels could discuss them in terms of a man's relation to a woman, or in terms of whether you're going to help a slave run away. Or in terms of what to do about a man obsessed with fighting evil, nature, what have you, in the form of a white whale.

ELLISON: Well, your own work seems to have this explicitness, and without being literal, Jack Burden in *All the King's Men* is a conscious center and he is a highly conscious man. Furthermore, he's not there as an omniscient figure, but, like each of us, is urgently trying to discover something. He is involved.

WARREN: Burden got there by accident. He was only a sentence or two in the first version—the verse play from which the novel developed.

ELLISON: Why did you make the change?

WARREN: I don't know. He was an unnamed newspaperman, a childhood friend of the assassin, an excuse for the young doctor, the assassin of the politician, Willie Stark, to say something before he performed the deed. When after two years I picked up the verse version, and began to fool with a novel, the unnamed newspaperman became the narrator. It turned out, in a way, that what he thought about the story was more important than the story itself. I suppose he became the narrator because he gave me the kind of interest I needed to write the novel. He made it possible for me to control it. He is an observer, but he is involved.

ELLISON: To follow this line a little farther, I was struck by the great flexibility of method you allowed yourself in *Brother to Dragons*. With ghosts coming back and reenacting their lives, and commenting on the action. You have several worlds of reality operating there. Everyone spoke, if I remember correctly, but the slaughtered slave. Why is he silent?

WARREN: He did have three lines toward the end:

I was lost in the world and the trees were tall.
I was lost in the world, and the dark swale heaved.
I was lost in my anguish and did not know the reason.

Then Jefferson says, "Reason, my son . . . how could I show you the light of reason, when I had lost it when your blood ran out." [12]

ELLISON: I'm probing here—maybe the character of R.P.W. in the poem spoke for him, too, in the scheme of the book?

WARREN: I didn't want George, the slave boy, *not* to be there, *not* to speak. I wanted him to be there all the time. I wanted his presence to speak, his experience to speak. I wanted the fact of his experience to ricochet off something. I wanted to make a bank shot like in billiards. The relation of George's experience to other people, not the experience itself, merely, was what I wanted to play up. If somebody, a character, is in the position of George, is pure victim, what can he say? He has nothing to say. All you can do is bounce him off other people, those with various kinds of moral involvements and responsibilities. But—to change the subject perhaps—those three lines which George does speak were the first lines of *Brother to Dragons* that I composed—four years before I began the consistent composition of the poem.

ELLISON: Would you say that you really come to grips with the problem of George in *Band of Angels*, in the person of Manty?

WARREN: No, I don't see it that way. George is just a boy caught in a maniacal piece of direct brutality. He had had a world to live in, with relations he could accept. It was a world he knew. Then suddenly it was upside down, and he was caught in the increasing terror and couldn't understand it.

ELLISON: And Manty?

WARREN: Oh, she's different. One difference is the degree of consciousness. Manty has read books, is educated. For another thing, she has—or I tried to make her have—an inside story. She is striving for identity, for enlightenment. George, however, is not highly conscious, and he has no inside story. He is victim. Manty is, of course, a victim too, but in one perspective at least, her view of herself as

victim is what stands in the way of her achieving identity.
But George—he isn't a subject for a story, has no personality, no problem. He's just a little boy caught in a terrible
fix. *Brother to Dragons* isn't *about* him.

ELLISON: Well, what about Manty's problem in her relationship
to Hamish Bond (Alec Hinks)? So, here is a young girl
trained as a white gentlewoman who suddenly finds herself
on the slave block, where she is bought by a man bearing a
false name and who, though wealthy through his own efforts, is escaping from his mother, who in her turn is obsessed by her myth of aristocracy.

WARREN: About that mother, I had somebody in mind—a real
person, as I don't usually do—but I'm not going to tell you
who it was.

ELLISON: Were you implying here that both Manty and Bond
have false identities, especially Bond?

WARREN: Yes, and even the false name and false identity were
forced on him by his mother.

ELLISON: His mother—who insists that she is by birth an
aristocratic Buckingham, who were great slave owners.

WARREN: That's her myth. The stick she beats husband and
son with. So the son's going to fix her, he says. He's going
to get a million slaves, he says. He's going to be "ass-deep
in niggers," he says. Bond makes her lie come both true
and untrue. He sinks himself into the lie in order to escape
from it—and to explore it, to know the truth of the lie.
And of course, he is out to avenge himself on his mother
for giving him a false identity, and on his father for being
a weakling, for having no identity to give him, to give the
son.

ELLISON: That's a great scene where the boy makes the morose
and beaten old father laugh by denouncing and rejecting
the mother.

WARREN: Bond has to escape them both. He gets away from
her by making the lie come true, but true in some shocking,
not respectable way that would violate her need for respectability. He becomes a slave-runner, and isn't respectable, even though he is a king of the coast. But somehow

he can't quite get away from her. He has to become respectable in the end, blackmail his way into New Orleans society. Stuck with his lie, he has to live it all the way through before he can speak an honest word, even though he's an old man.

ELLISON: It sounds like the last part of your book on *Segregation*, where you speak of the necessity of achieving moral identity.

WARREN: I hadn't thought about it that way. Maybe it's in the cards, though.

ELLISON: Another thing that strikes me about Hamish Bond is that he has know-how. He has initiative, he is inventive, self-assertive. Capable of great violence and revulsion from that violence.

WARREN: If it hadn't been for his mama, he might have gone West.

WALTER: Is it significant that he gets his start by tying in with an old Yankee slave-runner?

WARREN: To mention that in the book was just Confederate nastiness.

WALTER: But would it be historically true? The Yankee slave-runners?

WARREN: Would it! I guess the last of the numerous breed was a man named Gordon hanged in 1863 in New York. He was, by the way, the only one they ever got around to hanging. But in 1863 they, and Gordon, were sort of stuck with it.

ELLISON: Do you feel that—in terms of national morality—that we're the oldest country rather than the New World—that we've become the Old World in the sense that we've been grappling longer with the problem of industrialization, the increasing anonymity of the individual, plus the tortures of the race problem in its most intense and intimate form. Aren't we the Old World now in the sense that we've been coming to grips with these problems which European nations are only beginning to encounter in their crucial forms?

WARREN: We've been through some things, or are deeper into some things, that are just beginning for some other nations. In industrialization, for instance, France and Italy haven't even touched problems that we've got to the other side of, by luck and national resources, I guess. Not that I want to say we're home free. I've got my fingers crossed.

ELLISON: For ten years or more it has been said in the United States that problems of race are an obsession of Negro writers but that they have no place in literature. But how can a Negro writer avoid the problem of race?

WARREN: How can you expect a Southern Negro not to write about race, directly or indirectly, when you can't find a Southern white man who can avoid it?

ELLISON: I must say that it's usually white Northerners who express this opinion, though a few Negroes have been seduced by it. And they usually do so on aesthetic grounds.

WARREN: I'd like to add to that here that what I said about the historical element seems important. The Negro who is writing protest *qua* protest strikes me as anachronistic. Protest *qua* protest denies the textures of life. The problem is to permit the fullest range of life into racial awareness. I don't mean to imply that there's nothing to protest about, but aside from the appropriate political, sociological, and journalistic concerns, the problem is to see the protest in its relation to other things. Race isn't an isolated thing—I mean as it exists in the U.S.—it becomes a total symbolism for every kind of issue. They all flow into it. And out of it. Well, thank God. It gives a little variety to life. At the same time it proclaims the unity of life. You know the kind of person who puts on a certain expression and then talks about "solving" the race problem. Well, it's the same kind of person and the same kind of expression you meet when you hear the phrase "solve the sex problem." This may be a poor parallel, but it's some kind of a parallel. Basically the issue isn't to "solve" the "race problem" or the "sex problem." You don't solve it, you just experience it. Appreciate it.

ELLISON: Maybe that's another version of William James' "moral equivalent of war." You argue and try to keep the argument clean, all the human complexities in view.

WARREN: What I'm trying to say is this. A few years ago I sat in a room with some right-thinking friends, the kind of people who think you look in the back of the book for every answer—attitude A for situation A, attitude B for situation B, and so on for the damned alphabet. It developed that they wanted a world where everything is exactly alike and everybody is exactly alike. They wanted a production belt of human faces and human attitudes.

ELLISON: Hell, who would want such a world?

WARREN: "Right-thinkers" want it, for one thing. I don't want that kind of world. I want variety and pluralism—and *appreciation*. Appreciation in some sort of justice and decency and freedom of choice in conduct and personal life. Man is interesting in his differences. It's all a question of what you make of the differences. I'm not for differences *per se*, but you just let the world live the differences, live them out. I feel pretty strongly about attempts to legislate *undifference*. That is just as much tyranny as trying to legislate difference. Apply that to any differences except between healthy and unhealthy, criminal and noncriminal. Furthermore, you can't legislate the future of anybody, in any direction. It's not laws that are going to determine what our great-grandchildren feel or do. And you can't legislate virtue. The tragedy of a big half of American liberalism is to try to legislate virtue. You can't legislate virtue. You should simply try to establish conditions favorable for the growth of virtue. But that will never satisfy the bully-boys of virtue, the plug-uglies of virtue. They are interested in the production-belt stamp of virtue, attitude A in the back of the book, and not in establishing conditions of justice and decency in which human appreciation can find play.

ELLISON: Getting back to fiction—what's the relation of sociological research and other types of research to the forms of fiction, to the writer's view of social reality?

WARREN: I think it's purely accidental. For one writer a big dose of such stuff might be fine, for another it might be poison . . . I've known a good many people, some of them writers, who think of literature as *material* that you "work

up." You don't "work up" literature. But they point at
Zola. But Zola didn't do that, nor did Dreiser. They must
have thought they did, but they didn't. They weren't
"working up" something—in one sense, something was
working them up. You see the world as best you can—with
or without the help of somebody's research, as the case may
be. You see as much as you can, and the events and books
that are interesting to you should be interesting to you because you're a human being, not because you're trying to be
a writer. Then those things may be of some use to you as a
writer later on. I don't believe in a schematic approach to
material. The business of researching for a book strikes me
as a sort of obscenity. What I mean is, researching for a book
in the sense of trying to find a book to write. Once you
are engaged by a subject, are in your book, have your idea,
you may or may not want to do some investigating. But
you ought to do it in the same spirit in which you'd take
a walk in the evening air to think things over. You can't
research to get a book. You stumble on it. Or hope to. Maybe
you will, if you live right.

ELLISON: I see certain parallels between the development of
your work and its movement from *I'll Take My Stand* to
Band of Angels and *Segregation,* and Faulkner's Lucas
Beauchamp. He appears first as an aged and lecherous coachman who molests young maids and cooks, and who eats
ice cream with either spinach or turnip greens. Then in his
final metamorphosis he is an estimable symbol of human
courage. [This coachman is actually Simon Strother of
Sartoris; Lucas Beauchamp came much later in *Go Down,
Moses* and *Intruder in the Dust.*]

WARREN: Total courage and dignity.

ELLISON: This you have to pay something for, don't you? For
a view of the world that's that complicated. Is this something arrived at through taking a liberal stance, or is it a
product of what Henry James called "felt life," a wrestling
with reality?

WARREN: Not long ago a very bright, well-informed lady was
talking to me about some novels by Southerners. She finally

burst out: "Well, I think it's far too high a price to pay for good books to have people live like that, the way they live down there." That lady, I reckon, would "approve" of Lucas Beauchamp as heroic symbol—but I bet she'd stop that nonsense of eating ice cream and turnip greens mixed up and pinching the housegirl on the can.

ELLISON: Turnip greens and ice cream and all, elements of stereotypes and individual complexity and ambiguousness, Lucas Beauchamp comes out as one of the most dignified men in the Faulkner gallery. This seems to me to be a question that has been confronted by most writers whether they know it or not—you start out with certain assumptions given you by the culture into which you're born, and—

WARREN: You're stuck with certain things. Either you can see them and appreciate them or you can't. By the way, Lucas reminds me of something. More than twenty years ago I spent part of a summer in a little town in Louisiana, and like a good number of the population, whiled away the afternoons by going to the local murder trials. One case involved an old Negro man who had shot a young Negro woman for talking meanness against his baby-girl daughter. He had shot the victim with both barrels of a twelve-gauge at a range of eight feet, while the victim was in a crap game. There were a dozen witnesses to the execution. Besides that, he had sat for half an hour on a stump outside the door of the building where the crap game was going on, before he got down to business. He was waiting, because a friend had lost six dollars to the intended victim and had asked the old man to hold off till he had a chance to win it back. When the friend got the six dollars back, the old man went to work.

He never denied what he had done. He explained it all very carefully, and why he had to do it. He loved his baby-girl daughter and there wasn't anything else he could do. Then he would plead "Not Guilty." But if he got tried and convicted—and they couldn't fail to convict—he would get death. If, however, he would plead guilty to manslaughter he could get off light. But he wouldn't do it. He said he wasn't guilty of anything. The whole town got involved in the thing. Well, they finally cracked him. He pled guilty and got off light. Everybody was glad, sure—they weren't stuck with something, they could feel good and pretty virtuous. But they felt bad, too. Something had been lost, something a lot of them could appreciate. I used to think I'd try to make a story of this. But I never did. It was too complete, too self-fulfilling, as fact. But to get back to the old man. It took him three days to crack, and when he cracked he was nothing. Now, we don't approve of what he did—a status homicide the sociologists call it, and that is the worst sort of homicide, worse than homicide for gain, because status homicide is irrational, and you can't make sense of it, and it is the mark of a low order of society. But because status homicide is the mark of a low order of society, what are we to think about the old man's three-day struggle to keep his dignity? And are we to deny value to this dignity because of the way "they live down there"?

ELLISON: You feel, then, that one of the great blocks of achieving serious fiction out of experience is a sort of self-righteousness, the assumption that you're on the right side, that you're without sin?

WARREN: Once you start illustrating virtue as such, you had better stop writing fiction. Do something else, like Y work. Or join a committee. Your business as a writer is not to illustrate virtue but to show how a fellow may move toward it—or away from it.

ELLISON: Malraux says somewhere in his essays that "one cannot reveal the mystery of human beings in the form of a plea for the defense."

WARREN: Or in the form of an indictment, either.

WALTER: What about the devil's advocate?

WARREN: He can have a role, he can be Jonathan Swift, or something.

ELLISON: Well, back to what you call the "right-thinkers." I wonder what these people think, well, they confront a Negro, say, the symbol of the underdog, and he turns out to be a son-of-a-bitch. What do they do—hold a conference to decide how to treat him?

WARREN: They must sure have a problem.

ELLISON: The same kind of people, they have to consult with themselves to determine if they can laugh at certain situations in which Negroes are involved.

WALTER: Like minstrel shows. A whole world of purely American humor got lost in that shuffle along with some good songs. Some American art forms have been lost for the same reason.

WARREN: It's just goddamned hard, you have to admit, though, to sort out things that are symbolically charged. Sometimes the symbolic charge is so heavy you have a hard time getting at the real value really there. You always can, I guess, if the context is right. But hell, a lot of people can't read a context.

WALTER: It's like the problem of Shylock in *The Merchant of Venice*.

WARREN: Yes, suppress the play because it might offend a Jew. Or *Oliver Twist*. Well, such symbolic charges just have to be reckoned with and taken on their own terms and in their historical perspective. As a matter of fact, such symbolic charges are present, in one degree or another, in all relationships. They're simply stepped up and specialized in certain historical and social situations. There are mighty few stories you can tell without offending somebody—without some implicit affront. The comic strip of *Li'l Abner*, for instance, must have made certain persons of what is called "Appalachian white" origin feel inferior and humiliated. There are degrees as well as difference in these things. Context is all. And a relatively pure heart. *Relatively* pure—for if you had a pure heart, you wouldn't be in the book-writing business in the first place. We're stuck with it in ourselves. What we can write about, if anything. What you can make articulate. What voices you have in your insides—and in your ear.

An Interview with Flannery O'Connor and Robert Penn Warren

■■■

On the morning of April 23, 1959, Warren and Flannery O'Connor met with a group of students and faculty members during the annual Vanderbilt Literary Symposium. This transcription was published in the Vanderbilt student magazine, The Vagabond, *the following year.*

JOE SILLS: I would like to ask either or both of you: when you set out to write a story, how much of an outline do you have? . . .

FLANNERY O'CONNOR: I just don't outline.

WARREN: I had an outline once, and it took me two years to pull out of it. You think you've got your work done.

SILLS: What about the novel? How much outline do you work from? How do you write a novel?

O'CONNOR: Well, I just kind of feel it out like a hound dog. I follow the scent. Quite frequently it's the wrong scent, and you stop and go back to the last plausible point and start in some other direction.

SILLS: Are you aware of how it is going to end?

o'connor: Not always. You know the direction you're going in, but you don't know how you'll get there.

.   .   .   .

EDWIN GODSEY: Do any of you begin with the theme first, and hunt for the story, or do you do it the other way around?

o'connor: I think it's better to begin with the story, and then you know you've got something. Because the theme is more or less something that's in you, but if you intellectualize it too much, you probably destroy your novel.

WARREN: People have done it the other way, in cases: starting out with an idea, and hunting the fable, as they used to say. Coleridge is a good example of it. He says he had his theme for *The Ancient Mariner* for years. He kept casting around for the appropriate fable. He even made a false start or two, until he hit the right story. Those are not contradictory things, I think, because the theme was in him. He had at least reached some pretty clear intellectual definition of it before he started.

GODSEY: Theoretically, which do you think is better for the young writer?

WARREN: Let's don't say "the young writer." Just drop the phrase; not just for here, for always. Any writer who is not young had better shut up shop. He'd better be trying to wrangle through what he is up to, and pretend he's young anyway, or quit. Once he thinks he's an old writer who knows, he's finished. About which is better: I don't think there's any choice in the matter. It's just a matter of temperament. I think people can freeze themselves by their hasty intellectualizing of what they are up to.

.   .   .   .

WALTER SULLIVAN: Red, to get back to this novel business: your books are awfully well put together. The opening sequences contain so many images of the book as a whole, and prepare for so many things to happen. You've got to know a whole lot or you couldn't write that way.

WARREN: There's no law that makes you put the first chapter first, though.

SULLIVAN: Well, I know, but . . .

WARREN: Some of them have been written first, yes. I don't think it's knowing how the story comes out that's the point. As Flannery just said, you know what you want it to feel like. You envisage the feeling. You may or may not know how it is going to come out. You may have your big scenes in mind before you start. You may even be moving toward them all the time. You don't know whether they will jell out or not jell out. But it seems to me the important thing is to have enough feeling envisaged and pre-felt, as it were, about the way the book's going to go. If that feeling isn't there: unless it dominates your thinking, somehow . . . you know, be the thing that is behind the muse, the thing that keeps it under control: if you ever lose that feeling, then you start floundering. But as long as that feeling as to how the book is going to end is there, something is guiding it. And then your mechanical problems have a sort of built-in correction for error. I mean you have fifty ideas, but somehow you know they're wrong. If you keep this feeling firmly in you . . . I don't know how you will it . . . but as long as it is there, you have something to guide you in this automatic process of trial and error. You know what the book ought to feel like. Of course, you're going to modify that feeling.

SULLIVAN: I know exactly what you're saying, and I think you're exactly right. But it seems to me that there is a considerable danger in not knowing enough about where you're going, especially insofar as the structure of the book is concerned. In *All the King's Men*, did you write the first chapter first?

WARREN: No, it was the second chapter originally. There was a shift in material there which the editor did. The present opening chapter was the second chapter, or part of the second chapter. The original opening got off to a very poor start, with the narrator talking about the first time he had seen Stark, the politician. He goes back into the scene which now appears later, in the second or third chapter, when he comes into town to get a political favor, make a political connection, in a restaurant or beer hall in New Orleans. There is this portrait of him coming in, the boy with the Christmas tie, you know, and his hat in his hand. Well, that was a very predictable kind of start. It had no urgency in it. So expository in the worst sense. I was trying to step that up by a kind of commentary on it, and the commentary was pretty crude, and that's the way the thing remained when it went to the publisher. And Lambert Davis [13] said, "Look here, this is a very poor way to start a novel. You've got a natural start in the second chapter, and what's in the first chapter that's important, you can absorb very readily." And I think he was right. I know he was right about its being bad.

SULLIVAN: Well, now look, when you started the book, certainly you knew that Judge Irwin had been very culpable in his financial dealings.

WARREN: No, I did not. No, I didn't know it at all. That came quite a while along the way.

SULLIVAN: Well, then, did you know that Adam Stanton was going to kill Willie?

WARREN: Yes, I knew that.

SULLIVAN: You knew that Sugar Boy was going to kill Adam?

WARREN: Yes. The point is, I am mixing up two things, the novel and the verse play which preceded it. There you had the germ: the politician, his wife, his mistress, her brother were in the play. It was a very small cast, you see, and then it became a novel, but there was no Judge Irwin in the play at all. There's no mother, nothing of that personal stuff. In fact, there was no Jack Burden. He came in as a nameless newspaperman with two sentences to speak, a boyhood friend without a name as the assassin is waiting for Stark, who is then called Talos. The newspaperman just meets this man and says "Hello, Hello," just a few words between them, a way of killing time, of having a little nostalgic reference to their boyhood. Kind of a hold, you know, until the action could happen. You've always got to do that, you know. If a man goes to kill a man, if a man goes to get an ice cream soda, you can't just let him go and get it, or go and kill him. You have to stop it, hold it a minute, distract it a little, delay it, get a focus from the side, and nudge it a bit. You try to make the reader forget what you put the man there for. If you say, "I am going to get the ice cream soda," and just go do it, there's no story there. Jack Burden came in there just the way I described. I just can't go shoot him. I've got to stop him. I've got to do something, and so this guy appeared there to stop him. Having him in there filled a dramatic need of fiction, a need of pace. When the novel idea started out some years later, I couldn't do it as a straight dramatic novel. I tried that. I thought on an idle Sunday afternoon: that newspaperman might be useful. The moment of nostalgia might be made into some kind of feeling by which to tell the story. That was how he got in there. I remember that distinctly.

. . . .

o'connor: When you write the thing through once, you find out what the end is. Then you can go back to the first chapter and put in a lot of those foreshadowings.

warren: . . . If a person just does ordinary, hard, common-sense thinking about writing in general . . . I don't mean about writing only, but about books, novels, poems, stories that he's acquainted with—if he asks himself what he likes or doesn't like about them: that sharpens your wits; it goes deep down into your innards somewhere. It stays there, and is supposed to come out and affect your whole view of things, your whole practice, isn't it?

harry minetree: Can you really be that objective about something you're writing?

warren: I think you have to be at some stage. People are different, you know. Some people pour it out and it is fine; some people pour it out and it's awful. And some people grind it out very hard, and it is awful; and some people grind it out very hard, and it's good. I don't see any generalization. I do think one thing is always true: the degree of self-criticism is only good for a veto. You can throw out what you've got wrong, and you can even try to say why it's wrong, but you can't say, "Now I am going to do it right." At that point you're alone with the alone, and the alone had better come and do it, because you can't. Where the alone happens to be living, I don't know; he's backed up in your nervous system, or a must, or something. You need help at that point. It's got to happen to you, but the way you can make it happen to you, it strikes me, is just by keeping your eyes open about the way the world operates about you, and the way a piece of writing operates that you like or dislike: some know of an awareness as to how they operate. All the critical thinking you can do has to be forgotten as critical thinking whenever you sit down to write. It's bound to affect you, bound to be in you somewhere. Just as everything else is bound to be in you. I'm not disparaging hard critical, or other, thinking, but I think there's a right time and a wrong time for it.

JAMES WHITEHEAD: Sir, may I ask a question in two parts? You said that your nostalgic feeling about Burden may have been central. I wonder first, how much of that first chapter, after you had seen it as such, you felt was in a sense the enveloping tone of the novel. It struck me that this is the music that comes before the action in a sense you never forget, and that's in the first chapter. The other part of the question is: were you living in Louisiana when you got that out—from your inside, so to speak?

WARREN: I had been living in Louisiana for several years when I started to write. I started the play there, and I finished it in Rome, and then I laid it aside for several years and wrote two other books in between.

WHITEHEAD: It is the man who is the referent, the kicking-off place, not the sense, the sense of the land which you got across in the first chapter.

WARREN: No, I can't choose between those two things. It started as the simplest kind of idea. A man who has the gift for power gets his means and his ends mixed up, and gets some power, and there's a backlash on him. He gets killed. It starts with that. Huey Long and Julius Caesar both got killed in the capitol, and there you are. It's as simple as that. It's a germ, an anecdote. And teaching Shakespeare in Louisiana in 1935, you couldn't avoid this speculation.

CYRUS HOY: It's appropriate that you should have finished writing the play in Rome.

WARREN: Yes. The troops were under the window every day. But the tone of the play had not been the tone of the book. For better or for worse. And the tone of the book turned on the question of getting a lingo for this narrator. I remember that fact quite distinctly. It was a question just of his lingo, and fumbling around with how he's going to talk—he's got to talk some way. A straight journalistic prose would not do. That is the trap of all traps. There has to be an angularity to any piece of writing that claims to have a person behind it. The problem was to find a way for him to talk. It was really a backward process. The character wasn't set up—aside from the lingo, and trying to find a way for him to talk.

WHITEHEAD: Then the man saw that the country existed.

WARREN: His ambivalence about what he saw—as a road, as people, as things—was a start. His division of feeling was the way it came out of the start of the lingo. That was the germ. It didn't start with a plot, or conception. This guy gets power, and he gets shot. All the details of Burden's life were improvised. They were improvised in terms of some envisagement of his feelings about everything at the end. But I didn't know what the last chapter was going to be until I got there. I didn't know how I wanted it to feel. Just as Flannery was saying: you go back a little bit, and keep looking back. After you are along the way, keep looking back, and your backward looks along the way will help you go forward. You have to find a logic there that you pursue. If you can't find it, you're in trouble.

. . . .

WARREN: I must say that I don't want to nag at a point here that has nothing to do with the one we're discussing, but thinking of oneself as a young writer: it's wrong. I mean, stop boasting. You see, you think you know everything, and you've got to put it down. Don't play yourself for a coward, play for keeps. I think you have to do it that way. Not that nice little exercise I am doing because I am young, and ought to be forgiven. Nothing will be forgiven. It will stink just as much if you did it as if Hemingway did it. It will be just as bad. "I am a young learning writer, and I mean well" is a terrible way to think of it. You're full of urgency and wisdom; you've got to spill it, and set the world aright.

A young man I knew some time ago was such a talented young man, really, and so bright. He knew everything. He knew about Kafka and Aristotle; he had read everything. He was the most educated young man I had encountered in years. He was twenty-one years old, a senior at Yale, scholar of the house, prize product of an expensive educational system, and he was leaving his studies, he was so bright. "You just go write a novel or novelette for your project, no more classes for a year," and things like that. He wrote well; he knew all about how he should feel as a young writer of twenty-one. Like that cartoon I saw in *The New Yorker* some years ago of two little boys reading a book of child care, and one little boy saying, "Jesus, I'm going to be a stinker two years from now." This boy was writing just like that, that kind of self-consciousness, you know. He had dated himself, you see, along the way.

He was writing a novel, a love story, and the boy got the girl after certain tribulations that were casebook tribulations, it seemed to me, because I am sure he couldn't have gotten them out of real life. Nobody acts like that. They were all so right, intellectually. He knew what people should feel at the age of eighteen, nineteen, twenty, and twenty-one, and fifty-three, and fifty-nine, and seventy-six. He had it all worked out—the life pattern for the fruit fly there at his fingertips. He had a wonderful last paragraph. They got in a clinch and everything was fine, and then they were going to get married. Then this last paragraph: I found it sort of chilling. He said he knew of course this was not really love; he knew that love would come after years of shared experiences: you know, walking the baby with the colic, and the mortgages. Now, just imagine a young man twenty-one years old who knows all about Kafka and Aristotle writing like that. The girl ought to run screaming into the brush. He's dated himself as a young writer, you see, a young human being, a post-puberty adult, some kind of thing like that. His life, everything, was all dated and sealed up. Romeo would never have thought of himself in that way: "This is not true love—that would be seventeen years from now, when we pay off the mortgage." I think it's a dangerous way to look at things. You've got to feel you know the truth, got to tell it—it's the gospel. Hate your elders.

MINETREE: What term would you suggest in preference to "young writers"?

WARREN: I don't know. That's not my problem.

SULLIVAN: What do you call yourself, Red?

WARREN: I say I am trying to be a writer.

GEORGE CORE: Mr. Warren, how did you finally hit upon the form of *Brother to Dragons?*

WARREN: This is awfully like a dissecting room, where the corpse is scarcely able to fight back. To answer your question: by fumbling. It started out to be a novel. It clearly couldn't be a novel because the circumstantiality would bog you down, would kill off the main line. And then it started off to be a play. I was doing it in collaboration with a dramatist and producer, and we couldn't quite make it, couldn't agree. I couldn't get a frame for it—the machinery got too much in the way for me. And I was thinking of the wrong kind of problems at the wrong time. But what I was concerned with were the characters, and the emotional sense of it; I didn't want to be bothered by the pacing of it, that technical side. In other words, I didn't naturally think in dramatic terms. The next step was to throw away the notion of the stage play, and keep what was to me the dramatic image, which was the collision of these persons under the unresolved urgency of their earthly experience. All the characters come out of their private purgatory and collide; everybody comes to find out or tell something, rehearse something; it becomes a rehearsal of their unresolved lives in terms of a perspective put on it. That is what the hope was. Then there was the need to tie this to a personal note, putting the writer character in so he could participate in this process, the notion being that we are all unresolved in a way, the dead and the living. This interpenetration, this face [fact?] of a constant effort to resolve things, came back to the idea of a play again.

RANDALL MIZE: Miss O'Connor, yesterday you spoke about the problem of introducing a definite theological motivation in writing in a society which is somewhat religious only on the surface. Do you think it is possible to write from a definite theological point of view?

O'CONNOR: Yes, if you're a writer in the first place. If you are a writer, you can write from any point of view. I don't think a theological point of view interferes in any way unless it becomes so dominant that you're so full of ideas that you kill the character.

WARREN: Flannery, would this be true about theology or anything else: that by the sort of deductive way of going at it—illustrating the point—you're a dead duck before you start?

. . . .

BETTY WEBER: Miss O'Connor, I was interested in what you said yesterday about the grotesque in fiction writing, particularly in Southern writers. You say that the South can still recognize what a freak is, but perhaps thirty years from now we will be writing about the man in the gray flannel suit. I wondered if you would talk a bit more about that. Perhaps you'd explain why you think that's true.

O'CONNOR: I think as it gets to be more and more city and less country—as we, everything, is reduced to the same flat level

—we'll be writing about men in gray flannel suits. That's about all there'll be to write about, I think, as we lose our individuality.

WARREN: Did you like *Augie March?*

O'CONNOR: I didn't read it.

WARREN: In Bellow's book I had the sense, particularly in the first half, that it was very rich in personalities. An urban Jewish South Side Chicago world, and the people had a lot of bursting-off the page. They were really personalities. They were anything but people in gray flannel suits. That he could in that particular work catch this vigor—this clash— of personality: that's what I liked best about the book.

O'CONNOR: I shouldn't say "city" in that sense. I mean—

WARREN: Suburbs, yes.

O'CONNOR: I mean just the proliferation of supermarkets.

WARREN: The city has sort of a new romance after the super-market civilization of the suburbs; it's the new Wild West. I think Saul caught that in a way. Certainly there's a richness in his book.

O'CONNOR: That's his region. Everybody has to have a region, and I think in the South we're losing that regional sense.

WARREN: Well, you can't keep it for literary purposes.

O'CONNOR: No, because everybody wants the good things of life, like supermarkets—

WARREN: —and plastics—

O'CONNOR: —and cellophane. Everybody wants the privilege of being as abstract as the next man.

WALTER RUSSELL: We've talked a good bit about this flattening out of personality. For reasons that are undefined to me, I have a good bit more faith in—what do you want to call it?—the resilience of individuality, and I think it must find its way of cropping out between the divisions of the coun-try some way. Do you?

WARREN: I think there is danger in our talking about it at all. In a way, as individuals, or people who live in one place or another place, we can't avoid talking about it, I guess. It's clearly a dehumanizing of man. All the philosophers know about it, and we've heard about it, too. And you see it going on: the draining away of all responsibilities and identities and those things. But it is a little like that scholar of the house, you know: the plan he got from the mental health center, or the university, or wherever he got it, and this is a kind of self-consciousness again. Anybody who sets out to be an individual, a real character, is intolerable. You can't bear the posiness of the crusty old character. "I have a role. I'm going to make my dent on society by having a role. I know my function, my kind of joke, my kind of this, my kind of that." It can run off in that direction. Then you have professional Californians, and all sorts of highheeled-boot boys.

RUSSELL: But they're working at it.

WARREN: Everybody is working at it. Every place has its own kind of professional exponents—those who are going to be characters. Characters are the last thing in the world, it seems to me. They're the anti-individuals. They're substituting something for the notion of individuality, for fundamental integrity. We begin to talk about this, and we're singing the swan song. The mere fact that we're talking about it is a danger signal. We're made too self-conscious about it.

WHITEHEAD: I've a feeling that it's an unfortunate thing if some boy in Manhattan hasn't seen a cow or smelled a cedar tree. I'm not quite sure why—

WARREN: He feels pretty sorry for you, too.

WHITEHEAD: Yes, I know. That's the thing that bothers me.

WARREN: Maybe you're both right.

THOMAS MCNAIR: I think that what Miss O'Connor and Mr. Warren have been speaking about, this dehumanization, becomes a problem to the writer, because he perhaps is one of the surviving individuals. Perhaps, like Huxley in *Brave New World*, he may write about the whole man, he may write about other individuals, and his dehumanized readers can't even recognize his creation. They can't understand what he's writing about.

WARREN: I think maybe we're giving ourselves airs to think we're writing about the whole man.

MCNAIR: Well, comparatively speaking.

WARREN: I think it's really what Flannery was talking about yesterday. You write about the whole man by writing about freaks. If you want to write about the whole man, write with this negative approach. By "freak" I mean anybody you know who is worth writing about.

MCNAIR: You shifted the terms around, but I think you mean the same thing.

WARREN: You occasionally get a very complete man, and he has no story. Who cares about Robert E. Lee? Now, there's a man who's smooth as an egg. Turn him around, this primordial perfection: you see, he has no story. You can't just say what a wonderful man he was, and that you know he had some chaotic something inside because he's human, but you can't get at it. You know he was probably spoiling with blood lust, otherwise he wouldn't have been in that trade, wouldn't have done so well at it. We can make little schemes like this, and try to jazz it up a bit, but really what you have is this enormous, this monumental self-control, and selflessness, and lots of things like that. You have to improvise a story for him. You don't know his story. It's only the guy who's angular, incomplete, and struggling who has a story. If a person comes out too well, there's not much story. Whoever wants to tell a story of a sainted grandmother, unless you can find some old love letters, and get a new grandfather? In heaven there's no marriage and giving in marriage, and there's no literature.

MCNAIR: Don't you think perhaps it is easier for us in the South to recognize what is important in the freak to be written about?

WARREN: We've gotten some good documents.

MCNAIR: Easier for us than for a person in New York, in Manhattan.

O'CONNOR: I don't know. I had a friend from Brooklyn who went out to school in Indiana some place, and he said all he saw out there were healthy blond youngsters. He went back to Brooklyn and he saw a little old man about this high with a cigar in his mouth, and he said, "Ah! I'm home."

SULLIVAN: There's Cheever. He knows some freaks.

WARREN: And he knows he knows them. I think his point is, they don't know they're freaks. Until they read his stories about themselves. They think it's the man next door.

WHITEHEAD: In a sense, we're trying to say we can't get too involved in geography. You never know—you make a value judgment on something like that—you speak of something you never have seen—

WARREN: I think there's a real problem about your relation to your own world, but I don't think it's a matter of saying what's better and what's worse, because everybody is stuck with his own skin, and his own history, and his own situation. I think he's got every right to think about that, but I don't think it's a matter of choosing up sides for this purpose, this idea that you have to be chosen for this point or that point. I think self-congratulation is a mighty poor way to celebrate human nature. Joyce didn't hang around Dublin pleasing the Dubliners, yet Dublin is always there. Flattering yourself and your community is a mighty poor way, it seems to me, to write anything, or to be a good citizen, for that matter. Your own concern is in the defects, the jags.

WHITEHEAD: Yet it's possible you can find a piece of geography which makes you more aware of your own skin.

WARREN: You're just stuck with it. You can't choose it.

MCNAIR: That may all be true, and theoretically you can say that a writer in one place will write about the people in his place, bringing out the man in man, as well as the writer in another place.

WARREN: He has to.

MCNAIR: But is the best literature written in the South today or not? And why is it best?

WARREN: It is not our business to speculate about that point. It's not my business, at least. I am second to no man in admiring a lot of writers that happen to be born in Mississippi and contiguous states, but this sort of speculation doesn't do a writer any good. It leads right away to "Where's my piece of cake?" Something like that. It seems to me it's a very poor way to think about it, unless you want to be a social historian, or a critic, or a literary historian, or something like that. But it's no one's business to think about it very much. To think of how a person is related to his society is a very important point, but I think it should be thought about not as a writer but as a person. Thinking about it as a writer is the wrong level for going at it. Any important question should be thought about on its own merits, and not in relation to one as a writer.

CHRIS BONER: When a writer sits down to write, should he be more conscious of himself as a writer, or as a person?

WARREN: He shouldn't be conscious of himself at all. It seems to me he ought to be trying to do his job. A guy learning to catch a baseball has to learn by trial and error. A guy doing a broken field run has to have some training in this. When he's in there he'd better not stop and say, "Am I pretty or not?" When the tackle is bearing down. His business is speed at that point, and nothing but speed—and a little deception.

. . . .

WARREN: There's no stupidity it seems to me, at one level, in saying "All right, there are 'Southern writers' (in quotes)," and start saying what they do share. That is a reasonable thing to say, and a reasonable field of speculation, just so long as you don't equate them. Some clearly are synthetic, and write by imitating, trying to pose as another writer; some are purely imitators and have no personality except a synthetic one they're attached to. They use the group label as a way of trying to achieve some identity, of trying to be writers at all. But that is universally a problem; he's got to learn from somebody else. It is very hard for him to find any kind of voice of his own. That's his big trouble, it seems to me. But he can't find it except by saying he's going to find it, he's got to work around the problem, not head on into it. If he heads on into it, he's probably going to be the worst kind of imitator. Or he'll invent something to get a difference. But I don't see anything reprehensible in grouping a whole lot of—no use naming names, you know all the names, just say the "Southern writers." They do share something; what they do with what they share is a very important thing; what they are from one to another is a very important difference. That is what makes the fact that you can group them together a rather piquant thing. If you look at the next step, an ordinary writer on the subject says what they share, and then makes the group. The interesting thing is, having made the groups, seeing then what the differences are within that, in terms of all sorts of things: kinds of talents, temperaments, philosophy, and God knows what. But that is the next stage, and it's rarely done.

SULLIVAN: There seems to be some sort of tacit agreement here that the South is a rich land of images. Could you say something about the dangers of this attitude of not transcending the image. It seems to me that the great danger here is that the Southern writer will be so busy being Southern that he won't be anything else.

WARREN: It's certainly a trap.

SULLIVAN: Do you think it's as great a trap as I seem to think it is?

WARREN: Well, it couldn't be worse.

SULLIVAN: How about that, Flannery?

O'CONNOR: I don't know. I think if you're a real writer, you can avoid that kind of thing. There are so many horrible examples of regional writers, and the South is loaded. There's one behind every bush. So many awful examples. It's the first thing you think of avoiding.

WARREN: Yet you're stuck with your own experiences, your own world around you.

O'CONNOR: You have to keep going in deeper.

A Conversation with Robert Penn Warren

Frank Gado based this interview on an exchange between Warren and faculty and students of Union College, Schenectady, New York, February 8, 1966. Warren later edited the interview himself. It was published in Gado's book First Person: Conversations on Writers and Writing (*1973*).

. . . .

INTERVIEWER: Thomas Hardy was happy when he could put aside his novels and write poetry. Do you prefer working in one genre more than the others?

WARREN: Depends on what I'm working on at the time. I've thought about this some, and I think that writing poetry is more fun for me. It's so much more personal. I don't mean the material is necessarily more personal, but that it's a closer, more private activity. And technically it's a more exciting challenge: getting the words into the arc of the line and coordinating the meaning with the rhythm. I write poetry until it runs dry and the lines stop coming. Then

I'll switch to a novel and ride along with that, sometimes for six or seven years or maybe more. I don't have any theories about this beyond riding with the impulse.

. . . .

INTERVIEWER: It seems historical events have a special hold on you. *At Heaven's Gate, All the King's Men, World Enough and Time,* and *The Cave*—there may be others—all contain recognizable historical figures or occurrences. Why is this?

WARREN: Recognizable figures? I don't think they are recognizable from my treatment of them. I'm not being facetious. Writing a story about an actual person and using him as a kind of model are really not the same. I don't pretend that Willie Stark is Huey Long. I know Stark, but I have no idea what Long was really like. I heard him speak once at an enormous official luncheon celebrating the seventy-fifth anniversary of the founding of Louisiana State University —he had not been invited but walked in anyway and took over, and he was very funny. Then on another occasion I saw him—or I think it was he—in a passing car.

I knew stories about Long, but that's quite different. What happened with the real Long and what his motives were is between him, his God, and his conscience. There's no way in the world for me, or you, to know that. But I know water runs downhill; and if a bomb explodes, I know that someone lit the fuse. Events don't cause themselves. I saw the end products of Long and I know that men's motives and actions are triggered and operate in certain ways.

INTERVIEWER: Ducking the question . . .

WARREN: I'm not ducking it . . .

INTERVIEWER: No, I mean, let me ask the question in another way. What was it about the Kentucky tragedy that caught your eye?

WARREN: That came right out of a historical situation. Sure, there is a relationship in almost all of my novels with something that was a germ of fact. Individual personalities become mirrors of their times, or the times become a mirror of the personalities. Social tensions have a parallel in the personal world. The individual is an embodiment of external circumstances, so that a personal story is a social story. The mirror business has always struck me as being pretty interesting. I didn't frame this concept early in the process of writing novels, but I have discovered it works as a principle over a long time. . . .

My choosing the "Kentucky tragedy" tale was an accident. I was at the Library of Congress—I had the chair of Poetry—and Katherine Anne Porter, an old friend, who was a Library Fellow in American letters, had an office near mine. One day she said, "Look, here's something for you," and handed me the *Confession of Jeroboam Beauchamp*, and I read it. I had vaguely heard of this before, I guess through the two novels by William Gilmore Simms. It has been treated by others, too. Poe wrote a play about it, in Renaissance disguise. Then there was a book called *Greyslaer: A Romance of the Mohawk* by a fellow named [Charles Fenno] Hoffman—from this neighborhood [i.e., New York State] as a matter of fact. He changed the scene from Kentucky to the Mohawk Valley. He had earlier reported the trial in a book called *A Winter in the West*, a travel book published in 1826. This story, you see, has had a lot of literary adaptations, but I didn't know that before I got interested in it and began to look around. Without realizing the story had played such a role in American letters, I was caught right off by the character and by the situation, the conflict between what was called the "New Court" party and the "Old Court" party in Kentucky, between new and old, and by the "mirror" thing I mentioned before. Then, too, I shouldn't underplay the importance of the fact that it had happened around my home section. Beauchamp got into trouble in my home country, and I had some sense of what that world had been like. I could bring to my surmises a certain body of feeling.

INTERVIEWER: When you write novels based on history, do you think of your reader as knowing the stories in the way

that Greek audiences knew the stories on which the trag-
edies were based?

WARREN: Well, no. You can't, really. You have to carry a
context. Oh, at a certain level, yes, you expect some fa-
miliarity with the period, but hardly anybody would know
about the Old versus the New Court party in Kentucky
in 1820.

Incidentally, the New Court party reminded me of the
New Deal. The issues were somewhat the same: adjustments
of debts, economic crises. You can sometimes see one political era in terms of another.

INTERVIEWER: I hadn't realized that your use of history also
involved a dialogue between the real and the ideal.

WARREN: If I understand you, this would mean adjusting historical "fact" to fictional need. I can give you an instance in
which such a change was deliberate. I found that my historical man, Jeroboam Beauchamp, who killed his ex-spon-
sor and benefactor, Colonel Sharp, had belonged to the Old
Court party and that Sharp belonged to the New Court.
Now, that didn't suit my scheme. The older man should
be with the Old Court, the young man with the New—the
"idealistic." In terms of my theme, that was the wrong
layout, so I shifted them around. I had no compunction
about doing this, because the historical Beauchamp was
merely a prototype of my hero, and besides, was of no
historical importance.

INTERVIEWER: Your comments about a dialogue with history
remind me of Faulkner. Faulkner said somewhere that there
were only two nations in the United States—the South and
New England. At least in part, he seemed to have meant
that this sense of nationhood, of a people united by a common body of myth, was tied in with the region's closeness
to its history.

WARREN: Americans in general have a more highly developed
sense of history than the Europeans because our history is so
short. A man my age has known, right in his own family,
people whose memories go back farther than the midpoint

of our history as an independent nation. Now, that's bound
to have an effect on our thinking about the past.
   The South is a special case. It lost the war and suffered
hardship. That kind of defeat gives the past great importance. There is a need somehow to keep it alive, to justify
it, and this works to transform the record of fact into
legend. In the process, pain, dreariness, the particulars of the
individual experience become absorbed in the romantic fable.
The romance, you see, becomes stronger than the fact of
any one story and changes it; even if you are only one or two
generations removed from the event, it's hard to see through
the romantic haze. Maybe that's one of the reasons Southern
writers are so concerned with history. They've heard the
stories since they were kids and later on they try to understand them in terms of their own range of experience as
human beings. And in terms of scholarly history.

INTERVIEWER: *All the King's Men* was first written as a play.
What virtues did it gain in its recasting in novel form?

WARREN: My approach to the question would not be abstract.
The changes had to do with how the recasting happened.
As you said, I wrote the play version first. I showed it to a
friend who knew about drama, Francis Fergusson, who
worked on it quite seriously and gave me a brief con-
centrated course in drama based on my play. But then I
laid the story aside and wrote another book. It kept nagging
at me, however, and I decided to revise it and make it a
novel.
   It was a tight little play. When I read it over, I missed part
of my feelings involved in the original idea. The significant
context for the action, the world in which these things
could happen, was not there. Formulation of the context
grew in the process of writing a novel. It was this instinct
for a context that drove me on. Besides, I knew more about
novels than I did about plays. The notion—or *a* notion—
behind the play was that a man gains power because he is
drawn into a vacuum of power. In one sense, is a creation
of history. There was the germ of this in the first version,
but in the novel this became more and more important—as

"context." The narrator, Burden, has a "vacuum"—purpose-lessness—that Stark can fill. The bodyguard stutters, and Stark "talks so good." And so on with the mistress and others. For each individual, the "strong man" is a fulfill-ment. Here the individuals are the mirrors to society, in a sense.

But to return to the narrator, as an aside. He was the key in this respect. But he originally came into existence as a kind of accident. As a matter of fact, technical requirements often dictate character and meaning. It may be an aside here, but I'll tell how this particular character came about. In the play there is, of course, the assassination scene, in which the young doctor waits in the lobby of the capitol for the political boss to appear. You know he's outraged and that he has a gun in his pocket, and so you know he's going to shoot this guy. Now what happens? Let's take the play. A man comes out onstage, hand in pocket, hat drip-ping rain. He stands there. Stop. Let's pretend we're in the audience; we have all the information—couldn't have missed it—and as we sit there watching we say, "Go ahead and shoot him." Well, he hasn't come out yet. To which we say, "Come out and get shot, coward." Of course, you see the problem. The author has to satisfy the demand to get on with the play, yet he can't go too fast or it would kill the play. It can't happen rapidly—automatically, according to the expectations. A barrel, rolling down a hill, hits a tree, breaks up. That's action, but it's not drama. You've got to find some way to make the barrel bounce off here and bounce off there. Will it hit? Will it not? In short: distract attention. Throw something across the path of the driving object. A competing interest which serves as a "hold" to make the inevitable, when it happens, come as unforeseen.

This principle of a "hold" and distraction is rudimentary to dramatic art, to any form of telling which is not pure lyric poetry. It's as natural as breathing, but still it's very difficult to devise. You are not working out a syllogism or adding a bridge score; you are trying to fool people. You work toward something which is *expected* and at the same

time *not expected;* you want a double take on it. You want
shock or surprise, and yet a sense of its being logical. You
want variety, and you want the obvious line of a simple plot.

So here we are in this scene: "Come on out!" If he comes
out and it's bang-bang, then there's nothing to it, nothing
but a blank spot. If you wind up this way, the play is dead.
So I had to find something to fall across this moment when
the assassin is waiting. Something both natural and dis-
tracting. So I brought in someone and tried to get a conversation under way. "How are things going?" "All right,
I guess." "We had a lot of good times when we were kids,
didn't we? Sure had good times." And the assassin says,
"We certainly did."

That's the sort of thing you build on. Now, even at the
moment before the act which means his own death too, he
takes a backward look on life—boyhood, innocence, and all
of that. "Yes, we had nice times"—and in that little moment of speech there's retrospect to a lost world. Then out
comes the victim. Bang! Bang! But you've gotten something across there, some current of feeling running counter
to the other drive.

So when I first began to think of starting over with a
novel, I had to decide on the "voice." The idea of an all-
knowing author felt all wrong; no principle for dramatizing
development, no internal dramatization of the "vacuum."
So out of the air I pulled the nameless newspaperman, an
old friend. Give him a role—"vacuum." Why not make it
complicated? Make it an employee of the victim: his hatchet
man. I've known men from the newspaper world and
their theatrical stances. So, okay, put him in and let him
start talking. You're on your way.

So, you see, the play got switched over to a novel because
of a defect of meaning, because it didn't have a context, and
because of a technical consideration. But told this way,
things sound a bit too deliberate. They are arrived at by
trial and error usually. You rule out one possibility and then
grope around for something else. You follow some hunch
rather than a line of abstract reasoning.

INTERVIEWER: Did you recognize the problem with the play before or after it was first produced at the University of Minnesota?

WARREN: That production took place after the novel had been out six months or so. A friend of mine, Eric Bentley, who is now an eminent critic of drama, was one of my colleagues there. He asked me, "Didn't you write this as a play once?" I said, "Yes." "Let me see it," he said. So I did and he took it around to the drama school, where they decided to introduce it. It was a very splendid production.

. . . .

INTERVIEWER: When the movie was made, was there any use of the play version?

WARREN: No, but when I sold them the book, I had to sign the play over to them, too, to prevent any chance of my coming out later and claiming that they had taken something from the dramatic version.

INTERVIEWER: Perhaps you could settle an old argument. When I was in graduate school, a girl was writing a thesis on *All the King's Men* which maintained that Burden was the existentialist hero of an existentialist novel. To me, this was nonsense, and I was secretly delighted when our adviser, on returning from a colloquium with you at Yale, told her the underlying philosophical scheme was Hegelian. She almost assaulted him physically. Practically called him a liar.

WARREN: It's instructive for me. I wish I had known it.

INTERVIEWER: Neither existential nor Hegelian?

WARREN: I didn't know about it, either way.

INTERVIEWER: Didn't using Burden as narrator change the novel's center of gravity? In one way, he's more important than Stark.

WARREN: There is, of course, a vast difference between the two. Stark is the control point of the narrative, the first impulse, so to speak. But I had to set him within the context of a world. I needed an efficient cause. Power moving into a vacuum. So I got my vacuum fellow, or, as it were, my partial vacuum fellow, into the story. But the real center of gravity in the novel is the dynamics of power. The newspaperman helps illustrate it.

INTERVIEWER: Burden is fundamentally a decent man. What leads him to be an agent of evil?

WARREN: He is a man with a grave defect of character and personality—and he knows it. He's blind in certain ways and he's ready to be a tool, to enter someone else's magnetic field. Sounds awful, doesn't it? But it's a constant thing—power operates that way. Even nice people like Adlai Stevenson operated that way. All the people I knew wanted to do something for him in their spare time, even if they had to push doorbells. They were in love with Adlai. He filled their "vacuum." I voted for him, too. In 1952, that is.

There is a natural need to build something, to be part of a cause, to gain meaning. This can get to be an evil thing when the great blankness of life is filled by terrible forces. Look at what happens when this sense of cause is stimulated by a Hitler or Mussolini. I was in Italy when I was writing the play—I finished it in Italy in the first year of the war—so I couldn't help but relate these things, being right in the middle of it. I was cut off from my own world and I suppose this made my senses more acute. I was bound to wonder what made these events, what blankness had made it all possible.

INTERVIEWER: I'm still confused. Which theme struck you as most important: Burden's quest for self-knowledge or Willie's political corruption?

WARREN: Well, it wasn't so back and forth, you know, in the process of composition. Things don't come as clear options—rather, as aspects of a single complex process.

INTERVIEWER: Which one provided the forward movement?

WARREN: Well, I wanted them to be related. I wanted to make a story, rather than have the story make the relationship. It never crossed my mind that Burden . . . No, that's not true— I guess it crossed my mind. Let me put it this way: Stark was the conscious focused image.

Maybe I didn't succeed very well. I remember going to

see Bernard Berenson and being quite shocked when he said, "I want to tell you about your book. That fellow Stark is not very interesting." Well, I was taken aback because I thought I'd done my level best by Stark. He gave me a real lecture on this, a real lecture. The book, he said, was all Burden; for him, Stark was an excuse for Burden's existence. He liked the book fine, but not for my reasons.

INTERVIEWER: You were also criticized for doing too well by Stark, weren't you?

WARREN: Well, I've been called a fascist off and on all my life. That's what happens to a Jeffersonian Democrat in this crazy world we live in.

INTERVIEWER: Why did you choose Huey Long as a model? Was it because the events of his life made for an exciting novel, or was there a particular moral issue about Long himself?

WARREN: What I say might sound rude, but I don't mean it to be. It's not at all a matter of choosing in most cases, but of being chosen. The natural thing is for the story to be about you—it's always about you. You don't really start off: It's time to write a novel, what shall I write about? Now, there may be instances—Hollywood or some commercial writing —where the writer is that objective. But I don't think most writers, good or bad, work that way. They tend to have a lot of stories available to them just because they are human beings. Anybody here knows a lot of stories—whether he knows he knows them or not, he knows them. Now, when a writer decides on one of the many stories he has encountered, he doesn't just say: I'll take the third from the left. He sees his material in terms of a type of story that somehow catches hold of him, like a cockleburr in his hair. Why it's this story instead of that one that he picks to work on may be accidental, but waiving that consideration, it's really because it has a germ of meaning for him personally. An observation or an event snags on to an issue in your own mind, feelings, life—some probably unformulated concern that makes the exploration of the connection between that thing and the issue rewarding. This can happen without your being conscious of why some particular scene makes it happen.

I don't for the life of me know why the Long cockleburr got hold of me, but the accidental reason is easy: I was living in Louisiana where there was a world that was very dramatic and about which I had very ambivalent feelings. One gang was saying, "Oh, this savior!" and another was saying, "Oh, this son-of-a-bitch!" You couldn't help but speculate on what accounted for this social situation. But you could be certain of one thing: it didn't happen out of the blue. There had to be a context beforehand. When you have incompetent or bad government long enough, you get Willie Stark. Somebody had to move in to fill the vacuum. It doesn't have to be a vacuum of power; it can be thought of as a vacuum of social goods. A felt need will be satisfied, one way or other, and it doesn't matter whether Stark is just making promises or is actually trying to deliver on them.

Now, this was going on in Louisiana in a very dramatic way. But it was happening everywhere in the world. The New Deal—same thing. You see, somebody has to provide the bread and circuses; if not, there's going to be real trouble. You won't just have bad government but maybe no government at all. And I don't mean to sneer at the democratic process. When the voters have a need they want immediately satisfied and somebody says, "I can do it for you," why, it's natural for them to elect him. Of course, you can have a leader who is fulfilling justified needs merely as a means of seizing power, or who uses corrupt means to fulfill the legitimate needs, and that raises the question of what price tag you're willing to put on the fulfillment.

The situation in Louisiana prompted my amateurish speculation about history and morality. It feels strange talking about it now—it was all so long ago; it's like talking in your sleep.

INTERVIEWER: You suggested before that the method of narra-

tion in *All the King's Men* presented a problem. Did any
of Conrad's works furnish a guide?

WARREN: I've known Conrad since I was a boy of fifteen or
sixteen and I like him very much. He's a wonderful novelist.
But I don't think he influenced me, not so I was conscious
of it. But that sort of thing enters the public domain—after
Conrad, novels could never be quite the same; he was in
the air.

INTERVIEWER: Getting away from fiction for a moment, would
you comment on your view of political power as something shaped by an existing vacuum as it relates to the
desegregation of the South?

WARREN: Sure. In 1954, if there had been any leadership out
of Washington—that is, if old Ike had been even half aware
of his obligation to exert his authority and leadership—a
great mess would have been avoided. But he retired from
the issue, and instead of giving a rallying point for moder-
ate and liberal opinions, he put his head under a blanket
for almost a whole year. There was a vacuum in leadership
from Washington and on the local level too, and this en-
abled a hard-nosed segregationist minority to charge right
in.

I remember talking to the Secretary of Education in one
of the Southern states at the time. He said, "Look. Shut that
door and I'll tell you right now that sixty percent of all
my county superintendents would like nothing better than to
be desegregated tomorrow. They're all bankrupt, and inte-
grating the schools would save them no end of money.
What they need is for somebody to get up the right legal
suit so they can turn around and say, 'I didn't do it—they
made me.' If they could save face, they'd be glad. We can't
afford segregated schools. But if you print that I said this,
I'll call you a liar."

I remember, too, going up into a little county in Arkansas that had desegregated voluntarily. It was 1955, late '55,
and there had been a lot of violence there. The people were
poor; I remember seeing people lining up in the streets for

government beans. I spent a very long time with one of the officials—chairman of the school board, I think he was. I asked about the decision to desegregate, and he said, "We didn't have any theories. We were broke. It cost sixteen thousand dollars a year to move them niggers to a Negro school and we didn't even have sixteen thousand dollars, so we figured if we integrated, we'd save sixteen thousand dollars a year. But then the speech-makers started stirring things up and soon my business was being boycotted. They were getting ready to bomb my house, my wife was threatened, and my kids were being chased by little ruffians. I reached the breaking point. One day I was coming out of the post office when some guy stopped me and called me a nigger-lover. Well, I let him have it. Now I don't care—I'll take the consequences." This is an interesting story, you see. This man had a problem in responsibility. He worked it out logically and defended his position, even to standing up to the bomb throwers. In the end, he came out on the side of a principle. If there had been some real leadership in the land, his story might have been multiplied many times over.

INTERVIEWER: But if a man is a convinced segregationist from the start, how much of a possibility is there for his conversion on the basis of principle? Doesn't prejudice rule out logical deductions?

WARREN: You can ask a man, "Are you for segregation?" and he may answer, "Yes, suh, segregation forever." Well, what he's really saying is that he's for segregation—everything else being equal. Would he be for segregation if it cost him a considerable amount of money? If it meant not educating his kids? If he had to go to jail? When things get sorted out, segregation is probably not at the top of his list of priorities—and leadership should sort things out.

There's danger in looking at the white Southerners and writing them off as Negro-hating segregationists. People, you must remember, are awfully complex creatures, and you may be in for some surprises if you divide the cast into heroes and villains. History plays some pretty cruel jokes. Remember when all the liberals in England were wringing their hands over the plight of the poor Boers in South Africa? You should: it's in the history books. Not too long ago the Boers were the persecuted people. Not much sympathy for the Boers nowadays. The same Boers are now the prime racist villains of the world. And remember that wonderful book *Let Us Now Praise Famous Men*, with pictures by Walker Evans and James Agee's text? Everybody's heart bled for those poor people—the white sharecroppers of Alabama. The book exposed the poetry and pathos of their lives for us to weep over. Now those who then were doing the weeping go down to Tuscaloosa or to the march on Montgomery and see those same people and they become the hounds of hell in the public eye. They're no worse and no better than they ever were, but you change the question and you get a different perspective.

INTERVIEWER: Getting back to novel writing: have you ever used actual persons in your writing and then been embarrassed when you met them again later and they told you they recognized themselves?

WARREN: No, they don't know it at all, and I don't tell them about it. Sure, you use things—you even use yourself and try not to tell yourself about it. You use whatever you can get your hands on; but you're not really using a person, you use something attached to a person—some suggestion, some episode, some quirk or trait of character. Take Jack Burden. I used a model, but he doesn't know it yet. I know him very well indeed. I even know that he doesn't know what I know about him. And that's knowing a man mighty well.

INTERVIEWER: Why did you have Stark start out as an idealist? Was it because one of the stories you heard about Huey Long was that he began this way?

WARREN: In a way, it seems there was a deep mixture of impulses in Huey, which is only a way of saying he was human and stuck with himself. But Huey aside, dramatic considerations would have dictated the "idealism." I remember a lawyer I was interviewing in Arkansas. He said something like "I started out to make a little money—to study law and make a little money. Then I wanted to square things up and I got caught up in it, you see." This man simply stumbled into idealism. You encounter such things all the time.

INTERVIEWER: If you draw on real people you know, doesn't your novel, when you reread it, have a depth it doesn't have for us who aren't acquainted with the models?

WARREN: Oh, I know where the materials come from and I could trace them down, but the people in the book aren't the people I drew on. Bits have been projected, whole aspects of character have been filled in, basic changes have been made.

INTERVIEWER: I'd like to ask a question about criticism. People are always asking, "What does this mean?" And critics write all their articles trying to explain away the confusion. Now, I don't read a novel to get at any real meaning behind it. I read for enjoyment. Is that so wrong? Isn't there a danger that literary criticism will get to be like logical positivism in philosophy: a concern with meaning that winds up just being a study of words? Maybe a book should confuse you just to make you think.

WARREN: Do you mean you're confused when you think?

INTERVIEWER: No, I mean that confusion inspires new patterns of action.

WARREN: I'm not trying to make a joke when I say I'm so confused that I would welcome some clarity, or some help towards clarity. What we want, I think, is not added confusion but a mental experience that gives a sense of moving from disorder to order, to a moment of poise. It isn't a matter of just getting to some resolution tagged on at the back of the book. What we basically get out of a novel or play is an imaginative involvement in experience. The novel, say, starts with "confusion"—that is, with a problematic situation; otherwise, there would be no "story." But you must move through the "confusion" to the point when you can say, "Ah, now I see." This is an image of the possibility of meaning in life. It's a metaphor for meaning. To me this is a key notion. There is a satisfaction, a lift, a liberation in reading a good novel, seeing a good play, or reading a good poem. I feel, "Oh, things *do* work, after all!" Most of life is a hodgepodge in which it's very hard to feel meaningful. Seeing life in some way reflected in a guise that implies order gives a heightening of energy, of relief. It's a liberation. *Not*, I should emphasize, because of particular "solutions" offered, but because the process is an image of the possibility of meaning growing from experience—an image, that is, of our continuous effort to make sense of our lives.

INTERVIEWER: But I can't construct a philosophy in books. What they do is to make me seek more, to give me new ideas.

WARREN: Not by confusing you, though, do they?

INTERVIEWER: Yes. If I'm complacent, I won't go anywhere.

WARREN: Oh, but that's another matter. Every story, to be a story, must put you in trouble. The other day I read a remark attributed to—I think—Kathleen Norris. She said writing her novels was perfectly simple: put a good girl in bad trouble and then get her out. Well, she may not write the best novels, but she had the best idea. You want somebody in trouble and you want to wonder if he'll make it through or not. No trouble, no story.

INTERVIEWER: Let me try to synthesize a bit. You maintain that significant fiction deals with trouble and that art represents an attempt to lead from confusion to understanding; would you be subscribing to the theory that great periods of art coincide with periods of stress in history? And might this help account for the Southern renaissance my colleague John Bradbury [14] has been writing about?

WARREN: I don't think there's much doubt about it. But let me try to say what I mean here. Certain kinds of stress do not permit immediate artistic manifestation. As the seventeenth-century poet Abraham Cowley put it, troublous times are the best times to write of but the worst to write in. When the house is on fire, you don't sit down to write a sonnet. But a period of cultural and moral shock, short of the final cataclysm, does breed art. See New England of the great days, or Elizabethan England. Deep conflicts of values can release tremendous amounts of energy. When the pieties are shaken, you are forced to reexamine the whole basis of life. A new present has to be brought in line with the past, and the other way around.

The rapid rate of industrialization of the agricultural South had profound and sweeping effects. Smokestacks were rising—right in the bosom of the Jeffersonian ideal, and, it should be added, in the bosom of a good deal of poverty, pellagra, and illiteracy, not to mention the local variety of racism.

INTERVIEWER: When you've written a book, do you feel you've surrendered it to its audience? Should a reader be at all concerned with what you meant when you wrote it? I guess I'm really asking: Do you believe the so-called intentional fallacy is a fallacy?

WARREN: Stated that way, it's primarily a question of semantics. I would prefer to approach it from the other side. A writer doesn't know what his intentions are until he's done writing.

INTERVIEWER: So, in a way, writer and reader are approaching the work on a similar footing?

WARREN: If you look on a work as the writer's exploration of possibilities, then the question takes on a different complexion. A work represents a growth of meaning. You, the writer, are chiefly involved in finding, in growing toward meaning, but you haven't got a fully organized intended meaning when you start off. You have a certain body of feelings you are hoping to control, but not a specific intention. Intention is closer to result than to cause. A reader can infer an intention—that's well and good and part of the way we react to art—but that doesn't mean it was created according to the reader's impression of intention projected into form. I should add that this impression is exactly what the writer wants the reader to wind up with.

INTERVIEWER: Guide us a little further. When you are writing, are you directing yourself to the work of art, or are you using it as a means to approach your audience and reveal something of yourself and your view of the world?

WARREN: I don't think about my audience when I'm working. This doesn't mean that the audience isn't important. It is, but not right then when I'm concerned with trying "to make it right." I've heard many writers say the same thing. Now, making it right, of course, means making your vision available to somebody. But if you see it's not being made available, if it's going off the rails, it's not because it isn't grasped by an audience but because the thing isn't right itself. You are your own audience, but because the thing you've written doesn't conform to what you think you wanted to express during the process, then it's wrong and you had better start over. No, I'm not saying what I mean. The question is not whether the thing being done fails to conform to a preconceived notion. It is whether—and let me emphasize this—the thing being done is violating a logic implicit in the process of composing it. Or worse, because you have not discovered the internal logic.

Conversation:
Eleanor Clark and
Robert Penn Warren

▬▬▬▬▬▬▬▬▬▬▬▬▬▬▬▬▬▬▬▬▬▬▬▬▬▬▬▬▬▬▬

Chicago book columnist Roy Newquist interviewed Warren and his wife Eleanor Clark for his book Conversations *(1967). Newquist provides no information about the circumstances and surroundings of the interview. Most of the talk not directly related to Warren has been deleted.*

WARREN: Born, April 24, 1905. Guthrie, Kentucky, in Todd County, fifty miles north of Nashville, Tennessee. Population, 1206 or 1305, I forget which. It's still the same—hasn't changed to this day. Half in Tennessee, half in Kentucky, half black, half white.

I went to public schools through my third year of high school in Guthrie, then went away to prep school for a year, and from there to the university. . . . As a writer I arrived fairly late. I wrote one or two things as a youngster. I remember an overwhelmingly passionate desire to write a poem when I was twelve years old and had a fever. This proves the pathology of art. I actually wanted to be a naval officer; I had an appointment to Annapolis, but had an accident and couldn't go, so I went to Vanderbilt University instead. For three weeks I intended to become a chemical engineer. Then I fell into bad company. I had a freshman English coach named John Ransom. He was the last man to recruit, to want to recruit, anyone to writing, but he couldn't help it because he made it so interesting.

Lots of young people took his courses and decided it would be nice to be a writer, and I was one of them.

I wrote a great deal during college, and went on to graduate school at Berkeley, California, for two years, then to Yale graduate school, then to Oxford for two years. . . . I came back to the South in the middle of the Depression. I had to go back. I wasn't programmatic about it; I just felt I had to go there. It wasn't really home, it was simply a part of the world I had a stake in. At Oxford, probably out of homesickness, I began to write fiction. . . . But something happened to me at Oxford that simply took me back to the South. Perhaps it was because of the fact that when I was in college in Tennessee I became so involved with the university world, and to misuse a big word, the philosophical world, that even when the Scopes trial was held a few miles away I didn't go to it. Five years later I thought I was a damned fool not to have gone to it, so I came back from Oxford and became wedded to the South again. I could have gotten a bad job elsewhere.

NEWQUIST: That was during the period when such a disproportionate number of our writers originated in the South.

WARREN: It's true, I suppose, that for a while we did produce more than our share. And you're bound to wonder why, if you have lived in the South a great deal of time. I think it happened this way: The world of the South was frozen from 1865 to 1917, when the First World War came along. Things happened there, but the pattern of thought wasn't disturbed. There were no new ideas, no basic changes in society. The First World War shattered the frozen quality of the South. The key element in the South, the most obvious element, at any rate, is the race business. Once the First World War had been fought the South had to recognize the fact of Negro mobility, labor mobility. The Negroes would move from one place to another in the South where they were needed, and leave the South for opportunities up North.

A comparison (a more drastic thing, but nonetheless a comparison) is what happened in fourteenth-century Europe, when the Black Death struck and the labor ratio was changed. Society couldn't be constructed along the same lines afterward. But all sorts of shocks came to the South, beginning in 1917. I remember the people I knew, the college students and older people of the 1920's; they didn't look to New York or the Middle West, wonder what they were like, admire their writers. I madly admired Dreiser, and still do; he's a great writer, but I didn't look to him for guidance. In a strange way the relationship with the Irish and French writers was more important. Particularly the Irish, because ours is a provincial area, speaking provincial English. Our attention was focused on the European rather than the U.S. Northern. The writers, the Southern writers, of my generation, had a European orientation; Pound, Eliot, Crane, Stevens. Yeats and Joyce and the French novelists were our world. I never heard the word "Marx" used except in Hart, Schaffner and Marx until after I left college. This was a strange contradiction; every Southern freshman, literarily inclined, knew *The Waste Land* by heart in 1922. We sat up all night reading Baudelaire, but Marx and Freud were only ugly rumors.

Then our insular world ended. Strange tensions and ferments were bred, running from the question of a "new conscience"—"new discomfort" was the better description—regarding the Negro situation, and new notions of economics, and a sense of a world existing outside us. Just acquiring a sense of the world outside was challenging.

Hope came, too. The poverty of the South was immense, and the mere fact that the possibility existed of improving one's lot was an exciting thing. Even the black man felt this, as the possibility of change took hold.

Actually, I should think that all literary or artistic revivals, or new states of awareness, are based upon shocks of consciousness or moral shocks. You stir a man to a point where he wonders what he can do about an existing state. This happened in New England in the 1830's and 1840's, and in Elizabethan England of the eighteenth century. The Renaissance was a period of change through shock.

Results are always evidenced at different levels and scales. The society that is frozen, fixed in its values and procedures, begins to think about itself in a new way when it is kicked in the can. In literature the society can objectify the issues it finds most urgent. It's not a parlor trick, not a game; it's both a cause and effect of the society waking up to its own problems, its own inner nature. The South had this experience. It was shocked out of what it was. But you can't shock people too much, as Toynbee has noted. Too much challenge is like shooting a man in the heart. It doesn't make him do anything; he's dead. The Civil War, with its dire poverty and total shock, didn't bring change. It had to be just enough shock, the right shock treatment. The war generation in the South during World War I was the real carrier of the shock. Younger people like me benefited from it. We were picked up in the backwash. But the generation of John Crowe Ransom, Allen Tate, William Faulkner—they made the real crossover.

World War II hasn't affected the South as much. Economically, yes—you can see the new prosperity. But there's been less social change. The big thing has been the civil rights movement of the 1950's, which could be regarded as a delayed backwash of World War II. The new mobility, the new investment of money in the South, has benefited Negroes in a backhand, corner-of-the-table way. Without World War II and the new education for whites and Negroes through the GI Bill, you wouldn't have had the civil rights movement as it is known in the South and elsewhere; so I suppose that the second war did have deep and significant effects, after all.

NEWQUIST: In *Who Speaks for the Negro?* you examined the

civil rights movement in an extremely frank and intimate manner. What motivated the book, and how was it done, and what did you hope to accomplish?

WARREN: In one sense it was a purely personal book. You can't be a Southerner and not have the whole race question on your mind in one way or another. It's bound to be there. I simply had an overriding interest. I have my own feelings, and they were informing me of what was happening, but I guess I just wanted to know more, to really inspect my own feelings. I didn't go at it in a "Which side am I on?" approach; that wasn't the point. I knew where I stood at that time on that question. But I wanted to know the shades of feeling. You can't walk into Martin Luther King's office and say, "Let's go out to lunch and have a conversation." He'd say, "I'm busy; what do you want?" You have to have a reason for the project, a reason for yourself.

The key motive was to find out about that world as deeply as I could, to find out about myself as deeply as I could. The only way of "finding out" is to write a book or a poem; if you're a writer you will only do your thinking because you are writing. I must say that I have never had a more fruitful experience. The mere fact of seeing that number of people who feel such an extraordinary degree of commitment; the intelligence, the gaiety that sometimes entered. When you think of the great number of young Negroes of the highest intelligence, the strongest drive, devoting themselves to civil rights, you can only wish they didn't have to fight spooks. I'm not saying that what they've done and what they're doing isn't crucial and valuable, but what if all this energy was put to another purpose? To cancer research, for example? But they're committed to fighting the spooks of society instead of dealing with the real problems of nature, the real problems of man at another level.

America is a story of release of energy at different levels. One can see where each wave of immigrants has had a perfect release of energy, a sudden full entry into American life. The most recent and best-advertised release, artistically, is the Jewish literary impact. A Negro literary impact is just beginning; we are feeling the first stirrings of some extremely talented people. But think of this release of energy not in terms of just a few talented people, but a bang, a racial release. This is what has happened, stage by stage, to the various groups of immigrants. We don't even think about it any more. It is simply assumed. Now the last great reservoir of human energy, ethnically, is the Negro. Once that vast reservoir of energy is released we should run over with vast strengths and talents.

The Negro in a secret and suppressed way has made great contributions to American life, even when he was supposedly cut off from participation. The effect of the Negro has been enormous. We can't even guess what America would have been like without the Negro. No Civil War, a totally different structure of American life, different language, different music. Yet while the Negro has made an enormous impact racially, he's been cut off individually. This full recognition, the full release of energy, could come anytime in the next fifteen to thirty years. And it will be tremendous.

NEWQUIST: To turn to *All the King's Men*. Could you explain its genesis?

WARREN: I was writing novels and living in Louisiana, so there you are. It was just that simple. I was living in a melodrama. But all of my novels have come out of the same sort of thing, out of a world I knew something about.

If something doesn't interest me deeply I don't want to fool with it. It never crosses my mind to find a good story to write a novel about. I have to have enough interest in the subject matter to make me want to, have to, write the novel. Anyone knows a thousand good stories, but when you can get worked up about a thing that has a special rub, a special concern, then it simply has to be written.

NEWQUIST: As a poet and novelist are you aware of a conscious obligation, to whatever quarter that obligation might be owed?

WARREN: Yes, and I can say it very quickly. Two obligations. One is not to lie. The other is to write as well as I can. You're trying, imaginatively, to set up a world that feels like truth to you. This is the way it really is. It must be that way. And you have to do it as well as you can. You're not going to whip out something worthwhile without feeling it through. I think your obligation begins at home, always, where you're trying to tell the truth as you see or feel it. And I'll make a remark on the side: I think that if more obligations began at home there would be fewer public troubles. If home truths were applied we'd have a great deal less trouble in the world.

NEWQUIST: You've done a considerable amount of teaching at the university level, creative writing and literature courses. Has this been satisfying, on the whole?

WARREN: Let me go behind your question, if I may, without trying to undermine it. I don't see any difference between teaching classes in Shakespeare or classes in writing. It's all the same process: trying to teach people to apply their wits to the problem at hand. Fortunately, most of my teaching has been straight teaching; I can't imagine a worse fate than teaching just writing.

By and large, over the years, I've had an extraordinary range of talented, intelligent students. When you're teaching seniors or graduate students you expect this, of course. As for really memorable experiences in teaching, I don't recall a more extraordinary group of people anywhere than the students I had at Louisiana, seniors and graduate students. What this proves, I don't know. Perhaps I was lucky.

NEWQUIST: As far as your own body of work is concerned, which works have given you the greatest satisfaction?

WARREN: I have to take two views, a short view and a longer one. When you're doing something, you're committed to it and the work is it. To think beyond that would be death. As far as the long range is concerned, the novels that seem to have brought the most satisfaction to me are *World Enough and Time, Flood,* and *All the King's Men.* But when it comes to choosing fiction against poetry, it's more complicated. I have to change my metabolism. Many years ago I talked to Moravia about his first novel, and he told me that he thought of it as a poem. I know what he meant. All the novels I have written have seemed to me like big poems, with the chapters and events as metaphors rather than documents. This is the way I think of fiction, from one perspective.

NEWQUIST: How do you evaluate literary criticism and reviews?

WARREN: I don't. I don't know how to survey it or analyze. It's possible to pick up the paper on a day when something's right, another day when something's wrong.

On the academic side I think that "high-brow academic criticism" as opposed to straight reviewing has passed through a very strange phase where exegesis of a certain sort has become the order of the day, and this is a necessary phase, but it's about run its course. They're moving to something else.

You see this when the works of a particular writer are dealt with. Take the works of Faulkner, now. They've about done the exegesis of most of his novels, for better or worse.

NEWQUIST: To turn to the younger writer: what advice could you give him, or what would you hope for him?

WARREN: I'm not an advice-giver. I'm not even an advice-seeker. But I would, above all, make him an honest man. If he's a genius, I suppose he can be a little crooked now and then. But anyone who wants to write is going to pay a price, a damned big price. The gamble is big. Anybody with common sense and a reasonably solid character and reasonably good health can make a comfortable living these days, but the aspiring writer has to put a lot more on the line. The gamble is bigger, and I suppose the reward can be bigger, too. If he's honest and he works, advice is beside the point. He'll merely do what he must do, and that is everything.

NEWQUIST: In considering American literature as a whole, which writers or books or specific events do you regard as landmarks or turning points?

WARREN: This is a question I shy away from in my own mind, because I want to prowl around the question rather than plow right into it. The context swamps the question for me. I could pick off things for a textbook immediately, but I wouldn't feel the answer would be quite true. You can say

Huckleberry Finn, and be true and untrue at the same time. It was *the* novel when it came out, and it was and is important, but to regard its enduring popularity is one thing, and to try to evaluate its influence is another.

When Hawthorne wrote his first few stories, nobody read them. Now we look back at them and say, "Ah, that was a great moment," but nobody read them when they came out. They were published in obscure magazines. His best stories were published that way. So at what point do they become a turning point? We now say that those stories were new and fresh, extraordinary and revolutionary, but when they were first published nobody read them.

Melville's poems, published in 1866, now look like world-shaking events, but nobody read them then.

It isn't as simple as saying, "This particular writer changed things when he wrote such-and-such."

The fact that Hawthorne existed is the important fact, but we can't talk about his particular stories because they weren't read or understood or even thought about for years. They had a slow effect. It wasn't until 1850 that *The Scarlet Letter* had any effect at all, and then it was misunderstood. Melville's *Moby-Dick* is great, but 115 years ago, when it came out, it was a failure. Now it's a great influence. Conversely, for many years Longfellow was appraised as some sort of god, but nobody could be of less influence than Longfellow for the past seventy-five years.

This is the tangle I get into when I try to answer this question. Just look at the 1930's. *In Dubious Battle* and *Citizen Tom Paine* were talked about in American literature classrooms in the tone of voice reserved for Shakespeare. Now we have to think hard to recall who wrote them. And at the time, the same time, you couldn't get anyone to speak well of *Light in August* or *The Sound and the Fury.*

Note: Later in the evening Eleanor Clark, Robert Penn Warren, and I returned to the subject of the young writer who seems so inclined to seek help from older ones.

NEWQUIST: Perhaps it's from isolation that the young writer tries so hard to establish contact. There must be a feeling of working in a vacuum if you live apart from fellow writers.

WARREN: It's true that Eleanor and I were very lucky in having a lot of friends our age, and many who were somewhat older, who were very bright and literary. We didn't have to go out and knock on doors. Rapport was built-in. I don't think we felt lonely or dependent. I could talk about things, the important things, with people my own age, and Eleanor and her sister and their friend could even start their own magazine [at Vassar]. I suppose, if you're isolated in a non-literary community, it can be a different matter entirely.

CLARK: It's something else we're talking about, really. Who could have been more lonely than Sherwood Anderson as a young man? Or Dreiser? Actually, I don't know all the details of their early lives, but they certainly couldn't have lived in a very stimulating environment. And when you think of France, of the great writers of the nineteenth century, it seems they all studied in loneliness in some provincial town.

WARREN: They didn't stay there long, though.

CLARK: Even so, reaching out for communication is not the same as reaching for a handout. Let's make this distinction.

WARREN: I was speaking of the necessity for communication as a thing that comes first—

CLARK: But these people who write to us don't want you to talk; they're writing for a handout. They're writing for a synopsis of your own novels, or an introduction to someone here or there, or for help in getting a grant. This isn't asking for communication—

NEWQUIST: Or as your friend Peter De Vries says, "While you're up, get me a grant."

WARREN: Boy, that's true. You have to dodge getting grants, these days. They're like atomic bombs, all over the place. Few of us have survived the grants. The world is being blighted by them. It's a war against art.

CLARK: This is another important difference between now and

the time when we were making it, and starving in garrets. Nobody starves in garrets anymore; there's too much money around.

WARREN: There's no romance in art anymore. So many ways of getting an easy berth.

NEWQUIST: What do you think of the mechanics of so many best-sellers? The personality-oriented book that is sold to paperback and motion picture before it's ever written.

WARREN: And then turns out to be a bad book.

CLARK: The analogy of this very sort of thing is found in almost any poor section of Italy. People come to you wanting a job, and their idea of a job is this: Since you presumably move in a bigger world and have friends in Rome, your friends will know friends who know people in the ministry of something-or-other and, therefore, they will get a back-door job. This is the normal process of thought. Not to go out and do a job well. Of course, there are economic reasons for it, in these cases. And a certain involvement of historical procedures.

WARREN: Not as a saw, but as a way of life.

CLARK: It is, and it becomes a rather depressing commentary on a society. The business of today's young writer has become strangely analogous to this for very different reasons. There's no dire poverty behind their coming to the older writer to say, "Give me a hand." Something else is involved, but the psychology is the same. You go to somebody to get influence. Instead of sitting down and writing the best poem he can write, which is all that goddam well matters, all that matters. You write it or you don't. You're capable of it or you're not capable of it, and this should be all that matters. But in so many cases, it isn't what matters at all. They think first and foremost of climbing the ladder like some sort of awful worthless vine without roots.

WARREN: This is true. Most of them haven't written anything at all. They're not the compulsive writers who have to write. They are people who don't write, but who do want a swimming pool in California.

Albert Erskine[15] at Random House is a subtle and witty

man, and he would say that most writers he knows want to have been writers or to have written. They want the contract, the swimming pool, but they don't want to work. They don't want to live the process.

CLARK: We were talking to John Hersey[16] the other night about students taking LSD and all that. He remarked that what saddened him as much as anything was the way LSD, in so many cases he's seen, is a surrogate poem. It gives the illusion of being a poet and producing a poem without having written a bit of poetry.

WARREN: I wonder if it could ever lead to an A-plus on a term paper.

NEWQUIST: As far as the young writers are concerned, wasn't there more emphasis on the literary quarterlies—the *Southern Review, Antioch Review*, etc.—in the days when you, Mr. Warren, were an editor?

WARREN: You've got to remember that most of the wonderful things that appeared in the quarterlies and reviews weren't things that could be published in popular magazines. There were exceptions; the *Southern Review* published several stories by Katherine Anne Porter and two of her finest novelettes, *Old Mortality* and *Pale Horse, Pale Rider*. She could have published those elsewhere, but she preferred that they be in the *Southern Review*. We published five stories by Eudora Welty, five of her best. This was her choice, too.

CLARK: But a lot of us couldn't have published our stories anywhere but in those reviews and quarterlies. Someone once sold me on the idea of having an agent. It was a disaster. This poor agent looked at my things and she didn't know what they were all about, much less could she sell them for real money. Those stories were at home only in the *Kenyon Review* and the *Partisan Review* and *Life and Letters Today* and the *Southern Review*.

WARREN: Young writers may have had more patience then, more ambition; we had a natural set of contributors, and they seemed proud to have their stuff appear in our little magazines. In Louisiana we had the cream of fiction flowing into the office. Extraordinary first stories—they don't seem to be written any more. We never had a problem filling each issue with prose and poetry we were proud of. I don't really know if the young writer's approach to writing is that much different today. In the money sense everything seems more acute. The *Southern Review* has been revived, and they are paying. But money—I saw this during the few years I was at the Yale drama school. The shadow of Broadway fell over it. The students weren't aiming at writing the play they really wanted to write, or could write; they were trying to write next year's big hit. But perhaps the situation in the off-Broadway theater will change that prestige symbol.

NEWQUIST: I wonder if young writers get star-struck any more; fall under the influence of someone and worship—

CLARK: That could be so exciting. I remember when I was about seventeen, and discovered T. S. Eliot. I'll never get over it; I would say it was the guiding influence of my whole career. Eliot was the introduction to Marx and everything else. He broke up the conventional world I had known and presented a literature from which one could assemble a whole new fluctuating world. When he died last year I read all the obituaries I could find and I was absolutely overcome.

WARREN: Ralph Ellison says his life began with *The Waste Land* when he was at Tuskegee. That it changed his world.

NEWQUIST: A final question for both of you: If either of you were to chart your careers over again are there things you'd do differently?

CLARK: I'd have married him earlier.

WARREN: Very much earlier.

CLARK: As far as undoing career mistakes are concerned, wouldn't you make others?

WARREN: I'm sure I'd make worse mistakes. I think a man had best settle for what is done the first time around.

CLARK: I feel very lucky in my life. Woman, writer, and mother. I haven't formulated all this, not even to myself, but I'm sure it's a crucial sort of trinity.

Writing is removal; it's got to be. And being a mother is the opposite; it's an involvement. It's got to be, or you're a monster. A man is better able to remove himself from such involvement than a woman; perhaps it's the nature of the male.

But hardly anyone talks about one aspect of motherhood, and I haven't put it into terms for myself. When you have children you're surrounded by an endless and extraordinary creativity all of the time. It's a fantastic experience, and goes on at a pace adults cannot even remember. No experience as a single person can possibly prepare you for the barrage of creativity. It may be the total difference between being a single woman writer and a mother woman writer. Your time is chopped into: you're chauffeuring, you're worrying about colds and measles, you love them and practice piano with them and hundreds of things. And it's all time-consuming but it's lovely. But it isn't the big question as far as one's own writing life is concerned. You learn to accommodate your own impulses to this barrage, and it's a vital and difficult thing; yet if you are living with children who are pouring out inspiration by the mile every single day, it's as though you are looking in on God creating the universe. You somehow must accommodate the nature and proportion of your own creativity to this immense fact. How it is done, I don't know. One does manage—on some days.

WARREN: I think this matter of isolation and involvement is a constant struggle between poles, so to speak, for the writer. This is why we have to get away by ourselves, just to have a relaxation from conscience. But hasn't this always been true? The Anglo-Saxon artists, poets, painters of the nineteenth century were forever flocking to Italy. Now we're flocking to a village in France just to get away from too much social consciousness, and to have our children in a French school for a year.

But we're not expatriates. We're rather the opposite of that. We just have to live and work for awhile away from here, away from tension.

The Uses of History in Fiction

At a meeting of the Southern Historical Association held in New Orleans in November 1968, Ralph Ellison, William Styron, and Warren participated in a panel discussion moderated by historian C. Vann Woodward. The remarks here have been drawn from a transcription published in the Southern Literary Journal *the following year.*

WARREN: I want to say that I am appalled and honored to be invited to a group of historians. It makes you feel that the writing of fiction is more important than you thought it was, and that your writing is, too. I am honored to be here and it is a great pleasure to be among my friends—three old and dear friends.

What I want to do now is simply to try to state a few principles that occur to me about the relation between history and fiction—in a way, between history and art, as I see the problem, as a background to what may happen later.

First I should like to say that the word "history" is a very ambiguous word. Clearly it means on one hand things that happened in the past, the events of the past, the actions of the past. And the word also means the record of the past that historians write. So whenever the word is used, we have to sort out its meaning. I myself use it differently, in each sense, as the occasion may demand, and I'm afraid my friends do the same thing.

As Vann has said, history is in the past tense. That sounds simple enough. It is about the past. But it is not simple, because it is not merely about what happened in the past, it is also the imaginative past.

History and fiction are both in this past tense. History is the literal past tense. The historian says, "It was in the past; I prove that it happened." The fiction writer says, "I'll take it as it has happened, if it happened at all—which it probably didn't." But the mode of the past tense is the past tense of a state of mind—the feel of the past, not the literal past itself. It is a mode of memories. It's the mind working in terms of memory. The history of the past that the historians write is the racial past, the national past, the sectional past, all kinds of pasts, including economic history— but the past, always. To the novelist, say Thackeray writing about Becky Sharp, the past may be merely a little personal past. But it is past. Even science fiction is about the past; the writers tell about the future as though it were past. In science fiction, you get yourself to a point beyond the story that you are telling. It is never in the future tense. It is in an assumed future which has become a past.

This fact points to a particular stance of mind: it has *happened*, and we are trying to find its meaning. It's a mode of memory we are dealing with, an actuality as remembered. History is concerned with actuality; its past must be provable. The fiction writer's past is not provable; it *may* be imagined. His characters *may* be imagined. But historical characters are imagined, too. They are brought into the picture of an imagined world. For how do we know the world of "history" unless the historian has "imagined" it?

Now, the big difference here between history and fiction

is that the historian does not know his imagined world; he knows *about* it, and he must know all he can about it, because he wants to find the facts *behind* that world. But the fiction writer must claim to *know* the *inside* of his world for better or for worse. He mostly fails, but he claims to know the inside of his characters, the undocumentable inside. Historians are concerned with the truth *about*, with knowledge *about;* the fiction writer, with the knowledge *of*. And neither of these "knowledges" is to be achieved in any perfect form. But the kinds of "knowledge" *are*. This is a fundamental difference, it seems to me.

This leads to another distinction. Fiction is an art, one of the several arts. I want to read a little passage—the most radical passage I could find—about art as distinguished from other human activities. "Either art is a pure, irreducible activity, one that provides its own peculiar content, its own morality—it includes itself in its own meaning; or art is, on the other hand, a pleasanter form of presenting facts, meanings, and truths pertaining to other realms of reality like history, sociology, morality, where they exist in purer and fuller forms." This states the distinction quite coldly. For fiction is an art, like painting or music—with one difference. Its materials are more charged with all the human commitments and recalcitrances and roughnesses.

Now, here is where the rub comes, I think. The materials that go into a piece of fiction may be drawn from history or human experience, but their factuality gives them no special privilege, as contrasted with imagined materials. They have, as "materials" for it, the same status, and nothing more than that. But they come in with all the recalcitrances and the weights and the passions of the real world. The simplest example I can think of is this. Take *Hamlet*, or any tragedy we all admire and respond to. It is dealing with the recalcitrances of human pain, confusion, and error. We know these things all too well: the pain, confusion, and error of our own lives. But we come out of the play not weeping, but feeling pretty good, and we go down to the beer parlor and talk about it. Something's happened to the pain, confusion, error. It has happened only because we put the pain and error into perspective, and look at it—to see it and at the same time not quite feel it. We see it as if it had happened a long time ago—to us, but to somebody else, too.

There is, however, always a point where the exigencies and the pains of the materials of fiction or drama or poetry are too great to be absorbed. This recalcitrancy, which is the basis of contention between the form and the content of literature, can become too great. The really bigoted Catholic cannot read Milton; the really bigoted Protestant can't read Dante. In reading literature we have to make allowances for our theologies and our beliefs. But there is a point where it cracks. Let's recognize that. There is a form in which the recalcitrant material—that is, the practical commitment in relation to it—violates the vision of humanity, the long-range beauty of contemplation that is art. Let's leave it there for the moment.

. . . .

WARREN: Our little girl,[17] who is about eleven years old, was studying for an exam in American history, and she said to me, "Hear my lesson." I heard her lesson and she said things I thought were pretty preposterous, but I didn't say anything about it, because I knew she was saying her lesson for an exam. I was too smart to say anything about it, but she was watching my face. "Oh, Poppy!" she said. "This is for an exam; this is not the truth. I know better than this."

Now, this is not the historians' fault. This is the people who write textbooks of history. It's very different. Official histories may be tests, or orators at the Fourth of July, or textbook makers, but not historians. They are very different, you see. And girls of ten years old get this point quickly; they understand it perfectly. By the time they are seventeen or eighteen, in college, they may lose it. But they know it at ten years old. They watch things much more shrewdly than their elders; they have no stake in it except truth—truth, and grades. They are quite different: they know this, you see.

The historian is after this truth, and it's a good truth. So is the novelist. They are both trying to say what life feels like to them. They have different ground rules for it. Let's assume that both are conditioned by their societies at every given moment—at every moment in history, in time. Now, the breaking-out process is always an act of imagination for both the historian and the novelist. The rules are different, though, in this sense: the historian must prove points, document points, that the novelist doesn't have to document. Yet without that sense of documentation, the knowledge that It Is Possible, the novelist can't operate either. He is conditioned always by the sense of this documentation—that it is historically possible. He himself is tied to the facts of life. He must respect them. Insofar as he departs from them by imagination, he departs in terms of the possibilities laid down by these ground rules of fact—psychological fact, historical fact, sociological fact, all the various kinds of fact. Those are his ground rules. He can take a new view of them, but he cannot violate any one of them to a point which invalidates acceptance. That's the big proviso here. It varies a great deal. The materials that go into his work come from the rough-textured life around him, made up of beliefs and facts and attitudes of all kinds. A bigoted Catholic can't read Milton, and a bigoted Protestant can't read Dante, but a civilized Catholic can read Milton with joy. There's a point, though, where one's commitment to basic ideas and basic materials, by reason of bigotry or something else, makes one incapable of accepting the total vision of an art—of a novel or a poem, or whatever. Let's face this fact. The autonomy of the art is always subject to the recalcitrance of the materials and to your own lack of self-understanding.

WILLIAM STYRON: I don't know what I'm going to say to add to this confusion. We've been dealing in very intelligent abstractions, all of which make me feel that maybe we should get a little bit more concrete. I like that phrase of Red Warren's just now: "the autonomy of the art is subject to the recalcitrance of the materials." This is something that I have had preying on my mind for some time, in regard to a private argument, which became extraordinarily public, having to do with a book I wrote not too long ago. It occurred to me in thinking of this particular book, *The Confessions of Nat Turner*, that in all of the extraordinary flak and anti-anti-missile barrage that has surrounded it, no one, insofar as I know (and I don't mean only people who criticized it from the black point of view, but a number of my white commentators as well; and I bring this up not out of any immodesty, but simply because I'm more comfortable in talking about particulars rather than aesthetic abstractions)—no one has conceived of this book, which does deal with history indeed, as a separate entity which has its own autonomy, to use Red Warren's phrase, its own metaphysics, its own reason for being as an aesthetic object. No one has ventured, except for several people in private (bright people, whom I admire), to suggest that a work which deals with history can at the same time be a metaphorical plan, a metaphorical diagram for a writer's attitude toward human existence, which presumably is one of the writer's preoccupations anyway—that, despite all the obfuscation which surrounds the really incredible controversy about the rightness and wrongness of racial attitudes, wrong readings of Ulrich B. Phillips, Stanley Elkins, and so forth, a work of literature might have its own being, its own fountain, its own reality, its own power, its own appeal, which derive from factors that don't really relate to history. And this is why, again, I'm intrigued by Red Warren's phrase, "the autonomy of the art is subject to the recalcitrance of the materials."

I would like to suggest that in the endless rancor and bitterness which tends to collect and coalesce around controversial literary works, it might also be wise to pause and step back (I'm not speaking of my own work alone)—and regard a work as containing many metaphors, many reasons for being. This is true for all the literary works I admire. They are works (and I would include, among modern works, books by my distinguished contemporaries to my right) which do exist outside of history, which gain their power from history, to be sure, which are fed by a passionate comprehension of what history does to people and to things, but which have to have other levels of understanding, and have to be judged by other levels of understanding. It may be that in our perhaps overly modern and desperate preoccupation with history, which can be so valuable, we lose sight of the ineffable othernesses which go to make a work of art. At the risk of repeating myself once more, I would like to say that these factors have been forgotten.

WARREN: May I say something, Vann? It strikes me that the question is one of the basic tensions of our whole lives. We can't have an easy formulation for this, an easy way out of the question. We are stuck with the fact that life involves passions and concerns and antipathies and anguish about the materials of life itself—whatever goes on in our hearts and outside of ourselves. This is what good literature involves. If you couldn't carry these things into literature, literature would be meaningless. It would be a mere parlor trick. All this—the concerns, the confusion—goes into literature; it goes into the arts. It exists in terms of the experience that the writer describes in literature, presented there in and of himself. They are not the same thing for everybody; a little different, you know, for each person, frequently quite different. But they all go in as passion, as commitments of various kinds. Yet at the same time the thing described must be made objectively itself. Now, take Glendower, to whom Ralph was referring. Now, nobody here is a Welsh nationalist, I trust. If there is one here—

RALPH ELLISON: Ralph Ellison is.

WARREN: No, you're not; *you* aren't Welsh.

ELLISON: I'm a Welsh nationalist. But I also admire art.

WARREN: I'm a Confederate. So here we are. We have personal loyalties and problems, you see. But in *Henry IV,*

Part One, Glendower didn't bother us in terms of the great theme of the play. People are not living and dying over Glendower today. This is a purely pragmatic approach to it, you see; what can we surrender, what immediate needs can we give up, how can we withdraw our commitments in a given region of this play—in materials of the play—to gain a larger view? Now, I couldn't care less who won the battle at Shrewsbury, personally. It was a long time ago, and it isn't very important now. . . .

What I care about is the pattern of the human struggle there—as we know it in relation to Hotspur on one hand, and to the cold calculators on the other hand, and to Hal, as a kind of Golden Mean, and then, at last, to Falstaff, with all of his great tummy and great wit, and his ironic view of history and morality—outside of all schematic views. We are seeing a pattern of human possibility that bears on all of our lives, a pattern there that we see every day—the Hotspurs, or those cold calculators like Westmoreland, and then the people like Hal, who try to ride it through and in their perfect adaptability be all things to all men, and drink with Falstaff and kick him out at the end (in the next play, of course). We see this happening all the time. Shakespeare wrote a great vision of human life, but it's not about Welsh nationalism.

.   .   .   .

C. VANN WOODWARD: I'm interested in this question of fact my-self. One of our distinguished novelists present, Red War-ren, has written a novel about an historian. I think that Jack Burden was an historian, really. At least he was the narrator of *All the King's Men*, and he had two historical investiga-tions in his career. One of them, you'll remember, was the investigation of the truth about an ancestor, I believe a great-uncle named Cass Mastern, and he said that the in-vestigation was a failure. It was a failure because he was simply looking for the truth. The second investigation was about a man who turned out (though he didn't know it at the time) to be his father, Judge Irwin, and this investigation proved to be a great success. And he said that the reason for that success was that he was only looking for facts. The facts resulted in the suicide of his father, and a tragedy. So an interesting distinction was made there between facts and truth. Jack Burden, incidentally, was an historian, a seeker for a Ph.D., as some of us have been.

WARREN: He didn't get it.

WOODWARD: He didn't get it, and the reason, as you say, was he did not have to know Cass Mastern to get the degree. He only had to know the facts about Cass Mastern's world. I would be interested in hearing you discuss this distinction between fact and truth. I think it's to the nub of our discussion, perhaps.

WARREN: I'll tell you how it happened. I'll do it in two ways. One is how it happened to me, and the other is what could be said about it afterwards; they are quite different things. Jack Burden himself was a pure technical accident, a way to tell the story. And you stumble into that, because you are stuck with your problem of telling a story; you have to make him up as you go along. But that's another problem. The question about his peculiar researches, as I look back on them, is simply this. Being a very badly disorganized young fellow, he really didn't want the Ph.D. anyway. He stumbled on his family history, involving a character in his family, a couple of generations back, who had devoted his life to trying to find a moral position for himself. And this young man, without any moral orientation at all that I could figure out (he's an old-fashioned lost boy, not the new kind—there have always been these lost boys), didn't want his Ph.D., and he didn't know what to do with himself. He didn't know his mother, he didn't like his father, and so forth. At first he couldn't face the fact that in his own blood there was a man who *had* faced up to a moral problem in a deep way. He couldn't follow it through, could not bear to face the comparison to the other young man. Then, he couldn't face the truth otherwise, without this piece of research. Later, when he had the job of getting the dirt on a character in the novel, he did get all the facts. He gets all the facts, and the guy turns out to be his father, who commits suicide. It's a parable, I didn't mean it to be one; I wasn't trying to make a parable of truth and fact. It just worked out that way. You sort of stumble into these things. It's a parable, as you pointed out to me tonight; I hadn't thought about this before. Well, the facts Jack Burden gets are deadly things. Facts may kill. For one thing, they can kill myths.

An Interview in New Haven with Robert Penn Warren

Richard B. Sale, an editor of Studies in the Novel, *conducted this interview with Warren at Yale University on March 4, 1969. It appeared in the journal the following year.*

RICHARD B. SALE: We might start with your notion of place. I'm interested in your concept of place, especially since you've been here in Connecticut so long. So much of the fiction is involved with a feeling for place. How is it, for example, that you picked this area for a permanent residence rather than, say, the Tennessee-Kentucky "back home" country?

WARREN: That's accident, pure accident. There was a time—twenty years ago—when I considered going back permanently to Tennessee to live. I even got far enough to try to locate a place. I discovered the world had changed; it would have been artificial. That is, the world I'd be going back to would not be the one I was remembering. And then I settled up here. Again it's accident. I married up here.

That's not the decisive factor but is *a* factor. I married a Connecticut girl. The other thing was that I began to do a little teaching at Yale.

SALE: Your children feel, for example, that this is home?

WARREN: This is home. Of course it's home for them. It's the only home they know. One can't rewrite the script, you know, even if one wanted to. And one should be grateful, I think, for the favors one gets out of life without trying to rewrite the script arbitrarily. But as far as writing is concerned, the basic images that every man has, I suppose, go back to those of his childhood. He has to live on that capital all his life. There are grave defects if you *are* out of touch with your world, no doubt. It also has some advantages, I flatter myself to think—or encourage myself to think.

SALE: I was thinking of the novel *Flood* and its central character. Much of his dilemma is the business of going back.

WARREN: Yes, that's a part of the novel. Clearly that novel has in it a kind of tangential, peripheral reference, an issue of coming back and trying to pick up a world arbitrarily. That was not the germ of the novel; that was something at the end of the novel, later on.

SALE: Or that entered it.

WARREN: Almost inevitably entered the novel. But I didn't start with that notion. As far as that theme is concerned, the novel begins to deal with the question "What is home?" Ultimately home is not a place, it's a state of spirit, it's a state of feeling, a state of mind, a proper relationship to a world. It represents a— I don't want to use a big word; it can sound too ambitious, too grand—but the world view is your home. Your world view in one sense is your home. At least that's what I was trying to say in that novel, one of the things I was trying to say. That you're no more at home; you go back to the place and the place may not be your home any more. It may stand for whatever you don't like, for instance, or that place where you're not at home. I would not interpret that as being my case if I went back to Tennessee or Kentucky; that certainly would not be the case. But there would be something artificial in doing it by an act of will. It would be an attempt to reenact sentimentally a piece of the past, which I think is always false.

SALE: Was your imagery of "washing it away," the flooding of the country, saying this same thing?

WARREN: That is a part, but it was not planned into it. That was just happen-so, as it were; it was a given. The novel itself started simply from— I can tell you how the novel started.

SALE: I'd like to hear it.

WARREN: If you think it might be of some psychological interest. In April 1931, the anniversary of the Battle of Shiloh, I passed through southwest Tennessee. I saw the old house, hanging over the bluff of the river, which I think was Grant's headquarters during the battle—the second day of the battle, I think it was. Anyway, I forget the name of the house. I didn't go in; I just saw it, drove past it, and the village was the germ of Fiddlersburg and that house was the germ of the Fiddler house. I just caught a glimpse of it in passing, about a ninety-second glimpse. It stuck somehow. I couldn't describe the town now, only the impression I carried away from it. The—now, my God, what is it?—thirty or thirty-two years I've been writing that novel.

And another thing, I've seen one or two flooded-out places in the TVA system in Tennessee. For years and years I thought maybe somehow this was an image, this kind of doomsday to a community. Then, arbitrarily, *bang*, the community is gone. What happens to human relations in that context? This was something vaguely in the back of my mind, a speculation, no reference to fiction.

SALE: No reference to fiction in the original idea?

WARREN: No such idea then. As I began to move into the book the question arose of people who come back. I have friends who have arbitrarily attempted to come back and pick up a world by an act of will, and it's never worked for them, the ones I've seen—never worked for any of them. The sentimental reenactment without some practical justification—

SALE: —is somehow false?

WARREN: Those three things flowed in. Then the penitentiary, another germ from another place. I've seen a couple of prisons at different times. In fact, I started to write this novel, I toyed with it, twenty-odd years ago. And Elsa Morante, the wife of Alberto Moravia, wrote a novel [18] which had to do with a very similar situation: the prison inside and out in a small place, an island prison. And this novel, in a way, was so close to the novel I was then meditating that it killed mine off. I put it aside. Her novel came out in the mid-fifties. I've forgotten the title, but it's a very powerful, very beautiful novel. So I laid my book aside for some years before I began again. I thought I'd better let that one cook, get the other one out of my mind. I wrote two novels in between before I finally came around to my *Flood* novel.

This is rather funny; critics are funny people. The name of the family of mine in *Flood* is Tolliver. And I was vaguely modeling the character who became Maggie on a woman I used to know, who I thought was a terribly nice woman, terribly attractive and bright—vaguely this woman was in the back of my mind in making that character. I was casting around for names. I called her a dozen different things. I'd always liked the name Maggie, and I'd known some nice people named Maggie; so, you know, it sort of seemed all right. And so I gave her the name Maggie. The next thing I knew I saw a review or an essay saying the book was clearly derived from *The Mill on the Floss*, a rewriting of *The Mill on the Floss*, because there's a Maggie Tolliver in there. I haven't read *The Mill on the Floss* since I was twelve years old, and I don't intend to, furthermore. A big construction of interpretation of some kind around Maggie Tolliver and other characters who have equivalents in *The Mill on the Floss*.[19] Well, you better watch it, boys!

SALE: The critic made a concrete set of parallels.

WARREN: Criticism is a dangerous trade. So is fiction writing, for that matter. Well, there it is. All right: Fiddler. Fiddler came from a movie columnist. I just happened to see the name on the column he had written. I said that's a good one. Put it down as Fiddler and Fiddlersburg. There we are. That's the novel I think I'd have to rest my case on, though, for better or worse. That's one of the two or three best I think I ever did.

SALE: I was going to ask if you had preferences or favorites among your novels. You say that's one of them. Do you have a similar feeling about *Wilderness?*

WARREN: No, no.

SALE: What reservations about that one?

WARREN: I don't think it's the same. That's really a novelette. It was conceived to be about thirty thousand words long; it's now about sixty-five thousand words long. It began to exfoliate and develop, and the incidental characters began to be more important to me than they had been in the beginning. The ratio of the main character's interest to the incidental characters shifted along the way.

SALE: They took up more space.

WARREN: More space, and they become more interesting in many ways than the central character. The wealthy Jew, or the old North Carolina settler, whom I was rather fond of. Of course, Southern abolitionists are a very complicated sect. I've known a lot of them, and maybe I'm even called one of them sometimes. But they're very complicated people. Anyway, the ratio of interest changed between Rosenzweig and incidental characters like the settler or the Negro, or the rich Jew in New York, or the girl on the Pennsylvania farm. They became more demanding to me in a way than the central character did. So you have two kinds of books going on at the same time.

SALE: But you knew where you were going to take the main character.

WARREN: Yes, yes, I knew roughly where I was going to take him, you see. But, oh, let's talk about something: now here's a question. The Wilderness was called "The Pizen Woods," you know. Literally, historically. When you put the Pizen Woods in there, which is what history gives you, this is called symbolism, arbitrary symbolism.

SALE: But you had it to start with.

WARREN: History gave it. It *was* called that. (Unless I read the wrong memoirs.) This is arbitrary symbolism, says somebody. But it's what it was called. Pizen Woods. But there, you see, you can't win. I mean you're historically straight, factual, and it becomes symbolism.

SALE: Are you saying you've been damned for it or praised for it?

WARREN: I was damned in this case. For using "arbitrary symbolism." It may have seemed so, but you shouldn't be too sure until you've checked it.

SALE: Back to *Flood* for just a moment, I was curious about your use of water and flood images. After the first three or four pages, the airline stewardess peeked out of the airplane like a bird with a sprig of olive branches.

WARREN: Did I say that? I've forgotten it.

SALE: Yes. Was it just an incidental image? You didn't refer to the flooding for the next fifth of the book.

WARREN: I hadn't remembered that. It may have been a slip.

SALE: I was really asking this: do you use the technique of consciously tying imagery together throughout a long piece, with incidental image branches running off the main lines?

WARREN: Well, I can tell you in my case those things are almost always—accidental is the wrong word—spontaneous. They're not planned, and I throw them out or keep them, as I choose. But sometimes I don't notice them; they'll be there and I won't notice that they're there.

SALE: Then the choice is going to be at the revision stage?

WARREN: It may or may not be. I may throw them out at the moment, but planning is a strange thing in these matters, anyway. How can you say that you plan a thing that happens in a flash? The word pops into your head. The whole notion of intention and planning in these matters is a very, very peculiar thing, it seems to me. And the planning and the intention are primarily negations insofar as they're conscious. You're throwing out something rather than saying, "Now I want something." Because you can't know what you want until it comes. You have no way. You can do only one thing, it seems to me. You can describe to yourself the kind of problem you have. And hope that by describing to yourself the problem that you're up against at the particular moment, that somehow this will help your unconscious, your guts, deliver you the right thing. But you can't plan the thing itself. It has to come completely fulfilled. Or have the germ of fulfillment.

A friend of mine, who is now quite an extraordinarily good Elizabethan scholar, Arnold Stein, used to be an undergraduate here at Yale. As an undergraduate, he said to me, he was mad for Housman's poetry and he wrote Housman. He was a sophomore at Yale then—it was a long time ago now: "Dear Mr. Housman, I am devoted to your poetry. Can you tell me please, sir, how you always manage to choose the right word? Thank you very much, et cetera. Arnold Stein." Well, the old curmudgeon up at Cambridge answered the letter, strangely enough. And I've seen the letter. "Dear Mr. Stein, I do not choose the right word. I get rid of the wrong one. Period. Sincerely yours, A. E. Housman."

SALE: That's the only answer.

WARREN: The only answer. Yes, about the planning. When it comes to the actual thing, it has to be a matter of saying "That thing is wrong," kick it out, and hope that God will help me make it better the next five minutes or five days or five months or five years. It has to be a negative, a veto. It's where you can be conscious and argue with yourself. Or you can describe the nature of the problem. You can envision the kind of book, but the envisioning is unplanned again. The envisioning is a thing that has to come out of something as a happen-so.

Now, here's a kind of planning I use that makes sense. You can plan to be the kind of person that might write a certain kind of book. Put it that way. If you want to write poetry,

you can study poetry, you can memorize poetry, you can
live with poetry. This is your planning. You can plan by
immersing yourself in poetry as many ways as possible. Your
planning can be done at this level. After that, the planning
is a very, *very* strange process. It's primarily a negative.
Or a process of envisionments which themselves must be
spontaneous. And I don't know how to put it differently
than that. But the cold-blooded planning I think is utterly a
matter of basics. It's a matter of willingness to soak yourself
in the world of the thing you're dealing with, both in a
literary sense of, say, soaking yourself in poetry, memorizing it, reading it, thinking about it, studying with your own
poems—all these things. And on the other hand realizing in
planning what for *you* can be the life that you can write
poetry. That is, trying to find the way in which you can
have the right kind of privacy of spirit to write the poem
or the novel. And this is different for different people. I
have to have some other activity going on to gain a kind of
privacy. I have to have a thing to flee from, pull away from,
the right ratio of that. That is, I like some kind of job now
and then, objective and simple.

SALE: That's one kind.

WARREN: One plan. The other kind of plan goes right with it.
It's trying to—by experiment, I guess is the sort of way—
figure out the kind of life you could live that allows your
mind this kind of privacy that is necessary for writing. It's
different from person to person. You can never be sure
you're quite right about *yourself* either, of course.

SALE: The kind of planning you were talking about rejecting
is that sort of cold-blooded, cold-headed planning—

WARREN: That's immediate. That's right.

SALE: —that would plot out patterns. This is what you said
you do not do or cannot do.

WARREN: I quit that. I did one novel by a carefully worked-
out synopsis. I had about an eighty-page synopsis—almost
paragraph by paragraph—of what I wanted to get accomplished in that novel. I had it all worked out. Practically a
book by itself. I spent a year or two in the planning, trying

to live the novel in the planning level. Put it that way. In other words, I was trying to compose the novel in my head without breaking fully into language. I was separating language totally from mechanics, from plot and characterization. I had a bitter struggle with that novel because I had done the one thing I found I couldn't do in my work. I was violating what I conceive to be, for me at least, a basic necessity: the thing of character, the thing of action—idea—must be in terms of the *language* of the novel.

SALE: What was the book?

WARREN: Oh, *Heaven's Gate*. I had a bitter time trying to feel fresh on the things that I had already planned out so carefully, that looked so beautiful in the plan. I was only saved by the mountain man because he got me free-wheeling again. I dreamed of that in a fever dream. So I was home free on that.

SALE: So it came together finally?

WARREN: Typhus. While suffering from typhus in Rome, I dreamed the whole part of the thing in a sort of long fever fit. And I was free then. It released me to think of the novel as really happening then, rather than as a novel to work out, executing the plan from a blueprint. I know that there are people, I know some of them, who can plan in the way I said I can't plan. I know them, and history would give us many cases of that kind of planning. I can't. I can only plan in two ways. I can only plan by seeing the action of a book or of a poem. By seeing the big basic movements of it, I will know ahead of time, and I'll say Roman one, Roman two, Roman three, Roman five, or whatever it is. Those are the basic movements of the novel, and there'll be certain key scenes I will have—germ scenes.

The germinal scenes that are to be there will be in my mind ahead with the various movements of the novel or the feeling of what each movement means emotionally for the novel. And the knowledge of how I want the novel to *feel* at the end. What the actual events are at the end may be very dim in my mind until I'm very close to the end. I have a very clear notion of how I want the novel to feel, and what I have in the germ scenes will have been very carefully worked, probably written, sometimes long before I get to them. That much planning I do do. I just finished a long poem, *Audubon: A Vision*. It's about Audubon's life as a kind of focus for a lot of things about humans. I hope it's the way life is. It's about his heroic solution of his problems and the problem of being a man. Well, after I'd written about one-third of the poem, probably a hundred and fifty lines, suddenly, in the middle of something else, I began to write like fury. Wrote the last two little sections of the poem just like that! I didn't know where they would fit, but those two sections of the poem are now the end, section eight or ten of the poem. The poem is about four hundred and forty lines long, quite a long poem. I've been working at it for many, many months, started it twenty years ago. But then this section came in a flash when I was about one-third through the poem. But having settled the end, I knew exactly what the poem was going to be, what I was shooting for. Actually, I wrote that passage totally formed, almost like dictation. And I hope I remain as pleased with it as I was then and am now. I may be quite wrong.

SALE: So there's gestation in everything you've mentioned, a lengthy gestation period somewhere either before or during the composition.

WARREN: That's right. It may be years. Sometimes twenty years, twenty-five years.

SALE: And you keep several things in that work stage?

WARREN: Have to. I let nature take its course. That's unplanned. Only one kind of rule I make: if the poem comes, the poem gets the right-of-way. Stay with the poem as long as it feels hot. That's why I have got a novel now I've worked on five years that I've not finished.

SALE: That's what I was going to ask. It seems like you've given more attention to poetry in recent years.

WARREN: Yes. I've had a long run of it. I'm not complaining.

SALE: No, I shouldn't think so.

WARREN: But there has to be some rule about this, and I have one more chapter to go on the novel. Then rewrite. But the last three summers—no, the last two summers in France in '66 and '67—I sat down and said I'm going to finish the novel this summer. And in three days I was writing poems. In a year and a half I had written a book of poems. Then the fall came and I had to revise the poems. Not much of the novel got done. But you have to take some kind of a vow about priorities, and the start of a poem is more precarious than the start of a novel. So therefore I think you ought to give it more priority.

Usually the poem gets started, a few lines or a few passages, and then it's laid aside and finished later. And I try never to crowd them. Let them rest. I don't believe in crowding things.

SALE: Can you feel it when you're pushing one project too long and too strong and it's not functioning properly?

WARREN: When I don't want to do it, I don't do it. If I don't feel like doing it, I don't do it. If I don't feel hot, I leave it alone. Fiction has certain craft elements, for me, anyway, that are more obvious than in poetry. I mean there are certain things, like having to do a certain amount of typing to begin with. You have to sit there with the fiction. You do have the problem of writing the expository paragraph. There are many things that are matters of intelligence and craft and, in a crude way, "know-how."

SALE: And not in any sense inspiration or flash.

WARREN: That's right. But it must be done in terms of an inspiration, with some reference to inspiration. But these matters are not inspiration. Now, the ratio of that material, that kind of material, to the whole, to inspiration, is much greater than it is in poetry. Certainly greater than in short or lyric poetry, where you depend on heat to keep it going. So you do, you can live through slack periods.

SALE: And produce fiction.

WARREN: By intelligence and will in a novel in a way that you can't do it in poetry.

SALE: And keep the thing growing.

WARREN: And keep it growing. And in other words, the ratio

of a mechanical and critical intelligence to a novel is a little different, I think.

SALE: This is what I was asking. I think the writing of long prose demands a certain dogged stamina.

WARREN: I think so. I think so, too. But it doesn't mean that fiction doesn't depend equally on the inspiration element or the other element. I think it *does* depend equally. But other things flow into it in different proportions, different relations; a portion of it may sound mechanical. You can because more hours go into the mechanics of it.

SALE: Well, it soaks up more energy, more will, to get a lengthy work finished.

WARREN: More energy and more will. But to poetry. You have to be willing to waste time. When you start a poem, stay with it and suffer through it and just think about nothing, not even the poem. Just *be* there. It's more of a prayerful state than writing the novel is. A lot of the novel is in doing good works, as it were, not praying. And the prayerful state is just being passive with it, mumbling, being around there, lying on the grass, going swimming, you see. Even getting drunk. Get drunk prayerfully, though.

SALE: Then you had the kind of life in recent years where you could do this, when you chose. Is that correct? Or is there always limited time?

WARREN: Well, if you can't do it that way, you'd better not try. If something seems to be there to rob, always rob Peter to pay Paul. If anybody's going to be a writer, he's got to be able to say, "This has got to come first, to write has to come first." That is, if you have a job, you have to scant your job a little bit. You can't be an industrious apprentice if you're going to be a poet. You've got to pretend to be an industrious apprentice but really steal time from the boss. Or from your wife, or somebody, you see. The time's got to come from somewhere. And also this passivity, this "waitingness," has to be achieved some way. It can't be treated as a job. It's got to be treated as a non-job or an anti-job.

SALE: And you have to block out those other responsibilities completely.

WARREN: Block out the other obligations and responsibilities. And if you can have a job where you can fudge a little bit, so much the better. But I have known people that got up at five o'clock in the morning and wrote from five until eight before they went to the job. Five days a week. That's heroic. I've known people who've done this, done this for years.

SALE: They're novelists in the dark hours of the mornings.

WARREN: That's right. Or at night. Shut the door late at night and get at it. I know many people who have done that.

SALE: After a day of reporting, or whatever they were doing.

WARREN: Whatever they were doing. It just has to be done. One thing about this—I don't want to sound nasty—but I think that everybody who means to be a writer should go through a short period, anyway, where he does not have everything done for him, by a foundation or something else. Where he actually has to suffer a *little* bit, just a *little bit*, mind you, just enough to know what it's like to steal the time to give up something, in some way. And to offend wife or child or mother or father or best friend. Just to do what he wants to do. Just to know this: that he is able to make this reservation in life. To know how to achieve his inner privacy. If he doesn't make a try at it once in his life, he doesn't know anything about whether he wants to write or not, really, unless he's paid a price for it, a little price for it.

But I think there is some sense in the matter that I think a person should find out some place, somewhere fairly early along the way: How much effort is he willing to put in there to gain this inner privacy, this blankness, this right relationship to what he is doing, by giving up something? So he knows then exactly how much the process of writing is worth to him. Something of that. It doesn't have to be the financial thing. That was sort of half kidding. But that's putting it on the line, though; it is a matter of that.

SALE: With many people, that sacrifice comes in the business of making a living.

WARREN: It does in making a much better living, getting a better job. Getting promoted in the university or getting a better job or pleasing the boss—all these things, you know, enter into it. Also, it's the problem of what *kind* of life you can subject other people to. I know a young man— he's not young any longer—who shall be nameless. An extraordinary, talented writer, he married the wrong girl. Well, he's had a great success at life. But I know him well, and he sat there and told me, "I just can't do it. It's killing her. She's gonna leave me. I know it. It's gonna happen. She can't take it." She married a man when he was in a military uniform and was a heroic young man. And suddenly he put on those old clothes and locked the door to write. It was different, and she couldn't take it. So he quit writing and has made a great success of another kind of life.

SALE: That satisfied her?

WARREN: That satisfied her—and now they're divorced. Just recently, after twenty years.

SALE: There are all kinds of ways not to win.

WARREN: Lots of ways not to win. You can't win by losing, it's a cinch.

SALE: There has constantly been, there still is, a sense of history in your fiction. Now, I don't know how to phrase the question around it other than this way: Has there been any change in the part that historical reality plays in your writing of fiction?

WARREN: Well, the time, you mean?

SALE: The time, perhaps. I was thinking of such comments as Woodward makes about the soul of the South. What the Southerner is, what his milieu is. Have your attitudes changed any over a period of decades?

WARREN: Well, my attitudes on a particular question have changed very greatly and I hope they will continue to do some changing. I'd hate to think I was frozen. But on the question of historical relevance of history to my way of thinking or feeling, I don't think there's been much change.

You know the habits, how things were in the South. If you lived, say, in my generation, you still live in two kinds of time. The element of the past, the tale told. The things that happened before were told by older people, particularly if the older people were big in the Great War of '61–'65. A different feeling toward the present event and the past event somehow overlap in what was like a double-exposure photograph almost.

SALE: And the real world was one picture?

WARREN: The real world was there and old world was there, one photograph superimposed on the other. Their relationship was of constant curiosity and interest.

SALE: Which did they consider the more real? The old or the current?

WARREN: It would vary, I think. But the relations are the same, the two things.

SALE: Oh, but both were there constantly?

WARREN: Both are there. Both are there making a world of unfulfilled chances and unfulfilled options. This was always very important. The boyish imagination was always supposing: suppose, you know, suppose that Albert Sidney Johnston hadn't been killed at Shiloh the first day. Always supposing like that. Suppose that Jeb Stuart hadn't been on that city raid at Gettysburg? All these things the boy supposes. This is his sacred boyhood we're thinking about.

SALE: But adults use this pattern, too.

WARREN: They do! They do it all their lives. They continue their boyhood. The sense of the past and the sense of present are somehow intertwined constantly. This was a cultural factor in the South; the telling of tales was part of it. And the analyzing of other people's character, from malicious gossip on to high discourse about moral values, was involved in this thing, too. And the fascination with heredity: "You couldn't expect anything better from a son of Mr. Jones," or "Why do you suspect Mr. Jones' son is trying to be so good?"

SALE: You still see it in popular biographies: "His Welsh blood proved itself when . . ."

WARREN: Right. "Mr. Jones' Welsh blood came through." And there was the sense of a community being composed of individual people—on one hand, graybeards, on the other hand, babes. So the time sense was ingrained. You saw the object of time around you, the gray hair and the mewling baby. They were both there before you.

SALE: Where did the young man growing into awareness fit into that pattern of those people you were talking about?

WARREN: In between them; he looks both ways, toward age and toward childhood, to the past and to the present, and to his own dream of the future. This sense of time is a very important part of that. The time sense has changed, is changing. There's a very interesting passage in Alfred North Whitehead's *Adventures in Ideas* [1933] on the question of time, the change of the time-sense. This was written a long time ago now; it was written forty-five to fifty years ago, this passage. But the passage is something like this. He said that before the industrial revolution men had one time-sense; after it, quite a different one. Before 1800, say, there were disasters but no changes. No one man could recognize a change in the nature of life. Disasters could be war, famine, plague—they could happen like that. But the world began again roughly the same, at roughly the same point, the same techniques. The changes weren't demonstrable. They weren't obvious. They were so slow no man could notice them in his own lifetime, really. Disasters, yes; acts of God; but not acts of history. And after the industrial revolution we're going to have another world of change. Acceleration was constant change so that no man from 1800 on had the same world in his fifties as when he was one year old. Think what's happening more lately in the last fifty years since Whitehead wrote that. There's a real change, it seems to me, in the gut-time-sense of people. This means for many people disorientation profound.

SALE: Oh, I think so.

WARREN: Profound disorientation. Don't you think so?

SALE: And I think it stretches down to just what you were

talking about a moment ago. In that sense we're not a poetic age.

WARREN: We don't know yet. The human being is capable of great flexibility, and since we're the watershed, we don't know what's going to happen to the young. That's always the option. We have adapted to this. We can always see what we were like. What we are like, even!

SALE: And I know I'm not what the young are like. I was not in my childhood what they are like now.

WARREN: I am more like my father than my son is like me.

SALE: Yes, but there's a big jump between my son and my father.

WARREN: Yes. Between my son and my father there's a jump so great I don't know what it is. I'm much closer to my father, or even my grandfather, than I am to my son. Let me add that my son and I are very close in terms of affection and relationship. We are.

SALE: Oh, yes, I know. I know what you're saying.

WARREN: But the world he's come into is so different from the one I came into. So different. My father could vote when the last Indian battles were fought with artillery. That is, he was a young man of twenty-one when the Battle of Wounded-Knee was fought. Three regiments and a battery against the Sioux. And my grandfather, whom I knew well, fought the Civil War. And now my son reads in the morning paper about the astronauts. That's no relation between those worlds.

SALE: Let me jump to a new idea, about prose style. Because I was coming to see you, I read most of the novels again and was amazed to see the difference between the styles of the novels. Of course, the stories and their characters set the tone of the telling, but I'm speaking of the expository passages, the descriptive parts. I wanted to describe some of the prose in *World Enough and Time* as having a "brilliant" style as compared to, say, the "stark" style of the last book, *Flood*. Is there a conscious picking of the style in your work?

WARREN: Well, consciousness is negative again. The *World Enough and Time* book is based on a counterpoint of style, a counterpoint that has to do with the theme of the book. There is the modern man writing the book, the "I" of the book. Then there's the Jeremiah narrative which is a period piece, and a period piece in more ways than style. It's a period piece in psychology and other things. It's in a way a set historical piece, the whole thing. But the interplay of the two things offered me the reality, the interest of the novel. I'm speaking of the stance toward the novel rather than the content of the novel, if you can make that distinction. And the stance was a given; the material gave it. There was a document written by a man. The prototype of my character and the me who read that document were the germ of the novel. So me, a modern man, reading that historical document, was the germ of the novel itself. Katherine Anne Porter put that document on my desk and said, "Read it, Red. This is for you." I read it as a man of a certain period and a certain age, a certain education, a certain world. That was the middle of the Second World War when I read it, a strange time to be reading that document. So just that contrast caused the contrast of styles in the book. It was a given, in other words; the situation of writing the book gave the contrast.

SALE: I was asking because in the "I," the modern-man portion of the book, there was a sort of flash and irony throughout that I didn't find in the two more recently published books.

WARREN: Well, I see what you mean.

SALE: What I was asking for were your comments on the style rather than the intent of the whole novel. It's artificial to do that, I know, to completely separate them.

WARREN: No, it's a perfectly legitimate question, and I think I can answer it. I say I can try and answer, put it that way. I was about to say this: there was an interpenetration of the two styles in *World Enough and Time*, the historical style and, some would say almost a parody of that, the modern-man style. Now, that is a kind of mirror-facing-mirror thing.

SALE: That's what I was calling irony in the modern-man style.

WARREN: The technique was conscious, but it was conscious only after a time. It happened originally by accident, by impulse. Then it became, to a degree, conscious and methodical.

SALE: And continued throughout.

WARREN: Continued throughout. But at what point I became aware of it as a possibility I couldn't remember.

SALE: Well, I caught it on the early pages even. It was there.

WARREN: It probably was. It's somewhat similar to that in *All the King's Men.*

SALE: Yes, it is. As far as the general writing style, I would put the two close together.

WARREN: Well, Jack Burden and Cass Mastern have the same relationship as the "I" narrator and the Jeroboam Beauchamp-Beaumont fellow in *World Enough and Time.*

SALE: Well then, further, Jack Burden's ironic worship of Willie—

WARREN: Yeah, that doubleness—

SALE: —causes his misery.

WARREN: Yes, that's right. The method of treating the two groups is not too far apart.

SALE: I wonder if you sometimes found yourself writing in a style that didn't fit either your temper or the book you were working on.

WARREN: I do indeed, I do indeed. Of course, I try to spot that and do something about it. This is where the negative comes in again, the veto.

SALE: When you find yourself practicing "fine writing," or whatever?

WARREN: Well, fine or any kind of writing that is wrong for you. Poetry is even more disastrous, and I've made some very bad slips, such as in the volume of poems called *You, Emperors, and Others.* When I came to do my *Selected Poems* a few years later, I discarded many of those poems entirely. I was on the wrong track; I was writing poems that were not on my line, my basic impulse. I got stuck with a lot of sidetrack poems. I hadn't caught them early enough. Now, you can write—it isn't a question of being good or bad, you see—you can write a *bad* poem, by some kind of standard, you know, off the mainline. But the good poem off the mainline is the poem you ought to get rid of.

SALE: When it's out there by itself.

WARREN: A little bit of that's all right, but you can't do it too much, I've found. Several years later, now, I found myself throwing away most of that book. At least, quite a lot of it. The poems didn't belong to the mainline; this is something that happens. With poems, you see, you have a particular object you can spot. Now, if you were writing along in a novel, you see, a part here and a part there, and maybe you throw this out and that out. But of course you can't be throwing out pieces of the novel like you can throw out individual poems, unless you throw the whole novel away. You can throw it out if you're still writing it. But it's more obvious in poetry; you've smaller units. The whole poem is involved, and sometimes you can see one sentence or one line in a poem that is right, but the whole poem may somehow feel wrong. You can't neatly save that phrase, put it up in a notebook to use if the occasion comes up again. Oh, it stays back in your guts somewhere. The constant problem is to keep on the mainline. It's a real problem, now.

SALE: Do you have a feeling that some ideas simply suggest themselves as short pieces or poems rather than material for novels? Can you tell pretty well now what you're going to use certain ideas for?

WARREN: A poem or a big thing, fiction? Well, short stories are out for me. I haven't written a short story in, now, let's see, since '46. That's twenty-three years. The last two I wrote were my best ones, and I may never do another one. But I discovered that the overlap between the short story and the poem was very bad for me. I didn't finish a single short poem for ten years, from '45—God, it must have been '44 or '45, along in there—until '54. I didn't finish a single short poem, not one. I was working on a long poem during that time, *Brother to Dragons*, but I didn't finish it then. I must have started fifty short poems. Not one panned out. I threw them all away, and some of them were going okay. I couldn't finish them; they died on me. For ten years every one of them died. Which is all to the good!

During that period I reassessed my whole feeling about the question you were asking me. I began to see that I had, in a way, too abstract a view of what constituted the germ of a poem *for me*. I mean that when I went back to writing short poems, the poems were more directly tied to a realistic base of facts. They're more tied up with an event, an anecdote, an observation, you see. They were closer to me, closer to my observed and felt life. They had literal germs. That doesn't mean they were autobiographical in the rigid sense of the word. But they were tied more directly to the sort of thing that might become a short story. And once this sense of using such material for poems became clear, I said, "I don't want to write another short story." It was killed just like that. I'd never write short stories again. I just didn't want to have any more to do with them. They felt cramping to me, and I just didn't want to fool with them any more. Happy I was to quit. But this decision somehow seemed to be related to the notion of a poem that is tied closer to the texture of casual life, incidental life, incidental observation, direct experience. There's that. They moved into that world, poetry did. So most of the short poems—that is, many, many, many since then—could very easily have turned at one point into a short story.

SALE: But now poetry has come to take the place of the short story.

WARREN: That's it, that's right. When I wrote the last two short stories, I really liked them. I've only liked three or so that I've written—maybe four at the most. I was thinking the best at the very end, and I suddenly got nauseated with the whole idea of doing short stories or novelettes. And there it was. The poems and a complete change of attitude toward what constituted the germ of a short poem happened in that period.

SALE: But writing the short poem continues to give you considerable pleasure?

WARREN: Oh, sure. That's central to me. I love it; I love working with that. That's a central fact of life for me. Writing poetry to me is bread and meat.

SALE: And the novels as long as they come. Is that what you're saying?

WARREN: I've got a novel going right now. I'll write novels as long as they'll come; I love writing novels, but there's no pleasure writing short stories any more. I wouldn't touch them. There's none, and therefore I won't do it. And I have a positive feeling, no pleasure—anti-pleasure—for writing critical prose.

SALE: Do you still get trapped into writing it sometimes?

WARREN: I trap myself into it, in a sense. Because there are things you want to say. It's like conversation, you see, where it has cultivated, "made" pain. You have to write and you have to struggle. You have to work so hard at it for such small pleasure in the doing. Occasionally I've had great interest in prose; I wrote a long piece on John Ransom for his eightieth birthday. I wanted to do it, and I wanted to say certain things about him to clarify my own mind about certain things as best I could. I wanted to do the piece, but I hated the process. You see what I mean?

SALE: Yes, you wanted to get the piece done.

WARREN: I wanted to *have done* the piece. I don't feel the "had done" about a poem. I want the doing. I want the process.

SALE: Otherwise, you wouldn't keep producing them.

WARREN: Or the novel. I like the process of doing it. I want to be in with the novel, you see. But I don't feel that way about the stuff that's one dimension of drudgery.

SALE: Well, you obviously did have a period where it was pretty exciting at one time. The textbooks.

WARREN: I didn't really enjoy it that way. The textbooks were sociable. That is, they came out of collaborations and arguments and teaching in the classroom. There is the dimension of social life to it. It wasn't the other, the creative thing. It had a lot of drudgery.

SALE: Well, the texts continue to have a life of their own very nicely. I was thinking of *Understanding Poetry* and *Understanding Fiction*. Don't your publishers ever push you into revisions, forcing you back to these things?

WARREN: I do revisions, but that's still sociable. We've done *Understanding Poetry* three times; it's been out thirty-odd years. But the point is, again, that it's a social event. We work together. It's a world of argument, a world of discussion, a world of—the chore aspect is reduced. It's a matter of one's social life in the deepest way.

SALE: And it's separate from your creative activities.

WARREN: Totally separate because the creative side isn't in the conversations. In having this person you like to argue with, you disagree enough so that you're not just saying yes to each other. You are arguing back and forth, trying to explore something in terms of friendship and old association and differences of intellectual attitude and emotional attitude. So you come out with a text. This is fruitful; this is social life; that keeps it alive. If I were sitting off in a room alone, it could get pretty dreary. The actual drawing it out would be pretty horrible for me.

Let me shift to another subject. Put it this way about writing: If it isn't a kind of way of life, it's not fun. I'm not talking about textbooks now. I'm talking about the poems or a novel. If you can't feel this is the way of your living and feeling, a way of finding your own feeling, doing your own living, I don't see why else anybody does it.

SALE: Part of it is a romantic glamour that the beginner may expect.

WARREN: Oh, people start for all kinds of reasons. But once you're into it, the need is there. If it isn't there, to hell with it. Or as a friend of mine—my publisher, in fact—said, "The trouble with most writers is that most of them want to *have* written, not to write."

SALE: That's what I mean about the glamour surrounding the trade.

WARREN: And some of it is the rewards. But if the process itself is not your process of trying to find your way into your own life and life in general, to learn respect for your own feelings and your own values, then to hell with it. A writer's real nightmare is a fear of being trapped in repetition without that vital experience connected with it. That would be a terrible experience. It's the panic I think all writers get when they get to middle life.

SALE: The feeling they've done this before?

WARREN: That's right.

SALE: And they're just repeating themselves.

WARREN: They can't change. Now, John Ransom told me something astonishing years ago—and I think he was wrong. He's rarely wrong, but I think he was wrong that time. John and I were just carrying on a conversation, and he said, "I'm gonna quit writing poetry." I said, "What do you mean, quit?" He was at the height of his powers, maybe thirty-six he was. I was appalled. He said, "Well, I want to quit while I'm still enjoying it." He said, "I don't want to be a pro, a professional." He said, "I want to be an amateur. To me poetry is something I love." He said, "I can go on writing poems, better than any I've written. I know more about it all the time. They'd be better. But I wouldn't have any fun with them. I'd have no fun with them." He said, "So I'm gonna quit." Now, he has a very tidy mind and a very tidy life. He controls himself consciously and thoughtfully. His methodical, philosophical mind makes him say to himself, "I'm gonna quit." He did quit. He did quit indeed. Now, I think he was wrong. I think he was a better philosopher than a psychologist; put it that way. He said, "When I get a new way in, I may start again. A new way in, and I may start again." Here's where I think his psychology was defective. The way you gotta do is be there when the rain hits you, Randall Jarrell said.

SALE: Yes, I would think so, too.

WARREN: That, or else writing poetry sitting in the rain. Lightning hits you once, you're good; hits you six times, you're great. You have to be in the rain to be hit by lightning. Well, John was going to come in out of the rain, so an inspiration couldn't hit him. If he were with the medium out there, he might be hit. Stay in the rain, as Randall would put it.

SALE: Even if it was just a long, dreary drizzle.

WARREN: Just being out there in the rain and hoping for the best.

SALE: It's the old boxer analogy, isn't it: he's going to quit before he gets punchy.

WARREN: Yes, that's right. Everybody's afraid of himself. Every writer's afraid of being a writer. Some people want to quit. Some people don't quit in time. But it's a pattern.

SALE: Who's to know when it's time to quit?

WARREN: Well, you don't. You don't know when to quit. There's a poet whom I'm very close to, a very good friend of mine, one of the very best poets in the country. I'd say one of the most appreciated. In a letter he wrote to me last spring, he said, "I still feel it when it comes on. I like my new poems." He's right. The book with those has come out since then and the book has three or four beautiful poems in it, at his very best level. And so he's right.

SALE: And how long has he been practicing his trade?

WARREN: Well, he's in his sixties. He's my generation.

SALE: So there are many poems before this last batch.

WARREN: Oh, absolutely. He's sold quite a few volumes. But he's in his sixties, and he's thinking about it, too, you see.

SALE: Yes, "Is it time now?"

WARREN: Makes you nervous. It's bound to be a nightmare.

SALE: When a man decides he's found his stopping point, does this resolution necessarily mean leveling off? Couldn't it mean a continuing exploration?

WARREN: I don't think it means necessarily a leveling off. I think you have to find out, reassess and regroup. In its simplest terms, young poets have a great way of coming together. They should. Young people feel the necessity of a passionate friendship, association. They have the willingness to think each is great. They give roles for everybody to play. This is fine; they're getting into real life. There is a drama of youth, and that dims, has to dim. Deeper commitments take place in individuals, about individuals.

But this sense of shared experience is gone, in a way. The fragmenting of life is happening. The deepening of individual affections takes the place of it, in a way. Family things come in, too. Love in the family is something quite different again; it's another form of privacy, really. But excepting individual affections and family, there's something else that people need. They need some rational sense of a general communion. But the drama's gone.

SALE: But it can still be a world of action and realization.

WARREN: Yes, that's right, the sense of your relation to society. The sense of obligation, of patterns of values, which is more abstract, more rational than this sense of solidarity in the young. As an aside, the old have another kind of clubbiness: "Ain't they awful now." That's the worst thing they can do. That's using this attitude as a substitute; the old coming together and berating the young is a substitute for what they had when they were young, when they had this sense of a communal drama.

SALE: That's a very poor substitute.

WARREN: It's a poor substitute, a great temptation but a poor substitute, I think. But the need to find a rational set of values which enables you to keep some contact with the general world is the important thing.

SALE: That idea was working in two novels, *Wilderness* and *Flood*. It wasn't their main theme, but the new awareness of pain made the characters able to continue.

WARREN: That's the idea. Yes. I hope that's visible in the novels.

SALE: I also thought it was Wordsworthian that a new, more philosophical awareness took the place of the "animal spirits" of the young.

WARREN: Well, *The Cave* was the book where it was most explicit in my mind. The old man who is the old hellion, who is really jealous of his son and can't die because of his jealousy, can't take his role as a dying man. He can't accept himself being the age to die. He is the enemy of his son and the son knows it.

SALE: He can't give up the juices of youth.

WARREN: All of this is the father-son business; the old man can't, will not be a father and take his biological role. He's playing another role all the time. He has to learn to, well, take a sedative for his pain. He has to learn how to give his box to the boy. All these things he has to do. But that was quite the very center of the book. That notion of how this man is to learn his painful role. And I'll tell you this. I was working on that book when I wrote the essay "Knowledge and the Image of Man." Toward the end of the book, I wrote the piece. It came out of the book.

SALE: They worked very nicely.

WARREN: The piece came out of *The Cave*. Well, let me just say this on the side about these people who are finding allegories everywhere. *The Cave* goes back to the Floyd Collins case which happened around my home, that part of Kentucky. When it happened I was so deep in John Donne and the Elizabethans, I didn't bother to go up there. Only several years later, after I'd been away from Tennessee for a little while, I began to discover Tennessee. The working title of *The Cave* was originally *The Man Below*, and the man below is the man inside, of course, inside you. The submerged man in you and the man in the ground. Somewhere along the way this became the point. When the novel was finished and going to press, it had to be settled, titled. Albert Erskine, the editor, said, "This is a terrible title. You can't use this title. It's terrible. Find a title." The last day, the last afternoon in his office, closing date, no title still, I said, "Oh hell, call it *The Cave* and be done with it."

SALE: You said this?

WARREN: Well, I think I did. Maybe he said it. It was just like that. Get rid of the goddamn thing.

SALE: That sounds pretty satisfactory.

WARREN: Then I said or he said again, "What about Plato's Cave? We can have a little epigraph here to stick on it." So we went to Hiram Haydn's office next door to Albert's at Random House, got Plato down, and hunted the passage. Stuck it on like that. Impulse. Last minute.

SALE: That's fun.

WARREN: That's the story of the notion of this deeply plotted allegory from the start.

SALE: Someone has said that your book on John Brown was a step toward fiction. Do you think he's right, or do you know of any further explanation of that? Was it, in your mind, a move in that direction?

WARREN: No. I hadn't. It may have been true, but it wasn't in my mind. At that time fiction was beneath contempt in my scale of values. I had written, when I was a freshman, a story or two. They were terrible. I didn't begin writing fiction until after *John Brown*. But poetry was all, and I was a reader of history. I read a lot of history, and I have continued to read a lot of history. But *Brown*, I guess, was an approach to fiction because it presented a psychological problem to deal with and the question of narrative. It worked out that way but it was not programmatic. It just happened so. Well, once you sit down and write a long book all the way through, you're different. You know you're just different. You know you can do it. You know you can suffer through it, I mean. You can type that many words. Period. The kind of narrative in there became the stock in trade of my fiction. Issues that book raised remain in the fiction.

SALE: And maybe even the character.

WARREN: And sometimes the character, yes.

SALE: The passionate man—

WARREN: I think that a Frenchman first pointed that out. It hadn't occurred to me till later, long years after. But in reviewing *Night Rider* a Frenchman said it was the John Brown story over again. But it's true the world of rural violence which that novel had always remains in my work. It was part of my generation, caught in my imagination. It was there. My God, I saw it myself with my own eyes. With my own eyes, as they say, early image. This is an aside too: Someone will say, "Why do you write historical novels?" I say, "I don't. I write very few." They say, "*All the King's Men*." Well, historical, my foot! I was a grown man. I don't think they're historical novels. What I'm trying to find is what happened, something that has the distance of the past but has the image of an issue. It must be an image, a sort of simplified and distant framed image, of an immediate and contemporary issue, a sort of interplay between that image and the contemporary world. That's the only historical novel of interest to me. It must have this personal reference, a feeling of something, whatever that strange thing is that's making that story relevant for you, that involves something that is in you.

SALE: What about the problem of getting into a character who has some fanatic dream or commits great acts of violence?

WARREN: I don't know. I suppose you do it because you have that potentiality, I guess.

SALE: And you can depict it because you have it.

WARREN: I think you have to assume that there are no psychic accidents. You have to assume that in ordinary life I wouldn't want to be fanatical and force that to the point of mania. But there's something that makes an issue interesting to you; otherwise you couldn't live through the writing of the book. There's some issue there, concealed or not concealed, that involves you deeply enough to make you stay with it. I don't mean identification in any simple-minded way with you and the protagonist. In fact, every man is many men. And he's always splitting himself up, anyway, in his social life. Social life, ordinary life, no man is the same man to everybody unless he's a saint.

SALE: And you don't manifest all these possibilities to other people.

WARREN: No, and you'd better not or you'd be in jail, you'd be crazy. I'm not talking about some simple sublimation; I just mean that every man has only one story. He doesn't know what his story is, so he keeps on fiddling with the possibilities of that story. Every writer, no matter how trivial, and every writer, no matter how great, has only one tale; and the great writers have more versions of it. Shakespeare has more versions of it than Milton does. And Dickens has more versions than F. Scott Fitzgerald. And Faulkner has more than Hemingway. But you have to assume the central story.

SALE: Well, you've answered one of my other questions, about your intentions of writing poems and novels rather than criticism.

WARREN: It's not a matter of choice. I just don't think of myself as a critic. As I said, criticism is a kind of conversation or speculation that gets into writing. I have no critical sense. I've never had a critical sense, never had the ambition. By ambition I mean desire to force a thing through to the last ditch, as far as I can. Such critical pieces I've done were one way of thinking about issues that concerned me. Now, I'm not denigrating criticism. The critics are systematic, want to force the thing through to its ultimates. I. A. Richards, Cleanth Brooks, or Ransom, they are people who must try to drive the thing through, you know, and whose way of study and effort is in that direction. Now, for me it's a very different thing, whether it's reading criticism or an essay I'd written. Because it's usually *ad hoc*, usually came out of the classroom, or it's come out of my interests. Such work has been side efforts, excursions looking back on what my main interest was, rather than things in themselves. I have no professional commitment to it. It was subsidiary to the other, creative process for me.

SALE: An interested man's comments.

WARREN: That's right. That's good to put it that way. Oh, I'm sure that criticism has modified my writing, which is a way of thinking about writing. It's the way I think about my reading.

SALE: It's played a good auxiliary role.

WARREN: I'm the same way with drama. I started too late to make a career out of it. But I was interested in it. I think it had a very definite effect on my poetry. The interest in theater, which was always limited with me, had a very tremendous effect on the poetry and on the novels. *All the King's Men* was a play first, and this is a sort of submerged interest that I fool with in experimenting, felt my way into. These are probings into the nature of things and the nature of yourself. Even now if you stumble on something, well, all right. But there's no sort of the abiding commitment there.

I had a play on last fall. *Brother to Dragons* was done extremely well at the Providence Repertory Theater, Trinity Theater at Providence, an extraordinary production of it. Well, I worked on it a little bit; I sold it, and I was delighted with what they did with it. I have a big stake in it, a particular stake in it, but this doesn't mean I'm going to write another one. It was a special thing. I just feel it's a way of whetting your tools for something else, for fiction, for the novel, or for poetry. No, what I'd like to do is just write some more novels and write some more poems and nicer ones.

SALE: You mentioned several writers just in passing at different times. What of your early interest in other writers, in Faulkner, say. When did you first come across William Faulkner's works, do you recall?

WARREN: Exactly. Every detail of it. When I was a student at Oxford, I knew John Gould Fletcher in London, and John Gould Fletcher came up to Oxford for a weekend visit with me and brought me several books as presents. One was Hart Crane's *The Bridge* in the Black Paris edition, and one was MacLeish's *New Found Land* in the Black Paris edition and one was *Soldiers' Pay*, just out in England. He gave me this book and said, "You want to read *Soldiers' Pay*. It's wonderful writing. You'd better read it right quick." I read it and I remember on the back it had a blurb by Arnold Bennett which said, "An American who writes like an angel."

SALE: That's one of those generation bridges you were talking about before.

WARREN: That certainly is one of them and how ironical that one is. And I read the book and I thought it was just great. Of course it's not great but it set well. What was wonderful about it was the scene in that book—a certain shock of recognition to see a certain aspect of the South that you were aware of but never formulated. I'm not a Mississippian, but somehow there's enough generalized South for this to be interesting and important to me, and I read it at a time when I was starting to write. I'd already started my first novel, and my first piece of fiction was being published:

Prime Leaf. I was writing it at the request of Paul Rosenfeld for *The American Caravan*. He'd asked me to do a piece of fiction along the line of the tales we've been talking about. I was living back into my South, and here comes a novel about the South bringing a real shock of recognition. This hit me at the moment when I was puzzling with the question of what to do with Southern tales. And Katherine Anne Porter's tales about the South had been very important to me and so had Caroline Gordon's and some others. I got to know some fiction writers, you see. They talked about fiction the way I'd always heard poetry talked about.

SALE: With the same excitement.

WARREN: Same excitement, same sense of being a complicated, rich thing inside. You know about it. That's the excitement they brought to it.

SALE: When you were at L.S.U. in 1934, was Faulkner a popular author there?

WARREN: Well, again, I read him. I read the short stories when they came out and was mad for them. I read all the books when they came out. Yes—I, and all of my friends were this way, my historian friends were. Yes, the people who were interested in history had a passionate devotion to his work. I don't mean uncritical devotion, but a passionate interest in it. People had read him there. I felt I'd discovered him, but everybody I know practically had discovered him.

SALE: I guess a lot of people had privately discovered him.

WARREN: A lot, yes. Well, you know a few years later you couldn't find one of his books. I've recently read all, practically all, the reviews of Faulkner from 1929 to 1941.

SALE: And it didn't take too long.

WARREN: Incredibly, to the whole Marxist school, he was the Southern fascist. They polished him off.

SALE: Not to be read.

WARREN: It's incredible. It's one of the saddest, most humbling and distressing pieces of intellectual history I know. About then *Strange Fruit* came out. You had a pack and chorus, even being led by the Roosevelt administration, of praise for that book. And what a cocky book. *Go Down, Moses* came out then, too. "The Bear" was in it. Nobody mentioned it. That book died a-borning. And *Strange Fruit* was a great big thing.[20]

SALE: Yes, it was.

WARREN: Now, after that you couldn't buy a work of Faulkner's. They were all out of print. There were a few paperbacks floating around, but you couldn't get one through a regular channel.

SALE: You could in England, but you couldn't in the United States.

WARREN: You could in Italy.

.   .   .   .

SALE: Oh, about Katherine Anne Porter. Have you got any comment to make about where *Ship of Fools* fits into the total work?

WARREN: I don't— Let's see. *Ship of Fools* is a big, important book, but I think its powers are powers of a series of novelettes imbedded in it. I couldn't put the book down when I read it. I read it right straight through in two solid days of reading. Didn't get out of my chair to eat and go to bed. It is faulty, but I was expecting it; the end is not the end of a novel. You've had some wonderful novelettes on the way, I think. This is nothing against it. I say it's nothing against her. She's a terrific writer. Of the world's best twenty novelettes, she might probably have two of them. They're really great. I mean they're at the world level, you know. I would think "Old Mortality" and "Noon Wine" or maybe "Pale Horse" would be at the top level, you know, in that collection of the world's short novels. She would have one or two. She's bound to have one. She may have two in there. And several short stories are absolutely first rate. I'm not talking about wonderful; I'm talking about really the first-rate ones, you know. She's a terrific writer. She's natural for it. She has a genius for short fiction. The amount of density, of philosophical density, the human weight that she can get into things like "Old Mortality"! It's as big as a big novel. Or what she could get into "Noon Wine."

SALE: Or—what's the phrase?—to *get away with* having that much in it.

WARREN: That's right, that's right.

SALE: To get away with it, not just packing it in.

WARREN: Having it there, having it totally absorbed in its own scale. The resonance and the drama and the echoes of it. This is terrific. Now, I don't think about her personally. She's one of my oldest and dearest friends, and I don't think this is just friendship making me say this. But she has this power of getting these ranges of meaning into the short form. I think these same powers are in *Ship of Fools*, but not as a *novel*, not in *Ship of Fools* as novel, but in elements of *Ship of Fools*. They're not digested in the novel, they're not digested. But the novel, the novel thing does not hold all that's in that novel.

SALE: Would you put Eudora Welty in her category?

WARREN: I think Eudora is a terrific writer. I'll say that, yes, I think Eudora's best stories are in the top level. There are not many first-rate short-story writers, not many natural short-fiction writers. Eudora's one of them. In this country, how many do we have, really? We've had—Faulkner. He's had several short stories and "The Bear" which are top level. Katherine Anne, Eudora Welty, Hemingway. Fitzgerald has a couple of them, I think, that are real beauties. The rather long one called "Winter Dreams" is a beauty and "Rich Boy" is gratifying. And then you begin to thin out fast, you know. You begin to grope around. Now, you will find many fine stories, men of two or three stories.

SALE: Single stories.

WARREN: A single story or maybe two by somebody who's a novelist. There's a wonderful story by John Peale Bishop, quite a wonderful story. Caroline Gordon has two beautiful stories. Let's see—John O'Hara, now, he is a short-story writer. The same kind Moravia is or that Pirandello was. The same kind that Chekhov was or de Maupassant. He pours them out. Just pours them out automatically. And the problem is reading him. I've come rather lately to this view, but I got to reading a lot of them in a great run when I was in France last year just because they were available there in paperback. I was detached from them so far, I began to see that some of these are quite wonderful. But you have to read ten to find the good one. This is the way with de Maupassant. He's a very great writer, I think. He's much out of fashion now. He also was a fine novelist. And Pirandello or Moravia, but you have to read through so many to find that one because the good ones look like the bad ones. And the bad ones are so well turned out. They are so close to the good ones, don't you see. You have to take three or four looks to see the difference. And I've come to think that John O'Hara is really a superlative short-story writer. I think you have to look, try to see the bad from the good, the almost good from the really good, but there's some quite powerful things he's done. He's a natural. He's a natural-born story writer; anyway, I think he's underrated. There are two or three novels that really matter, but he's also a real short-story writer.

Oh, I also wanted to record my admiration for Flannery O'Connor. I would put her name in that same group of the best short-fiction writers. She's written some beauties, much better than her novels.

SALE: Did you know her?

WARREN: I knew her slightly. I spent one weekend as a guest in the same house with her. That's the only time I ever saw her, in Nashville. She was a fascinating woman, wonderful writer. The short-story psychology is a strange, strange thing. It's as different from a novel in a way as poetry is. Well, not quite, but there's a real difference. She was a wonderful writer. She's going to be permanent, I think.

SALE: Yes.

WARREN: Well, Peter Taylor's done some excellent short stories.

SALE: Okay, one more writer. How does Hemingway wear on you, looking back?

WARREN: Very well indeed, I think. In my fiction class here I use Hemingway, and now nobody's read him. The students haven't read him. Five years ago everybody read him. Now they have not and they don't even want to because he's dead.

SALE: As far as being one of the in-vogue writers, he's out?

WARREN: Right, but they haven't even read him. You see that even when his books are required. Hardy's out. Nobody's read Hardy. Year after year I've asked the students in my classes, and these are bright-to-the-roof boys, especially bright and very literary, who have never read a single poem of Hardy's. But the real virtues of Hemingway become more apparent, now that the gulf becomes more apparent too.

SALE: But they're separating now.

WARREN: They're separating now. I think the real power is there and the real qualities are more impressive than they were before.

SALE: So you wouldn't change any of your earlier estimates?

WARREN: No, no, I would change apathies here and there about a particular work, yes, but I would still think of *A Farewell to Arms* as a very, very powerful book of the same kind I thought it was twenty years ago. Same order of book, I haven't changed my mind about that. I find certain clichés of it more offensive than I found then, or I find Catherine even less of a character than I thought she was then. She's a sort of onanistic dream, in a way, more so than I thought then.

SALE: You've mentioned that Hemingway, for example, is not in vogue with your students. Are there others on the blacklist?

WARREN: I've started taking my census every year, my poll, my questionnaire, by which I've discovered that not one of this class of twelve, the finest flower of Yale literarydom, had read a single novel by de Maupassant or by Dreiser, by Balzac, by Zola. They don't know anything about Zola. The total realistic-naturalistic tradition, including Dickens, is out, totally out. Stendhal, yes, Gide, Kafka, in. Proust is going out. Gide and Kafka are hot; market firm. They are holding steady, and Faulkner's in but he won't last long. The whole tradition of the realistic-naturalistic tradition, the whole meat-and-potatoes school, is out in favor of Kafka, Camus, and Gide.

SALE: Maybe Herman Hesse.

WARREN: Hesse's coming in steady, God help us, and then Salinger, you see—

SALE: Is gone, is long gone.

WARREN: He's long gone, and five years ago he was taking the place of Balzac or Zola. Isn't it funny, but the fancy-fancy, arty-arty fiction with the psychological complication has driven out this other type almost entirely in colleges as far as I know. Now it may be changing back a bit. They only read *An American Tragedy* or Zola at gunpoint.

Zola's a wonderful writer. In '61 I was in France and I read a novel by Zola every week. I could buy him in the Livres des Poche edition at thirty cents, and I read one every week. In the middle of that summer of Zola, I read Camus's *La Peste*, a fine book; but reading it in the middle of Zola made me feel very strange.

SALE: I can imagine.

WARREN: It was just like coming out from a guillotining and seeing somebody tatting baby socks or something. It just seems so trivial—all that totally created world of Zola, the populated world. Then to come down to *La Peste*. I went back to Zola with an air of relief.

SALE: Back into the world.

WARREN: Back into the real world, all kidding aside.

SALE: Thank you very much—

WARREN: Not at all. I feel I've been yelling my head off. Let's go to the Beinecke [Rare Book and Manuscript Library at Yale] and take a peek there.

Robert Penn Warren:
An Interview

▌▌▌

This interview by Marshall Walker was recorded on September 11, 1969, at Warren's home in Fairfield, Connecticut, and was first published in the August 1974 issue of the British periodical Journal of American Studies. *Walker reprinted it in his book* Robert Penn Warren: A Vision Earned *(1979).*

MARSHALL WALKER: I'd like to begin with a question about the Fugitive group. Would you say that there was any special critical emphasis in these early Fugitive discussions of poetry? You have said before that there's a fallacy in assuming there was a systematic program behind the Fugitive group.

WARREN: That would certainly be a fallacy. I think the best way for me to talk about it would be by referring to how the group began. It began some years before my time as a group of young college instructors, and men in the city of Nashville with no connection with the university, who found a community of interest in discussing philosophy. They met at each other's houses and talked philosophy till a late hour. Bit by bit, some of the people involved began to write poetry and show their poetry to each other. By the time I came along, writing poetry or discussing it was the main interest. The group was very small, ten or twelve or thirteen people, with no formal organization, simply a matter of friendship. And then they began to publish a little magazine called *The Fugitive*.

WALKER: There was a certain resistance to that magazine, wasn't there, by the authorities at Vanderbilt University?

WARREN: Well, certainly, the head of the English Department was embarrassed by it and begged his instructors not to do it.

WALKER: Why should that have been embarrassing to him, do you think? Because it published a *new* kind of poetry?

WARREN: I think so. But after all, some businessmen in town put up the money for it. A comic situation. Maxwell House coffee gave the prize—which, I think, Hart Crane won. That was the first year.

WALKER: There is a notion that the Fugitives were a group of people who went in for *close reading* of one another's poems and whose critical standards were what we would call objectivist. This I take to be a fallacy.

WARREN: There was no theorizing that I can think of around that point. If you are going to criticize individual poems, you have to talk about the actual words on the page, this line or that line, this word or that word, but as I remember the discussions, they were very far-ranging and all sorts of implications might come in. It was hit-or-miss. There were many temperaments here, and certainly some of the people were very much concerned with history in the relation of literature to the historical materials, or how one state of history emphasizes one kind of poetry. For instance, some of the people in the group were very deep in balladry, which would be anything *but* biased toward formalism. Then there were people like Ransom, who was trained in classical philosophy and often led the discussion of a poem off into the world of general aesthetics. Many lines of approach came together in particular applications, in discussing particular poems. But there was no general theorizing that I can remember.

The next phase of the group's interest—several years later—moved over to the matter of society and history. So this would, in a way, refute the notion of this being a little group of formalists working out a theory of pure, limited, objectivist poetry: the group became more and more oriented—almost paradoxically—toward history (American history) and at the same time toward aesthetic theorizing.

WALKER: Your own orientation was, for a time, distinctly historical, wasn't it, with *John Brown: The Making of a Martyr* as your first major publication?

WARREN: Yes it was. But this was, in a way, a question of homesickness, I guess. As long as I was *living* in Tennessee and Kentucky and knew a great deal about various kinds of life there from the way Negro field hands talked or mountaineers talked, what they did and what they ate, on up to the world of Nashville, Tennessee, I had no romantic notions about it. I was just naturally steeped in it and I knew that world. I also had read a good deal of Southern history and was partly raised by a grandfather who was a great reader of history and talked it all the time. He was a Confederate veteran, a captain of cavalry with Forrest and full of that and things like *Napoleon and His Marshals*, and military history generally. I had a deep soaking in that as a little boy. But this didn't seem to apply to the other half of my life, in which my whole passion was John Donne, John Ford, Webster's plays, Baudelaire. Then, as soon as I *left* that world of Tennessee and went to California, and then to Yale and Oxford, I began to rethink the meaning, as it were, of the world I had actually been living in without considering it.

WALKER: And this led to your first book, *John Brown: The Making of a Martyr?*

WARREN: That's right.

WALKER: To an outsider the book also looks like part of a campaign: it seems to fit in with the whole motivation behind *I'll Take My Stand*. Quite apart from a simple matter of interest in this piece of history, is it at all reasonable to see the book as an Agrarian's attempt to demythologize a Northern martyr?

WARREN: I think that's a fair account of it, but it wasn't a conscious motive. It preceded my connection with the whole Agrarian business. As for the immediate provocation, a publisher proposed a contract to me for it, and I grabbed it. I began the book when I was a graduate student at Yale in 1927–28 and I finished it at Oxford. It overlapped with but began before I had much share in the Agrarian conversations.

WALKER: You were at Oxford when *I'll Take My Stand* came out. So you weren't really in on the Agrarian conversations, were you?

WARREN: No, only in passing through on a visit to Nashville.

WALKER: So the interest in John Brown was something you developed independently?

WARREN: That's right. But it was tied in this way. Other friends of mine, by this time, were ferociously restudying American history. I wasn't alone in this. Allen Tate was doing it, you see—

WALKER: And Frank Owsley?

WARREN: Frank Owsley was a professional American historian, so he was doing it. In fact, I didn't know Frank at that time except most casually. But this was happening to a number of people. It was part of a turning back, a turning from their interest in poetry to try to see the setting of the kind of poetry that interested them. The notion of Ireland was deep in this too, though it was not specified often—the notion of a somewhat backward society in an outlying place with a different tradition and a rich folk-life, facing the big modern machine. This notion was in the background, talked about not as a model but as a parallel somehow. There were three factors in this: on the one hand there was the new poetry—Pound and Eliot—which was appreciated very early there and read in Nashville when it was not read in New York, and then Yeats and the Irish. Young Tennesseeans who had been off in the First World War, or had studied at Oxford or in Paris, seized on this parallel.

WALKER: So that poetry was very intimately associated with the concept of a small outlying nation with its own history and its own problems?

WARREN: The folk and the international were the two elements that entered into it.

WALKER: Was Yeats rather specially the poet who embodied all that these people in Nashville were thinking about, i.e., an international poetry but with a national root?

WARREN: The folk element for some of the Fugitives was very important, and in that case, yes, Yeats would have had a special importance; but also Hardy, for instance. Ransom was mad for Hardy. So was I as a boy, and still am.

WALKER: Could one explain that in terms of Hardy's anti-establishment, anti-religious stance, his notion of fate, his liberation from the whole nineteenth-century set?

WARREN: Well, I think that may be true, though I'd never thought of it. I *would* single out the notion of fate: a fatalism was deeply ingrained in the Southern mind. Things could not be changed—things lay beyond any individual effort to change them. A sense of entrapment. I think you can probably make a case that Hardy touched this nerve. Another thing was Hardy's use of folk materials, his portraits of little ironies of folk-life. This touched some of those people very deeply. I'm sure they touched Ransom.

WALKER: There is a Hardyesque quality about Ransom's poetry, isn't there?

WARREN: Indeed there is. It's very dramatic in the way Hardy's poetry is dramatic.

WALKER: I'm thinking of the deceptive way in which a Hardy poem—"In the Moonlight," for example—can appear very slight, and yet contain TNT. Ransom is very like that, I think.

WARREN: He's very like that, and I think this is not so much a matter of modeling yourself on that, because Ransom's classical training is, I'm sure, as much behind his poetry as anything—perhaps more than any other single thing—but

Hardy played right into this. His simplicities and the folk element played into it, plus this bias toward poetry as coming from the *event* in life rather than being a beautiful abstraction.

WALKER: I'd like to turn now to your most famous book, *All the King's Men*. This is not only the most widely read and most highly regarded of your novels but also the story that has occupied you longest—from the original play in 1937 until the published version of the play in 1960; so it's something that you've been involved with for a very long time. Could you explain this at all?

WARREN: Let me make a slight comment on that spread of time, which I find almost embarrassing to think of—twenty-three years. The point is that a lot of the involvement with the later phases of it—the play aspect of it—came by a kind of accident. I was drawn back to it by a producer wanting to do it. With this, of course, there was my own dissatisfaction with the original version of the play—a verse play then—that preceded the novel by some eight years. The reason I never tried to produce the first version [26] was that I never felt happy about it, and in fact, the novel was written because I wasn't happy about that play. The original version of the play was a tight play about the dictator, the Huey Long figure, and the people around him. Now, the theory of that play was that the dictator, the man of power, is powerful only because he fulfills the blanknesses and needs of people around him. His power is an index to the weaknesses of others. In other words, his power lies in the defects of others rather than a thing existing in itself, and so he fulfills the needs of people around him. The idea that gradually developed in the course of writing the play was the contrast between the "hero" as a person and the "hero" as a reflex of history. In the original version my politician was not named Stark, but Talos—[Talus is] the name of the "Iron Groom," the robot, the servant to the Knight of Justice, in Spenser's *Faerie Queene*. This was a sort of private joke, but it indicates the line of thought, and Talos does sound like a "Southern" name.

But this notion did not work in this little tight play, and the choruses did not quite carry it. It was a tight personal story and I did not feel satisfied with the range of reference to the world outside, to society and to the history outside of it. And, as I say, behind that play and the book there was a sort of soaking in Machiavelli, a little Guicciardini and William James and just a lot of reading of history. Now, I don't mean to suggest that after a certain amount of reading I said to myself, "I think I'll write a play about all this." It just happened. And the biggest part of the "happening" was probably that I lived in Louisiana—that "banana republic," as I think Carleton Beals called it—at the time when Huey P. Long held it as his fief and when he was gunned down in the grand new skyscraper capitol which he had built to his greater glory.

But back to the original play: my dissatisfaction with it led a bit to the novel, to get some sense of the world *around* the man—the man as *seen* rather than the man as presented. The strong man should be seen through the weaknesses of others, or the needs of others, rather than taken as an abstract power presented directly.. That was, I suppose, the shift of interest that made the novel; but then, afterwards, problems became more technical.

WALKER: So that this is one explanation, anyway, of the long preoccupation. And a technical interest in getting it right as drama.

WARREN: Part of that, yes. And that process of being interested in the stage for a while, I'm sure, changed my poetry a great deal.

WALKER: Many of the themes and preoccupations, particularly in your fiction, seem characteristically American. Do you think there is any sense in seeing your work in terms of a tradition, a kind of American dialectic that runs, I think, from Hawthorne right down to the present time? To put it very crudely, you have first of all the Puritan dichotomies, then you have Transcendentalism, and for the Transcendentalists life becomes a Blakean affair: all life is holy. Emerson cancels evil out of the human algebra; Hawthorne brings it back; Melville says "No" in even greater thunder, and points out through Moby Dick—perhaps the most eloquent of all American symbols—that truth is this *doubleness* of the whale. I would like to suggest that you are concerned with this kind of problem in *All the King's Men*, and elsewhere. Willie Stark himself is a mixed man: Jack [Burden] calls him "the man of fact" and Adam Stanton "the man of idea," but virtue lies in wait for Willie just as virtue lies in wait in those lines in *Brother to Dragons*, "More dogged than Pinkerton, more scientific than the FBI." This seems to explain Willie's inability to stay remorseless: Willie as human simply *cannot* continue to be monovalent.

WARREN: No he can't; he says so himself at the end, "It could have been different." This is his acknowledgment of that fact.

WALKER: Now, isn't this an acknowledgment of the truth of fusion, of the oneness of opposing categories of value and the way they inevitably cohabit? You *can't* split one off from the other. Ahab's great sin—his tragedy too—is that he tries to split the moral atom and blows himself up in the process. Now, I think this notion of doubleness enters the American spiritual bloodstream. It's there in Faulkner too: Joe Christmas is really a kind of Moby Dick. As Ahab forces the whale to become *all* evil, imposing the demonism he sees in the world on the essentially ambiguous hump of the whale, so the community of Jefferson forces Joe Christmas to become all Negro, all black, and thus forces him into the abyss. So they split the moral atom too. In *All the King's Men*, Willie Stark realizes—he feels it on the pulse and he feels it in the bullet—that he *has* to be a mixed man.

WARREN: I think what you're saying is perfectly true about the American system. Or not *system*, but the central *tension* in American literature, I think, is pretty well described by what you are saying. Not pretty well; it's extremely accurate, and beautifully put. When it comes down to *me* in this little footnote on that grand picture, I wouldn't say that anything as grand as that was in my mind. I *can* say that a certain kind of *issue*, both a moral and psychological issue that's implied by that, *was* in my mind—an approach to it. I was not thinking of anything I was trying to do as "belonging *to*" anything, you see. By the way, when it comes down to Hawthorne and Emerson meeting on the wood paths of Concord, I'm strictly for Hawthorne. I really have something that's almost a pathological flinch from Emersonianism, from Thoreauism, from these over-simplifications, as I think of them, of the grinding problems of life and of personality. So I'm all for the Hawthorne in the picture.

WALKER: Your early book on John Brown certainly deals with a grinding problem of personality.

WARREN: I have puzzled a great deal about this—the man had some kind of constant obsessive interest for me. On the one hand, he's so heroic; on the other hand, he's so vile, pathologically vile. Some fifteen years ago, when Edmund Wilson was working on *Patriotic Gore*, we'd meet at parties and he would say, "Red, let's go and sit in the corner and talk about the Civil War," and we always did. And the subject of Brown once or twice came up, and he once said, "But he's trivial, he's merely a homicidal maniac—forget him!" Now this is *half* of Brown. In a strange way the homicidal maniac lives in terms of grand gestures and heroic stances, and is a carrier of high values, but *is* a homicidal maniac! This is a strange situation; and the split of feeling around Brown makes the split of feeling in a thing like my character Stark almost trivial. Brown lives in the dramatic stance of his life, rather than in the psychological content of it; he lives in noble stances and noble utterances, and at the psychological and often the *factual* level of conduct was—it's incredible—brutal. Perfect self-deception—yet "noble." Now, on this point, I suppose, the people I have chosen to write about—or rather, who have chosen me to write about *them*—are trying to find out some way to make these things work together, come together: somehow they are trying to get out of this box. This would be true of a man like the hero of *World Enough and Time*, who *must* find a *cause*, an ideal cause, in order to justify some of his most secret and destructive motives—no, that's not accurate—*needs*.

WALKER: I think in *At Heaven's Gate* the most interesting character is Slim Sarrett. His ruthlessness—albeit a tormented ruthlessness—and his efforts, finally successful, to *create* himself, make him appear as a kind of criticism of Sartre's existentialist ideas about the nature of the self. Is this a possible influence, direct or indirect, or is it just coincidence?

WARREN: It's pure coincidence. I didn't know anything about Sartre at that time. Except a review of Faulkner's *The Sound and the Fury*—or some other odds and ends, maybe. As a matter of fact, that character was almost a portrait of a person I knew, the closest portrait I've ever done in a piece of fiction; but I felt that he was in a way peripheral to what the book is really about. All the novels I've tried to write—published novels, anyway—are concerned, I discovered later, with some *mirror* thing—the mirror of the psychology of the people over against the society they are living in, so the story of the society is reflected in the *personal* stories, the moral and psychological stories of the individual characters, and the other way around too: society then enacts these private dramas. This book in its scheme—not in the inception of the scheme but as it developed—was much influenced by my long immersion in Dante, as I think may be obvious. There are the usurer and the homosexual—the crimes against nature: here is a society where nature is being violated one way or another, and all the characters are somehow *denying* nature. The relation of the father and son in the Jerry character and his father—Jerry is committing a crime against nature; he's impious.

WALKER: He denies his father—and takes a phony father.

WARREN: He takes a phony father. He's not following the Dante scheme; it developed bit by bit—these various crimes against nature. But the usurer, the great banker, and Sarrett, the homosexual, are straight out of the Circle. But it wasn't *conceived* this way; it *developed* this way. If I didn't think of Dante for quite a long time, it could be back in my head, you see, because in those years I was reading him almost daily.

WALKER: This question of the true and false father is also there in *All the King's Men*, isn't it?

WARREN: I've been told, and I think it's true, that the true and the false father are in practically every story I've written. Now, what that means, I do not know!

WALKER: What is so interesting is that the alignment of the true *father* and the truth of the *situation* is very close.

WARREN: That's right. If I were asked (I haven't ever said this before, or even thought it, I guess) to relate that fact to what we were talking about before, I should say, probably, this attempt to put the two halves of the world together, the halves being the fact and the idea, or these various splits of this kind, the Emersonian and the Hawthornian, all these things we were talking about in Brown—the perfect father will do that, but the perfect father is only in heaven, of course. This story is about an attempt at finding the true model—

WALKER: You mean the point where fact and idea coincide, the perfect fusion?

WARREN: Well, it's not in our world, I guess. But we constantly want to have it in our world, and we only find it by finding a new father, I guess, beyond us, beyond this world.

WALKER: Does this make our case hopeless, do you think?

WARREN: No. It just makes it interesting, gives us something to talk about! But this question of *finding* the father, this perfect father, is, in one way or another, in the various stories.

WALKER: I'd like to ask you a little about the process of redefinition that's gone on in your work. Part of the 1957 interview with Ralph Ellison puzzled me a little, and I wonder if you could say something more about it. He asked you about the progression from the essay on the Negro in *I'll Take My Stand* to the stance of, say, *Band of Angels*, and then, of course, to *Segregation* and *Who Speaks for the Negro?* Now, in your reply there, I think you suggest that you were writing the essay at the same time that you were writing your first serious piece of fiction. I felt that possibly you rather glossed over the question of what was happening to your own *beliefs* by talking about a new interest in a different *form:* not the form of the socio-political essay or analysis, but rather, the form of fiction. Did you, fairly soon after that essay in *I'll Take My Stand,* begin to rethink the whole question of the position of the Negro?

WARREN: I didn't begin to "rethink" anything systematically. It was by accident. Put it this way: I wrote the essay on the Negro for *I'll Take My Stand* at the same time as I was writing a novelette—*Prime Leaf*—which was also about the South. The connection, let's say, is this: thousands of miles away in England, doing these two things—both are ways of looking back at your origins, your homeland, and all of that. They both had great emotional charges, as it were, more than I realized at the time, I'm sure. On the essay—this is part of that fatalism that was deeply engrained in the Southern mind. Nobody—except Negroes—saw anything except some system of what the sociologists then called super- and sub-ordination based on and modified by all sorts of legal guarantees of "separate but equal." This is what the Supreme Court saw. This is the way the world was. At the same time, many people were uncomfortable with it, many whites. Of course, you can be damn certain a lot of *Negroes* were uncomfortable! But a lot of whites too. It's a question of trying to rationalize the inevitable—what seemed to be the inevitable—structure of the world. Now, at the same time, in writing fiction for the first time, in this foreign country, about the world of my boyhood, the *feelings* then came into it, not in the essayistic frame, not in terms of a social apology, but in terms of, simply, *response.*

WALKER: I don't quite follow.

WARREN: Not *interpretative*—the *essay* was a social apology, an analysis and an apology, but *fiction* involves, simply, your reseeing in your imagination a world, and this brings the problem of your immediate response, your immediate *feeling* about what you are seeing, without justification, without intellectualization.

WALKER: Just what's to be seen there?

WARREN: Just what's there, and having to face it as *there*. Its *thereness* is all. Now immediately after this, within six months, I was back in the South, and the Depression was coming on. I was living in the country a great deal—not in town—and you'd see more acutely than ever: first, from having been away from it for so long; second, from having to think about it during the years of absence, and then seeing this starvation-poverty that was coming on for whites and blacks and also certain aspects of the brutality of the system in its psychological way, which I'd been too young when I'd lived there before, or too stupid, to be aware of. So there was this long drift for several years of looking at that world again and seeing two things: one, the immediate kinds of degradation involved, personal, psychological, and spiritual degradation, plus the poverty. At the same time the effect on the Southern white society became more and more obvious—the great cost, both money cost and spiritual cost. Also, I made acquaintances who were aware of this. It was being *talked* about more. At the same time, certain friends of mine, like Davidson, became more *frozen* in their opposition to change, and the issue became drawn for me. So I had to see it, bit by bit.

Five years later I couldn't possibly have written that essay because I had lived into the world now in a different perspective and a different age. Also, one other thing I'll say. The Depression did a great deal to destroy the sense of historical fatalism, because you *had* to have action or die. There was a crisis there which *demanded* action. You could not accept history as finished, which is part of the Southern disease, and you had to reorder society, and this meant you had to reorder all sorts of relationships. The fact that you thought things *could* be reordered opened the whole question, psychologically. At the same time, your acquaintance with the old, the Civil War, generation, like my grandfather—their attitudes toward race had been very different from attitudes toward race in the 1900's in the South.

WALKER: More paternalist?

WARREN: Well, they were more deeply aware of certain splits. My grandfather was against slavery—at least, he said that he had thought it was a bad system—but held some slaves.

WALKER: Why would he hold them?

WARREN: Just like a socialist who is a banker now, you see, or hired by a business. It was the only structure of actual living. If you're going to farm, you have to have labor. That was the only labor available.

WALKER: So right in there, there was a split between fact and idea—in the Southern inheritance.

WARREN: Right there. In the whole question of the Southern story this split is deep, from Thomas Jefferson right on down—to take it at the grand level—to Robert E. Lee, who was an emancipationist; and Grant held the last slaves legally held in the United States, I think. There are no *morals* in this, it's just part of the comedy of our history; but segregationism was a very late development in the South, it only became legal quite late, and the old people had been *against* segregation because they didn't have that kind of racial antipathy. They might be the boss but they had no racial antipathy. It was a question of the structure.

WALKER: The two books that seem to me to have been most adversely criticized are *Wilderness* and *Band of Angels*, leaving aside *Flood*, which I think has been generally misunderstood. It seems to me that there's a very considerable clue to the way your imagination quite naturally operates in the discussion of "Pure and Impure Poetry" in that early essay: this notion that an ideal or a purity has always to withstand the blast of irony. Perhaps what is lacking in *Wilderness* and *Band of Angels* is this Mercutio in the underbrush. There's something, somehow, too *straight*, too "pure" about them. I would like to suggest that one of the strengths of *Flood*, and something that has apparently been missed by the critics, is that in this novel the conversion of Lettice Poindexter is something we *can* accept precisely because it's *earned*, because throughout the whole novel Mercutio has been sniping from the underbrush. We accept this as more than mere sentimentality because of the book's continual scrutiny of every ideal posture that comes up. This kind of running skepticism is lacking in *Wilderness* and it's lacking in the melodrama of *Band of Angels;* but I think that Mercutio returns to the underbrush of your fiction with real power in *Flood.* Now, does this make any sense at all?

WARREN: I hope it does.

WALKER: Does this notion seem to you to say anything about what happens?

WARREN: Well, I think it does. The problem of *Wilderness* involves a technical matter too. It started out to be a novelette, and began to exfoliate in terms not of the central character, but in terms of the objective world, so that the development of the central character did not keep pace with the development of the experiences he went through, objectively considered. I became enraptured, as it were, with the world outside of him, the people outside of him, and he never developed to go along with this development of the story. You have the strange effect of a central *hollowness* with a rich context, with the central character as an observer who is a *mere* observer. He's involved *intellectually*, but *only* intellectually. The story is never fleshed out in enough depth so that the world of context is related to his experience in the right way. And this is partly scale: it started out to be a novelette, say twenty-five thousand words, and it winds up as a novel; but the character does not develop to fit the context.

WALKER: Would you agree that this quality of irony—what I've said about ideal notions or ideal stances continually being undercut and evaluated by, say, the voice of a Jack Burden or by the counterpoint of an Ashby Wyndham narrative—is characteristic of the novels that are really strong?

WARREN: It's characteristic of many of my novels, anyway, and it is not true of this book.

WALKER: Do you think it's true of *Band of Angels?*

WARREN: Well, I think you're right about that. One thing there: the narrator is wrong. There's not enough richness and depth in the experience of the narrator—at least, it isn't brought out—and the same is true of the other book.

WALKER: Would you say that in your writing life there have been phases in which prose, or the imagination associated with prose, has been dominant, and other phases when poetry has been dominant? It seems to me, looking down the list, that after *Band of Angels* there is a poetic phase, and then again, after *Flood,* a very strong poetic phase. Is this so—is it phased like that?

WARREN: It worked out this way as far as I can tell: poetry was my *central* interest for many years, up until the middle 1940's. I read it all the time and worked at it all the time, and fiction was definitely a secondary interest. Of course, when you are in the middle of a novel it *can't* be secondary, it becomes your life for a year or so. But behind this, the novels I was writing, came the notion that somehow they might be poems: the first conception of them. *All the King's Men* started as a verse play, you see, and the other novels had very much the same background of feeling—came out of a sense that they might *be* poems if one wrote long poems like *that.* So the composition of novels didn't feel like a break between prose and poetry. Of course, there are obviously *great* differences, but they are tied to the poetic interest or commitment, or whatever you should call it, in a very definite way.

Now, something happened about 1945. I got so I could not finish a short poem. I wrote, started many over that period of years. I never finished one—I lost the capacity for finishing a short poem. I'd write five lines, ten lines, twenty lines—it would die on me. I lost my sense of it. I was working in those years, for five or six years, on a long poem, *Brother to Dragons,* and that was absorbing, I suppose, all the juice. But anyway, the short poems did not work out. Then, some little time after I had finished *Brother to Dragons,* I felt a whole new sense of poetry. I felt freer than I had felt before. The narrative sense began to enter the short poem—as a germ, that is. So in the summer of 1954, when Eleanor and I and a then-baby daughter were living in the ruined fortress in Italy, there was suddenly just this new sense of *release*—so the short poems began to come in that year.

WALKER: Of course, a lot of the poems are about that place—

WARREN: —about that place, because the place and the events all tie together in this sense of a new way into poetry. Look, I could start it from the immediate thing freely, or the immediate thing might be something I was thinking about that happened twenty-five years before. This has been a whole different kind of feeling for writing poems.

WALKER: You once made a rather Jamesian statement about getting the *germ* of a story in a flash. Would you be prepared to say anything about the germ of the new novel, *Meet Me in the Green Glen?*

WARREN: I don't know how I'd put it. The germ—I know exactly what it was: it was on a hunting trip with my brother, in Tennessee, some years ago. We went up a stream bed in an old army jeep. It was a wilderness, but had once been a prosperous valley. We saw the ruins of a nice house in there, and this totally abandoned valley, now a game reserve, a park, began to grow in my mind—this sense of a lost world in that valley. Then some other stories that I knew began to flow in and populate it with other echoes of episodes I had known.

WALKER: Episodes in real life?

WARREN: Some, yes; and in just that way, you see, it came as the feel of a place.

WALKER: Place is very important to you, isn't it?

WARREN: I think so, that's why I'm so tied to that world there—*one* reason. Let me say one thing on the question of start. Almost all, I guess *all*, of the novels I've written and many of the poems get started years before they are written, many years before. In fact, the Audubon book was started twenty years ago, and all the novels—*Flood* went back twenty-odd years. Usually there's a long period of thinking the story over, staying with the story or staying with the poem. These things flow along and the actual finishing may come quite, quite late after the idea, or after even the starting of the writing. It's a very slow process that way.

WALKER: When you look at the current American novel—Bellow, Malamud, Barth, Pynchon—do you feel very much that these writers are of a different generation? Do you feel that they're talking about a different world, concerned with different things, interested in different techniques? Do you feel apart from them?

WARREN: Well, one *has* to feel apart—I'm older—apart from them in that sense. But I feel very close in my *interests*. I feel very close imaginatively to Saul Bellow's work. He's a wonderful writer, a powerful imagination. And of course, in one sense he's writing about a strange Jewish world which I know only by report and through friends like Saul Bellow or through the work of people like him. But I think there's a strange kind of possibility of rapport: Jewish writing in America has a minority psychology to it, so does Southern writing. As my wife once said, "You're just like Jews, you Southerners," and I think there's some truth in that. This is reflected, I think, in the literature. There's a certain *insideness* of the *outsider*, and intensities of inside effects sometimes look queer to those who are not inside. Malamud, I admire greatly, and Styron. I think Styron's last book, *Nat Turner*, is very powerful and deeply felt.

WALKER: This caused a lot of argument about the authenticity of Negro feeling that Styron had been able to imagine. There was a lot of criticism, wasn't there, by Negro intellectuals?

WARREN: Oh yes, there was. This is politics. Put in its simplest form, as one black graduate student said to me, when he asked me how I liked the book and I told him, "Well, it wasn't fair; he took our boy and ran with him." Simple as that. That is not the whole question—*part* of it is this, crudely stated. It's part of a historical moment, of a political moment. At the same time, deeper than that, there is the fact that the sexual treatment makes the white woman the dream girl of Nat, who refuses the black women, you see, who are available to him. Now, this was offensive and you can see why. At the same time, I think there are some grounds for accepting this as valid. Also—I don't want to go into an elaborate discussion of the book, but this is part of this historical moment—one little item which was attacked by one of the black militants was taken by Styron out of the autobiography of Frederick Douglass—a very cunning little device of taking something out of a legitimate autobiography of a slave and a hero of the blacks and embedding this as part of Nat's story, and *this* being singled out for attack then by blacks. By the way, my sympathies are with Black Power—as I would interpret it. The psychological need I'm deeply sympathetic with, and I think Black Power, in terms of its long-range meaning, is essential. I was in no sense sneering at that, except that the manifestations of it in some particular cases, I think, are somewhat short-sighted. Sometimes viciously short-sighted. I would say also, I think I know quite enough about Southern chauvinism to understand black chauvinism.

WALKER: How do you view the contemporary scene in criticism? I'd like very much to know how you respond to McLuhan.

WARREN: I haven't read him enough, but I respond negatively. I think that this is not going to stick. He is a terribly clever writer—I've read at him some—but I'm not going to have any long-bearded theories about this. I just don't think it covers the case.

WALKER: Do you think there's anything on the critical scene that *does* cover the case?

WARREN: There's *never* anything on the critical scene that covers the case. I think good criticism usually is almost inevitably *ad hoc* in some deep sense; it's trying to make sense of some *particular* thing before it, in terms of values that are much broader than that.

WALKER: Well, that's a good Coleridgian position to take. Are there any particular vivid contemporary ideas or technical notions that you feel attracted to?

WARREN: Well, there are certain things you can't avoid as being important whether you like them or not. What's happening to modern America, maybe the modern world, is something that is appalling and inspiriting, I suppose, at the same time. My guess is that nothing has happened like this since the rise of Christianity—a fundamental change. Human sensibility, human instinct for value, is changing. Now to *what*, nobody knows yet. It's the world of the Roman Empire again. Things are falling apart, and we don't know quite how to define this. You can make some guesses—but at the same time that you make the big guesses, I think you have to quote two authorities: one is Jefferson, that liberty is gained by inches, so you have to nag along inch by inch. And I was talking to David Riesman a few weeks ago, and he was saying that apocalyptic solutions and apocalyptic analyses and diagnoses don't interest him, really, because it's the little things, day by day, picking up the garbage in this village, that makes life *work*, and the values will finally take their shape from these thousands of little efforts, of little decencies, little organizations that give the *ground* for social continuity.

WALKER: It's interesting that so many of the recent novels, especially from America, have been, in a sense, apocalyptic. One thinks particularly of books like *Catch-22*, which is a kind of comic apocalypse, of Thomas Pynchon's books, or of John Barth's *The Sot-Weed Factor*.

WARREN: Yes, quite a wonderful book, I think.

WALKER: They're all comic apocalypses, contemplating a total revelation, spoofed at the same time as it's presented.

WARREN: Yes, that's right.

WALKER: The apocalyptic mode is something that has certainly occupied very intelligent writers recently.

WARREN: And politically too. For instance, Tom Kahn, the student power man—SDS—some years ago, writing about the black movement, said there are many young blacks who would rather fail apocalyptically than win, and be stuck with the responsibility of running society. The great tragic moment—to fail with a great bang—is more satisfying than winning and then having to hack along to put the world together.

WALKER: So they would opt for the fire rather than the daily gray.

WARREN: That's right. But this is very human and it's very young. We all have this impulse in our youth and we keep it in our age. There are two aspects of this that have crossed my mind: one is, a sense of time is fundamentally so different now to what it was even thirty-five or forty years ago. . . . And the other crucial thing is the hereditary attitude toward nature which is tied to this. More and more there's no relation between physical nature and man, and man's life, and this does something to us.

WALKER: You mean less and less garden and more and more machine?

WARREN: That's right. Man's role in nature, as being part of nature, is no longer felt, and this is tied to the sudden passion now in America to save something, save a patch of green, save a few acres of forest. The "hippies," in their blundering and uninstructed way, represent a protest at being uprooted from nature. Theirs is a last effort to restore not the patch of green for picnickers but something to the soul. This effort is important; don't forget that there are many people who actually *hate* the idea of the green place, the hill, the woods, the stream; they hate it with a passion, loathe it because they are afraid of it, are afraid of it because they don't understand their relation to it. They hate it the same way they hate a library.

And we don't know the end of this story; but something is happening deep in the gut or the soul of modern man that we just don't know the meaning of now. The social structure is such, this impotence is so great, that you feel what's the use, why vote, why do this, why do that? The minimal activity, though, is important. Bertrand Russell, years ago, was saying the only hope is to find the small organization that will allow man to feel important, significant within it. This is the only hope. It's the inches business again.

WALKER: Two more small points. Saul Bellow, a year or two ago, repined that the writer today has sunk, he said, from the curer of souls, which was his proper business in the nineteenth century, to the level of the etiquette page, advice to the lovelorn, something of that sort. Would you agree with that?

WARREN: The writer now gives a handbook of fornication— the number of positions is what the novel has, in most recent times, taken as its subject.

WALKER: Yes, well, that, I suppose, is a form of etiquette! Do you think that the writer *might* reasonably regard himself as a curer of souls in the twentieth century?

WARREN: I think he had better not take himself too seriously in that role. The soul he ought to cure is his own, put it that way. Literature springs from the attempt to inspect one's own soul rather than from the attempt to cure the souls of others, although it happens that good literature may cure souls, but not because it set out to do that.

WALKER: Round about when you were thirteen, I understand, you read Buckle's *History of Civilization*.

WARREN: Oh, somewhere around then. Later, I expect. In those days there were not many books to read.

WALKER: But this was on every educated shelf, wasn't it?

WARREN: That's right.

WALKER: And after believing for a while in Buckle's great geographical key to everything—

WARREN: Everybody wants a big solution to everything. For a long time I would stop people in the street and explain to them what made the world change!

WALKER: Well, you became disenchanted with this one-answer system. Now I wonder whether you found any describable substitute for the one-answer system?

WARREN: No. I didn't. Marx didn't serve. Me, anyway.

WALKER: Has anything else worked?

WARREN: Neither did the church.

WALKER: Any other contestants?

WARREN: No.

WALKER: Do you anticipate finding any describable substitute?

WARREN: No. Hack along. Inches, again.

A Conversation with Robert Penn Warren

▆▆

Ruth Fisher and Warren had this conversation in Warren's office at Silliman College, Yale University, on November 18, 1970. Later Warren made editorial changes before it was published in the May 1972 issue of Four Quarters.

RUTH FISHER: Both Leonard Casper (*The Dark and Bloody Ground*) and Victor Strandberg (*A Colder Fire*) apparently feel that many critics have approached your works unprepared and with very little perception of your method of persuasion and what you are really trying to say. Therefore, what we find in the evaluations of your works are many incomplete explications and inadequate critical analyses by some critics. I wonder if you could give me a basic framework that could be used in the approach to your works? Are there some general assumptions about man that you feel are essential to an understanding of your works?

WARREN: Let me say this. In general—and I have certain reservations about what I am going to say—if a man's work does not deliver something, there is no discussion about it that is going to make it deliver. Now, discussion, or background information, can sometimes make it possible to go beyond what had been written in the work. But you can't simply talk a good game of bridge; you have to *play* the game of bridge. Neither your intentions nor the theoretical assumptions behind your work are really relative to the work, in one sense. The work has to deliver itself. So you can't undertake to apologize for your work and try to make the apology take the place of your work. All work does need context to be fully understood. But context doesn't necessarily make the work any better. It may lead to fuller understanding, but it may lead to a fuller understanding of the errors of your work, the failures of your work.

But to answer the question, I don't want to put it on the level of apology. And I don't know how I would go about saying that there is some particular image of man that I have in mind. The books that I have written, for better or for worse, are a record of the various kinds of images of man that I have had at different times. Of course, I have changed my notions, or at least changed my feelings about my notions along the way.

And this leads me to another point. I should think that in most cases, in most cases, anyway—I don't want to be dogmatic about this—the process of writing the novel or the poem is a process of trying to find out what the writer thinks. He is not working deductively from a highly articulated image, a careful scheme of values; he is trying to find the values, find the ideas, by a process of trial and error, as it were. Life is a process of trial and error about our own values. We may have certain assumptions about our values. We do have them. But at a certain age, say twenty-one, we feel one way; by the time we reach thirty-one, we feel quite different. Our ideas have changed. They may be more firmly established by experience; they may be completely blown up by experience. Certainly, they won't be the same; they can't be the same. They will have gone through, to a greater or lesser degree, the test of experience. They can't be the same after just a little bit of living.

And the writing is the process in which the imagination

takes the place of literal living; by moving toward values and modifying, testing, and exfoliating older values. So, since I see the whole process as one of continuing experiment with values, I don't know how to answer that question about setting up a framework at any given moment. My ideas have changed so much over the years. My feelings have certainly changed about many things.

But critics have to set up this contextual world in order to understand the writer in question. They do this in order for the reader to better understand the work of the writer in question. By setting up the contexts, the critics may come to *like* the writer less or may come to *like* him more. But there is no guarantee that fuller understanding' brings one to fuller liking.

My notion of criticism is that its purpose is to deliver the reader back to the work. All the study *about* a writer or a work, all the analyses of background, of ideas, of the structure of a work—the purpose of all this is to prepare the reader to confront the work with innocence, with simplicity, with directness. The purpose is to remove difficulties that stand between the reader and the work. Otherwise, it is busy-work and nothing more—and a job, sometimes with a pay check.

FISHER: Don't you find that this happens quite often, that a critic or even a teacher will bring something into a poem or a piece of fiction that is totally irrelevant to the work being examined?

WARREN: Everybody is going to make this error sooner or later. But you have to take the risk of making it. Because a critic or a teacher of literature has to try to set up this contextual world for the work in order to see the work in different perspectives. Some of these are bound to be wrong along the way.

But to return to what I was about to say. This process may lead to false tracks, but even the best tracks, the most right and fruitful, have to be forgotten in the end. For example, let's take a simple case. Clearly, to read Shakespeare we must learn something about the language he wrote in.

We study a book on the subject. We read the footnotes to the plays. Our purpose in doing this preliminary work is to be able to read Shakespeare naturally, simply, innocently—without being *aware* that we are using a learned language. You are not worrying about the nature of the language you are dealing with. Insofar as you have done your homework, you can forget the homework. It is in your bloodstream and you are simply reading Shakespeare. This is the innocence that comes from knowledge. The purpose of criticism is to bring the reader to that happy condition. It's rarely ever achieved, of course. Perhaps never achieved. But it's the ideal we aim at.

FISHER: Has being a teacher of literature had much influence on the way you write? Does it, for example, encourage an analytical approach to structure?

WARREN: This is a question that in one sense is unanswerable. Because I can't say what I would be if I weren't me. I don't want to dodge it on that basis, though. I won't dodge it at all. I'll try to answer. I would have to answer by saying how I would like to go at it, and how I trust that I do sometimes.

To take a preliminary notion, whatever we do—teaching or reading criticism or practicing it a little—has an effect on us. It gets inside us. We can't throw it away, except by a feat of total amnesia. Even then it's lurking in your brain somewhere, and you are different because of its presence. But to turn to the general question of how ideas may affect the process of writing—we have to recognize that they can appear at different levels of consciousness. Some writers, and some very good ones indeed, are intensely self-conscious in the practice of their art. They bring a great deal to bear at the level of "knowing." For better or for worse, I try to forget, not remember, what little I know. I try to "feel" into the structure of my story. Literally, I want to get the kinetic sense of the plot movement, of the swell and fall of action, of the intense moment and the relaxed moment. But—and this is a big *but*—when things begin to feel wrong, that is when I try to analyze the reason why things are wrong. Finding out the reason for the wrongness will not give you rightness, but it clears the way, perhaps, for rightness to come. In general, however, I try to immerse myself in the immediate concerns of the thing I'm doing. You have to pray that what you have learned and thought in the past will, by instinct, as it were, bear fruit now. But of course, once you have a draft, you must become "critic"— must try to estimate, analyze, explain to yourself. That is, insofar as things have gone wrong.

It's the same—learning to write, if you can ever say you have "learned"—as learning to drive a tennis ball. A coach can look at the action and analyze it into various stages, say body position, placement of feet at the moment of contact, grip on racket, shoulder position, et cetera. All these things can be separated out as problems. Now the coach may say, "Do it again, your racket is wrong, you turned your arm too far down." In other words, he is trying to analytically break up the action. The coach wants the player to know intellectually each phase of action, because the player, left to himself and acting *naturally*, has failed to strike the ball correctly. The player failed naturally. Therefore, he analyzes the failure by taking the parts of action and locating the source of error. The player may drill himself on these actions and, *bang*, the ball comes and he has a beautiful return. But when he hit the ball, he was not thinking; he had gone beyond thinking; it was in the bloodstream. There is total unawareness in the moment of action.

FISHER: Is that how you write?

WARREN: That's how you want to write. Writing is not caught in a single motion like a tennis ball. You can stop and look back and assess as you go along. But the principle is the same, I think. Certainly, if you study four or five years in college and then take two years to write a certain book, you are not trying to remember everything that you learned in college. You are trying to write a good book. You think about the actual process as it exists in the moment of action. Now, the moment of action in writing a book is longer than that of striking a tennis ball, but the parallels are real in the significant moment of action. You want to be able to have the right flash of "inspiration." Where does it come from? It comes from all of you, all of the things you have learned, the kind of man you have made yourself by the time you are twenty-five or fifty. You have lived into this moment of inspiration. Let's take the case where people get total inspiration, like a revelation from on high.

Take the case of Coleridge and "Kubla Khan" and the laudanum. Coleridge takes the laudanum and goes to sleep and has a dream. The dream is both visual and verbal. He sees the things and the words are there, too. He is awakened by a man at the door, and he writes it all down.[22] That's a lovely way to write poetry. But this doesn't happen often. How did it happen?

Let's take the case of a famous chemist. Kekulé had been working for two or three years trying to arrive at a formula for the benzene ring. He couldn't work it out. He tried intellectually for several years. One night, after working on his chemistry textbooks in a stuffy room, he fell asleep over his work. He had a nightmare about snakes biting each other. He woke up with the snake images in his head, and said, "My God! That's the formula." He spent the rest of the night working out the mathematics for the snake formula—

FISHER: And you do this, in your writing?

WARREN: Now, wait—now, don't rush me.

What happens to Coleridge and what happens to Kekulé: Coleridge can dream a poem, the chemist can dream a formula; but Coleridge could never dream a chemical formula and Kekulé could never dream "Kubla Khan." The dream can only come out of the person who owns the dream already. The dream work is done on the material that is already available in the man. There can be no revelation to a man to whom the revelation would not be a summing up of his own experience. His conscious, intellectual efforts may have failed to solve his problem (or write his poem), but the solution, thanks to all his past history and presumably recent efforts too, is "in" him and emerges fulfilled. There's nothing irrational about such a process, for the end product—that of Kekulé's formula or Coleridge's poem—embodies the law of the medium appropriate to it. This can happen because we, at the conscious and the unconscious levels, are all one piece. Now, what I am trying to get at is this, insofar as writing is concerned. You try by all your strength to be rational, to study, and to think (as well as to be open, receptive), to prepare yourself for the moment when all your work will—apparently—become superfluous. When the idea will take over, effortlessly. But as Pasteur put it, Fortune favors only the prepared spirit. The idea "comes" to him. These ideas come mysteriously. You can't say I'm going to have an idea now. You have to be in the condition to have an idea. The trick in writing is to get in a certain condition to have an idea. In other words, it won't come by logical manipulation. You have to find what for you may lead you to these happy moments. You have to learn the art of blankness.[23] And learn to "live right." Whatever that is for you.

FISHER: Do you feel that the creativity required by you as a major poet and fiction writer has enhanced your role as a critic? Is criticism as an art as creative as fiction or poetry?

WARREN: You have two questions there.

It seems to me there would be one kind of advantage for a critic in having some experience of the art he was criticizing, some inside experience. For certain kinds of criticism it would be almost essential, and for others almost irrelevant. It depends upon the kind of criticism you are talking about. Let me interrupt myself to say that there are many kinds of criticism, and this is where the problem really gets a little difficult.

Any kind of criticism that has to do with the nature of the process by which a work comes to exist is bound to profit from some experience with the business of creation. Any kind of criticism that has to do with the nature of the thing created in the sense of its technical aspects, its formal aspects, is bound to derive value from such experience.

Paul Wiess, a professor of aesthetics lately retired from this university, undertook to dabble in all the arts in order to get some sense of the inside feel of the art, the nature of art. He studied dancing, for instance. Now, Paul dancing is not going to become the great event of the ballet season, I can promise you that. And Paul painting pictures is not going to drive Michelangelo off the Sistine Chapel ceiling. But Paul wants to get a feel of the art in order to understand the relationship between the hand and the thing the hand did. These are attempts to heal the gap between man's rational nature and man's emotional nature, artistic nature. And physical nature, too, for all arts depend on that physical base.

It is inevitable that if you work seriously, or dabble unseriously, in an art, it is bound to have some value for whatever criticism you do. It won't guarantee that your criticism will be good, but it may prevent certain kinds of errors. It may prevent certain kinds of intellectualism that haunt criticism. It has one limitation, though. If you are a writer yourself, it is very hard for you to free yourself of your own preconceptions born from your experience as a writer. You see, there is a liability here, too. But the liability is much less great than its advantage. In ordinary run-of-the-mill criticism, though, it may cut you off from certain writers. You can't understand them because you are too much yourself. But these are risks you have to take.

FISHER: Is criticism as an art as creative as fiction or poetry?

WARREN: May I criticize your question?

FISHER: Yes, please do.

WARREN: Criticism when it really functions in the full sense of the word leads to a creative act in the sense of appreciating the work of art, whatever it is. You have to redo the work. You repaint the picture, rewrite the book, recompose the music, by going inside, if you are really experiencing it properly. You are writing the book; you are painting the picture; you feel the whole process is yours. This is clearly a creative act, and it's a very difficult creative act.

Now where do you lay the line between the creative elements of criticism and the uncreative. Sometimes it's hard, sometimes it's not clear. What I object to in your question is the phrase "as creative." It is creative possibly in its effect. It can be creative along the way when the person is analyzing the nature of the thing created or the way it can affect one. But that's being specifically creative. But it involves all other things, too, that may be in themselves not creative. It's how you approach the nature of criticism.

. . . .

FISHER: Is there a difference, then, in the writer's mind in the relationship among the three—short stories, poetry, and novels? What is the relationship? What is the difference in the level?

WARREN: Well, I can only tell you what's in this writer's mind. Me.

FISHER: Because you have written all three and quite brilliantly.

WARREN: Well, thank you.

The short stories were always a kind of accident for me. All young people write stories first, so I wrote a few stories. But I wrote poems for years before I wrote short stories. I published a lot of poems before I wrote any fiction seriously. But short stories always seemed to have a way of limiting your risk in fiction. I was trying to write the best story I could, of course. I started writing novels before I wrote short stories. I wrote a novelette first, and then I wrote a novel before I wrote any short stories at all. I came to them almost . . . well, I don't know how I really came to short stories. Except, maybe, I was very hard up and hoped for the quick buck. Which didn't come.

I wrote quite a few short stories, but I never had the same feeling for them as I had for poems or novels. This is me. I am not theorizing about anybody else. But for poetry and novels, I feel that they are not so distinct in certain ways. I really think of novels when I am trying to compose or conceive of them the way I think about a poem. I don't see the conception as being different even if the materials you work with are different. I feel, for instance, about a big episode in a novel the way I feel about the question of rhythm in narrative composition—I don't mean the prose style—the relationship there of its swoops and valleys of action, the way I feel about the meter of a poem. Exactly the same way. Just another kind of rhythm. I really think of the novel as composed in the same spirit as a poem is composed. I have had cases where I started one form and went into another. *All the King's Men* was a play first, a verse play, then it became a novel. *Brother to Dragons* started, in idea, as a novel first, then a play—prose play or verse play, undifferentiated—then it became the thing that it is, another kind of thing in verse.[24]

I don't feel the form is an absolute distinction. I tend to think of a novel in the same spirit as I think of a poem. But there is one important difference, at another level. The novels are much more objective for me. The poems have a much deeper and more immediate personal reference. This does not necessarily mean autobiography. I have been amused to see, in a few cases, critics using poems as a source of biographical material. What balls! It's very naïve —for a professed critic, too.

FISHER: In your novels, you use the technique of a story within a story. In *All the King's Men* you have the Cass Mastern interlude. What is the function of this technique? Is it necessary to the structural pattern of your novel?

WARREN: I can tell you exactly how it happened; I remember distinctly. Take *All the King's Men*. The novel went along to a certain point in the full swing of action. The narrator of the novel then got stuck (and I got stuck) with the problem of trying to make sense of his own feelings about his role in relation to Willie Stark, the political dictator in my novel. I could have stopped the action and made my narrator, Jack Burden, have a moral debate with himself: "I don't approve of all that's going on, and I must discuss this with myself, my God, and my kindly pastor, et cetera." He could, in other words, have gone at the question abstractly. But this is not his character. He is, in fact, trying to live a life avoiding all moral issues. But anyway, the abstract way would have been death to the novel. At this point I suddenly had an idea. I gave Burden a Civil War relative (about whom he had been trying to do a Ph.D. dissertation)—Cass Mastern by name—and invented a story for Cass, in which Cass struggles for, and finds, moral awareness. The Cass story stands as a kind of mirror image for Jack, but not, I trust, merely as a device. Jack responds to the contrast, it has a part in his development. What I was trying to avoid was the abstract approach. I wanted to give the reader the sense of meaning emerging from experience. That, anyway, is the essence of fiction—the image of meaning emerging from experience.

FISHER: Many literary critics and teachers regard Eliot's *The Waste Land* as a kind of watershed in American literature. How do you feel about this? What effect did a poem like *The Waste Land* have on young writers in 1925, particularly the ones at Vanderbilt University?

WARREN: It certainly was a watershed in my life and the lives of many of my friends. It came out in November 1922, in the *Dial* magazine. That's where I first read it. I was completely overwhelmed by it and didn't, I promise you, understand it at all. There was no model for it. Your generation is different, much later. There were models for it and by then criticisms about it. The college students of my generation—I was a sophomore in college—my friends were all hit by it. The boys memorized it. The professors didn't like it. They came to it very slowly, if at all. Even my most revered friend and then professor, John Ransom, didn't like it. He was very tepid about it entirely. This is nothing against him or *The Waste Land*. But my generation—we memorized the poem and went around quoting it all the time. We intuited the thing as belonging to us. This generation later wrote the exegeses about *The Waste Land*. F. O. Matthiessen's book *The Achievement of T. S. Eliot* came out ten years later. Cleanth Brooks' work on Eliot was written in the early thirties. Now, Brooks is one of those boys who fell in love with a poem in college. This is an old story. They thought about it, worked at it, pondered about it, and they wrote the books about the poem. There were no courses about it, thank God! They took it to their hearts and minds. It came out of their experience with the poem.

FISHER: So it was a big watershed!

WARREN: I'm trying to get at something beyond that. How a generation should discover and appropriate certain works— as the Brookses and the Matthiessens appropriated *The Waste Land* and then wrote the books about it. If they had taken a quickie course in Eliot in the 1920's, the process would have been very unnatural. What the boys did was to give each other courses in it. To pool their responses, their intuitions, the little bits of learning—and the sense of poetry they had gotten from reading Shakespeare, Keats, Baudelaire, et cetera. But it's very unhealthy and passive for students to want a university to do for them what they should do for themselves. Right here at Yale there are a number of students who clamor for courses about young writers—writers under thirty years old—and this to me is the height of absurdity, even vicious absurdity. The students should make their discoveries of the "young" and then tell the professors. And they shouldn't want some damned credit for this—some class certification that it is "important." This is passive—craven—obsequious. As when a student says to me, "I can't write next year because there's no writing course for me." Well, one thing is clear, such a student is not born to be a writer.

There's a strange paradox here. This generation of college students wants independence, self-reliance, et cetera. But on some matters they are simply craven. They want courses even to tell them how to breathe, as though you couldn't breathe without a course, or believe breathing to be important. One university even has a course in how to date. But I want to add something here. In general, in the last five years I've had the best level, intellectually and otherwise, of students in my life. Level, I said, not necessarily individuals.

FISHER: What do you think of contemporary writers?

WARREN: We have some fine ones. Many I admire greatly.

There are quite a few young poets who are awfully good. If I make a list, I'm bound to forget the ones I like best, but I'll name a few at random.

William Harmon just received the Lamont Poetry prize for a first book of poetry. This book is very impressive. He is clearly good. Ann Stevenson, one book published. It's very good. Anne Sexton, of course; she is older. She has published two or three books now. And Sylvia Plath, of course. There is Mark Strand. He is a very powerful poet. He's about thirty-five. There are others I like very much. Let me see. I'll remember as soon as this tape is finished. Oh! There is one I just recently read. Nikki Giovanni. I think she has real talent. She is a black girl, by the way. I think she is on the wrong track in some of her poems and theory—I don't want to get into criticism here. But she has real power. Mark Strand has real power, too. W. S. Merwin, he's around forty now and has published five or six books. But his book *Lice* was a very powerful book. Very original. I like other books of his, too. Then there're Adrienne Rich and Gary Snyder, John Hollander. There are lots of poets around who are good. Oh, I just mention a very remarkable work by a man who is in his sixties, Raymond Guthrie, *Maximum Security Ward*—a wonderfully strong and moving book.

FISHER: Does it matter if you are young or old?

WARREN: Well, I'm not talking about people who have been around for a time. People like Shapiro, Wilbur, Lowell, William Meredith, Eberhart, James Dickey: that's another generation. I'm talking about people under forty. There are a lot of good young poets around. I don't see a big single overwhelming intuition of the age, though. Why should I? No one has hit it yet. That is, to correspond to *The Waste Land*.

FISHER: One that would epitomize the entire age!

WARREN: No. I don't see it yet. But I don't care about that, though. In the meanwhile, there are many good poets around. Very fine poets, doing really powerful work. Some of these people are going to be awfully good poets.

FISHER: In your interview with James Farmer, in *Who Speaks for the Negro?*, you were speaking of Ralph Ellison. . . .

WARREN: Put me on record as saying that Ralph Ellison is a really fine writer.

FISHER: Yes, he really is a fine writer. I like his work.

In your interview with James Farmer, the question was raised concerning the use of literature as a device for protest as opposed to "art for art's sake." What do you think of today's black writers using their fiction or poetry as a form of protest?

WARREN: This is awfully complex. I'll try to put my thoughts in order about it. The subject for poetry or fiction is what makes you feel like writing. What you can make a poem or novel out of. Good poetry or fiction comes out of something that you connect with in a very deep emotional way. It is something that matters to you in a way worth commemorating and at the same time worth analyzing, defining.

But here the problem begins to take shape. There are various ways in which you may connect emotionally—and intellectually—with a subject. There are many kinds of "mattering."

With that thought in mind, let's change our approach. There are kinds and kinds of occasions. When the house is on fire, you call the fire department, grab the baby, and get out. You don't sit down and play a sonata on the way out. Certain moments in life are simply incompatible with art, and this would be true of any moment of urgent action. There is a time to murder and a time to create.

The "art" of urgent action in its simplest terms has one and only one function: incitement to a special end. Such art is an instrument used for a practical purpose, and the practical end dominates all other aspects. When the bugle is blown for the charge, it is not being blown to delight music lovers by the expert performance of the bugler—even though, if the bugle is inexpertly blown, it may not serve the purpose of inciting to the charge. To put it a little differently, a certain degree of—shall we call it "artfulness"—is required to achieve the practical end, but the end has nothing in itself to do with art. This is true even if the end is worthy, moral, and urgent. And here we face the painful paradox that the good end may often be taken to justify the evil means—including the limiting or the distorting of truth. And so, emphasis on the "simple truth" may often end up with the "complex lie." As good an example of this as I can think of is wartime propaganda: the enemy is always presented as a monster of all iniquities, totally dehumanized and therefore to be guiltlessly destroyed by any means available. Then when peace comes you have to start unsaying all you said. Japanese now versus 1942.

I have been talking about the crudest and most simplistic use of art—or artfulness—to promote action. As a basis for the discussion of your question. But having taken this as a base, let me move away from it by saying that all art—like all ideas—may be said to imply certain consequences, certain eventual possibilities of action. A particular vision of life—and such a vision is what a piece of art is—implies certain particular modes of action. But insofar as the piece of art is most fulfilled as art, it enlightens us about the values on which action may be grounded rather than inciting us to a specified action.

When we come down to "protest art" by blacks, here and now, I should say that we have to distinguish between mere incitement and the incitement that is grounded on enlightenment, works in which passion and wisdom, in some degree, meet. For a practical end, mere incitement may be all an author aims at, but he should try to be clear as to what he is doing: the house is on fire and I'll do anything to get out. But enlightenment-as-incitement is something quite different. If the protest is (as it is for the black American) against injustice, then the protest that is enlightenment-as-incitement would imply something about the nature of justice—and in its artistic quality, something about the human depth of the issues involved. Ultimately, I should hope that the most powerful protest against injustice is an assertion—or implication—of human solidarity. I do not mean that the particulars of outrage are not available for art, but I do mean that they should be in context. Here let me add that powerful works of racial protest have been written by black Americans, works that are what I call works of enlightenment-as-incitement—or we may reverse the phrase, incitement-as-enlightenment. For instance, some of the work of Ralph Ellison, LeRoi Jones, and James Baldwin—different as these writers are from each other.

Thinking back on what I have said, I feel I have barely scratched the surface, but I've tried to indicate the way I'd go about the question. And we must remember that the question raised by black protest starts all sorts of perennial questions about art and life. And in such cases, the beginning of virtue is, I feel, to start by making distinctions rather than judgments. Let me say something else. Passionate involvements are fundamental to strong art, and times of trouble give us our most powerful images for art. But part of the artist's job is to understand his own passion. And the fashionable, even in passions, is the enemy of all art.

FISHER: When you, Mr. Brooks, and Mr. Pipkin founded *The Southern Review*,[25] you published some very fine writers. How did these writers come to your attention, since most of them had yet to make the reputation they later achieved?

WARREN: Let me say one general thing first. In the thirties there were a lot of good writers around who had a hard time getting published. Two things were in our favor. First, there was no money around—and though we didn't pay much, we paid something—and second, we didn't have to try to please a mass market. We only had to please ourselves.

Then, something else: In that period and the decade earlier, the period of the little magazine, the distinction between the little magazine and the slicks was important. The big slick magazines, things like *The Saturday Evening Post*, were totally different from literary magazines, which were out for ART. Commercial magazines and little magazines were very distinct. That's no longer true today.

Esquire, among the pants ads, would publish (they invented this thing, you know, about mixing things up) Fitzgerald and a few big names of literary value and mix them with the pants ads, men's styles, and a few pinup girls. Now this hash is all over the whole country. *Playboy* . . . the editor of *Kenyon Review* became fiction editor of *Playboy*. That's how far it has gone.

FISHER: That seems almost inconceivable.

WARREN: This is the world we are living in. And for better or worse, there is a less obvious role for the little magazines in contrast to the official magazines. But in the thirties there was rarely any place for a serious writer to go except to the little magazines. There were some writers like Katherine Anne Porter, who was already an established writer, but not the great name she's become since. She could have published her stories elsewhere. But she wanted to publish with us. We published five or six of her short stories and two of her best novelettes in a few years. She said, "I choose my friends." She said, "I like the company I keep, I won't publish in those magazines." Of course, don't forget, everyone wants to make a living, too, and anybody would be glad to get well paid for his work—but there was a sharp distinction then and you could get people you wanted, sometimes simply because nobody else wanted them. Also friends and the grapevine helped a lot.

FISHER: Are the epigraphs used in your novels intended to set the primary theme of that novel, or should those epigraphs be used in a nonrestrictive manner, more or less as a touchstone?

WARREN: I can tell you what happened. That's the only way I can put it. I don't think there were any in my first two or three novels, two of which weren't published.

I remember *All the King's Men*'s epigraph perfectly well. That was a period when I was deeply immersed in Dante for five or six years. And I was pretty sure that when the novel was finished, people were going to misread the meaning of my main character. The epigraph was a way of signaling my view of the thing. And I was right about the misreadings. It came out right away—this fascist stuff all over the place.

This epigraph in *All the King's Men* is from the *Divine Comedy*, "The Purgatory." Manfredi had been killed in a battle against the papal army, and his body had been thrown out, not buried in sacred ground. Therefore, Dante is surprised to find him in Purgatory. Manfredi says, "But I crossed my hands on my bosom as I died. No Pope can deny you repentance. Nobody can deny you your relationship to God." The epigraph says that there is always that little bit of green, of hope.

Now, Willie Stark's deathbed reversal of feeling is like Manfredi's. I didn't think of Manfredi first. I finished the book before I thought of Manfredi. It (the epigraph) is a secret indicator of what I meant in my book.

FISHER: Is that the same case with *World Enough and Time*, where you use a quotation from Spenser's *Faerie Queene?*

WARREN: Yes it is. That's a more elaborate case of trying to let the epigraph interpret the book. The hero in *World Enough and Time* is a young man trying to create a world for himself, not belonging to this world. He wants to find a cause that will justify a violent and heroic act, as it were. He wants to create a romance for himself to be in. (The book is, in a way, about the pathology of romanticism.)

And Spenser talks about antique times in this quotation. Also, this reference is to Book Five, of Artegall and justice, the Knight of Justice. And this young man—of an antique time—is trying to perform justice. He is being the just avenger. So this is a little commentary on the theme of the book.

FISHER: Do you have a novel that you feel embodies all the essential qualities necessary for a successful novel, both from a philosophical and a technical point of view?

WARREN: God, no! I don't even want to think about that!

FISHER: Would you say that there is one book more than any other that best exemplifies your philosophy?

WARREN: Well, the trouble is you write a book, then you change yourself. I wouldn't say . . . I don't think of a philosophy as a finished product. Certainly not for a man like me. It's a way of thinking about your life as you live.

FISHER: Many people feel that the philosophy espoused in "Knowledge and the Image of Man" represents your basic thinking in life. But in view of what you have just said in the previous statement, I suppose you have changed?

WARREN: Well, I would be hard put to say in any three ways or five ways. But a basic change in my feeling about the nature of life would mean that if you have thought about it intellectually, then you would have to reset it intellectually. But I honestly don't think abstractly. I wish I did think more abstractly. But the poems . . . I write the poems and the novels trying to find out what I am feeling now. This sounds romantic and I don't want it to sound romantic. A writer is trying to think that way, rather than making up a philosophy and trying to illustrate it.

FISHER: So, in other words, then, critics are wrong when they place you in one particular specific philosophical position and say you are this or you are that?

WARREN: No. That may or may not be the case, you see. They don't all agree, so they can't all be right. But in any case, the ideas you have expressed or embodied in your work have their place in your history. And they (critics) are right trying to explore these things. But I am always struck by the attempt to freeze any writer in a formal philosophical position when the essence of the process of writing is to constantly modify and enrich or maybe narrow or do something to it. But it's a life process, and as long as the life process is going on, there are going to be reexplorations and modifications of the work by the writer himself.

FISHER: The statement has often been made that one should not confuse the writer with his works, that one should separate the author's own philosophical views from those espoused in his works. Can a writer really separate his views from those of his characters? Or do you put into your characters what you really believe?

WARREN: I can't put it into all of them because all the characters don't agree with each other.

FISHER: Yes, but one of them?

WARREN: No! I never think of one as speaking especially for

me. Never! Never! I feel myself as, in a way, outside of my book, my characters. Though, of course, you are always using little secret bits and pieces of yourself, your friends, and your experiences, usually distorting them.

FISHER: What about the idea of the whole thing? Can you separate the man from the entire book?

WARREN: The idea of the book is different from any one man in the book. There is no man in the book that has the idea of the whole book. The book embodies that. I'm outside the book.

FISHER: By being outside, then, you separate yourself from any one character in the book?

WARREN: From any one person. You want to feel with them. But nobody is my spokesman. I never think of any one man being R. P. Warren who is saying so-and-so right now. I don't think that way. The book is my way of trying to "say" the idea, that is the book. The whole book. Now, there are some writers who identify fully with their characters and the characters speak for them. I don't think that way at all. It's not my temperament.

Speaking Freely

▬▬▬▬▬▬▬▬▬▬▬▬▬▬▬▬▬▬▬▬▬▬▬▬▬▬▬▬▬▬▬▬▬

Warren was the guest on Edwin Newman's television program "Speaking Freely," WNBC-TV, January 3, 1971. The interview had been taped the month before, on December 17, 1970, soon after he received the National Medal for Literature.

. . . .

EDWIN NEWMAN: In one of your books, you quote Hawthorne on the Civil War: "It was delightful to share in the heroic sentiment of the time," Hawthorne said, "and to feel that I had a country—a consciousness which seemed to make me young again." Is that missing now, do you think? Missing from many of our people? Obviously, we don't want to have another war to achieve that, but—

WARREN: We haven't got that kind of war right now [in the Vietnam conflict]. The war is different.

NEWMAN: Do we have a sense of country at all? Is that still with us?

WARREN: I'm quite sure we have a sense of country, at a level not evoked by this war. This war doesn't evoke it. Pearl

Harbor evoked it. Overnight, automatically. This war doesn't evoke it. This is a policy war, and a policy war can never evoke a sense of country.

NEWMAN: There must be a more fruitful way to evoke a sense of country than by war.

WARREN: Indeed. I should say. But it's a very painful fact that usually a war evokes it more than anything else. William James said, "The only tax men pay willingly is a war tax." This applies to the emotions, too. And quite rightly, I think, in one sense. In peacetime you should be critical of everything your country does. You should try to keep it straight. And in a moment of great crisis you forgive your country its errors, in order to let it survive. But William James is right. The war tax is the only tax men pay willingly. This applies to your emotional relationship too.

NEWMAN: You're willing to have your emotions taxed, as well as your—

WARREN: That's right. That's right. And normally, I think, any intelligent person is inclined to criticize his country more strongly than he will criticize anything else. And he should. He should. It's a way of criticizing himself, too. Trying to live more intelligently, and more fully.

NEWMAN: During the Second World War, when you were the consultant on poetry for the Library of Congress, were you not telephoned one day to advise on what was represented as poetry by a general?

WARREN: I sure was. I was feeling pretty well out of it, because the Navy didn't want me, and the Army would have to come and get me if the Navy didn't want me, and so I was waiting. They never came. But a general called me up one morning and said—rather, a captain called me up and said General So-and-So wants to talk to the consultant on poetry. The general is writing a poem for a song to inspirit our boys—

NEWMAN: To inspirit . . . ?

WARREN: To inspirit our boys, he said. This is what the captain said. He was a very educated captain. And a very fancy captain, clearly. And the general came on, and he said,

I want to find out about the meter. What do you think of the meter of my poem? And he read the meter on the telephone, from some place—and he tapped it out, and I tapped it out, and we tapped it out. Did four or five times. I thought it was fine meter for his purposes. So we didn't go into anything beyond that. I remembered part of this. I remembered a lot of it at the time, but it tends to leave my mind now. Well, all I can remember now is a couplet, which was a refrain. It kept coming back in. "We are the boys who don't like to brag, / But we sure are proud of the grand old flag." That's good wartime poetry.

NEWMAN: Is that poetry, by the way?

WARREN: No, it's wartime poetry. It's a general's wartime poetry, you might say. It's about as good as General Patton's poetry, though. Did you ever hear his poetry?

NEWMAN: No, I haven't.

WARREN: I read a fragment of it once. And Sitting Bull was a pretty good military man; he wrote some poetry too.

NEWMAN: Patton's poetry was all addressed to the God of War, was it not?

WARREN: Um-hm.

NEWMAN: God of Battles, I think.

WARREN: Something like that, yeah. Very much like very bad Kipling.

NEWMAN: Mr. Warren . . . the American South gives the impression of being a particularly rich, fertile field for literature. If it is, if indeed it is, what is it that makes it so? Why have so many celebrated American writers come from the South? Is it the climate? Is it the War? Is it the fact that it had slavery? Or is it possible to say?

WARREN: Yes. I'll make a guess. If you have a very—a firmly organized society, aesthetically organized, fixed, rigidly fixed, with little sense of change in it, and little opportunity —limitation of opportunities of various kinds, with unremarked, unobserved, undefined pressures there, building up, usually moral pressures of one kind or another, or partly moral pressures—you suddenly introduce other forces that are very shattering to this, morally shattering, morally disturbing, plus a sense of shifting ranges of opportunity for feeling, for all sorts of things—you are apt to get some reaction. It may be literary in part. Some kind of cultural shock, cultural collision of a rather static world, against a world more fluid and provocative, which involves a moral issue of some kind, it's apt, very apt—probably, you can judge from history—to get some kind of literary expression.

NEWMAN: So the more flexible society is less likely to produce—

WARREN: Well, I wouldn't say that, exactly. I'd say a society waking up is more apt to write than it is to do anything else. . . . In the earlier part of the nineteenth century you have something almost parallel to that—a very rigid society suddenly brought in contact with European and Eastern thought, and suddenly money was also a different part of it. And a whole shift took place in the structure of New England society, from the old, the preacher-teacher-farmer, you suddenly had State Street and finance, and people going to Germany to study, like—like Longfellow being sent to study and coming back to teach—this world, shock of ideas, plus people taking those ships out to the Orient. Suddenly a great shock and a change of the social center of gravity. There is a whole theory about this, how firmly based I don't know, but it's a theory backed by a very eminent historian,[26] that you have this shock of a change of the nature of power in New England. It's the key to the whole ferment of ideas from 1830 on.

NEWMAN: It's the flowering of New England.

WARREN: That's right. From that point on. In the South, with its deep, very deep moral ambiguities around slavery—it being a very democratic country, with terrible slavery in the middle of it—and the home of our republic—because Jefferson was Southern, and so was Washington—carrying on a tradition outside of the American tradition. Slavery again. This whole question of an internal struggle, usually glossed over, but central to the whole life of the section; and then a very frozen world, cut off from modernity up until the First World War. And the First World War, you had this great, great shock of meeting the outside world, really meeting it. Also the shock of meeting the black man for the first time, in a new role. In one of Faulkner's novels, a returning black soldier (one of the early novels)—a returning black soldier was a shock. He was wearing a uniform. It was a different world. From that time on, it was a different world. This whole encounter with the outside world from Ireland—this is very important to the South, some part of the South, anyway—the image of Ireland as a rebellious minority, and the South as a rebellious minority, or French educations and experience in the war, and England—the explosion suddenly in all different directions. And I think you can make a case for this. You have the same thing in different ways happening with the sudden great burst of Jewish literary genius in this country; and black, the same way. The same kind of shock—the breaking up of a fixed situation, where some people have been more or less enclosed, brought into a fruitful relation and a shocking relation to the world outside.

NEWMAN: And that's what we're having now, this—well, the Jewish outburst has been going on for some time.

WARREN: For some time, and the black outburst is now in full swing. The release of all sorts of submerged and hidden capacities. Brought about by some strange, shocking relation to an outside world. It's a certain kind of shock, of course. But we see it, stage after stage. We see it in the first breakthrough of the immigrants, with Dreiser. He was the first immigrant writer in America. In the long time since America was established. And a whole new vein of feeling came from American literature with Theodore Dreiser.

NEWMAN: I suppose you see it in another way with Willa Cather—in the West?

WARREN: Yes. But that society was firmly fixed. It was rigid, you see, and it wasn't in the sense of minority society, as Southern society was, or Jewish society, or black society, you see. These are fairly firmly fixed, enclosed groups, with their own order of life, and their own special kind of limitations and deprivations, and their own inner problems and tensions.

NEWMAN: In your own case, Professor Warren, both your grandfathers fought for the South in the Civil War—

WARREN: And a grand-uncle, too, may I add. He got shot in the leg.

NEWMAN: And I think you heard first-hand accounts of the fighting. Is that correct?

WARREN: That's correct. Yeah, sure.

NEWMAN: What effect did it have on you? Did it make the Civil War seem a very romantic thing? What notion did it give you of the South in which you were living?

WARREN: It was very double. At the first, of course, a small boy of six or seven hearing about battles, it's all very romantic because he doesn't understand blood, but I do remember very distinctly the shock of discovering that the old man, my grandfather, who had fought battles, wasn't romantic about it. I remember that shock very distinctly. It was a story, an important story to tell, but it wasn't romantic. This was a great shock, because I wanted to make it all very romantic in my childish way. This shock was quite real. I even wrote a poem about it, called "Court Martial"—about that moment when the old man was not romantic at all, and I had been romantic, and suddenly he was realistic about it. So it carries a double thing with it. Though any defeated society is going to romanticize its war, that was done by the U.D.C., not the old men.

NEWMAN: That's the United Daughters of the Confederacy?

WARREN: Yes.

NEWMAN: —who romanticize it?

WARREN: Well, they are the carriers of piety, and they are the carriers of romance.

NEWMAN: You yourself have written, in dealing with Herman Melville, an American writer to whom you've paid a great deal of attention—

WARREN: Yes. Twenty years of attention.

NEWMAN: You quote a line—I should say, you quote a line from Melville, in one of his poems that refers to the Wars

of the Roses: "In legend all shall end." Melville thought
that would happen with the Civil War. He said, "North
and South shall join the train of Yorkist and Lancastrian."
Do you think the Civil War is going into legend? Has it
gone into legend?

WARREN: It's there, I think, now. It's a legend, and a forgotten
legend, in one sense.

NEWMAN: May that legend be changed by the black revolt?

WARREN: It'll be forgotten by it. It's being changed by it, yes.
But it suddenly seems so remote, you know. It'll come
back again as something not remote, but it's a great Homeric moment of our history, I think. You can't forget that
story, but we lay it aside for the moment.

NEWMAN: We can lay it aside politically, can't we?

WARREN: Yes. It's now overlaid with so many ambiguous and
confusing and, I think, destructive issues that have nothing
to do with the War itself. The War is incomprehensible
now to most young people who haven't made themselves
historically instructed in it. They see only a kind of gross
symbol, not a human experience of infinite complication.
But I say this without grief or pain or surprise. It's an
observation.

NEWMAN: I suppose it was inevitable. It's usually thought to
have become inevitable because of the industrialization
of the South, but it probably happens for much less predictable reasons, doesn't it, when you get an historic development of that kind? It happens in ways that nobody
can foresee.

WARREN: You mean the role of the Civil War in the American
consciousness?

NEWMAN: Yes. There certainly have been times in American
history in this century when it seemed that the Civil War
would never cease to be a political factor.

WARREN: Nineteen sixty-one, for instance. And suddenly it's
only a thing in New Orleans to wave a Confederate flag for
reasons that would have embarrassed Robert E. Lee. He
would have been the last man to have been cheering on
Governor Faubus in Arkansas. But his flag is being used by—

was used for the school in Arkansas, in Little Rock, or in New Orleans several years ago when desegregation proceeded in those two schools, those two places. But it takes time to reorder symbols, and that's the symbolism it now has. Only history courses will remedy that. Back to Melville. May I cut back there a moment?

NEWMAN: Please do.

WARREN: That particular poem—a wonderful poem, with some awful bad lines in it. It's such a poem of fundamental insight to me. It's called "The Battle of Stones River, Tennessee, as Viewed from an Oxford Cloister," and this bloody battle, fought outside of Nashville in the Confederate drive to retake Nashville late in the War, seen by the Oxford Don, a historian or a man aware of his own history, with thousands of miles of distance, it looks like time—he looks back to the Wars of the Roses in England, their Civil War of centuries before, and the poem really says (paraphrased and boiled down) that what we remember from history is human stances, the sense of human values, rather than issues. What remains is the nobility or ignobility of the human stance, the human gesture, the human passion. Not politics or even the moral issues. And this is what happens ultimately: All becomes legend. We see an image of human values, I think. I mean, all the past—I don't mean the Civil War—we have to analyze to bring back the issues. We are really concerned with the image of the passion, the devotion, the courage of human beings in any cause, rather than the weighing . . . distributing right and wrong in the cause. This is the romance of the enemy we always find. The brave enemy is always our best friend, not the rather ordinary fellow who is our ally.

. . . .

NEWMAN: Again, coming back to Melville, in *The Selected Poems of Herman Melville*, which you edited, you refer quite early in the Introduction really to poetic value. Is that something that can be defined?

WARREN: Well, if I could define it today, I wouldn't accept

the same definition tomorrow. Put it that way. I made a remark in the Introduction of this sort: In the course of years of reading Melville—sporadically, but off and on for many years—I took a different view of what conscious poetic values that I had when I started twenty-five years earlier, in '46, with my first piece on Melville; and I began to feel more dimensions in the question, just by living very closely with the work of that poet (and other poets). This is, I suppose, inevitable. I change in things all the time. But I was more— For one thing, Melville is a very imperfect poet. He was very unsure technically. And I was forced to think more and more about what survives imperfect techniques. An intuition somehow survives groping formulation, the imperfect formulation of it. And sometimes the imperfection of the formulation actually gives a peculiar poignance to the intuition. But I wouldn't have any clear-cut formula for this. I can report a certain shift in my basic feeling about poetic values, but my whole life, and, I suppose, all lives of people who read poetry, must record a shift of taste. A poet who is great when you're twenty-five is not great when you're fifty. You still admire him, but the infatuation is gone. . . .

NEWMAN: Does this have anything to do with the growing sophistication on the part of the reader?

WARREN: I don't think so. It's deeper than that, I would say, individually considered. It wouldn't be sophistication; it might be a new innocence, even, instead of sophistication. But the difference I would insist on, and what I would say about this, out of my own experience, is two symbols that make much sense. It's what nourishes me. There are certain poets at certain times that are necessary to me. And I soak in them. I feed on them. They are saying something to me, or giving me a way of life, a feel of life which another poet will not do at that time, that period of years. The poet I have known before may be remembered with affection and great admiration, but I don't want to read him then, any more. He's not for me any more. I may come back to him. Of course, there are a few poets where the reference is more or less steady—with different degrees, but more or less steady. But very few, I think, for me.

NEWMAN: I remember at a news conference once, General de Gaulle was asked who his favorite poet was, and he replied, "The poet I am reading."

WARREN: That should be the way it is, in a way. What you are wrapped up in. I mean, really reading, not just scanning.

NEWMAN: May I go a bit further in this? You have written, with Cleanth Brooks, what I suppose is the most celebrated textbook on poetry in the English language, *Understanding Poetry*, so I don't hesitate to ask you. You take an example of Melville's poetry, and you quote the line "Like the fish of the bright and twittering fin," and you say that the word "twittering" converts that line into poetry. Is it possible to say how it does that, or is it just something we know from reading it aloud, or rereading it—really reading it, not scanning it, as you said?

WARREN: Well, I think I could say why for me. It's not going to be why for you, you see. How does the line go now?

NEWMAN: "Like the fish of the bright and twittering fin."

WARREN: If the fish has a bright and twitching fin, it's not poetry, you see. It's not poetry then. That's dead. Couldn't be worse. But "twittering" gives a new dimension to the whole thing, gives a new sense. It's not the only thing that makes poetry, but it discovers a new dimension of feeling. It's like—that little trill of a bird on the bough, as it were. The busy little twitch of the fin in the bright water, and the little warble or twitter of a bird on a bough are now tied together. We see a relation, feel a relation of the density and of resonance in nature. We have expanded our sense of life a little bit, just a little bit, by the twittering, [not] by the twitching.

NEWMAN: It's an image, in the old sense of image.

WARREN: That's right. It amounts to a concealed metaphor, a concealed simile of some kind. It opens up our sense of a vital density of the world, the resonance of life. Just a little bitty bit, you know; just a little bit. But enough to make it feel as poetry. A new dimension of feeling has been opened up to experience. And that is just a trivial little line; it's a nothing of a line. This is where he started, though, before *Moby-Dick*. He could write *Moby-Dick* and write the great poems of the Civil War, and the other big poems he was supposed to write.

NEWMAN: Professor Warren, you have said that the hope was once tenable that a volume of poetry could sell like a popular novel, but that any poet who entertained such a hope today would have to be—would be marked out as a certifiable lunatic.

WARREN: Barring Mr. McKuen, of course.

NEWMAN: Yes, Rod McKuen, but what is bad about this change in taste, then?

WARREN: This is a long and fumbling answer. If you— It's not a change of taste. It's a change in the world which is behind this. When Tennyson's *In Memoriam* was published, in the middle of the last century, the publishers gave to Tennyson (for a poem he published anonymously, I think) enough money to marry Emily. He was engaged fifteen years; it was time to marry her. But he set up housekeeping on this poem. Imagine that. The advance on this little poem set up housekeeping for Alfred and Emily. But now I suppose that doesn't happen. Tennyson's poems were published over here during the Civil War. They couldn't keep count of the sales. They couldn't keep count. The bookkeeping broke down in the thing so fast. Unbelievable. Unbelievable. Right in the middle of the War. And also, a very small percentage of the public was literate compared to now. But those who could read, read. That's one difference. Everybody reads now, and nobody reads. Or few read. But in any case, why? For one thing, poetry—it wasn't a matter of taste. It was a matter of what kind of needs poetry fulfilled in the broadest sense. It fulfilled the needs of our columnists, the daily columnists. It fulfilled the need that now gives us our weird news. It took the place of novels. It did everything. It was a jack-of-all-trades then, really. If Tennyson wrote a poem called *Maud* about women's rights

—but Kate Millett does not write in verse, you see. All right, there we are. *Maud* is a poem. I must say it's not much of a poem. It's a lot of verse, with a few nice lyrical touches, like the bugle, I think, is in there nicely, but by and large this so-called poem, *Maud*, was, officially speaking, a poem, while Miss Millett does not write in verse. She writes in a, shall I say, sober prose. But that's one example right there. Or if you talk about science in the modern world, you don't write a poem like *In Memoriam*. Tennyson writes about science in the modern world, and he calls the poem *In Memoriam*. There are other things there, too, in the poem. Now, if you get Mr. Mumford, and Mr. Reich, and all the other pundits of science and technology—they don't write in verse. Some don't even write in prose. Some do. It's another world, you see. We have specialized out the needs which once put us in a lump. However imperfectly we acted, we acted in a lump, all together. Now we have specialized it out, so poetry is poetry, only poetry and very little else. Now, back in the 1930's you had a little social-consciousness poetry; in Vietnam you have a little Vietnam poetry. But by and large, poetry goes on being poetry, bringing to all of us some special satisfactions which are poetic.

NEWMAN: There's even an enormous difference between World War I and World War II, wasn't there?

WARREN: There certainly was. There certainly was. Now, I am not applauding this specialization entirely. I think we have lost certain things by it. And I would guess we may regain a broader base, a richer poetry, by coming back to poetry as a fuller reference to life than we have had it for a long time. Without the awe. Let's look at it this way too. The poetry of Pound and Eliot and Yeats, the three great masters of our century in English—they were writing about fundamental issues of our society, of our whole world. They were the people who suddenly made the image of a glimmer of a technological world emotionally available. Scientists . . . like Bertrand Russell had written about it; several others had written about it. But it hadn't affected

anybody. But once the image of the Waste Land is there—
You see, it's the Waste Land. That's where it is. Why is it
the Waste Land? So, however recondite and specialized we
figure the poetry of Eliot was, it also gave us the big,
dominant image of an age. It is now a catchword among
eighth-graders, and lies behind street riots and hippie com-
munes and group-gropes. Now, that irrelevant poem is a
very difficult poem. It took people a long time to understand
it. But what they finally understood was the very world
they were living in. It's very hard to say, in a way, that *The
Waste Land* is more specialized or irrelevant than *In Memoriam*. It didn't sell as much. It has sold an awful lot over
the years now to this time.

NEWMAN: Against the background of what you've just said,
then, Professor Warren, let me ask you to explain something else you have said or written. You say there has
never been so much poetry in existence as there is now. You
find poetry on the air, on the hustings, in folk ballads, in
advertising copy and public relations. What do you mean
by that?

WARREN: I don't mean good poetry. Sometimes it happens to
be good. But I mean the use of the language emotively to
compel assent and arouse feelings. This aspect of language
is always there, except among scientists doing a specific
job. And it's organized, highly organized, the advertising
business. We know this, you see. They are very, very
clever fellows. They know a lot about the techniques of
poetry, and they make very good livings out of it. Some
of them do, anyway.

NEWMAN: That's poetry in the sense of emotive language?

WARREN: The manipulation of language to arouse emotion,
in that sense. Emotive language, or controlled for effect—
poetry in that sense—or expressive of emotion. In its broad
general sense, the world is always full of it. That doesn't
make it good or bad. It may be used descriptively only.

NEWMAN: Professor Warren, you have been teaching for many
years. Everybody talks about how different young people
are nowadays. Are they different from what they used to

be? Have the students you've taught noticeably changed over the years in a fundamental way?

WARREN: Well, "fundamental" is a trick word there, you see. It's a trick word.

NEWMAN: That's emotive language, perhaps.

WARREN: I don't think it's emotive language; it's a word we have to deal with, I think. I think we have to deal with that word. There are differences. There are real differences, but I would have to preface any remark about that by saying that I don't want to put them in a lump. "The young" is a word. The actual young are people. They are all different, in their ways. Now, to break them into certain groups, you can generalize about—more than about the individuals—I mean, about the group as a whole. And I think, if you are going to have a kind of precocity, a kind of intellectual awareness before emotional maturity, you're going to have a certain number of liabilities with this. At the same time I say that, my observation is in a small range of students I see. I have very few students, really. But I know them pretty well, those I have, because I see a lot of them in a face-to-face way. In five years the level of what I've seen is remarkably higher. The best is no better, but the level is so much higher. And the kind of basic seriousness. I will say this, too—this is surprising to me, and painful to me, that more and more I see a lack of vocation among even very, very brilliant young people. No direction, no passion for life. And this is, I think, a very shattering thing to watch.

NEWMAN: Is that the so-called dropout . . . ?

WARREN: I am talking, now, not so much about dropouts, though it applies to dropouts. I mean the bright dropouts—the young man who has taken his degree, has his B.A. with honors, and says, "Where do I go now? There's no place I really want to go." Or the senior saying, "What do I do next? I don't really care." Now a man with an expensive education, a first-rate brain, feels there's no place for him in the world—this is not an uncommon situation. Not uncommon at all. And expanded and multiplied, it can be tragic. At the same time, I know so many people of the same generation who have found the most rewarding lives, so far, in direct action of poetry, writing poetry, or giving two days a week out of his law practice to slum practice, and so forth. These are going on together. They are side by side. And we don't know what's going to happen out of this. But I do resent the notion that the young are put in one package. There are many kinds of young. And the articulate young, or the noisy young (they're not the same thing, necessarily—noisy and articulate is not the same thing), aren't always fair samples. Think of all the boys in laboratories or libraries who are truly changing the world. The guys in the chemistry laboratories, the guys in the medical schools, the guys— Karl Marx, sitting around reading a book—

NEWMAN: In the British Museum.

WARREN: In the British Museum. We don't know where the world is being changed.

. . . .

A Conversation with Robert Penn Warren

Warren was seventy—three weeks away from his seventy-first birthday—when he was interviewed for educational television by Bill Moyers. The conversation was taped at Yale University and broadcast on WNET Thirteen April 4, 1976.

WARREN: I'm in love with America; the funny part of it is, I really am. I've been in every state in the Union except one, and I'm going there within a month.

BILL MOYERS: Which state is that?

WARREN: That's Oregon. And I've traveled in the Depression in a fifty-dollar car, broken-down, old green Studebaker. I wandered all over the West. I spent time on ranches here and ranches there and have been in all sorts of places. And I've had change given back to me for gas in the Depression. Some guys say, "Oh, keep the change, buddy; you look worse than I do." I really fell in love with this country.

MOYERS: *He is a rarity in American letters. The only writer to win Pulitzer Prizes for both fiction and poetry. And he loves the country he often rebukes. We'll see why tonight in a conversation with Robert Penn Warren.*

. . . .

MOYERS: The novel [*All the King's Men*] became a classic when Robert Penn Warren wrote it at the age of forty-one. Almost three million copies have been sold around the world . . . in twenty languages. The movie became a classic, too. It won three Oscars. Its subject was politics; its theme, corruption.

. . . .

WARREN: It sort of grew out of circumstances. Grew out of a folklore of the moment where I was and I guess also because I was teaching Shakespeare and reading Machiavelli and William James. Everything flowed together. That was a world of melodrama, the world of pure melodrama. Nothing like it since, well, until Watergate, as far as melodrama's concerned.

MOYERS: Oh, you think Watergate was melodrama.

WARREN: Obviously, it was melodrama, tragedy. It was tragedy, too. You couldn't believe it. Well . . . only it happened to be true.

MOYERS: Did you think that *All the King's Men* would become a classic?

WARREN: I never gave it a thought; I just try to make an honest living.

MOYERS: *It has been a prolific life since Robert Penn Warren arrived in Guthrie, Kentucky, seventy-one years ago this month. Since then he's been almost everywhere, and written just about everything. Nine novels, ten volumes of poetry, short stories, essays, two studies of race relations. There's hardly an award he hasn't collected. The National Book Award, the Chair of Poetry at the Library of Congress, the Bollingen Prize, the National Medal for Literature, and of course, those two Pulitzers. He's still writing. Increasingly intrigued by the fate of democracy in a world*

*of technology. We talked at Yale University, his base for
writing and teaching this past quarter-century.*

As a poet and a novelist, as opposed to being the author
of *All the King's Men,* how do you explain the vast dis-
enchantment of our modern times?

WARREN: I don't know. It's touched every country in the
world; we're not alone, it's part of the modern world.

MOYERS: Is there something in . . . ?

WARREN: There's something in the modern world going on,
and I don't profess to understand it. We can make guesses
about it.

MOYERS: Make some guesses.

WARREN: Well, we are, for one thing—the whole Western
world is undergoing some deep change in its very nature
in what it can believe in. And one of those things is clearly
how democracy can function in a world of technology.
That's one thing. Another thing, it just seems the massive
number of people involved. Government's designed, the
modern liberal democracy is designed, to function within a
certain limited world.

MOYERS: How successful do you think we are in keeping some
notion of democracy, and some concept of the self, alive in
a highly technological, scientific age of huge organizations?

WARREN: Not successful enough. I think you can see many
indications of that.

MOYERS: What are some of the manifestations you see that
deeply trouble you?

WARREN: Now, this is a small academic matter in one sense:
the death of history.

MOYERS: The death of history?

WARREN: Yes. History departments are on the decline, I'm
told. I don't know the statistics. But certainly they . . . the
sense of the past is passing out of the consciousness of the
generation.

MOYERS: What do you think will be the consequence of that?

WARREN: I don't know how you can have a future without a
sense of the past. A real future. And we have a book like
Plumb's book, *The Death of the Past,* which is a very im-

pressive and disturbing book. As Plumb puts it, in the past people have tried and learned what wisdom they could from history. They have tried to learn from what has happened before. Now, he says, social science will take the place of history. And the past will die . . . and the machine will take over . . . done by social scientists. That's his prediction. He says only history keeps alive the human sense, history in the broadest sense of the word. It might be literary history or political history or any other kind of history. It's man's long effort to be human. And if a student understands this or tries to penetrate this problem, he becomes human. If he once gives that up as a concern, he turns to mechanism.

MOYERS: The machine.

WARREN: The machine.

MOYERS: Process?

WARREN: Some process to take charge. Now he may have . . . there are many kinds of machines, there're many kinds of processes he can turn to. But the . . . the sense of a human being's effort to be human and to somehow develop his humanity, that is what history's about.

MOYERS: Do you sense among the students you teach, and among the young people you know, this loss of the past, this disconnection from history?

WARREN: Yes, I have. I have indeed.

MOYERS: What is the effect of it?

WARREN: It's a certain kind of blankness. A certain kind of blankness. But the past is dead for a great number of young people; it just doesn't exist.

MOYERS: I know you once wrote that Americans felt liberated from time, and that it gave them a sense of being, gave us a sense of being on a great gravy train with a first-class ticket.

WARREN: Well, we had the country of the future, the party of the future . . . we had the future ahead of us, and we had this vast space behind us on this continent. We had time and space. We could change the limitations of the European world. Such a simple thing as a man's hands becoming valuable. A man on the American continent in the eighteenth century was valuable, neighbors were valuable, hands were valuable, there were things for hands to do. And so the whole sense of the human value changed . . . right . . . beginning with the value of hands, what they could do. Or the value of a neighbor down the road a mile away instead of twenty miles away. These things made a whole difference in the sense of life. And it's a fundamental stimulus to our sense of our own destiny.

MOYERS: They also were a power incentive, were they not, to human dignity?

WARREN: To human dignity because the hands mean something. They're not just things owned by somebody else. They belong to that man. And then, all of the rest of the factors that enter into the creation of American . . . the American spirit. All of those things are involved.

MOYERS: You said once . . .

WARREN: We could always move, and the sense of time—being time-bound and space-bound—disappeared, but mitigated, anyway. A whole psychology was born; it'd never been in the world before.

MOYERS: A very optimistic philosophy of progress.

WARREN: That's right. As Jefferson said, in writing to his daughter Martha, he said, Americans—I think it was his daughter Martha, anyway—Americans fear nothing, you see, cannot be overcome by earnest application, you see, and what's the other word? Ingenuity.[27]

MOYERS: Ingenuity.

WARREN: Americans assume that there are no insoluble problems.

MOYERS: We've really been—we've really been trapped, in a sense, by Thomas Jefferson's definitions of America in those terms, haven't we?

WARREN: That's right, we assume that we can solve anything rather easily. And we're always right. We think we're usually right about it. Since we can solve things, we're the ones who are right.

MOYERS: I remember you wrote once that America was defined by one man in an upstairs room. Thomas Jefferson writing "all men are created equal," giving this great metaphysical boost to the American self-image.

WARREN: Yes, he gave more than any one person, gave us our self-image. I think he was wrong about human nature in his emphasis on it. He wasn't a fool, of course; he knew that there were bad people. He knew there were stupid people because of six, I think, siblings in his outfit. Four had something wrong with them in the head. And the other one died young. Jefferson's genius was the only one of this brood of children who was even—I think this is right now—who was not in some way deficient. And so he was probably aware of the fact that all men are not born equal, right there at his own fireside.

MOYERS: How do people who still live with that mystique of democracy, that mystique of the self, how do they come to terms with the world you have described as being large, impersonal, driven by science and technology?

WARREN: They say that's the way to solve it, by and large. They say somebody will fix it up, the expert will fix it up some way. The magic cancer cure, there'll be this, there'll be that. The expert will come along and fix it up. And our faith has gone from God to experts. And sometimes experts don't work out.

MOYERS: Well, you've written a lot about how to hold on to the sense of self when the world is changing this way. What do you say when the world enforces a beating upon us from many directions, forces we can't understand, forces we can't change, forces we can't even define? How do you . . . ?

WARREN: Some forces we don't . . . even want to change; we want our technology and we should have it, should want it. It's how we use it, that's important. It's the attitude toward it, it seems to me is important, not its presence. From scientific speculation to the applications in technology represents a great human achievement. It's how we approach this and how we wish to use it.

MOYERS: Well, I wouldn't want to abandon, would you, this material progress we've made, the things that make life so much more amenable.

WARREN: God, no, I don't want to abandon it. My grandfather said he took a very dim view of the modern world—he was born in '38.

MOYERS: Eighteen thirty-eight . . .

WARREN: Eighteen thirty-eight, and fought the Civil War and wound up life as . . . he died in 1919, 1920, something like that—'21. He looked around the modern world and found it not all to his taste. But he said they have got two things that make it worthwhile. Fly screens and painless dentistry. Well, I'm for fly screens and painless dentistry too. I want that and I want some other things to boot.

MOYERS: What is the proper posture or attitude from all the years you've lived?

WARREN: The problem is finally a human problem, and not a technical problem. And we're back to the history again. The sense of the human as being the key sense. As we talk about education, this means the so-called humanities is the only place for students to find the point of reference for the application of their science and their technology. That is the sense of the struggle to define values.

MOYERS: What are the values that are most important to you now?

WARREN: Well, I can tell you what my pleasures are.

MOYERS: What are your pleasures?

WARREN: Put it this way. Because I'm selfish and want to fill my days in a way that pleases me. Well, it so happens that my chief interest in life, aside from my friendly affections and family affections, which is another thing—though they're related—is the fact I like novels and poems, as I want to read them and I want to write them . . . as I have an occupation which to me . . . I can go beyond that—now, why that occupation? It's the only way that I can try to make sense to myself of my own experience . . . is this way. Otherwise I feel rather lost . . . in the ruck of my experience and the experience I observe around me. If you write a poem or read the poem—somebody else has written one that suits you, that pleases you, this is a way of making your own life make sense to you. It's your way of trying to give shape to experience. And the satisfaction of living is feeling that you're living significantly.

MOYERS: Does it . . . ?

WARREN: That doesn't mean grandly; that means it has a meaning, it has a shape, that your life is not being wasted, it isn't just being from this to that.

MOYERS: It also means imposing . . .

WARREN: And understanding.

MOYERS: . . . and imposing order, doesn't it?

WARREN: Order.

MOYERS: Some sense of order.

WARREN: Some sense of order on it, yes.

MOYERS: What does poetry and literature offer people in an age of technology and science?

WARREN: I say it offers an inward landscape. Now, I've been talking about outer landscape, but it offers an inner landscape . . . it offers a sense of what man is like inside. What experience is like, he can see perspectives of experience. This may be in poetry or it may be in history or it may be in political science; it may be taken in historical perspective. Man's view of how he should govern himself over a period of time has changed.

MOYERS: But how does it help us to see ways to deal with technology, with organization, with size?

WARREN: It makes us ask the question how that light or this object or this automobile or this plane will serve our deepest human needs. Or whether it's a gadget, whether it's a toy. Now, when Coleridge has the Ancient Mariner shoot the albatross for no reason except he has a crossbow to shoot the albatross, he's dealing with that problem. The problem was already there, you see. A machine defines the act. The man shoots the bird only because he has a crossbow. Why should he shoot the bird? He has no reason to shoot the bird. It's a gratuitous act. The machine defines the act. Because the machine will do so-and-so, therefore it must be done. See what I'm getting at there? Coleridge's poem is a criticism . . . man as victim of technology.

MOYERS: How do we get control?

WARREN: It's a constant struggle. It means trying to inspect the things that shape us, that make us. Once we understand it, we can sometimes do something about it. Now, I'm not talking of psychoanalysis; I'm talking much broader than psychoanalysis, which is one—is a special kind of application of a principle that's always been functioning in the world. People look at what made their world tick or made them tick, and they achieve, may achieve, some sense of freedom from mechanical forces. I mean forces of machines, of mechanisms, but forces that have them into machines and give them habits of doing this thing this way and that way. Religious conversion is one of the most obvious examples of this.

MOYERS: Reconversion?

WARREN: Religious conversion.

MOYERS: Religious conversion.

WARREN: . . . is an old-fashioned way of looking at it. A man's been one kind of man; he suddenly understands life differently . . .

MOYERS: Do you believe that's still possible?

WARREN: I think so. I think it can exist; it exists for certain people.

MOYERS: Well, give us some help. How do we do it?

WARREN: Try to see how you came to be the way you are. The poem of Randall Jarrell's "Change" ends "change me, change me."

MOYERS: And you think it's still . . . is part of the creative process.

WARREN: I still believe in such things as religious conversion . . . though I'm a non-believer, I'm a non-churchgoer, put it this way: I'm rather a common type, I think now, of a yearner.

MOYERS: The yearner?

WARREN: The yearner. I would say that I have a religious temperament, you see, with a scientific background.

MOYERS: Pilgrims sought God and looked for a promised land in the hereafter. What do you yearn for?

WARREN: I yearn for significance, for life as significance. Now, if I'm feeling with a poem or a novel I'm, in a small way, trying to do the same thing. I'm trying to make it make sense to me. That's all. That's one reason why I like teaching . . . I have a real passion for teaching.

MOYERS: How's that?

WARREN: I think there's nothing more exciting than seeing a young person moving toward the moment of recognizing significance in something. The inner significance of something.

MOYERS: And it happens under what occasions?

WARREN: It can happen under— In a classroom, it can happen in any classroom any time and very often. And very often, indeed. And I'm a parent and I've seen it happen to my children.

MOYERS: How does it happen in an urban, complicated, interdependent city where life is crowded and services are poor, and a feeling that one is being acted upon by men and events over which he has no control? How does this yearning to signify find the creative satisfaction?

WARREN: It means a whole regeneration of the feeling of our society. And it's not going to be done by just making a few appropriations. I knew one man whom I rarely see now—he used to live in this neighborhood—whose job was to explain the background of the National Merit Scholarship winners. What could he find in common among these boys and girls who were spectacular intellectually, you see, and had great drive. And he said he had worked on it for years. He had found one thing only was in common: there was always a person behind that child. It might be a friend or a teacher or an old grandmother who's illiterate. It has nothing to do with education. With some sense of recognition by an older person of this child's worth, this child felt valuable, felt valued. And some one person or maybe, maybe more than one had made him feel this was worth sitting at night reading, studying his book.

MOYERS: And you're saying somehow we have to get that personal touch back into . . .

WARREN: Some sense, something that will correspond to that. To humanize education, or to . . . maybe you can't create the home life again, maybe it's gone. I don't know. Now, I don't . . . I hesitate to be optimistic. But he said at least if they do anything, they know there was always one person or more than one behind that child . . . who suddenly seems like a miracle. He might be coming out of some lowly, illiterate, starving ranch in Wyoming and suddenly this child appears and it looks like a miracle. But no, the old grandpa was there, talking to the child or some . . . or some teacher spotted him. Now, Dreiser was the most unpromising boy you can imagine. He was just the most totally unpromising. He was a ferocious masturbator, he tried to get a wealthy girl, got money and . . . and sex tied up . . . tangled all his life. He was a poor student, he scarcely read a book, but some schoolteacher, a Miss Field, spotted him and said that boy has something. And she let him go on and graduate from high school. He got a job in Chicago as a clerk in the basement of a . . . of a hardware store as a stockboy. And she hunted him up a year or so later . . . said I'm going to send you to college. This old-maid schoolteacher said I've saved my money and I'm going to send you to college, you've got something. She sent him to college for a year. He wouldn't go back, said I'm not getting anything here, said I'm just not learning anything here at all. So he . . . he wouldn't take her money any more, said I'm wasting your money. But that's the one person that put the finger on him, though, and says you've got something. Anything that will cultivate the sense of the value of a human being is the hope that'll make that man feel valuable, and that'll make . . . make it easier for someone else to feel valuable.

MOYERS: Well, we've been for two hundred years a country that grooved on more and better progress, and that hasn't been all bad. It's had a big price. But the question, it seems to me now is, how do you hold onto the material abundance, spread it around so that more people share in it, but at the same time keep what you've written about so often, that sense of self and dignity and individual responsibility?

WARREN: Also, we've got to quit lying to ourselves all the time. Now, the Civil War was the biggest lie any nation ever told itself. It freed the slaves. Then what did it do with them? And the big lie was told, and also, we're full of virtue, we did it, we freed the slaves and it came home to roost a hundred years later. But we lie to ourselves all the time.

The lying about Vietnam was appalling. There was an awful lot of lying about Vietnam. There've been all kinds of lying. Now, there's the lying about our dealing with Mexico from the very start. I'm not saying give California back to Mexico; if you have to give 'em somethin', give 'em California, is my motto . . . which I used to know very well. But the point is you cannot keep lying to yourself indefinitely. And my daughter studying her history lesson in American history several years ago when she was a little girl in school—not now; she's a senior at Yale—but I was hearing her lesson for the examination. And she said something that was so appallingly wrong, I must have flushed . . . she said don't say anything, Daddy (Poppy, she called me), don't say anything, Poppy, don't say anything, I know it's a lie but it's what you have to tell the teacher.

MOYERS: Well, that was . . .

WARREN: And this is the way half of our life is led in America. We have the right lies to tell ourselves.

MOYERS: But haven't we stripped ourselves now of that pretense? I mean we were never innocent, but now the pretense is gone.

WARREN: The pretense is . . . is going, anyway.

MOYERS: You don't think it's all . . .

WARREN: I don't think it's all gone, no. You're going to hear more lies the next six months than you ever heard in your life before.

MOYERS: The stuff of another novel.

WARREN: Well, the lies are going to be told. But see . . . I'm in love with America . . . the funny part is, I really am.

MOYERS: What do you like about it? What . . . what does America say to you? Affirmatively.

WARREN: Well, the story is just so goddamn wonderful. I mean the whole thing from the . . . the little handful of men, you know, who pledged their lives and sacred honor and set off the world. It's a great story. And it's the plain sweat and pain that went into this country . . . and integrity, the incredible integrity.

MOYERS: Integrity.

WARREN: There's just lots of it. The people . . . history's full of it.

MOYERS: This is the man I'm talking to who wrote that piracy and go-getterism are part of this country.

WARREN: They are. But at the same time, you find the other thing is there too. But even the evil is part of the story.

MOYERS: It's the story you love.

WARREN: I love the story, but also, you can't have a story like for the . . . you know, from babes and sucklings, all life is evil against good. And American history is interesting because that's the way it is.

MOYERS: And often the evil and the good reside in the same personality.

WARREN: In the same personality. On the one hand you have a man like Houston who is a . . . is a pirate and a brigand but . . . but a boy who will read Homer by the fireside of the Cherokee chief when he's . . . when he's thirteen, fourteen years old and say that's pretty good. And he ran away from home and was living with the Cherokees in east Tennessee when he was a boy in his teens and reading Homer. And he turned out to be great.

MOYERS: Well, he was very lucky because when he headed west he stopped in Texas.

WARREN: He stopped in Texas, he stopped at the right . . . in the right place at the right time. But he started out . . . he and the same old Indian chief he met later on after he had been governor of Kentucky . . . I mean of Tennessee . . . and had this trouble with a woman there . . . with his wife . . . his wife had left. But he lived with the Indians again. Now, he and the Indian chief plotted to conquer the whole West, including Mexican west. And Jackson stopped him. Well, this is almost verifiable, there's some doubt about it, but it's almost certainly true. And when he crossed the river, when he plunged across the river into Texas, his friend rode with him to the river and gave him a new razor as a parting present. Razors were hard to come by in those days. And he turned around and said this razor'll shave the President. Well now, this is . . . this is America. I mean . . . I like these romantic stories of America. And the incredible energy and the incredible humor of America.

MOYERS: Humor?

WARREN: Humor. The whole tale of the . . . the folk tales, incredible number of folk tales, just an incredible number of folk tales. The whole sense of the . . . the whole Southwest . . . it's incredible. But it's the complexity that is . . . is engaging. But what I hate is they destroy the complexity, to wipe out all that past and see us outside the past like that. I know we've had heroic ages, that it's Homeric.

MOYERS: Is it over?

WARREN: Well, that's up to us. Now, I . . . I felt a thrill with the moon shots. I know that's not very sophisticated. But I think that's not the whole story, though. Moon shots and poems are not very different. They're both totally irrelevant to the ordinary business of life. The guy that devotes his life to fiddling in a laboratory or fiddling with a poem, they're both outside the ordinary common-sense world. And they're both a little crazy.

MOYERS: And yet you value them.

WARREN: I value them, indeed. I . . . I think if you once get rid of the craziness in the world, you haven't got anything left.

MOYERS: I remember in one poem you once asked yourself, "Have I learned how to live?" Have you answered that question?

WARREN: I haven't answered the question, no . . . no, of course I haven't answered the question. How would I? I know certain things about myself that I didn't know one time. Some things I don't like, too, I've learned. But don't ask me which ones.

MOYERS: I was just about to.

WARREN: But I do know that I have to have a certain amount of time a day for myself . . . they're kept for special occasions, I mean I . . . I want to be alone with my scribbling, my writing . . . my swimming or something. And I don't know why. I . . . but I guess it's a lonely boyhood, I attribute it to that, anyway.

MOYERS: But filled with the presence of ideas and people from the books you read.

WARREN: That's right. I had a very happy . . . very happy boyhood actually. My summers were very happy, anyway. On an old run-down farm where old Grandfather was very bookish and quoted poems all the time when he wasn't reading Napoleon and His Marshals . . . or drawing the maps of Civil War battles with his stick in the dust. And reading military history.

MOYERS: Most people don't know that about that part of the South. They still think of the violence and the terror of the South, and the racism. They don't realize that in the world, even when I grew up, it was filled with writing and reading and . . . and presences beyond the known and seen.

WARREN: There was a lot of reading; it has declined a great deal too. It was declining already in the . . . my boyhood. But you can tell by the books in the house, the kind of books in the house, you know. Or the . . . or the correspondence of a family. I'd get hold of the correspondence of a family for a hundred years. And an old house being torn down, several times I got the papers . . . the contractor tearing it down said got some papers for you. And I said I'd read them. But one thing that's impressive, at least in middle Tennessee and Kentucky, was the will toward, well, education or bookishness in the strangest communities. Well, even kidnapped . . . a schoolteacher went to another at gunpoint to get one, you know. And a certain man named Allener, I think, had a big revolutionary grant near Bowling Green, Kentucky. He was a wealthy man with a vast estate; he . . . he had built himself a fine house, but he couldn't get a schoolteacher. So he . . . a man who had commanded a regiment, you see, of regulars in the Revolution, and a man of great wealth . . . said well, I can do something useful, I can teach school. So he taught school for no pay for the rest of his life. Any child that would come, could come. He was a schoolteacher. Now, that is a kind of heroism.

MOYERS: Time to be alone, you say, is essential to answering that question: how to live. Do you have a television set?

WARREN: No, I don't. I apologize. There's just not enough time in the day, you see . . . there's not enough time in the day . . . so much to do. And if it's television or books . . . what it would come down to be.

MOYERS: And you've made your choice.

WARREN: I made my choice. Also, I didn't want my children having passive enjoyments.

MOYERS: Passive enjoy . . .

WARREN: Passive enjoyments.

MOYERS: Explain that.

WARREN: I'll be honest with you; I didn't want TV around small children. Have the problem of discipline, you know . . . in monitoring it. And they took it; they'd never ask for one. They'd rush to one in any other house, but they would say to the teacher, if he said to you use this program for your course: But our family's not like that, my father won't let me. And there it was. But I . . . this is eccentric, I know.

MOYERS: I remember now that you wrote somewhere about the danger of our becoming consumers not only of products but of time not wisely used. Is that what you mean?

WARREN: That's part of it, yes. And children are very vulnerable.

MOYERS: Well, that provokes me to think that most people aren't poets and writers, most people can't flee, and most people live in systems and institutions that give them very

little time to themselves. And yet, as I travel the country and
listen to people, they're saying, How can I create myself,
how can I signify? Do you have any thoughts?

WARREN: I think part of it is will . . . to look into something
that opens the inside, that books or, oh, I could say perfectly well . . . I could see it perfectly well being done by
TV, you see. I'll be arbitrary about that. But . . . I don't
know, I'm not trying to remake the human race, I'm reporting myself as best I can to you . . . and what I find necessary
to me.

MOYERS: And pleasurable, you said.

WARREN: And pleasurable, uh-uh. And pleasurable, yes.

MOYERS: What about the process of writing, of creating poems
and novels? Was it painful?

WARREN: It's a kind of pain I can't do without. I can't say I
like it, but I can't do without it. It's the old thing of scratch-
ing where you itch. We're trying to find out what the
meaning of your experience is. I phrase it that way to myself now. I've already done it to you early today. I've been
trying to find out some meaning of your own experience.
Now, I often write about other people; of course, this is
part of you too. I find . . . I find I can't do without it
so far.

MOYERS: Can you teach it? Can you teach a young person to
write?

WARREN: I don't think so. In one sense you can. I think you
can teach shortcuts and what to look for. I think you can
teach certain things which are peripheral to the actual
process. You can't create the kind of person that will be a
writer, but you can help a little bit. You can open eyes to
certain things and you can show how certain pieces of . . .
of literature work a little bit . . . can be helpful. What to
look for . . . you can modify a taste to a degree.

MOYERS: In more than thirty years of teaching, have you
noticed any significant change in the ability of young people
whom you teach to write and express themselves?

WARREN: I find increasing illiteracy.

MOYERS: Illiteracy?

WARREN: Illiteracy. Yes, I do . . . right in Yale University.

MOYERS: Kingman Brewster's not going to be very happy with that.

WARREN: Well, I'm sorry. That's just true.

MOYERS: Well, all of this: increasing illiteracy, discontinuity with the past, size, complexion, technology, even television —how does it all make you feel about the fate of democracy?

WARREN: I'm an optimist. And I think God loves Americans and drunkards . . . keeps them out of the way of passing cars . . .

MOYERS: But not of themselves.

WARREN: Not of themselves, yeah. We're part of a whole great process, we're part of the whole Western world, we're part of the whole drive of technology, and we have a very tenuous . . . a very tenuous hold on our . . . our goods and our chattels right now in this world. It's a very dangerous world we're living in. And I wish to God I had some wisdom about it. But I think there is a streak of contempt in the American life . . . of things that are very valuable and . . . not only are valuable, are essential to our survival. We're driving fairly straight for a purely technological society, and with technological controls. And our government is in the hands, in the control of technologists who are not concerned about any value except mere workability . . . immediate workability.

MOYERS: Utility.

WARREN: Utility. And I'm not . . . not by any sense sneering at the . . . at the useful things of the world. Even the pleasant things of the world, I like 'em a lot. I met a young man a few years ago . . . a few years out of Princeton, such a nice young man, the nicest kind of a young American. He said [when] we were introduced . . . he said, "I'm Xerox." Now he has given up his identity already; he says, "I'm Xerox." He's not Mr. Jim Jones any more even in his own mind; he has no self.

MOYERS: He's the organization of which he's a part.

WARREN: He's the organization of which he's a part. I'm Xerox.

And this is a symbol to me of the whole state of mind of the self ceasing to exist . . . it's part of a machine.

MOYERS: Is there an antidote?

WARREN: I think there is. I don't know whether anybody's gonna use it or not.

MOYERS: What?

WARREN: Well, I think the proper kind of education. I mean education that has something of the humanistic about it.

MOYERS: That says you matter.

WARREN: That says you matter. And the human being is this kind of a creature.

MOYERS: You're talking about a rebel. What is it that makes a rebel? Aren't you?

WARREN: I guess I am . . . I guess I am. Well, let me read you a little poem about the perfect citizen. I love this one by Auden, the man who is the perfect citizen. He was not a poet and not a scientist and not anything else, he's just simply a good citizen. "The Unknown Citizen": *

To JS/07/M/378
This Marble Monument
Is Erected by the State

He was found by the Bureau of Statistics to be
One against whom there was no official complaint,
And all the reports on his conduct agree
That, in the modern sense of an old-fashioned word, he
    was a saint,
For in everything he did he served the Greater Community.
Except for the War till the day he retired
He worked in a factory and never got fired,
But satisfied his employers, Fudge Motors Inc.
Yet he wasn't a scab or odd in his views,
For his Union reports that he paid his dues,
(Our report on his Union shows it was sound)
And our Social Psychology workers found
That he was popular with his mates and liked a drink.

The Press are convinced that he bought a paper every day
And that his reactions to advertisements were normal in
every way.
Policies taken out in his name prove that he was fully
insured,
And his Health-card shows he was once in hospital but
left it cured.
Both Producers Research and High-Grade Living declare
He was fully sensible to the advantages of the Instalment
Plan
And had everything necessary to the Modern Man,
A phonograph, a radio, a car and a frigidaire.
Our researchers into Public Opinion are content
That he held the proper opinions for the time of year;
When there was peace, he was for peace; when there was
war, he went.
He was married and added five children to the population,
Which our Eugenist says was the right number for a parent
of his generation,
And our teachers report that he never interfered with their
education.
Was he free? Was he happy? The question is absurd:
Had anything been wrong, we should certainly have heard.

MOYERS: Chilling.

WARREN: It's chilling.

MOYERS: Shades of George Orwell. What about the role of
writers in our history? The writers who have shaped or
questioned, contributed to these two hundred years. What
can you say about . . . about writers in American history?

WARREN: Well, I'll say this, anyway. If we start pretty early
. . . let's start with Cooper. You find a man who creates the
first great myth of America.

MOYERS: James Fenimore Cooper.

WARREN: James Fenimore Cooper. Now, he's . . . on one
hand, he says, you see, you have the rape of a natural land
. . . the destruction of a natural land. On the other hand,
you have the destruction of man and brutality that he's
aware of and talks about. And also the paradox, which he
has no solution for . . . between the values of nature and
those of civilization. He has no easy solution for them. Let's
take a case or two and look at [it] right quickly. In *Deer-*

slayer you have two characters, named Hurry Harry, that's
the go-getter, that's his name for the go-getter, the guy
who's out to exploit anything, and Hunter, an ex-pirate
who's been driven off the seas . . . hidden away on Lake
Glimmerglass. Now, these two guys are partners in the American story. The ex-pirate and the go-getter. Now, this is
too pat, it sounds almost too pat. And then this deerslayer,
the young deerslayer, he has never killed a man. . . . There's
a camp of Indians, women and children at some point on
the lake. There's a bounty on Indian scalps. So Go-getter
Hurry Harry and Hunter set out to go into the camp—it's
abandoned by all the braves—and kill all the women and
children and sell their scalps. Now, this is Cooper's view
of . . . of a myth of America. And . . . or another case,
in running back to his first novel, that series of pioneers
with people bringing cannon out to kill . . . to kill passenger
pigeons—no reason except the killing of pigeons—with a
cannon. They're not going to eat them; they let them rot.
At the same time, they lock up in jail the now very old
Leatherstocking because he's killed a deer out of season
to live on. That episode appears in the first one of the books.
But over and over again you have this. He's attacking; he's
going at the things in the American society that he sees as
incipient and with the same problems we're dealing with
now.

MOYERS: Well, other writers forged those myths.

WARREN: It started with Cooper. You can go right ahead with
William Faulkner and Cooper agreeing right down the line.
And Frost not far off that line. And then you have another
approach which is represented by . . . well, I mean most
recently, most famously, Pound, who was concerned with
American philistinism of another sort. And lack of a spiritu-
ality, if you want to call it that. You have a whole series of
the major writers who are violently critical of America.
Melville, for instance, violently critical, and they simply are
not ordinarily read straight in school. They're just not read
straight in school. What they say is not being . . . is not
being told to the student. Over and over again you find it's

true. And what the implications are of our American literature. It's an extremely critical literature, critical of America
and constantly rebuking America and trying to remake it.

MOYERS: And yet that's so American—to be critical, to take to
task, to challenge.

WARREN: That's right, that's American too, you see . . . the
fact that they've produced the writers who could take this
violent attitude toward their own people or to their own
society. Let me tell you something . . . just an anecdote.
A man I used to know in Italy—still know—he was a lieu-
tenant in the Italian army when Italy got in the war in the
summer of '40. He took to the hills with two friends. A rifle
each and a few grenades and some pistols. And finally joined
the partisans, finally found some other discontented people
to join with. And as a major with an armored train and an air
fleet of his own. But he said that what got him off—his
father had fled Italy earlier as anti-fascist (his father being
a musician . . . concert conductor). This young man said
I left because such a stupid fascist government allowed
them to translate American novels. And all the novels were
translated because they attack America, these American novels attacking America, you see. The Faulkners and God knows
who. And he said to himself, "A country that strong that
could afford to attack itself and criticize itself must be very
strong, so I think I'll leave the Italian army." He did.

MOYERS: We're right back to that fundamental division again.

WARREN: Right . . . right back.

MOYERS: Now . . . we've always seen ourselves, if we read the
novels, as we are. And we know now that the masks have
been stripped off in the last few years, and yet I still find,
Mr. Warren, hosts of people out there who want to believe
. . . and want to affirm.

WARREN: Well, I'm in love with America. I . . . I want to believe and want to affirm, too. And I just literally—I don't
know any other way to describe it—I just fell in love with
the American continent.

. . . .

Talk with
Robert Penn Warren

The New York Times Book Review *published this interview by Benjamin DeMott on the front page of its January 9, 1977, issue. Sharing the page with the interview was a review of Warren's* Selected Poems, 1923–1975.

BENJAMIN DEMOTT: How does the poetry establishment take to a poet who regularly produces best-selling novels?
WARREN: Everything is appearances. It could look as though, having had some best sellers, I decided to write a few poems. That's not the way it is. I have ten books of poems, the same number of volumes of poetry as novels—twelve if you count two novels that are unpublished, thank God. I began with poetry. It's where I am still. At first I thought novels were beneath contempt. It wasn't until I began to know some fiction writers, Katherine Anne Porter, Caroline Gordon, Ford Madox Ford, that I realized they had the same sense of the insides of fiction that John Ransom and Tate had for the insides of poetry.

· · · · · · · · · · · · · ·

WARREN: Anyway, I don't see a split between fiction and poetry. Both originate in a certain feeling—a governing emotion. Both are coming from the same place in the gut. For me the common denominator is always an ethical issue. *All the King's Men* began as a verse play. *Brother to Dragons* was once in my mind a novel. My poems start with a feeling that could become poem or story. Everything starts from an observed fact of life and then the search begins for the *issue*—the ethical or dramatic issue—in the fact. It's no different in novels. Both fiction and poetry became—poetry very early—for me a way of life. I had to live into them, had to have them. But there is a difference. Poetry is a more direct way of trying to know the self, to make sense of experience . . . freer from *place*, so though all my novels have Southern settings, I have poems involving Crete, Italy, France, and even Vermont—or rather, involving me and a relation to my life there.

DEMOTT: In the *Selected Poems* everything seems to change when you come into the sequence called "Promises." A poem called "The Child Next Door" and a half dozen after that. A change in intensity—in the "interior."

WARREN: I remember the time. There was a time in the middle of the forties and for the next ten years almost when I couldn't finish a poem. I started and I'd do three lines of one. Then another few lines—of another I could never finish. Then for some years we lived, in the summers, in a ruined sixteenth-century fortress on the Mediterranean, and it was an Eden—but an Eden with a bloody history of centuries. Everybody needs an Eden—at least once—but a special kind of complex Eden. Anyway, I began to finish my poems, for the first time in ten years.

DEMOTT: They're family pieces really, aren't they? They feel close to the bone. It's as though you changed your relation to poetry itself, as though . . .

WARREN: Look at that! [*Focusing sternly on the coffee table, something offensive.*] Your drink, it's empty.

[*Drink repairs interval. Campari fruit juice for R.P.W. Pause.*]

DEMOTT: The day after the election the new President—I think he was talking to Plains—said it would be nice having somebody in the White House that didn't "talk funny." Those awful Northern accents. What else does it mean, the country having a Chief Executive from Georgia?

WARREN: It's a part of a long picture of the amalgamation of the country, one small thing in a very large process. I'm surprised the country has kept as many of its differences as it has over the last thirty-five years, with wars, TV, and all the rest of it, the mobility it's had. But this is part of the process that's going to even everything out eventually.

DEMOTT: How do you feel about the amalgamating? I only hope history can endure to tell people what the world, from 10,000 B.C. to now, was like. Imagine never knowing anything different from 2076!

WARREN: I don't have any emotion about it. History is going along the way it goes, whatever way it goes, whether you grumble or not. And my notion is to try to live—live life now and make my little comments and bear an honest witness to my time. Here or elsewhere. Because nobody's going to change it.

DEMOTT: Is that what "living with it" means to you?

WARREN: Yes, personally, there came a matter of great crisis in my life. . . . My wife's a Yankee girl, she's as Yankee as they get, they don't get any Yankier, and she said, "With the kind of boyhood you had, and you seemed to enjoy it so much, to have your children never, never, never to have known that world seems odd, and it will seem odd to them some day." Even before she spoke I was thinking of going back. I have a brother in Kentucky, and he said, "I'll put a man on a farm for you to run things." I began to look for a place down there, but suddenly I saw it was a different world. The people aren't the same people. Oh, more prosperous and all that, but not the kind I had known—with a civic sense, you might say, and a certain personal worth. So we are stuck with a new world. With certain virtues, I'd be the first to grant, but perhaps some fatal defects. Maybe our children can save it. Many young people have that dream, thank God. Or at least the dream of saving themselves by making something useful or beautiful and loving the world God made.

Back to the subject we were on. In much of the South you have a straight TV culture superimposed on a vacuum, or a new kind of money culture. Something survives—but how long? against what odds?—and inner odds? If I had a farm there now, I'd have to go get in my car and go somewhere to find somebody to talk to. Nobody to just sit on the corner of the fence and pass the time of day with. And things like the new drinking parties, you know—I suddenly realized I would be a stranger forever. It just would not be the same world. It's part of the natural course of life in this country, but it's very special in the South because there was more for the South to be specially against. I love the South because it is "real" to me—my "for-ness" and my "against-ness"—when things go wrong there, it hurts me. When they go wrong somewhere else, it's "the course of history."

DEMOTT: It's hard not to think about "against-ness" in the context of *I'll Take My Stand* [the 1930 volume in which John Crowe Ransom, Allen Tate, Donald Davidson, R.P.W., and others set out a case for Southern naturalness and simplicity, for an economy of subsistence farming, and for avoidance of Northern rapacity, rationalism, and rat-racing]. Have you put that whole episode in perspective?

WARREN: On the matter of what the Agrarians stood for—as I look back, I see two sets of things, negatives and positives. And I think we were right on one set of those and very ignorant on the other. We were right on man and nature—the problems run to nature, not to man. Things have new names now. Ecology and such. People talk a great deal about man and nature—philosophers, hippies, retreats—but do they see the base? Of course, we didn't invent it either, but we had an early version of it—arrived at through experience, personal experience and Thomas Jefferson. It was the broad general idea of man's place in nature, his relationship to the whole natural world, people wanting a world where making their living and drawing their first breath in the morning and the things they do during the day are pleasures to them.

DEMOTT: This for the positives. There were some fantasies, though, no? I mean, a fantasy about what the character of life on the small subsistence farm was like. How really sustaining would it have been to any of the Agrarians themselves?

WARREN: You couldn't build a society on it, but you could take up a lot of slack. Would you rather see a man living on a small farm (if he knew how) or drawing relief? You might have had a more balanced society. As it was, what you had for a hundred years in America was internal imperialism. The money was drained to a certain central point.

DEMOTT: *Who Owns America?*—you mean that argument? [28]

WARREN: Who owns America? That might have been mitigated or spread different. But it's all speculation.

DEMOTT: You have a brand-new novel coming soon?

WARREN: In two months. It's called *A Place to Come To.* You can't summarize a novel—not this, anyway—but it is about the Southerner who hates (or is ashamed of) the South (at least that's the germ idea), and it is my observation that such a Southerner, even if a great success in the world, is always a "placeless" man—so we come back to the "modern man"—in his motel room and his TV program. But that's not fair to my story.

DEMOTT: I understand that it's the sense of the deep-down moral issue that controls the way a book by R.P.W. works out. But for the reader . . . for me it's the voice of the countryman in your books that holds the mind. It seems effortless and it's everywhere. I remember a little piece—casual, offhand—you once did about how *All the King's Men* got started. You were remembering some comments by a redneck hitchhiker relishing Huey Long outwitting some private toll-bridge owner. I could hear the man's voice the minute you began telling his story. Suppose you were telling a young writer what it takes to get that, would you come out for genius or love?

WARREN: [*Blinks, grins*] My goodness, here we're gabbing along and . . .

DEMOTT: You'd admit that you had to care about the sound?

WARREN: Oh, yes! Caring matters. It's the same in a poem. And I've got a new poem going right now. But now [*rising, interview glass in hand*] let's tend to business—these are holidays. . . .

An Interview with Robert Penn Warren

Warren the poet was the focus of Peter Stitt's attention when he conducted this interview at Warren's home in Fairfield, Connecticut, in early March 1977. The Sewanee Review *published the conversation that summer.*

PETER STITT: You entered Vanderbilt at an early age, which leads me to think that you grew up in a home where the life of the mind was fully lived. Is that so?

WARREN: Well, both my father and my maternal grandfather had books everywhere. I've got a lot of my father's books right over there. I recently reread Cooper for the first time since I was a boy, using my father's copies. And each book had the date he finished reading it—1890, '91, and so on. I spent my boyhood summers with my grandfather on a tobacco farm. He was an old man then. . . . He read poetry and quoted it by the yard. He was wonderful, an idol. His place was very remote, and he allowed nobody on it except our family: he was totally cut off from the rest of the world. For one thing, it just didn't interest him. I mean, he read books all the time—Egyptian history or Confederate history or American history, and poetry. But there was nobody to talk to: there were very few people in the community who had any interests like his. So I got the benefit of his conversation. I spent hours a day with him and I found him fascinating. He was against slavery but a good Confederate. He said, "I stand with my people." . . . He loved to relive the war with me: we'd lay it all out on the ground, using stones and rifle shells.

STITT: Was it the literary activity at Vanderbilt that drew you there?

WARREN: What I actually wanted to be was a naval officer. I finished high school at the age of fifteen—no great intellectual accomplishment where I went—and got the appointment to Annapolis. But then I had an accident. I was struck in the eye by a stone, and couldn't pass the physical. So I chose Vanderbilt. Then I had to wait a year; they wouldn't take you at fifteen unless you were living at home. I started out to be a chemical engineer, but they taught chemistry primarily by rote: there was no theorizing, no sense of what it was about. At the same time, I had John Crowe Ransom as a professional English teacher. He made no effort to court the students, but I found him fascinating. He taught ordinary freshman expository writing, but he had other things to say along the way, and he would shine. At the end of the first term he said, "I think you don't belong in here. I think I will have you go to my advanced class." There was only one writing course beyond freshman English at Vanderbilt. A few people in their sophomore year would study forms of versification, poetry writing, essay writing—things like that—with Ransom; and this is what I did the second half of my freshman year. He was also the first poet I had ever seen, a real live poet in pants and vest. I read his first book of poems and discovered that he was making poetry out of a world I knew: it came home to me.

Ransom was a Greek scholar by training. He had never taken an English course in his life except freshman English, which was required at Vanderbilt, where he had gone. And he always said, in a tony way, "I don't see any reason to take a course in literature when the language is native to you." He laughed at himself for being an English teacher. "I find myself completely superfluous."

STITT: Was there much literary activity among the students at that time?

WARREN: It was a strange situation, and I really can't understand it even today. There was just a tremendous interest in poetry among the students. There were two undergraduate writing clubs, junior and senior, where people would read poems and essays to each other. And there was an informal poetry club which met about once a week. We'd read each other's poems and booze a little, crack corn, and talk poetry. All kinds of people wrote poems then—I remember two all-American football players, a future U.S. senator, a man who later became chairman of the Department of Romance Languages at Wisconsin, and another who later became the only Phi Beta Kappa private in the Marine Corps. It is hard to believe now, but this is literally true: if an issue of *Dial* would come out, people would line up to get the first one. Freshmen were buying the *New Republic* or *The Nation*, to get the new poem by Yeats or the new poem by Hart Crane. This didn't last for very long, but it did last up to the thirties, when I was teaching there and people like Randall Jarrell were in as freshmen. And all this was going on outside of the curriculum. That's why I think graduate programs in creative writing are stupid. Sometimes I've been peripherally involved in them, but if people want to write, they will write. It is nice if they can show their stuff to their elders; that's natural. But what we see is just an attempt to formalize what since the beginning of time has been natural.

STITT: How did you become a member of the Fugitive group?

WARREN: The Fugitive group was started before the First World War when some young professors, including Ransom, and some bookish, intelligent young businessmen got together to discuss literature and philosophy. But it really got going after the war, when the moving force became a strange Jew named Mttron Hirsch, an adventurer of no education whatever, except that he had read *everything*. He had been the heavyweight boxing champion of the Pacific fleet, and was a great friend of Gertrude Stein in her early days. He had also been a model for many of the painters of Paris: he was an enormously handsome man, very big, perfectly formed in his way—and he became the center, almost the idol, of the group. He was in his early forties then, and had, or claimed to have, a back injury. So he would lie flat on his back on a couch and be waited on by his kin. I think he made a good thing of it. He was the wise man of the tribe, and he liked to be able to talk with some learned friends, so he accumulated people around him. I guess that was the source of it originally.

I believe Allen Tate and Ridley Wills were the first undergraduates to be admitted to the group. They were five or six years older than I. Tate had been ill and had come back to college, which is why he and I overlapped. He couldn't pass, or wouldn't pass, freshman math and freshman chemistry, both of which were required. He had all A's in everything else, things like Greek and Latin; but he wouldn't do the others—it bored him too much. So he was around.

Then in my junior year, I guess it was, Ransom invited me to the Fugitive meetings. Greatest thrill I'd had in my life. By then it was mostly a poetry club—we read each other's poems and argued poetry. Everybody was an equal in that room; no one pulled his long gray beard. And it was a good time to be there: Ransom was writing his best poems then, and Tate was just finding himself. I myself was seventeen, and I said, "This is what I'm going to do." I had no interest in fiction, though, not until later.

STITT: John Crowe Ransom must have been a remarkable man and a strong presence in the group.

WARREN: He was an influence on everybody. He was a center of this without ever trying to be; we just automatically looked to him, you see. He was very learned and a student all his life. And not only that—he was also a great player of

games, a crack golfer; and he played tennis, poker, and
bridge. Sometimes he played bridge or poker for the
whole weekend. People who didn't know him well sometimes think he was an unfeeling man, but that just isn't so
at all. I recently had a letter from my goddaughter, who is
Ransom's granddaughter. She said, "He is so often por-
trayed as being cold and self-absorbed that I wanted to
write and tell you at least one thing that happened in my
presence. When you were ill"—this was in 1972; I had
hepatitis and they thought it was cancer—"Pappy either
went or sent someone to the post office three times a day
to see if there was any news, and he telephoned all over the
country." He was a man of great warmth. I wrote an essay
in celebration of his eightieth birthday, and the letter he
wrote me in return is incredible. He said, "I find myself at
last brushing away a furtive tear." He raised vegetables
and flowers, and every morning he would decorate the
whole house with fresh flowers. And he loved to cook
breakfast—better breakfasts than I've had all the rest of my
life. He always served them to his wife while she was still
in bed.

STITT: Why do you suppose Ransom stopped writing poetry
when he did?

WARREN: Well, I can tell you exactly what he said to me before he stopped writing. We were sitting by the fireside
one night, and he said, "You know, I think I will quit writing poetry." Now, he was at his very peak, and I said,
"You're crazy." He said, "No, I know what I'm doing." John
was, in everything he did, intellectual and introspective—he
knew his own mind. But this is one time when he did *not*
know what he was doing. He went on to say, "I know I can
write better poems than I've ever written; I know how to
write my poems. But I want to be an amateur"—and that's
what he was—"I want to love what I'm doing, to do it for
pleasure"—that's his game business again. He said, "I hate a
professional poet. I know people who have ruined themselves by being professional poets, because they end up
imitating themselves. If I get a new insight, a new way in,

if I grow into something different, I will start again, but I don't want to be same old John Crowe Ransom." That's the way he explained it to me. So I said, "Well, you're crazy," and I still think he was crazy.

Randall Jarrell had a different idea, and I think he was right. He said that being a poet is like standing out in the rain, waiting for lightning to hit you. If it hits you once—that is, if you write one really fine poem—you are good; if it hits you six times, you're great. Ransom wouldn't stay out in the rain.

STITT: Do you think he was wise to go back late in life and revise his poems as he did?

WARREN: I think frequently he did harm to the poems. He wanted to be back in touch with it, but he had lost the touch. The last time I went to see him was at the time of his eighty-fifth birthday. I went out there to give a reading and to see him. He was totally himself, not showing any sign of age. After we came back from the reading, we sat down and had a drink, and he said, "I've given myself a birthday present. I've written a new poem." It was a new kind of poem, you see—published in the *Sewanee Review.* He went back into the rain at the age of eighty-five. And that was that.

STITT: I want to talk a bit about how you compose your poems. What gets you started on a poem—is it an idea, an image, a rhythm, or something else?

WARREN: It can be a lot of things. More and more for me the germ of a poem is an event in the natural world. And there is a mood, a feeling, that helps. For about ten years, from 1944 to '54, I was unable to finish a poem—I'd start one, and get just so far and then it would die on me. I have stacks of unfinished poems. I *was* writing then—other things, *Brother to Dragons* and a lot of short stories. Many times the germ of a short story could also be the germ of a poem, and I was wasting mine on short stories. I've only written three that I even like. And so I quit writing short stories.

Then I got married, and my wife had a child, then a second; and we went to a place in Italy, an island with a ruined fortress. It is a very striking place—there is a rocky peninsula with the sea on three sides, and a sixteenth-century fortress on the top. There was a matching fortress across the bay. We had a wonderful time there, for two summers and more, and I began writing poetry again, in that spot. I had a whole different attitude toward life, my outlook was changed. The poems in *Promises* were all written there. Somehow, all of this—the place, the objects there, the children, the other people, my new outlook—made possible a new grasp on the roots of poetry for me. There were memories and natural events: the poems wander back and forth from my boyhood to my children. Seeing a little gold-headed girl on that bloody spot of history is an *event*. With the bay beyond, the sea beyond that, the white butterflies, that's all a natural event. It could be made into a short story, but you would have to cook up a lot of stuff around it. All you have to cook up in the poem is to be honest with your feelings and your observation, somehow.

This was a new way of starting poetry for me. I had been writing two kinds of poems earlier—one kind tended to start from a verbal and abstract place, and the other kind was a sort of balladry, based on an element of narrative. "Billie Potts" was the last poem I wrote before the drought set in. It was a bridge piece, my jumping-off place when I started again, ten years later. Now my method is more mixed. Some poems can start with a mood. Say there is a stream under your window, and you are aware of the sound all night as you sleep; or you notice the moonlight on the water, or hear an owl call. Things like this can start a mood that will carry over into the daylight. These objects may not appear in the poem, but the mood gets you going.

Then my most recent poem—I think it is one of my best —is a poem that was set off by a review of my work. Harold Bloom of Yale is kind enough to like my poetry, and he wrote a review for *The New Leader* in which he talks about the place that hawks occupy in my poetry. When I read it, I realized that it is all true. You don't know your own poetry, you know—working on it so closely, you see it differently. And so I thought about the fact that I had killed a hawk, a red-tail, in my woodland boyhood. I brought him down with what was a record shot for me. I was then a practicing taxidermist, among other things, and I stuffed the hawk and carried him with me for many years —I used to keep him over my bookshelf. This is the key to the poem, a factual event, a memory. It can be like that.

That's my most recent poem. Now I've had a break of several weeks—poetry comes to me in fits of a few weeks or a few months, perhaps a half-year, and then there is a break. I know when I am through with a certain mood, a certain thing—every book is based on a curve and I know when the curve is closing in and the book is over. It is purely intuitive. But I don't know whether this new book is over or not. I've got enough poems, but it is not quite the way I want it. But it will be a strange book and will look as if I've started all over again, in the way Ransom said. But I never know how the next poem will start; I don't want to fall into a formula.

STITT: You have said, "For me the common denominator is always an ethical issue." This is clearer, I think, in fiction than in poetry.

WARREN: It is much more obvious in fiction. But the relation between the abstract and the concrete is different in more recent poems. I have moved more toward a moralized anecdote—I don't mean to preach sermons, but I also don't want to be coy about it. I would like to show the problem of the abstract and the concrete in the construction of the poem itself.

STITT: Do you write your poems out in longhand or at the typewriter?

WARREN: Practically in my head. I do a lot of them when I am exercising. I find that regular exercise, any kind of simple repeated motion, is like hypnosis—it frees your mind. So when I am walking or swimming, I try to let my mind go blank, so I can catch the poems on the wing, before they can get away. Then when I have a start and am organized, I will sit down with pencil and paper, but never at the typewriter. I once had a bad shoulder injury, and must swim or exercise very heavily every morning in order to keep it functioning freely. And this I find is very conducive to writing my poetry.

STITT: Do you revise your poems heavily?

WARREN: Very heavily. I read them and read them, and do draft after draft. And I retain the drafts. Often if I am stuck I will go back to an earlier version to refresh myself—I may have been on the right track and taken a wrong turn.

STITT: Have you ever had this experience some poets speak of, where a poem just comes to you in a burst, as though by inspiration, and all you had to do was write down the words?

WARREN: The best parts of a poem always come in bursts or in a flash. This has been said by many people—Frost said in a letter, "My best poems are always my easiest." My notion is this: that the poet is a hunter on the track of an unknown beast, and has only one shot in his gun. You don't know what the beast is, but when you see him, you've got to shoot him, and it has got to be instantaneous. You can labor on the pruning, and you can work at your technique, but you cannot labor the poem into being.

STITT: As you've reprinted your collections, you have often left poems out, sometimes many of them. Why is this?

WARREN: Sometimes I think they are bad, and sometimes other people think they are bad. For instance, when I was preparing my Selected Poems of 1966, I consulted with Allen Tate, William Meredith, and Cleanth Brooks. If two of them were strongly negative about a poem, I would take it out, unless I had my own strong reasons for leaving it in. And my editor, Albert Erskine, is very helpful.

STITT: Do you feel that your two creative activities, fiction and poetry, are complementary to one another?

WARREN: I feel this: they have the same germ; they are very different in the way they manifest themselves, but they spring from the same source. I always put the poem first: if a poem falls across a novel, I will take the poem first. I will stop the novel and go whoring after the poem, as I have done several times. I mentioned earlier how writing short stories kept me away from poetry. *All the King's Men* is a novel, but it started out as poetry, a verse play. The original idea was implicit in a single word, the name Talos, my first name for Willie Stark and also the name of the groom in book five of *The Faerie Queene*. I was thinking that people like Hitler or Huey Long are machines, executing the will of Justice. Reducing it to one word is purely private. As for the verse play, I later saw that it left out the action and complication necessary to show that power—the man of power—flows into a vacuum: a vacuum in society, government, or individuals. So my man Talos became Stark, whose power fulfills the weaknesses of others.

STITT: Some critics feel that poetry has displaced fiction as your most important concern in recent years? Do you think that is true?

WARREN: I don't know—I still try to roll with the punch and write what needs to be written on a given day. But I started as a poet and I will probably end as a poet. If I had to choose between my novels and my *Selected Poems*, I would keep the *Selected Poems* as representing me more fully, my vision and my self. I think poems are more *you*.

STITT: You mentioned Harold Bloom earlier. Do you pay much attention to the critics and reviewers of your own work, especially poetry?

WARREN: I have learned things from some of them, but most reviewers are just filling space. Sometimes a foolish critic will tell you a very important thing, almost by accident. But you've got to learn to live without counting the good reviews and the bad reviews, because sometimes they are right and sometimes they are wrong. I understand there is a weak review of my novel coming out in the *Times Book Review*, when just a few weeks ago they devoted practically the whole issue to praising the *Selected Poems*. So you just do the best you can.

STITT: In rereading things written about your work, I found one critic who called your poetry cerebral and academic. How do you react to that?

WARREN: It depends who says you are cerebral. Compared to Sara Teasdale, I would say I am cerebral, but John Donne would probably think I was not. Speaking more generally, I think you've got to forget all the things you know abstractly when you start writing. Of course, you never forget what you know about novel structure or about the construction of a poem, but you put those aside and just do it. You may use material that is intellectual, but you are using it in another spirit entirely.

STITT: Another critic I came across said that Richard Wilbur hates the "things of this world." Now, I would say that Wilbur, like Robert Penn Warren, loves the things of this world, and indicates that love by investing physical objects with an implicit spiritual essence.

WARREN: I am a creature of this world, but I am also a yearner, I suppose. I would call this temperament rather than theology—I haven't got any gospel. That is, I feel an immanence of meaning in things, but I have no meaning to put there that is interesting or beautiful. I think I put it as close as I could in a poem called "Masts at Dawn"—"We must try / To love so well the world that we may believe, in the end, in God." I am a man of temperament in the modern world who hasn't got any religion. Dante almost got me at one stage, but then I suddenly realized, "My God, Dante's a good Protestant—he was! Where have I gone?" My poem reverses the whole thing, you see: I would rather start with the world.

STITT: How did you come to write your beautiful poem on Audubon?

WARREN: There is a little story about that. I never research a book, except if I get in a pinch on some detail, then I will look that up. But when I was thinking about writing *World Enough and Time*, I began to soak myself in Americana of the early nineteenth century, histories of Kentucky and Tennessee—that sort of thing. Well, Audubon appears in that history, so I went ahead and looked at his journals, and so forth. I got interested in the man and his life, and began, way back in the forties, to write a poem about Audubon. But it was a trap; I couldn't find the frame for it, the narrative line. I did write quite a bit, but it wouldn't come together, so I set it aside and forgot about it. Then in the sixties I was writing a history of American literature with Dick [R.W.B.] Lewis and Cleanth Brooks, and I did the section on Audubon. We all read everything, then one person would write up a given section and the others would rewrite the first draft to their hearts' desire—a continuing process. So I got back into Audubon. Then one day when my wife wasn't here, I was making the bed, when suddenly there popped into my mind a line that had been in the version of *Audubon* that I had abandoned. I never went and hunted the rest of it up, so I only had that one line to go on. But I suddenly saw how to do it. I did it in fragments, sort of snapshots of Audubon. I began to see him as a certain kind of man, a man who has finally learned to accept his fate. The poem is about man and his fate—all along, Audubon resisted his fate and thought it was evil—a man is supposed to support his family, and so forth. But now he accepts his fate. Late in his life he said, "I dream of nothing but birds." Audubon was the greatest slayer of birds that ever lived: he destroyed beauty in order to create beauty and whet his understanding. Love is knowledge. And then in the end the poem is about Audubon and me.

STITT: Since the fifties your poetry has been mostly optimistic and affirmative, emphasizing the glory of the world and its promises. And yet you also have poems on ugliness, death, racial violence, and so on. How do these poems fit into your vision?

WARREN: That's all part of the picture, just the other side of it. You have people like Dreiser, who are monsters humanly but who make great things. There is Flaubert,[29] whose main goal in going to Egypt was to get the clap, and yet he had this inspiration for *Madame Bovary*, and he thanks

God to be alive, approaching the curve of the wave. It is the complication of life—nothing more complicated than that.

STITT: Do you think of a book of poems as a cohesive unit or as a collection of individual pieces?

WARREN: I don't see them as pieces but as a kind of unit. Some time back I began to write poetry in suites of three or four units, and that has become more and more a mark of mine.

STITT: The subtitle of *Or Else—Poem/Poems 1968–1974* would seem to indicate that idea.

WARREN: Yes—it can be considered a long poem, or it can be considered a group of short poems. Some of the poems were written with my being unaware of their place in the sequence. It wasn't undertaken as a planned sequence; the true sequence grew. This kind of structure is related to how you feel your experience—I couldn't tell you exactly how, but is related.

STITT: You have done a good deal of editing. I think especially of the editions of the poems of Melville and Whittier. What impelled you to undertake those tasks?

WARREN: I don't know. Melville I have always been crazy about; one of the first critical essays I ever wrote was on his poems. Then someone asked me to do a little Melville edition for a series of poets in New York, and I said yes and started work on it. But when I showed it to them, they said it was too much, too big, so I thought to hell with you, and took it to Random House. I was just fascinated by Melville. Then Whittier: I had been rereading Whittier and felt that I had done him a wrong—I found his complexity more interesting in a cumulative text than what I had seen before. Now, Dreiser is an old passion. I've read all of Dreiser and have had many different opinions of him along the way. Humanly he was a monster. I have a psychologist friend at Yale whose chief study is the act of creativity. I got him to read first the autobiographies of Dreiser, then some of the novels, and he was very helpful. He would say, "Okay, this is a lie, and that is a screening device for something else." But those are ways of being in contact with things that interest me—I'm not making a career of it, although I enjoy the work. I could spend my life very happily studying Coleridge, studying Dreiser, and so forth. I just like something else better. I have more need for something else.

STITT: Do you find the writing of criticism a pleasant task?

WARREN: Well, it's a little bit like teaching. I like to talk about books I have read, and I always liked the association with the students. I think that only in the university can you find a certain kind of humanistic temperament to deal with —I don't mean that everybody who teaches has it, but some people are quite wonderful. They know something disinterestedly, and know how to apply it, and it is a privilege to associate with them. But I couldn't have stood teaching beyond a certain point—I got sick of myself for one thing. And I have ceased to have any interest in writing criticism, even though there is a new edition of my *Selected Essays* in preparation. I have sworn that I will never write another line of criticism of any kind. I will write some fictional prose; I want to write a couple of more novels that are in my head, but I really enjoy writing poetry more now.

STITT: Do you still consider yourself a Southern writer, even though you have been away so long?

WARREN: I can't be anything else. You are what you are. I was born and grew up in Kentucky, and I think your early images survive. Images mean a lot of things besides pictures.

A Conversation with
Robert Penn Warren

███

John Baker interviewed Warren for the initial volume of the Bruccoli Clark series Conversations with Writers. *The conversation took place at the author's home in Connecticut in the spring of 1977. Warren has revised the interview extensively since it was first published.*

JOHN BAKER: I'd like to start, as one should, at the beginning—about when you were growing up as a boy in Kentucky. Were you always a big reader?

WARREN: Yes, both at my father's house and my grandfather's house—I spent my summers with my maternal grandfather—and both houses were full of books. My grandfather was a great reader and had a wide range of reading in poetry. He quoted it if he found somebody to quote it to. . . . He was interested in military history and American history; he talked American history a great deal. He knew a great deal about it in a very unacademic way, particularly Civil War history—he knew that very well. He had fought in various battles, and he would draw the ground plan for the battles of Austerlitz and the Bridge of Lodi—*Napoleon and His*

Marshals was favorite reading—and would explain the tactics of battles that he had been in, various battles of the Civil War.

He was a very entertaining old grandfather to have, you know. He was very bookish, in an old-fashioned sense. He loved to read Egyptian history, for some reason—Breasted was one of his favorite authors. So I spent one summer building a pyramid and putting everything in it—then made a discovery of it all the next summer. It was a lovely life. I'd see a white boy once every month, maybe. It was a very remote farm, had a lot of woods on it, a ramshackle house, and this prowling the woods or reading or talking to my grandfather—that was about all there was.

BAKER: Where did you get the books? Obviously, it was too remote for libraries. Did he have many, many books in his house?

WARREN: There were books in the house, not a big library, no, but lots. He was, I think, rather a failure at this stage. He had been a farmer—a tobacco farmer—but he also was a tobacco "buyer" at one time. His daughters always said that their father was "visionary"—didn't put his mind on practical matters. He was always wrapped up with books or something. At one time he had some barns full of tobacco on consignment, you see, which he forgot to insure, and they burned. So rather than go bankrupt, which was the easy way out, he stuck by his debt and paid it off, as I seem to remember the tale—but that took a long time and set him back deeply. But that's why they called him a visionary. They also called him an inveterate reader, the daughters did. I thought they meant Confederate reader.

BAKER: I can see the confusion.

WARREN: I had it quite mixed up at that age, six or eight. Confederate reader was a special kind of reader. I didn't know what kind it was.

BAKER: Now, Kentucky was a border state; which side would he have been on?

WARREN: Oh, our people were all Confederates. And, in fact, he wasn't a Kentuckian; he settled there after the war. He

couldn't go back to Tennessee, because once he had been
ordered to chase down and hang guerrillas. At this time, or
shortly after, the "Parson" Brownlow government was in
control of Tennessee, or most of it. So the relatives of these
guerrillas (these outlaws—both sides were hanging them
without much trial—my grandfather said they gave them
a fair trial, it just didn't take very long) brought murder
charges against my grandfather. Also, his property, whatever it was, was confiscated—according to my great-aunt.
She, because he rarely talked about any personal matters.
So when peace came he was on the run. He couldn't go
in the state of Tennessee for years, until things had settled down. So he just took refuge outside. By the way,
he did talk about guerrillas to me and I have a poem about
it.[30]

But my father's people were native Kentuckians, and they
had come over early, pioneering into the southwest section
of the state and becoming farmers. My father was a very
bookish man, and much more so, in one sense, than my
maternal grandfather, because he had set out to be a lawyer
and writer and actually published some poetry in his youth.
I only knew this because I, when about ten or twelve,
stumbled on a big book once in the house called *The Poets
of America*. It was some big anthology from about 1895,
something like that. Looking into it, I saw a picture of my
father.[31]

BAKER: And he had never mentioned it to you?

WARREN: Never, because he felt that was a part of his life that
he had put away. He had never mentioned it; he never
mentioned it again. I showed him four or five poems there
and the picture and a little note—a little bibliographical
note. He took it away from me and it disappeared, so he
must have destroyed it. But when he was an old, old man,
way up in his eighties, he sent me a poem or two he had
found in his papers—on old yellow paper falling apart, and
the old purple ribbon that he had used back in the nineties
—without comment; he just sent those to me in an envelope.

BAKER: How old were you when he sent them to you?

WARREN: Oh, I was then fifty years old, or so. But his had been a well-concealed literary career. In fact, I didn't know him well until long after. I left home early; I was fifteen when I left home. I didn't get to know him well until after I came back from graduate school and then taught at Vanderbilt. After my mother died, then he and I traveled a great deal together and got very intimate in that last phase of his life —about 1931 until his death in '56, when he was eighty-six years old. He was a gentle but very strong man. Sick once in his life. Never another day in bed. At eighty-six he had cancer of the prostate, told no one, certainly no doctor, fainted from pain, fell down and died the next day. Tough, all right.

BAKER: So he lived to become aware that you had become a major writer?

WARREN: Oh yes. A writer, anyway.

BAKER: And at the last, I guess he was responding to the notion that you had carried on what he had wanted to do.

WARREN: Well, this is rather intimate and I think not that relevant, but it created a strange kind of . . . His own life, his youth, was spent taking care of a whole brood, a stepmother and half brothers and a half sister. His mother died when he was quite young; his father remarried quickly— the farmer married the first girl down the road, as it was common to do in those days—having a house of children. Then he died when he was very young. So he left a house full of children. He was a veteran, too, of the Civil War. But there was never much communication or connection between the two families. They lived in the same community but they had no connection. They never visited; they never saw each other. My father's stepmother and her children had no connection with my mother's family at all. They met on the street and they said, "How do you do?" That was it. But then, by the time I knew my grandfather he had cut himself off rather thoroughly. Only one family, not kin, ever came to visit in my time.

As was so often the case in farming in those days, a man didn't know where he stood financially, and my Warren grandfather was a man of some little property, had a good place. But he had debts as well, so that when he was dead, he left very little. My father was then about fifteen or sixteen. He dug in, but his older brother took one look and ran away to Mexico and made a good life for himself as a mining engineer. My father took over at home. He was the next son, and despite his responsibilities, educated himself in various ways, simply by ferocious reading, for one thing.

A few years ago I was writing an essay, a long essay on Cooper, and using my father's books. I noticed at the end of every novel there was the date when he had finished it—1891 or whatever it was. He was very methodical. And until he died he spent hours a day reading all sorts of things. He was reading Freud, Marx, and things like that as well as poetry and history. He kept on. He was totally alone in the last part of his life, and I've never understood this isolation that he imposed on himself. One thing about it, I think nobody around was interested in the things he was interested in. Nobody around with the same interests. So he would just rather read than talk about things that didn't interest him. He learned French from an Alsatian clerk, studied Greek with a professor he paid, at night—Southwestern Presbyterian University at Clarksville, Tennessee.

BAKER: But you were interested, anyway, as a boy.

WARREN: I was interested. My father had the old habit of reading to his own children in the evening, usually poetry or history. I'd listen by the hour, and that was all to my benefit. My father had set out to be a lawyer or a poet, and he wound up as the village banker. The bank failed in '27 and '28, and then he kept store and struggled a few years, then went personally bankrupt. During those few years of misery and struggle, aggravated greatly by the death of my mother in 1931, I was just getting my first job. It wasn't a very happy period.

BAKER: What did you think you would become as a child? Did you expect to become something like a writer?

WARREN: Well, I didn't expect to become a writer. My ambition was to be a naval officer and I got an appointment to

Annapolis. Well, it was political; a friend of my father's was a congressman and he got me the appointment. Then I had an accident. I couldn't go—an accident to my eyes—and then I went to the university [Vanderbilt] instead, and I started out in life there as a chemical engineer. That didn't last but three weeks or so, because I found the English courses so much more interesting.

. . . .

BAKER: An extraordinary place to have been. Was there anywhere else like it in America at that time?

WARREN: At that time, as far as I know, none. There were four or five small groups of writers' societies among the students, and that continued for years, up until right now. But then I was invited to join the Fugitive group, all grown men, and several of them already recognized as writers.

BAKER: Why did they call themselves Fugitives?

WARREN: It's explained in the first little editorial in this little magazine, the pilot issue: "We fly from nothing so much as the South of the magnolia." [32] They were rebels, in other words, against the apologetic Southern literature. They were quite unconcerned with the official Southern literature, quite contemptuous on the whole. One young man who later became a professor of French and head of the department at Wisconsin—who later had the biggest private collection of Baudelaire—well, he would keep you up all night reading aloud to you from Baudelaire and explicating poems. He had a little private university on Baudelaire. It was a strange kind of ferment going on there for fifteen years or more. But the university had no part in this; the university had no interest in it.

BAKER: So you published your magazine, *The Fugitive?*

WARREN: It was founded by older and wiser heads—Ransom, Davidson, Tate, et cetera. The prize money—the Maxwell House Coffee Company gave the money for prizes, believe it or not. But the group had started as a philosophy club, which was composed of young businessmen in town and several young instructors at the university, and they met in town in people's houses—they had no connection with the university. This was before World War I. Some began to write poetry, and then poetry became the main interest later.

BAKER: Were they critics as well?

WARREN: There was a great deal of argument about critical theory, and Tate and Ransom, of course, became well-known professional critics as well as poets. And Davidson and several others in the group became professional writers. But it was really a university outside of the university. They were the people who were moderns, chiefly Tate. The strange thing was that at Vanderbilt, I thought that Marx was a member of a firm that made clothes, and I thought that Freud was a man who cured Jews of syphilis or something like that. It was very retarded in some ways, and very modern in terms of poetry and literary theory. But I went to Berkeley then, and out there they knew all about Marx and Freud. But they hadn't heard the news about poetry. Even at Yale graduate school they hadn't heard the news.

BAKER: How about Oxford? You went to Oxford for a while, I believe?

WARREN: That's right, I wound up there. I was following scholarships; I was just simply doing that. Wherever I got the scholarship, the biggest scholarship, that's where I went. Oxford was a much more worldly place, of course, much more dispersed. At least to me it was. Most of my friends there were, with two or three exceptions, people who were aviators or people like that. I didn't even know Spender, though he and I were there at the same time. I was always aiming at the Left Bank.

BAKER: You didn't join the Poetry Society or anything like that?

WARREN: No, I didn't join it. I visited once or twice, but I wasn't very attracted by it. I wrote a big part of my first prose work, my first novelette, there—my first fiction.

BAKER: And then when you came back to America you began teaching, I believe.

WARREN: I went to Tennessee, because that's where I wanted

to live. I had a better offer in California. I wanted to live in the middle of Tennessee, and I had the idea held out to me that there was going to be a place at Vanderbilt opening up the next year—and there was. But I was finally fired in '34— let go. So I went to Louisiana State University and found a new life there with an old friend, Cleanth Brooks, who was already there.

BAKER: And you collaborated with him on a number of books, I know.

WARREN: Yes. We did those textbooks and books of that sort. They always came out of our class notes and just ordinary conversations; they weren't jobs. They just grew out of our normal life, and only by accident a publisher passing through saw it lying on my desk—Crofts, old Mr. Crofts of Crofts Publishing Company—and said, "This book shouldn't waste in here." He said, "Just let me—Where's the Press?" And he walked across the hall to the Press and came back and said, "I bought it from them." [33]

BAKER: An instant deal.

WARREN: And then another publisher passed through and saw some more notes, some of the poetry notes, and seemed to feel we had a book on understanding poetry. So, by a real collaboration, we put our notes together and argued the poems, which was fun. So we put that book together, and we loved that. So this was a natural development; we had no intention of setting ourselves up as a textbook factory, which, in fact, we did do.

BAKER: But what were the essential principles behind your teaching? Were you trying to teach your classes in a way that hadn't been taught before?

WARREN: Well, I guess one thing not to be forgotten is the kind of reading we had done and found to be profitable. This was the age when Coleridge was a great revelation— Coleridge's analyses of poetry—and the time Ivor Richards was just beginning to be known. And then both of us read fairly widely—widely being a relative term—in the history of criticism. Now, what we used to be given out in some of our own early classes as students was a piece of biography,

and the poem was always neglected or simply "admired."
You got the biography, and the social history, and everything else, but you didn't get the poem.

BAKER: Exactly. Then a few lines of quotation and that was it.

WARREN: A beautiful line, that was it. And the intent was to
answer that question—*Why* is it a beautiful passage? *Why*
is it an effective passage? Turn the cart around and the
horse around a little bit.

BAKER: So you were zeroing in on the text very closely?

WARREN: Not on the text very closely, but the text as a starting point, as well as the ending point. But now this brings
up a whole question that is often distorted, the question of
historical scholarship and the so-called New Criticism—to
my mind a term without a referent—many kinds of animals
under that tent. But back to technical scholarship—and
ideas and morality. Until a few years ago, when Brooks's
old tutor at Oxford died, he and the Oxford man were joint
editors on a whole series of eighteenth-century texts on
Percy, the Bishop Percy letters. Now, on the one hand,
Brooks is an eighteenth-century scholar; on the other hand,
he is interested in theology and is very deeply involved in
the affairs of the church. And he is, you might say, a
theologian and moralist, so he's concerned with anything
but the little cut of lines of poetry, you see. It wasn't a
question of one thing denying another. It's a question of
what is the strategy of teaching poetry. And the relation of
poetry to the other topics, to the other things in life, is
there, too. But you can't discuss the poetry as poetry unless
you know what *poetry is*, and how it relates to other activities. The main starting point wasn't trying to develop a
system for teaching poetry.

As far as the other side was concerned, there was never
any assumption which denied the history of it, or denied
social or moral reference, you see. I used Brooks as an
example because he's a perfect example of it: he's a professional scholar of the eighteenth century and known for
that. Now, I am not a professional scholar of the eighteenth

century, because I find the eighteenth century rather dull on the whole.

BAKER: Yes, I wouldn't have thought it was sympathetic to you, really. But I have read you on *The Rime of the Ancient Mariner* and also on Melville's poems.

WARREN: He's a wonderful poet.

BAKER: He's a wonderful poet. They very much neglect him.

WARREN: He's even now very neglected. But in a sense he has long since been rediscovered. It took so long; he was lost in general, of course. My wife's grandfather was a friend of Melville. He was a young lawyer with literary tastes who knew Melville and was one of the few friends Melville had. In the next room we have several of his last books which the widow sent to my wife's grandfather with her mourning card and with a note at the death of Melville. But for a long period there, Melville was simply not known. I didn't read a Melville novel until the movie [1930] came out, *Moby-Dick*.

.   .   .   .

BAKER: I didn't realize that he had fallen as far out of fashion as that.

WARREN: He fell very far out of fashion. And the poems weren't published until right before 1940, '38, or '40. A Princeton scholar published a few notes on them in an anthology in the late thirties. Then there was a small selection in '44, by F.O. Matthiessen, which I reviewed. I wrote my first piece about Melville on that book. That book hooked me; I got so interested in Melville I began working on a long essay then in '46.

BAKER: And during the thirties you also began to write on some of your contemporaries. I remember you did a piece on Thomas Wolfe, and you also wrote on some of Hemingway's work.

WARREN: I did the Wolfe as a review. I did the Hemingway because Scribner's asked me to do a preface to a new edition of Hemingway. I did a good bit of reviewing during that period. Every five dollars meant something for several years there, and reviewing was the way to get the five dollars. Now, sonnets could get you as much as ten dollars, but it took a long time to write a sonnet.

BAKER: So for most of the thirties you were writing reviews and poetry, side by side?

WARREN: Side by side, yes. And you could get liquor cheap at that time. For instance, a sonnet would buy about a gallon of corn, or maybe two gallons of corn, according to the sonnet. This was before Prohibition.[34]

BAKER: I'm amazed you didn't become a writer of epic verse, at that rate.

WARREN: Well, I wasn't ambitious.

BAKER: Did you see your role as a critic essentially as a didactic one? Did you see yourself instructing the reader about the work in question rather than simply delivering your opinion on it?

WARREN: Well, put it this way. In a classroom you are stuck with the idea of a point you are trying to put across to persuade your listeners. When you're trying to write a review, it's usually to make sense of the thing for yourself. The emphasis is different—at least it was for me. Writing about a poem for a review or for an essay, like on *The Rime of the Ancient Mariner* or the Melville thing, I'm trying to make sense to myself; and as a textbook operation, the classroom is different. You have a fixed audience for a special purpose. That makes it different.

Writing poems or novels, I'm trying basically to make the *thing right*—put it that way—to create the thing as it should be, as I want it to be, as I hope it will be, rather than trying to think of how many copies it'll sell, or whom I'm writing for. You're bound to have a few people in mind that you respect, whom you know well, whose opinions mean something to you, who are there somehow a possible audience. But that small, little bitty audience is all that you have to think about—that's my experience, anyway. You want to make a thing that "works," that fulfills itself, put it that way. How do you know whether it works? You don't know until you see it work on people. But you have to go with the nature of the thing in the process of writing the thing, it seems to me. It carries its own logic.

BAKER: Like a sculptor finding the actual form in wood or stone?

WARREN: Something like that, yes.

BAKER: And bringing out the inherent quality in it?

WARREN: That's right, that's right. Now, you want that to communicate, but I think communication is not your first thought—not my first thought. It's to make the thing right, that's my first thought. If it's made right, it will communicate, put it that way.

BAKER: Sometimes, perhaps, even to only a small group of people?

WARREN: Maybe a small group.

BAKER: But you've never consciously written anything with a view to scoring a popular success? You've never deliberately aimed at a large audience?

WARREN: No, I never have. I like a large audience, but it hasn't been aimed at.

BAKER: Has it surprised you on the occasions when it has come? *All the King's Men,* for instance, your first great success?

WARREN: It surprised me, quite a surprise.

BAKER: What first made you interested in writing fiction? Obviously, this was a long way from your thoughts when you started out writing criticism and poetry. What was the catalyst that made you want to become a novelist?

WARREN: It was an accident, although I think I can trace it now. I began to know people who were novelists, like Ford Madox Ford, Caroline Gordon, and Katherine Anne Porter —writers of fiction, rather; Porter wasn't a novelist then; she was doing novelettes and short stories. And Caroline Gordon and a few other people who were actual writers of novels. I saw a good deal of them. I didn't know Ford well, though he was a great talker. And hearing these people talk about the inside of fiction, how fiction is built, its subtleties, what it's really like, was like hearing Ransom or

Tate talk about the inside of poetry, back in the Fugitive group. I began to see that they—poetry and fiction—weren't so different. They had the same kind of art, with the same complications inside them and different purposes, of course. So as I heard people like that talk, I began to shift unconsciously, I think, in my own attitude toward fiction. And that's the general background.

. . . .

BAKER: These [first stories] are things that your grandfather had told you?

WARREN: The night-rider wars, the tobacco wars, yeah. And so I said why not?—when Paul Rosenfeld called Oxford to ask me to do a novelette for the old *American Caravan*.

BAKER: Was the story of Billie Potts in your famous poem one of the things that you heard from him, too, or did you hear that from somebody else?

WARREN: No, I heard that from an aunt, an old aunt, a great-aunt, who was the sister of his dead wife.

. . . .

BAKER: In terms of writing, do you find the writing of a novel easier than poetry, for instance?

WARREN: Well, you can write poetry lying down or swimming. You can't write novels lying down, that's one difference. You have to sit at a typewriter and type it out—that makes a big difference. No, a poem for me and a novel are not, otherwise, so different. They start much the same way, on the same kind of emotional journey, and can go either way. *All the King's Men* was a verse play first, before it was a novel—a complete verse play.

. . . .

And then I did a prose version which was done in New York a couple of little runs; and then it was done in Germany; and it has been done in Moscow for two and a half years, so I'm told. And three companies did it in Poland. It was done there in two companies simultaneously, in Warsaw and Krakow—the state theater in Poland.

BAKER: That's extraordinary, that they should be so fascinated by it in Eastern Europe and Russia. Partly because they see in it a sort of critique of the American system, do you suppose?

WARREN: Well now, it's hard to know. They also did a movie of it, their own movie. Now, I know this only because one of the actors . . . wrote me a letter and got it carried out, and he sent me stills from the movie. He was playing Jack, the narrator. He said they started out to have a very fine movie, because they had an actor playing the politician who understood the complexities of the role. But he died in the middle of the movie, and they had to get another one; so they got a Party hack, who took a naïve view of it. He said they did not get the movie they hoped to get out of it. No, it was the Russian version on TV.

BAKER: It seems to me that a lot of your most successful novels have been based in some way or another on a historical incident, which you've then imagined yourself into and, in a sense, reconstructed. Is this something that you like to do? *All the King's Men* is a good example of that, but it's not, by any means, the only one.

WARREN: No. I'm sometimes said to be a historical novelist. The first one was *Night Rider*, about the tobacco wars when I was a child, and I saw it, so I guess that's not historic.

BAKER: It's history now, but it wasn't then.

WARREN: It wasn't then, you see. And also the novel about Nashville in the thirties, *At Heaven's Gate*—it wasn't history then. I was living there when I was twenty-five years old, and I was seeing those same things happen. Then *All the King's Men* was not history. I never did a day's research in my life on these novels. They were coming out of the world I lived in, but not a historical one.

BAKER: *World Enough and Time*, for instance?

WARREN: Well, *World Enough and Time* was a straight historical novel.

BAKER: You even called it a romance, as I recall, a historical romance—or was that the publisher?

WARREN: No, I put the word "romance" on as a special meaning for me. *World Enough and Time*, that's about a case in Kentucky in 1825, which Poe had written a play about and many novels were written about it before. It's a story about the young idealist who can't find an object for his idealism, you see. He creates a dream world in which he can play the hero. It's a story about the romantic temperament, that's what it is. I was really thinking, I suppose, somewhere in the back of my mind about Hawthorne and some of his materials. It is a historical romance, but it's a philosophizing one—that's the difference. I have a modern man telling it and commenting on it as a modern man, you see. The modern man claims to have the documents—as I had some documents—and sees them in the modern way.

BAKER: Yes, you've got the dual sensibility working.

WARREN: That's the idea of that one. Now the other one, *Band of Angels*, is a Civil War story, which is a true story, or partly true, about two girls—they must have been octoroons—whose father was a rich planter near Lexington. His wife died quite young—she's not the mother of these children. He then takes into his house a yellow concubine—she may have been, say, a quadroon, but we can't be sure. The story is a very well known one in middle Kentucky, or was at one time. By this yellow girl he then has two daughters. He raises them as his own daughters. He drops all of his friends, so the daughters never see anybody except the father and their mother and the household. The father takes them on trips north and travels with them as his daughters, of course, and is delighted with them, fond of them. He then puts them in Oberlin College when they get big enough, which is the only coeducational school in the country—also an abolitionist school, but that doesn't matter, because he's never admitted their color, you see.

Then when they are big girls, grown girls, college age, he dies suddenly, and dies in debt. The two girls are seized at his grave by the creditors, the sheriff acting for all of the creditors. This causes a great scandal in the state. They are sold off to a downriver trader, and that's all we know about them. But that much is in the record. Of course, you can't have two, so I got rid of one of them right quick—I never had but one. And then the question is: Why couldn't the father admit that? You see, he couldn't bring himself to face the fact that they weren't white; but to make a manumission legal, he'd have to denominate them as slaves, and he couldn't face that situation, you see. He just kept postponing, thinking it would work out or maybe that they'd get married and live up North or something. But in my book she goes to the Civil War as a slave.

The whole story is about an investigation of the nature of freedom. I mean she's never free—you can't set her free from the fact of the relationship to her father. Until she can forgive her father, she's not free. You see, that's the nature of freedom as she experiences it. It's not just a piece of paper in the story, or the Battle of Gettysburg. The story is inside her.

The last two books are, again, different. *The Cave*—once again, that's a modern story, set in my lifetime, based on the Floyd Collins case in 1925, which I couldn't care less about then, because I was interested in John Donne and the Greeks by that time. I couldn't even be bothered to go see the place. But later on I crawled every cave in that whole region. I've done a lot of caving, just to see what caves were like—but only when I was writing the book. I'm afraid of caves.

BAKER: Yes, that comes through in the book, very powerfully.

WARREN: I'm afraid of caves, sure. But that happened a long time ago, in my lifetime. Usually it takes about ten or twenty years for me to write a novel. I carry it around with me and I try to talk about it to friends, and gradually tell the story to myself by telling it to somebody else, trying it on other people. I quit that now because I have nobody to talk to. You can't do it to your wife, poor woman; she's got her own troubles. You can't do it to your children; they're too busy, you see. And your friends all have their jobs.

BAKER: I can see your problem.

WARREN: Everybody knows a hundred stories, you know, a thousand stories—the question is: Why does this story pick on you? Why this story and not that story? My guess is now this: The story or the poem you find to write is the story or poem that has some meaning that you haven't solved in it, that you haven't quite laid hands on. So your writing—it is a way of understanding it, what its meaning, the potential meaning, is. And the story that you understand perfectly, you don't write. You know what the meaning is; there's nothing there to nag your mind about it. A story that's one for you is the one that you have to work to understand.

BAKER: So for you, writing is always an act of exploration, essentially?

WARREN: Exploration and interpretation. It's not just stenographic work.

BAKER: Which means that the people that you look for as protagonists, whether in a story that really happened or something you simply conceived yourself, have to be people who don't understand themselves?

WARREN: In most cases, yes. Who don't understand their own role, anyway, their own meaning. Or, perhaps, get misled by their own motives.

BAKER: Somebody once said he thought all your novels were essentially about idealists betrayed by their own ideals. Is that fair enough?

WARREN: That's pretty fair; that's pretty fair. That would certainly apply to the young murderer in *World Enough and Time*.

BAKER: It would. And in a sense it would apply to the man in *Band of Angels*, too, because his ideal was to create this world in which these girls could live.

WARREN: See also her husband and Seth. That's right, and it would apply to the hero, Mr. Munn, of my first published novel, *Night Rider*, and it would apply certainly to the last two novels I've written.[35] Now, *Flood*, I'm not sure of that one.

BAKER: You deny, with perfect justice, that you're a historical novelist in the usual sense of the word. Do you consider yourself a Southern novelist? Nearly all of your novels are set in the South.

WARREN: All of them are, without exception. There are scenes outside the South. My current novel has scenes in Chicago, and one other novel, *Wilderness*, has scenes in New York City—the draft riots in New York City in 1863. But you can't write with inner authority about a world you don't understand, and you understand your world usually by the time you're ten or eleven years old. Short stories are a little different. Now, I'm in awe of a writer like Katherine Anne Porter, who can write in various countries, with a wonderful sense of national differences.

BAKER: Yes—who can write about, say, a Mexican bandit leader. You, presumably, would find that very difficult to conceptualize.

WARREN: I find that difficult and I would simply take the world I understand best. And I've had to do that.

BAKER: Here you are living up in New England, and yet the landscape that haunts your mind throughout your novels and poems remains that of the South.

WARREN: Well, poetry's different. I have many poems about Vermont and a few about Greece and a lot about France and Italy. But poems are more personal transactions between you and yourself—and that land. There's no reportage, you understand. For a novel, you have to be able to tell what food to eat, what hour of the day—a thousand things, you know, that depend on information, and I just don't know that much about anywhere else. I lived in Minnesota, for instance, but I can't imagine myself writing a novel about Minnesota life, unless it was to get into the world of straight business or the academic world, where the occupation carries its own mores and habits.

BAKER: And where the setting doesn't count?

WARREN: The university could be Berkeley, or it could be the University of Minnesota, or it could be Yale. If I had to write a university novel, I wouldn't give a damn which one it was. They're all alike. Also, I guess I have an abiding concern with American history, but especially with Southern history. And I read a lot of history—for a nonprofessional I read a lot, anyway.

BAKER: You've never written a formal book of history of any kind? You've never been tempted to do so?

WARREN: I wrote a little essay for *Life* magazine and I published a book called *The Legacy of the Civil War*, but that was just an assignment—a request from *Life* magazine. The whole thing turned out longer than *Life* wanted, and so they used a part and I published the whole as a book. It's just a long essay. I wouldn't think of sitting down and writing a piece of history as just another piece of history.

BAKER: So the actual writing of history—simply reconstructing events and trying to make it colorful narrative—wouldn't have any interest for you?

WARREN: No, no. I wouldn't have any interest in doing that. Besides, I'm not qualified. I'm not Vann Woodward. I'm terribly interested in history, but writing it is not for me. It's a very demanding profession. But I'm entitled to my view of history as written. If you're going to be a good historian, it's a very demanding profession.

BAKER: Do you think the many-sidedness of your work as critic, novelist, and poet has meant, to a certain extent, that your reputation has become diffused? There are a number of people who regard you as a great poet, and another number of people who regard you as a great novelist, and yet your achievement itself is so varied. Americans love specialization, as you know, and you're difficult to categorize for that reason.

WARREN: Well, I have only two roles, essentially: poetry and fiction—and only a certain kind of fiction. But I don't regard myself as a professional critic. It's like teaching; it's part of my social life. I had to teach for a living in the thirties and early forties. I couldn't have managed without it. But I discovered that I enjoy teaching. I quit teaching entirely three times but always drifted back in. But I haven't taught more than one term a year and only two days a week at most for—since the 1940's. But I like to keep in touch with the young.

BAKER: So you'd never give it up?

WARREN: If I weren't paid to teach, I would pay for the privilege—as Jarrell once said. But it's also a way of talking about ideas. When I have an idea I want to talk about it, and the only way you can do that is to teach. Also, you can find in the academy certain people that you can't find outside. There are not too many of them in the teaching profession, but there are some—the real humanists—brave men who love their learning and who love ideas. Now, if you hang around the university, you can get some of that rubbed off on you, or at least you can talk to people like that, and you can profit from it. When I'm not teaching, I miss it very much. You get the same thing by social life at a party. You can't do it, say, having six people to dinner. Occasionally you can, but not very often. That sort of association involves teaching at a good university, and I've been very fortunate in always being in places where there were some people . . .

A real critic, like Cleanth Brooks or I. A. Richards, has a system—they develop a system. And it's a critic's main interest, and he's concerned with that primarily. I'm not. I'm interested in trying to understand this poem or that poem, but I'm not interested in trying to create a system. I'm interested in a different kind of understanding. You might say a more limited kind of understanding. I'm interested in my enjoyment, put it that way, more than anything else. I've certainly written some so-called criticism, but I usually take it from my class notes. I'm just not a professional critic. That business is just something that happens, like my garden. I like to garden in the same spirit. But writing fiction, poetry, that's serious—that's for keeps.

BAKER: But even that, I think, may have, shall we say, diluted the way in which you are regarded. There was a recent review on the front page of *The New York Times Book Review* of your latest collected verse in which the critic with an air of astonishment wrote that behind our backs Penn Warren has turned into our greatest poet. That was the gist of his review, it seems to me. He'd clearly been thinking of you mostly as a novelist, and perhaps a novelist to whom he wasn't particularly drawn; yet as a poet, he found you extraordinary. Now, other people are more interested in your novels. What I'm trying to say is: Do you feel that it dissipates your impact to be so active in both fields?

WARREN: I think it does, but it's something I don't worry about. It'll shake down, and it's nothing to worry about. And after all, novelists and poets are both fictionalizers, of course, and not such rare birds. I don't find an absolute difference, as I said before. At a certain level an idea takes hold. Now, it doesn't necessarily come with a form; it comes as an idea or an impulse. It may be one verse of a verse play. It isn't labeled when it comes to you. I've started many things in one form and shifted to another—quite often, in fact. Now I've quit short stories entirely—since 1946. Short stories interfere with poems. I was writing stories mostly because I needed the money, mostly in the thirties.

BAKER: These were primarily written for magazines and such, for immediate publication?

WARREN: I wrote them the best I could, but I wrote them for money. I found that the short stories were eating up poems, or what could have become poems. I got some very good prices for some of the stories. But usually a lot later when I didn't need it so bad. But I quit it quite deliberately, because I found the germ of a story might be the germ of a poem.

BAKER: Yes. Sometimes even in sets of poems you'll follow one thought through . . .

WARREN: Yes, that's right.

BAKER: A series of five or six poems.

WARREN: That's right. And it could at one stage have turned

into a short story. So I just don't write them as stories. Just quit, deliberately.

BAKER: Well, that's one habit you kicked, anyway.

WARREN: I kicked that one.

BAKER: If you had your choice and somebody said you could only be remembered for either your poetry or your fiction, which would you prefer to be remembered for? Which has been the more important to you? Is that a ridiculous question?

WARREN: Well, I think it's a question that has to be treated within certain limitations. Of course, one would like to be remembered, period. So I try to do work that is worthy of me—honest. But I feel poetry is much more personal than fiction. It's more personal for me—and I suppose that answers your question.

BAKER: Yes.

WARREN: You're closer to trying to investigate your own values and the meaning of your own life in poems than you are in a novel. At least I am. In any case, I think I'd make that choice if I were given a choice. But that doesn't mean that I don't feel that I could start a new novel now, with complete commitment to it. I'd do it because I felt I had to do it. I'm not just in search of a money deal, or so one might say, "He writes novels for the Book-of-the-Month Club and the Literary Guild." I try to write the best novel I can, period. But the interesting topics, the basic ideas in the poems and the basic ideas in the novels may be the same. They concern the same basic things.

The South: Distance
and Change

██▌▐█▌▐█▐▌▐▐▐▐▌▐▐▐▌▐▐▐▐▌▐▐▐▐▐▌▐▐▐▐▌▐▐▐▌▐▐▐▐▌▐▐██

*Louis D. Rubin, Jr., conducted this interview at the request
of the Voice of America as part of a project on the South and
its writers. Rubin traveled to New Haven to talk with Warren
and Styron in April 1977. The interview was broadcast over-
seas and later published in a book that Rubin edited,* The
American South: Portrait of a Culture (*1980*).

LOUIS RUBIN: The two Southern authors who are with me here
to talk about the South might be said to be of different
literary generations. Robert Penn Warren was born in 1905.
As a youthful member of the Nashville Fugitive poets he
was publishing verse in 1924, a year before William Styron
was born. Red Warren's first novel, *Night Rider*, came out
before the Second World War, in 1939. Bill Styron published *Lie Down in Darkness*, his first novel, in 1951. Yet in
addition to a close personal friendship, they share many
things together, among them a fascination with Southern
history. What is interesting to me here is that neither of

them has lived in the Southern states for a number of years. Bill, you left Newport News, Virginia, well before your first novel came out, didn't you?

WILLIAM STYRON: Well, I'll put it this way: there's a split. I spent my childhood, boyhood, youth, and education entirely in the South, and in my early twenties I left. I've visited a lot, but I've never really been back.

RUBIN: And, Red Warren, you grew up in Guthrie, Kentucky, and then you went to Vanderbilt University in Nashville, Tennessee . . .

WARREN: Fifty miles away. It was in the same part of the world.

RUBIN: But then when you graduated from Vanderbilt you went to California, and Yale, and then Oxford, and then you came back to the South to teach.

WARREN: In 1930. And I lived in the South until 1942, with some trips abroad and other trips around the country—a lot of trips to the Far West during that period, and abroad a couple of times.

RUBIN: You left Louisiana State University, where you and Cleanth Brooks edited the *Southern Review*, in 1942, and you went to Minnesota. So you've been away from the South for over thirty years.

WARREN: Yes, I left Minnesota for Yale, and I've lived in New England now for twenty-five years, for twenty-seven years.

RUBIN: And, Bill, you've been away almost that long yourself.

STYRON: Yes.

RUBIN: Yet what strikes me now is this: Red, you recently published a new novel, *A Place to Come To*. And, Bill, I've seen excerpts from the novel that you've been working on. Red's novel involves a Southerner who's been away from the South for a long time, going back and leaving. And while Bill's novel takes place in New York and Europe and involves a concentration camp experience of the Second World War, nevertheless the meaning of the experience is "happening," insofar as the narrator is involved, to a Southerner from Virginia. So obviously the experience outside of the South still seems to mean a great deal to both of you in terms of what it signifies to you *as* Southerners. Your imagination seems to be still very thoroughly grounded in an identity that geographically at least you abandoned a long time ago. Could you say that, as a fiction writer, Red, this is still the experience that is most real to you?

WARREN: Well, "reality," I guess, is one word to describe it. Actually, it seems to me that though your basic images and attitudes may change in many ways, they are always fundamentally conditioned by what you knew in small and large ways very early in life. This remains important, at least to me. Now take a small, trivial thing. If I were writing a story about a Connecticut farmer, I wouldn't know where to begin. But writing a story about such a family, rich or poor, grand or miserable, in the South, I wouldn't have any hesitation. It would be as natural as breathing to me. I'd know what they did, I'd know what they ate, I'd know what they'd say. And also the matter of landscape is extremely important. I suppose I'm bringing in something now that may be irrelevant, but the nature of the land itself, in relation to the landscape of other parts of the world, other places, is very important to me, particularly in poems.

RUBIN: . . . Red Warren, I notice that several of your recent novels have involved a man going back a long time later to the place where he grew up and noticing the difference, having had the experience of being out in the world. In one instance the old place has been covered by flood waters. In your most recent novel he comes back at the very end to the town he had been fleeing from all his life, where his mother had lived.

WARREN: She had driven him out, because she hated where she was.

RUBIN: In one of your poems there is an image that I find very striking—it has come to my mind again and again. It is the image of the man who has returned home and walks out by the railroad tracks at night and watches the Pullman cars on the train go by—that memory. In both cases it seems to me that so much of your experience of the South, and Bill Styron's experience of the South, involves this sense of "Who am I?" in terms of "How far have I gone from the

South and where did I start from and how did I come back?"

WARREN: There's one difference between us; I don't know how important it is. I wanted to live in the South, you see; I'm a refugee from the South, driven out, as it were. The place I wanted to live, the place I thought was heaven to me, after my years of wandering, was middle Tennessee, which is a beautiful country, or *was* a beautiful country—it's rapidly being ruined. But I couldn't make it work. When I went back to teach for three years there, I enjoyed living in the country and driving in to do my teaching, and this was fine. But I was let out of Vanderbilt University, and had to go elsewhere for a job. I went to Louisiana State University, which was quite fortunately a very exciting place. And I left Louisiana only because I felt I wasn't wanted. I felt pressure to leave. It wasn't a choice. I had settled myself down and bought a house in the country—settled down for life, I assumed. I left, shall we say, under pressure of some kind or another. I wasn't fired. I left out of pride. I went to Minnesota, which I enjoyed.

I've quit teaching several times—"never again." But I fell in love with teaching along the way, so I always drifted back in again. I was out as long as six years one time, two years another time, and again a year or so at a time. But that's not the point. The point is that I, unlike Bill, didn't make a choice of living outside the South. I always felt myself somehow squeezed out of the South, which is a very different thing from Bill's conscious choice. That is a generational matter, perhaps; I don't know.

RUBIN: But I wonder whether Bill's choice was entirely a free one? In other words, didn't the choice really mean: "Can I be myself and do what I want to do while living here?" And the answer was no.

STYRON: I think that was my decision. The decision I made had nothing to do with any antipathy toward the South; quite the contrary. It so happened that I didn't have many friends left in the South. I had very few connections in the South that I felt deeply. I was not in teaching. After I left Duke

University I hung around Durham for a while and enjoyed it, oddly enough, because it's not the most attractive of Southern cities. But I left simply because most of the profounder contacts I had made with other human beings were in the North, and that was my decision.

. . . .

WARREN: The South never crossed my mind except as an imaginative construct before I left it. I was raised on the battles and leaders of the Civil War by a grandfather veteran who had a very active part in the Civil War, but he was also mad for Napoleon's campaigns, so I got a great dose of Napoleon's campaigns and General Forrest's operations all mixed up together. . . . I had it all tangled up together in my earliest years.

RUBIN: That is also what the Confederates themselves did, you know. They thought of their Civil War experience, when they wrote about it, in Napoleonic terms. You know that story about the Battle of Shiloh, the surprise march, when the sun's coming up and the officers are saying "This is the sun of Austerlitz," and the soldiers didn't know what they were talking about—they thought they were saying "the Son of Oyster Itch."

WARREN: This leads to another question. The South has one peculiarity: it was a nation once, and that makes a vast difference, though it can be forgotten that it makes a difference. Another thing that's forgotten that makes a difference is that Southerners felt that they had created the Union—Washington and Jefferson had created the Union—and the North was going to take it away from them. There were many Unionists in the Civil War who were still fighting in the Confederate army because they were fighting for their country, which was the United States of America.

STYRON: Wasn't Robert E. Lee's conflict in 1861 based on that?

WARREN: I guess it was based on that; many were. It was a double nationality that was involved there, and there's a vast complication—I don't pretend to settle it now—an emotional tangle in the role of the South in fighting the United States, and the role of the South as an independent nation. This is a complicated issue, and it has strong emotional ramifications, even for ignorant people.

STYRON: The very idea that such an intense nationalism existed almost defines the individuality that the South still thinks itself to have, whether rightly or wrongly.

RUBIN: I think it's still very much there. I don't think it's eroding. The fact that the South is becoming urbanized and industrialized, so that, let's say, the suburbs of Atlanta seem to resemble the suburbs of Detroit, or something like that—I don't think that they *are* the suburbs of Detroit. I don't think the South is losing its identity at all.

STYRON: I don't think it's losing its identity, but I think it tends to be less well defined in certain areas. I've spent recently a lot of time in North Carolina, and I notice that in the larger urban areas there is a blur. I mean, except for the accents and so on, you find a kind of Northern overlay. On the other hand, the small towns, where I've also been, in eastern North Carolina, are maybe even more Southern than I once remembered, for some reason. A little town like Goldsboro, where I've spent a lot of time, which is in the heart of the Tobacco Belt, has barely changed an iota since the time I remember it as a little boy in the 1930's. So I think it's a matter of where you are in the South.

WARREN: That may be true. I think there are vast changes in the parts of the South I knew best—middle Tennessee and the Cumberland River Valley—vast changes and changes of attitude. Now some are for the good, and I would be the first to grant that. I faced the question, actually, when I started to buy a farm in Tennessee, where I would spend half the year. I felt I'd be isolated. A lot of friends are dead and gone. But I also felt a real change in the whole nature of the world. And I felt it would be an idle dream for me to go back there. It would be ridiculous.

STYRON: I feel the same way.

WARREN: The one friend I know who did so shot himself.

STYRON: *That's* the end of a dream.

RUBIN: Aren't you really talking about the nature of time,

though? I mean, about your experience of your childhood and the people you knew when you grew up as a child. If you had stayed there, they wouldn't have continued the same way, either. When you go back to Guthrie, Red, or you go back to Newport News, Bill, in a sense you are going back to your memories of a time. There are a number of physical objects around that can trigger those memories, but you're really going back to a time even more than to a place. You say that everything has changed. What you're saying is that so many years have elapsed, aren't you? As for the people who have been there all along and who haven't left, they've changed too. They're not the same. You're now fifty-one, I believe. Let's say you had been fifty-one in the year 1935 instead of 1977. Don't you think that if you had come back to Newport News in 1935 at the age of fifty-one, you might also have said, "This has all changed. It's all gone. It's not like what it was"? In other words, isn't part of what we're dealing with here the nature of time, and when you look back it always seems that everything has changed?

WARREN: Part of it is. That's partly true. But there are also other elements involved in it. One element for me was that I had no attachments to a town. My attachment was always to the country, and that made a difference. I was attached to the countryside, to rural life, not town life. I couldn't abide small town life from the start. I was always against it.

RUBIN: In some ways it seems to me that a good deal of the strength of twentieth-century Southern writing in general, and your own work in particular, may lie in the fact that the literature itself has had to, and still has to, confront the tremendous phenomenon of change in time. It becomes almost an exemplar of the American experience as a whole. The change has been so swift, so bewildering, and in so short a period of time—in your own lifetimes—that a good deal of the strength of Southern literature comes out of the intensity and the power of that change.

STYRON: I think you must include in that the quite obvious and single most significant social change in the South, which we haven't touched on yet—the rapidity with which the whole racial dilemma has been turned around, within the lifetimes of most all of us. Certainly that has been one of the most bewildering and, I might add, amazing and benignly revolutionary things that I think have ever happened in a civilized country.

WARREN: And now Jimmy Carter can be elected president by black support, as he was.

STYRON: Yes, of course.

. . . .

WARREN: Back in the 1960's I was traveling a great deal in the South, more than in the North for a while, interviewing Negroes for a book I was writing—all kinds of Negroes. More than once I heard Negroes say, "There's a personal relationship here, bad or good, which gives reality and holds some hope for the future. If a sheriff shoots you in Alabama, he probably knows your name. If a cop brains you in Detroit, he doesn't know your name. That makes a big difference." This was actually said to me by an Alabama black. "I see some hope in that," he said. "He knows what he's doing; he's stuck with it."

STYRON: He might be a black sheriff now.

WARREN: Yes, now he might be a sheriff himself. . . . Don't forget that segregation was a very late development in America, and it was not true of the Old South. There was slavery, but not segregation. Segregation did not come in until quite late. In the 1880's and 1890's, according to Vann Woodward's book *The Strange Career of Jim Crow*, the Charleston, South Carolina, papers, for example, were against segregation. They said, "After you segregate the trains, the next thing is there will be two Bibles to kiss in court." And it happened.

RUBIN: That's true. On the other hand, I think that can be interpreted a little differently. Isn't it true that laws demanding segregation, and all these little artifacts—the front and the back of the streetcar—came about because with the end of slavery there was no longer any enormous institutionalized social fact which would create the distance, maintain the barrier, and therefore the white South felt it had to enact these things into little laws, and things like that? It wasn't even questioned, before, so that there wasn't any need for it in that sense.

WARREN: Well, there was no need up North, because there was enforced segregation already.

STYRON: But there was also the fact of Reconstruction, which was a trauma in many ways to the South, with on the surface often a very shocking insult to white Southern sensibilities. The idea of black men being in power, and being artificially put in power, was a traumatic experience after the hegemony of the whites. Certainly one of the reasons for Jim Crow, at least one of the elements in Jim Crow, was a redressing of that grievance.

WARREN: It was also a change in the class system in the South, part of it.

RUBIN: Very much so.

STYRON: But all this aside, the fact still remains that for many of us, if we could have lived to be two hundred years old today, we would have known a phase in our lives when strict segregation would have been an unheard-of strangeness because in antebellum times it would have made no sense, emotionally or otherwise. But for those of us who are caught up in history, the experience of being brought up in the South, born and raised any time from 1900 right on through to World War II, was the equivalent—I don't think it's stretching it too far to say—of living in South Africa, certainly in the Black Belt part of the South where I was brought up. You had a total *apartheid*, and it had a severe, lacerating, and wounding effect on both races, black and white.

WARREN: I agree with you about that.

STYRON: And it wasn't our fault. I'm not trying to get off the hook. I'm simply saying that history treated a whole generation of us—maybe two generations—to this.

WARREN: One other very important element in it, too, is the flinch from black flesh, dark flesh. Now the flinch was not part of slavery. The flinch from black flesh was very strong in the North. The word "miscegenation," for example, was a word cooked up by Copperheads and New York journalists, according to the *Journal of Negro History*, which is my only authority for this. They tried to get Lincoln and various other people to sign a document saying it would be nice to have miscegenation. They couldn't get a signer.

RUBIN: What you're saying is that nineteenth-century America, North and South, was racist.

WARREN: What I'm saying is that in the South there was little flinch from black flesh compared to that in the North, where there was a great flinch from black flesh and concubinage occurred quite frequently.

STYRON: Aren't you saying also that this repulsion did not exist much in antebellum times, but did exist afterwards, even in the South?

WARREN: That's exactly what I'm saying. It grew up afterwards in the South.

STYRON: I remember noting this to my own surprise once, when I wrote an essay on this for *Harper's* a long time ago. When I reflected on my boyhood in a Southern town, not a Southern rural environment, in retrospect I was astounded by my total unfamiliarity with black flesh. I mean, even as a presence, even as a part of the ambiance of my life. It was nonexistent, except for the ones who worked in the kitchen. After the day was done they evaporated, they went somewhere else. The myth was quite the opposite. This miscegenation myth you're talking about *was* a myth, because after the modern South began and after Jim Crow began, everything legislated against any contact.

WARREN: In the earlier agricultural South, a lot of children played together. They had their black nurse. This was very common, in many segments of society.

RUBIN: It seems to me that in your imaginative writings and in your journalism, too, both of you have chronicled this change. I don't say that you sat down consciously with the intention of doing so, but this is what your work shows. In Bill Styron's case, his first novel involves someone growing up in the South and leaving the South. His next novel involves someone who again grew up in the South but is a long way away from it and is trying to learn how to go back, but not really back to the same place—how to find a place, or a place to come to, to use the title of Red Warren's latest book. And in your next novel, Bill, you took a black man, a slave; here is the Southern racial experience, but looked at from a completely different point of view. In the novel you're working on now there is a man brought up with Southern sensibilities, coming to grips with a different kind of horror, a completely different kind of horrible situation—the concentration camps of the Second World War. And he says, "The particular kind of injustices which I'm indignant about may not be nearly so important as what race hatred can do to people like this." That's the insight to be drawn out of that experience of separation. And, Red, it seems to me in your instance, there are few if any other authors who have written as much as you have, consciously, about the problems of the South and the Southerner, the Southerner going away and returning, the Southerner living in the change from the Old South to the New South, and the various problems this involves. If I were a social historian, let's say fifty years from now, and I wanted to chronicle how all this happened, in both instances your works would be one of the best places to look, even though I would doubt very much that either one of you, especially when you are writing fiction or poetry, ever sat down with that conscious intention in mind.

WARREN: Certainly it never crosses my mind. It's the story that counts. If it has a story it has a cocklebur in it that you can't understand and that you want to understand. It has a nag in it; that becomes the reason you write it, the nag in it.

RUBIN: You wrote your first fiction about the South when you were in England, didn't you?

WARREN: I did, and I did it because I was asked to write it. The farther I got away from the South, the more I thought about it. . . .

RUBIN: And you, Bill, wrote your first fiction at Duke, in Durham, though that was apprentice fiction.

STYRON: Yes, very much so.

RUBIN: And you wrote most of *Lie Down in Darkness* living in New York, didn't you?

STYRON: I wrote practically all of it somewhere in New York.

RUBIN: So in both cases it's been the fact that you were away from the scene that triggered the reexamination, and then you have kept reexamining it, and it's provided a sort of nourishment, an index of reality if you want to call it that, all the way. You can measure "Who am I?" in terms of the kind of ambiance that you grow up in. What I'm getting at is this: the fact that neither you, Red, nor you, Bill, has been living in the geographical South for a number of years, may make you into a different kind of Southern writer, but nevertheless that very experience itself is a part of the Southern experience—the moving out from and looking back at the past.

WARREN: I don't want to talk about myself too much, but something you've said triggers this thought. For ten years I couldn't finish a poem, even a short poem—I have stacks of them unfinished, four lines or six lines or eight lines, and then they go off in a folder somewhere. Now I began writing poems again in Italy, at a ruined castle over the sea. . . . That year I wrote *Promises* and two sonnets, and spent the winter revising them. That book is half Kentucky-Tennessee, and half Italy. There's medieval Italy and boyhood—they make a book. Do you see what I'm getting at? It's the long withdrawal from south Kentucky. But the book is really on that theme as much as any other theme, the other being father-child, father-daughter, father-son, as infants.

RUBIN: Don't you think the same thing is true of your most recent novel?

WARREN: It's quite deliberately true of it, though it's autobiographical only in the deep way that all books are autobiographical. I want to come back to one other thing. You said a Southerner asks "Who am I?" but "Who am I?" strikes me as ultimately the question all writers are asking. In the Southern case it's only an especially acute one; it's pointed up more sharply. But "Who am I?" is a basic human question. I just add that as a footnote to what you said.

RUBIN: That's quite true. But the extent to which it is a problem is what's involved, and it seems to me that when you look at the great body of nineteenth-century Southern literature, that question could be answered very easily, they thought, and the fact that it was answered so very easily accounts for the fact that the literature has so little tension in it, because the answer is rhetorical. In your generation and Bill's generation this is not a rhetorical question; the indices are all moved around and changed around and mixed up, and therefore you're wrestling with it all the time. You don't wrestle with it literally, in terms of the question "Who am I, Robert Penn Warren?" or "Who am I, William Styron?" but "Who is this person or that person in this dramatic situation?" It comes to the same thing, though.

WARREN: Yes, you transfer it.

STYRON: You're quite accurate when you point out the huge chasm between nineteenth-century Southern sensibility and twentieth-century. I'm speaking in general. Apart from Edgar Allan Poe and one or two others, don't we tend to localize nineteenth-century Southern writing in sensibilities like Thomas Nelson Page, who were delightfully satisfied with the status quo? And possibly for good reason—the status quo often looked pretty good to them.

WARREN: Or their dream of it.

RUBIN: That's really more like it. Thomas Nelson Page was writing about the beauties of life on the old plantation, and his best stories are told by the faithful black retainer. Here is a man who is married to the sister of Marshall Field, lives in Washington, D.C., travels abroad all the time, goes up to New England in the summers, serves as the ambassador to Italy during the First World War—a thoroughgoing cosmopolite, and yet when he sits down with a pen and writes there is the dream of the old thing—he's not looking at his own experience.

WARREN: It's a pastoral.

STYRON: He's not looking, because even at that time the horrors were commencing. To localize history in one single type of event, lynchings were very rare things in the first half of the nineteenth century. It was a post-Civil War phenomenon; it came with Jim Crow. Page was writing during the heyday of lynching. We in the twentieth century, let's face it, have had strange and unearthly experiences that were not dreamed of by and large by our nineteenth-century forebears. The Civil War is an exception to that, but I'm talking about the experience between black and white, the tension—the power and the glory and the horrors and all that reached their crescendo in the twentieth century.

WARREN: It's not black or white in the twentieth century, it's everybody.

STYRON: It's anybody. You're talking about the whole world.

WARREN: About the Dresden fire raid, and a lot of other such things.

STYRON: And to me that's another thing that my own imagination has been captured by—a thing that's totally extraneous to my experience, namely, what happened in the Nazi concentration camps, which seems to epitomize humanity at its nadir in all of its history. And I have been able I think to come at it through whatever sensibility I created in myself as a Southerner.

WARREN: This is an important point, Bill. It seems to me that the whole problem of modernity, of all modernity, is that of how can the person hang on to the fact that he's a person, and not become simply a thing being shoved here and shoved there, caught in a vast, complicated machine, and depersonalized in the process. The very strong personal sense in the South that makes tales worth telling—sitting around and talking about some*body*, Mr. Smith versus Mr. Jones, or why did this man do this crazy thing, because he's that kind of a person—is involved somehow in the question of how personality is preserved in the face of the more and more mechanized, computerized world of technology.

RUBIN: In other words, a gas oven is so much more efficient than a lash, isn't it?

STYRON: It's another thing that's just being apprehended, really. It's fascinating to me that a place like Auschwitz is in a curious way an extension of Western chattel slavery. It was of course a place for extermination, but it was equally a place in which slavery was practiced, of a monstrous sort, which was a logical extension of the *relatively* benign slavery practiced in the South—I say "relatively" because slavery in the South was not, inhuman as it was, practiced as a method to extract everything that one could out of a body and then let it perish, whereas Auschwitz was a place in which slavery was practiced with the idea in mind that people were disposable and that after you got the work out of them they died. I don't think it's possible to make any direct comparisons between Southern slavery and Nazi slavery, but the two are somehow linked in what you, Red, were describing as a kind of evolutionary dehumanizing process which is all around us.

WARREN: Yes, that's what I'm getting at.

RUBIN: The struggle to preserve one's humanity, one's identity, within this—a constant struggle which goes on all the time—in a sense constitutes the burden of a great deal of twentieth-century Southern literature.

WARREN: It becomes acute there because the mark of individuality was strong and old-fashioned.

RUBIN: It seems to me that your work, and the work of your generation of Southern writers, is a place to look to see this process going on, and continuing, and being imaginatively explored. At least, I know that's where I look.

Reminiscences:
A Conversation with
Robert Penn Warren

▐▐▌▐▐▐▐▐▐▌▐▐▐▐▐▐▐▐▐▌▐▐▐▐▐▐▐▐▐▐▐▐▐▐▐▐▐▐▐▐▐▐▐▐▐▐▐▐▐▐▐▐

*David Farrell interviewed Warren at his home in Fairfield,
Connecticut, in the fall of 1977. In his introduction to the
interview as it appeared in the* Southern Review *in 1980,
Farrell recalls the visit: "We began by talking about his children, a subject that Warren took to eagerly." Then they
turned to the subject of his early years in Kentucky.*

DAVID FARRELL: To begin with, tell me a little bit about your
earliest years in Kentucky and Guthrie.
WARREN: Well, I'll go back a couple of generations to really
make it make sense. . . . I found a big book, an anthology
of American poetry, published about 1895, something like
that.[36] I was a boy of twelve years. I happened to open it
up and I saw a picture of my father there, and some poems
by him and a biographical sketch, and I was unsettled by
this, in a way.
FARRELL: You'd never heard about this?
WARREN: He'd never mentioned it. He was a man who hadn't

had the life he set out to have, but in his old years he said
to me, "Well, I learned to take a joy in my obligations."

FARRELL: Did you show him the anthology?

WARREN: I showed him the book. He just took it away from
me and he showed some kind of an awful intensity in the
act of taking the book away from me and he said, "Give it
to me." Not in a mean way, but in a very firm way, and it
disappeared. He must have destroyed it. I never found that
book in any of his library. But when he was an old man in
his eighties, he sent me some poems written . . . it must
have been back when he was about twenty-two or -three,
because the typing was that of an old-fashioned typewriter,
purple ink and all that.

FARRELL: What were the poems like?

WARREN: They were poetry of a person who knew the techniques but I thought had no inspiration in them, you see.
And he was set on being a lawyer-poet, but he educated all
the children and took care of his stepmother and God knows
what else.

FARRELL: What kind of books did he read?

WARREN: Up into his last year of life, as long as he could sit
up in a chair, he was reading books. His house was full of
history; he was reading history. But all the books I would
leave in the house, or that my brothers and sisters from
college would leave in the house, he'd read them all—Jung,
and Freud, and God knows what.

FARRELL: Just keeping current . . . I'm wondering if you ever
had an image of your father as a poet as you were working
to be a poet.

WARREN: No, I don't think there was much connection. I was
ambitious, as a boy is ambitious, but quite different. The
whole thing I wanted to be . . . I had a great interest in the
woods.

FARRELL: Hunting . . .

WARREN: And in naturalists, men collecting things, studying
trees and butterflies and things like that. But I spent all my
summers in the country with my maternal grandfather. He
was a man of the same cut, in the way of my father. . . .

I have a lot of poems about my grandfather. He appears in one called "The Day Dr. Knox Did It," as one of the characters.

FARRELL: Was he interested in poetry, like your father?

WARREN: Oh, yes, he was soaked in poetry.

FARRELL: What kinds of poetry? Which poets?

WARREN: Primarily the English Romantics, and then he had some batch of Burns he was crazy about, and Byron, and quite a bit of Pope, and bits of Shakespeare floating around.

FARRELL: And he would quote these to you?

WARREN: He would quote them to me and for himself. . . . The whole family was bookish, and I could see from the kind of things they had, the books they had, they had gotten their state of prosperity; they had gotten these fancy English annuals for the children, you see. My mother was a very well-read girl; she'd gotten this from her family.

FARRELL: How about your childhood friends and your school experiences?

WARREN: I had a few friends, one very close friend, several years older than I. I had a poem about him in the *New Yorker* last year. It was, I guess, a rather long poem on a baseball player. He was the only neighbor we had. We lived sort of half in the country; the town was growing out to us then. Name was Greenfield.[37] He pitched for the New York Giants, later on. But we played together. We'd go to the woods together a lot. He was older than I and taught me a lot. He was the best shot I ever saw—incredible.

FARRELL: How about church? How did that figure in your early life?

WARREN: My people were very un-churchy. They were good citizens, but un-churchy. My father wasn't even a member of a church until very late in life, and that was just church as a worthy social institution. My father was in a way an old-fashioned freethinker. Put it this way: he was of a religious temperament and a man of the most ferocious sense of obligation. And great kindness to people, great kindness. . . . And I heard him say this, "I figure this whole country has made a mistake about the Negro, you see, this whole tragedy. The Negro. I've never known one that if you didn't treat him right he wouldn't treat you right." This was his attitude toward every man. I mean, he was a very rigorously ethical man.

FARRELL: Then you weren't taken to church?

WARREN: We went to Sunday school to familiarize ourselves with the Bible. Except as children under twelve, we weren't made to go to church. Now, my father made me read the Bible. He paid me to read the Bible.

FARRELL: He paid you to read the Bible!

WARREN: He was interested that I read it. He said, "Now, you ought to know this book. It's a foundation of society."

FARRELL: For him it was literature, a social, cultural document. This is why it was part of your education.

WARREN: That's right. He paid me to learn it. I read the whole thing, three times at least.

FARRELL: Did this kind of thing spur your interest in writing?

WARREN: No, I had no desire to write in those years. I wanted to be a naval officer. . . .

FARRELL: But you didn't go.

WARREN: No, I had an accident. . . . I went off to Vanderbilt, and there I made lifelong friends.

FARRELL: Who were they? Tate, of course.

WARREN: Yes, Tate and John Crowe Ransom. At that early time he wasn't treating me special, just like any other student, but later on he was much like a father to me, and advised me, but never aggressively. He never said, "You're my protégé," or anything, thank God. . . .

FARRELL: What did . . . [Ransom] tell you to read?

WARREN: I don't know. All the obvious things, I guess. He'd never studied any English. He was a classicist. He took classics at Oxford, concentrating on philosophy, and was one of the first American Rhodes Scholars who made an impression as a classical scholar.

FARRELL: That an American could do it in classics? He impressed them in England?

WARREN: Yeah. And he majored in Greek philosophy, so he was of a very speculative mind and widely read in philosophy, but never tried to get technical. Ideas were treated as, well, as the Greeks must have treated them.

FARRELL: Did this sort of classic background come out in his classroom all the time? Was he quoting the classic philosophers or speaking . . .

WARREN: He referred to them now and then, but there was never any "side" to Ransom at all.

FARRELL: Who brought *The Waste Land* to Vanderbilt? Ransom, because he'd been at Oxford?

WARREN: No, Ransom didn't even like *The Waste Land* very well. Tate was a great influence there; he invented modernism, you might say, for Vanderbilt.

FARRELL: But he was a student like yourself.

WARREN: He was a student—he was six years older than I—but he was also a genius. He taught modernism to Ransom. I mean, they quarreled about it all the time.

FARRELL: And Ransom came around to accepting the instruction?

WARREN: They both learned from each other. Tate would say that Ransom was great. And he was, and maybe the best kind of teacher, when he caught fire, thought out loud. We will have but a few that good, you know, when the roll is called up yonder. Ransom was a calm, gentle man, small, but extremely handsome in a kind of benign way, a good athlete, a crack golfer. He said he wanted to be known as a domestic poet, he had loved domestic life so much.

FARRELL: Home life.

WARREN: Yes, his home. It was a sort of second home to me, I was there so much. He and his wife, Robb Reavill, lived near the campus and had quite a few students over often. They had all sorts of games, volleyball, and bowling, and their whole life was a game. They all worked, but work was play, too. Just a different kind of play.

FARRELL: Quite different from your background, wasn't it?

WARREN: Yes, in that play was not a common thing—playful*ness* and humor. My background was rather lacking in humor. It wasn't lacking in this little streak of intellectuality.

FARRELL: No, no, I see that, but here they were combined; after all, Ransom was intellectual as well.

WARREN: Yeah, Ransom, he was a high-powered intellectual.

FARRELL: And here you began to make a number of friends and to write.

WARREN: And girls, don't forget girls. But the people I knew who were writers there, I liked best. . . . Tate, he was a rather learned man, and he was a very powerful personality, and he was a great influence on the Nashville group. There's no question about that. One thing I heard Ransom say about him once, "I wish I had Tate's gift of knowing my own mind in five minutes about a poem." Tate had an incredible range of reading and certitude and a real passion for thinking things through, you see.

FARRELL: Are you talking about a sharp, analytic mind?

WARREN: Yes, on the relation of literature to ideas, to society, those things, you see, he was very astute about them. He was a great reader; he forgot nothing. He would take a little poem of mine and he would give it a kind of treatment you couldn't believe, telling you what the poem was like, pointing out possibilities.

FARRELL: Did Tate continue to play this part in your career, in your literature?

WARREN: Well, even right now, I mean till he got so ill, we would always swap poems and write each other about each other's poems. One thing is happening as you get older: you get fewer and fewer people you can send poems to and who write to you and fewer people that want you to write about their poems. But Tate was my most powerful critic, because he was the one I knew best, at the time. Later I was at the Ransom house, almost a second home. But in the early times there were Tate and Ridley Wills, who took me out first to the Fugitives. Once there, I got something from all of them.

FARRELL: In this group of Fugitives, was Tate remarkable?

WARREN: Well, I wouldn't say he was more remarkable than Ransom, even than Davidson, but they were different. Also, he was the most modern. He had really made it up before he knew the work of Eliot or Crane. Tate was more my own age. He would take a poem on my typewriter and start giving me a lecture.

FARRELL: I suppose that what was remarkable about that group in Nashville anyway was that there was more than one. You often have one bright or special person . . .

WARREN: Yeah, but they all were all strong personalities. Very strong personalities.

FARRELL: This was the caldron you were dropped into at the age of seventeen.

WARREN: Sixteen, to be exact. And they were terrific personalities. Davidson was a marvelous teacher and a marvelously brilliant man and I think a damn fool in certain ways. But Davidson and I remained dear friends to the end, and I'd go see him every time I could, and he would always forgive me. Call me a damn fool, and then start the friendship over again.

FARRELL: Oh, he thought you were a damn fool, just as you thought he was.

WARREN: Yeah, on the race question, you see, and then we'd forget that and then talk about poetry. But Davidson was an extraordinary teacher, just extraordinary. I can't believe my own luck in having found these people at the right age for me.

FARRELL: And it was just luck.

WARREN: Pure luck. Why would I want to go to Harvard? These people, they were thinking beyond the time they lived in.

FARRELL: What interests me is this: did the South, did the Civil War have something to do with this new gestation that was occurring at Vanderbilt?

WARREN: I don't know. *The Fugitive*, you see, in its first editorial—this was before my time—they said they fled from nothing more than from the South of the magnolia.

FARRELL: And they weren't fleeing toward the Northeast, they were . . . what were they fleeing toward? You flee from something.

WARREN: They were trying to create something.

FARRELL: A new South, a new Southern tradition.

WARREN: Well, "a new South" has the wrong . . .

FARRELL: "A new South" has come to take on another meaning.

WARREN: Yeah, but some of these people were also much influenced by the Irish situation.

FARRELL: What Irish situation?

WARREN: The Irish were colonial people to the English, and a primitive people to the English, or a retarded people, against the great, powerful industrial organization, and they somehow managed to see through it and write their poems.

FARRELL: What particular Irishmen?

WARREN: You could take their whole Irish of the time, from Synge or Yeats or . . .

FARRELL: And Synge and Yeats were known to these people in Nashville and you think they consciously . . .

WARREN: Of course. They talked about the Irish and the Southern question. I heard them talk about it. They saw certain parallels. And also they saw great differences. For instance, there was no racial or religious cohesion in the South that would give the South the Irish stamina to keep on. And there were certain parallels. They were certainly aware of the parallels. Now they were skeptically and exploratorily aware of them; they weren't taking this as a model, you see. They weren't going to have an Easter uprising or anything like that.

FARRELL: But they were aware that Ireland had this magnificent literature and that the colonial status had something to do with this. And they were aware that the South had some parallel position.

WARREN: Mississippi, which is the most illiterate state in the Union, having all those riots . . .

FARRELL: And people like Hodding Carter,[38] you know, the Greenville . . .

WARREN: Yeah, I knew him well, he was an old friend of mine. But the primitive people—I say primitive in the sense of the South or Ireland—have some special human relation to each other, which is not possible in a great megalopolitan society.

And they know each other differently. They know families, they don't know persons. They have a sense of shared history.

FARRELL: Yes. They've known a family for generations.

WARREN: And they all have a common history. Black people have said to me, the Southern white man and the Southern black man have the same history. They've got the same problems and the same history. They can understand each other. Or, rather, there is a better chance there, in the end.

FARRELL: Whereas, the Northern black man and the Northern white man profess to be liberal . . .

WARREN: It's bullshit.

FARRELL: They can't understand each other. They're not speaking the same language.

WARREN: They're not speaking the same language. And I've heard several of . . . one girl who's gone through the mill, of prison in Mississippi and all the rest of it, says to me, "Well, if an Alabama sheriff shoots you, he knows he's killed a human being because he probably knows your name. And in New York City, he doesn't give a damn."

FARRELL: Another body, another animal.

WARREN: Another body. And I said years ago, it's not going to be too long before Mississippi's going to be sending freedom riders to Boston, and by God, they're already doing it.

FARRELL: So you had this great experience at Vanderbilt. Why did you go way out to California right after that, after graduating?

WARREN: As soon as I finished Vanderbilt, I wanted to go as many places as I could. So I went to San Francisco first, as far away as I could get. I was following scholarships by now, you see. I went to Berkeley, where I had a scholarship, and I went to Yale, where I had a scholarship.

FARRELL: You went to these places chiefly because of the scholarship? Or because they were far away?

WARREN: Both. I wasn't applying to a place nearby, anyway. I could have stayed at California, but I did what I wanted— I switched to Yale, just kept on the same thing at Yale.

FARRELL: Were there any writers at Berkeley? Was there any group like you'd left behind?

WARREN: There were a lot of writers there, but they hadn't heard the news.

FARRELL: What news?

WARREN: They hadn't any idea what modern literature was.

FARRELL: How about Yale?

WARREN: Well, at Yale, Tucker Brook, the Elizabethan, in Shakespeare, was just marvelous. And Old French that I took with [Robert] Menner. Menner was a great man.

FARRELL: How about the rest of Yale? Was it a stimulating place, more stimulating than Berkeley?

WARREN: Well, the students were not. I would say there were two men I met there with whom I became great friends. Dixon Wecter was one of them, one of the most brilliant men I've ever known. And I liked a man named Randall Stewart, who later became head of the department at Vanderbilt.

· · · · · · · · · · · ·

FARRELL: How would you contrast prose and poetry?

WARREN: Poetry to me is not something you do after you get it fixed in your mind. Poetry is a way of thinking, or a way of feeling; it's a way of exploring. I don't start writing a novel until I've got it in my head. Now, it's not going to be the same novel, but I've got *a* novel in my head.

FARRELL: You have a blueprint.

WARREN: But I don't write that way. However, one novel I did by writing a complete outline, from start to finish, and it was about eighty pages long. Almost every paragraph was indicated in the outline. I spent months doing that. And thinking it through, and trying to make notes on it, and then writing a consecutive narrative for it. And I hated writing the book so much that I threw the outline away. Because it was killing the sense of discovery in the writing of the book. But there is a certain kind of that preliminary work that must be done—the gradual growth of plot and the discovery of meaning, all in your head before you start writing. Anyway, by nature there is more cold, mechanical preparation in a novel than there is in the poems. In the poems, you are looking at a different level of your being.

FARRELL: Would you say there's more finish to a prose work, that poetry is less finished?

WARREN: No, I'm talking about the question of exploring the self and the world through the process of composing the work. That is, the poetry is more that process, and I don't plan a poem that way.

FARRELL: How about a big narrative poem, like "Billie Potts"?

WARREN: Then you do plan that in a way. You have to. But you can't plan until you've had the intuition of what you want the poem to mean. But you don't do an outline for it—no notes. I never wrote a note on a poem in my life. And I've long since stopped making notes about prose. After that one terrible experience with having a whole novel reduced to eighty pages and then just trying to type it all into words and expand it. I quit that and just tried to get my imagination going again. That turned out to be *Heaven's Gate*, and I'll never do an outline again. What I do is get the basic novel in my mind and think of it in terms of movements. Now these are not chapters, these are movements.

FARRELL: In the musical sense?

WARREN: In the musical sense, almost. Get it reduced to that and the equivalent feelings that are tied to these movements. And then I would sit down and on one page I would have my notes on the movements before I start. That's all I'll have written down. I want to be free to maneuver.

FARRELL: By movement, do you mean actually the plot and the characters?

WARREN: Yes, I involve everything. It's a stage of development, a stage of being of the novel, a stage in the dialectic, too. The content I carry mostly in my head. Finding these movements is the big thing that takes two or three years, sometimes twenty years, as in the case of *The Cave*. Then, I start writing, the simplest, most direct way at the first part of it. But then I carry three stacks of papers. I have my

typewriter with what I've been working on. Then after I've
got the first chapter done, I read it over. I read each page
over, too, each page. I want to write each page as well as
I can while I'm doing it. So I revise each page as I go along.
And then I get through the chapter, and I read it and I say
to myself, now, how could it be better? Is it something really
I wanted to do? And if I find things I want to add to it, I
make a stack of papers to add to that chapter. Sometimes
these notes may be four or five pages long, each one. Sometimes there will be a whole scene written out, free hand.
Those things *to be done* in revision. Then, as it gets longer,
then we have to look backwards, and then you also have to
be thinking forward all the time. So you accumulate either
a pile of notes, or more scenes, or analyses. You've got a
great stack of stuff saying go back through this much, and
you've got a pile looking forward, with you between at
the end. You go back to the beginning, turn the pile over,
and start all over, and go back. So this thing has grown, has
had a natural growth on which you then can bring your
intellectual criticism to bear in terms of what you had felt
to be at the time naturally growing out of the work you
were doing.

FARRELL: What is the process you go through in your poetry?
WARREN: Oh, I go through many revisions. Then maybe I
  throw the whole thing away. Often I do three or four versions. And then, there's *Brother to Dragons*. I had always
  wanted to rewrite the poem and I finally did.

. . . .

FARRELL: What motivates you to make all these revisions in
  your poetry?
WARREN: I always send poetry to friends. As you get older
  you have fewer friends to send it to who have the time or
  the inclination to reply. That's one of the terrible things
  about having bright friends when you're young who will
  write you long letters about your poems, as Ransom or Tate
  would. Now they're fewer, they're younger. The old ones
  are not up to it anymore.

FARRELL: Is the criticism as good, though, coming from the younger . . .

WARREN: Well, it can be good. It can be perfectly right, but I mean people like Bill Meredith and John Hollander and Harold Bloom and Mark Strand. I send them poems, and they blue-pencil it and write back letters about it, talk to me about it.

FARRELL: The process of putting this poem down. You've described it as, would you say, more experimental, or less structured?

WARREN: I would say it's less structured. I'm trying to see all the time the whole structure of the poem. I'm not just writing blind. There may even be a plot. The poem called "Red-Tailed Hawk," for instance, which appeared in the *New Yorker*. That had some sort of plot. I killed the damned hawk and stuffed the damn hawk and then the hawk was standing on my bookshelf for years, and then I burned the hawk (and I lied a little bit there; I didn't burn the hawk, I just threw him away). I didn't write that down as plot; I didn't want to commit myself to it. I wanted to write and see how the actions happened. You're dealing with something which is much more fluid and mercurial and you're trying to be open to possibility.

FARRELL: Could you make some remarks about your favorite poems—or ones through which you discovered some important things?

WARREN: Well, "Billie Potts" was a poem I found out something by. It's always been a kind of narrative streak in my poetry—or hints of narrative. It was primarily a philosophical poem—a poem about American history, philosophy of American history, and you can carry it farther if you want to, theological—and then a ballad. Now, I fused those two, but I began the process quite unconsciously. I remember the very day when I walked across the snow, across the campus of the University of Minnesota, when I began composing it. And I composed the first stanza or two while walking along, roughly, and rewrote later. Something else, you see, putting two things together that I had been fumbling at before but had never done.

FARRELL: Any other poems?

WARREN: I would mention one, much earlier, called "Monologue at Midnight." And another one—it's always anthologized—about the bearded oaks, a poem of two lovers: "Bearded Oaks."

FARRELL: How about anything in *Promises?*

WARREN: *Promises* was discovery, starting all over again. From 1944 to '54 I must have started fifty poems, had gotten three or four lines or ten lines and threw them away, couldn't carry them through. One thing, I was tied up in fiction. One thing, I had, I guess, more personal problems than I should have had, and another thing, I was fumbling stylistically, writing my fiction at that time, too. And I guess I was more deeply engrossed in fiction than I was in poetry at this time.

FARRELL: To the point of actually interfering with your poetry?

WARREN: Yes. But in '54, suddenly a new place, a new time, a new life. Also, I had been into more abstract subjects. Now I began poems more directly from the concrete.

·   ·   ·   ·   ·   ·   ·   ·   ·   ·   ·   ·

WARREN: And while we're on poems, I just finished a book of poems. [It appeared in 1978 as *Now and Then: Poems, 1976–1978.*] It's a big one. New ones. I've had two years since the other book was published.

FARRELL: You mean the *Selected Poems.*

WARREN: Yeah, I had a big period. Now I don't know if it was good or bad. I say a big one, getting a book done, a pretty good-sized book done.

FARRELL: How many poems are in it?

WARREN: I've got forty-five, I guess, but one of them is very long. Some of them are four or five lines long and one of them has thirty sections; it's big. The book is divided into three parts. The first part of the book is called "Nostalgic." Now they're mostly poems that go back, like the baseball player poem and things like that. And "The Hawk." I would say some of them are purely fictional, but I mean they go back to that period, they belong to a period of life. The second period is "Speculative," the second group. Now, they are less tied to place, and they are more tied to idea. They sometimes reach into place, and actually Vermont is the setting for most of them. And the third is the long poem which is a poem about . . . [When published, the book had only two sections.]

FARRELL: You had a close association with one of the most famous poets of our era, Robert Lowell. He was a student of yours at LSU, wasn't he? Why did he come to LSU? Did Ransom send him down?

WARREN: Oh, yes, Ransom sent him down, and subsequently his wife [Jean Stafford] became the secretary of *The Southern Review*. And Cal [Lowell] took graduate work with me and then Cal and I locked up the doors several days a week at twelve o'clock and had a sandwich and a quick Coke and then we read Dante for two hours. I had just learned enough Italian to read Dante, and he was then in the process of learning it, and we read, argued, and it converted him before the year was over.

FARRELL: Converted him to what, Dante?

WARREN: Catholicism.

FARRELL: You mean this is the point of his conversion? Dante was?

WARREN: Before he started reading Dante, he wasn't, and when he got through, he was. I was away part of that time, so I wasn't there when the crisis came, and Father [Maurice] Schexnayder used to lend us books, a Catholic chaplain, used to lend us books on certain saints and on certain theological points we would be interested in, and he got hooked about that time. I'm sure there was a lot of thinking behind that— I mean, including Allen Tate and including a lot of other people. Cal wrote a poem about me for the Vanderbilt literary magazine that began last year. The magazine had several poems by mostly poet friends of mine, including the poem by Cal.

FARRELL: Was this the poem that is in *Day by Day,* called "Louisiana State University in 1940"?

WARREN: A line about a class of mine appears, and . . .

FARRELL: He says, "And listen to Robert Penn Warren talk for hours about Machiavelli, Cesare Borgia, and . . . sitting in a green seminar room." And another place he speaks of you and quotes a line of yours that's in *Selected Poems,* a line that really struck him, and he says, "An old master still engaging the dazzled disciple." Is that the way he thought of you? Was he your disciple in that way?

WARREN: I never thought of it as such. We were on very different tracks altogether.

FARRELL: He speaks admiringly of you because you were both a poet and a novelist, and he says something like this, "I'm just a poet, so I'll just speak about your poetry."

WARREN: He was very hot about the last book, not the *Selected Poems,* but the *Or Else.* He was very high on it; I get that from certain sources. We saw each other a lot for a while. And he and I used to have lunch together in New York a lot. But there were reasons why we never saw each other's families . . .

FARRELL: Well, what was he like there in 1940?

WARREN: He was good company, eager and good company.

FARRELL: Was he naïve?

WARREN: He was always kind of naïve, he was always a naïf of one kind or another. And a calculated naïf, too. But he had charm and he had great intelligence and he read widely, and he could be wonderfully good company. I enjoyed my company with him in that period and later in New York I saw him quite a bit. But I think . . . but you talk about a man who was really mad, is what it amounts to, it comes to that, he was on his way. I don't know how you estimate it.

FARRELL: What hit him?

WARREN: I don't know anything about it. I can't know what hit him—what do I know about it?

FARRELL: It may not have been anything, it may have just been . . .

WARREN: It happens to people, whatever it is, it happens to

people, all sorts of things. All I can say is that I had a period when I saw a lot of him and I liked his society a lot, and we saw each other out and we talked and argued a lot. I loved his poetry; it was tremendously fine. But I think his last whole phase is just . . . self-exploitation, and I think it's pretty crazy.

The Oral Roots
of Literature

William C. Forrest and Cornelius Novelli of LeMoyne College interviewed Warren on the Yale University campus on October 21, 1977. The interview was published in The Sewanee Review *in the summer of 1981.*

WILLIAM C. FORREST: How important do you believe the sound
of poetry is?

WARREN: No sound, no poetry. We know the sound works on
us; we speak it or we hear it in more than one dimension.
We have a whole muscular apparatus working in the mouth,
for example.

There is a whole combination of experiences going on at
the same time. The semantic content of the words sets off
emotional vibrations—their tension or relaxation—in a person's being, whether the speaker or listener. There is also
the emotional effect of the imagery that is set off by the
words. And the imagery is of two kinds. One is felt imagery,
an imagery which is muscular and neural. Another kind of

imagery is that of the metaphors and references—this can come from a sensory reference to an object or from a metaphorical use of language. But all of these things combine; they all belong to language. And there is no way to separate these various aspects of the poem from one another—except by rapid reading, which is really a way of not reading except for pure information.

But literature, in contrast to journalism and science, is a use of language in its fullest dimensions. It's experience we're concerned with, and experience is a very complex thing—from what's being said on through all the dimensions of language itself. And the relations established among all the dimensions of language have the most extraordinary power, especially when we are dealing with great art.

CORNELIUS NOVELLI: Do you recall, when you were a child, having literature read aloud to you?

WARREN: Well, yes, from the very earliest. . . . I learned to read from "Horatius at the Bridge" because there must have been a thousand times my father had read it, and finally he said: "I'm not going to read that poem one more time; you must know that poem by heart; read it yourself." It was my favorite poem at that time—the age of six. I picked it up and, by God, I was reading. Slow and fumbling—but reading. It was a poem of sound.

My schooling—grade school, I mean—was old-fashioned, too. In some classes we had Friday afternoon recitations in which students memorized poems and said them by heart, badly or well, good poems or bad poems. The same thing was true when I went to Clarksville to high school. I remember "The Skeleton in Armor" to this day. Good or bad the poems may have been, but at least it was recognized that the poem existed as verbal art. It wasn't just something on a page; it was an *action* you took part in, an action that affected you, and affected your hearers. I'm not talking about elocution, about the way to render a poem dramatically in reading, but about simply surrendering yourself to the spoken possibilities of language, something as simple as that.

Let's go one step farther. Most readers of poetry and most poets don't read poetry aloud except off and on. But they have a habit of making the subvocal reading of poetry or prose as full an experience as the actual reading aloud. Their bodies are so trained, their feelings are so adjusted by experience, that they don't need it read aloud. The unspoken reading, the subvocal reading, which has all the physical responses and all the emotional responses, may actually be more effective than any oral reading you can muster.

NOVELLI: In other words, they're so well trained at reading poetry that, like well-trained musicians, they can hear it under the score.

WARREN: They hear it, but as an inner experience rather than as a performance aloud.

FORREST: Do you feel that before a reader gets to the stage in which the sensory qualities come through in a silent reading, a certain amount of learning has to take place by actually reading aloud?

WARREN: Yes, it must become a natural process. Even as late as when I was in freshman English at Vanderbilt, one quarter we were supposed to memorize seven hundred to one thousand lines of verse. We were tested on it, with a bonus for anything memorized beyond the assigned minimum. Then, being mad for poetry, I spent all my time memorizing and got a big bonus. Very easy: I liked that system. It wasn't tyranny; you had ordinary college students all memorizing, say, a thousand lines of Tennyson in a quarter. It was natural; that was the whole system. Life has changed; now it's tyranny to memorize a quatrain in a schoolroom.

FORREST: It seems to me that in the fourth edition of *Understanding Poetry* and in the fifth edition of *An Approach to Literature*, you and Mr. Brooks advise students to read poetry aloud more often and perhaps with more detailed advice than you had in the earlier editions.

WARREN: In the earlier editions we assumed that this was done. I assumed it because I had always done it myself. But in fact it was a real issue, you see; it was necessary to insist on it.

FORREST: And so you were giving that advice on principle.

WARREN: On principle. I guess we were just not previously aware how much the oral reading of poetry had fallen off.

FORREST: Can you spell out some of the advantages for the student of reading poetry aloud?

WARREN: Well, first I would say this. Most unpoetical children from, say, six to ten, once they begin to learn poetry, try to act it out. They want to convert poetry to a stance or a position. I've seen this happen over and over again with my own children and with other children too. They recognize immediately that this is a drama, that every poetic form is a drama of some kind. And every form of poetry *is* a drama. A speaker is speaking to some occasion and to some audience. Uncorrupted by bad teaching, the child will, if he has to memorize poetry, almost instinctively move toward the dramatization of it.

Now this is turning your question around. That is, the mere fact of knowing or reading out loud, or knowing the poem and memorizing the poem—and these things are tied together—gives you the sense of the poem as drama. It gives you a role, as it were, to act out, or maybe several roles.

A second advantage that comes to the student who reads poetry aloud, over and above the natural dramatic involvement, arises from the fact that the language of poetry, or to some degree the language of any real piece of literature, is not merely a set of verbal equivalents or equal signs. Literary language is a fundamental experience, a coherent experience; and it affects the body. The body naturally *wants* to participate in this thing and to get its share of the experience. The expression of any piece of good writing, prose or poetry, depends on this capacity of the writer to write in such a way that these natural responses are summoned up and are tied to certain emotional or intellectual effects.

NOVELLI: You think, then, that a writer should be acutely aware of his language as a physical action and a physical experience?

WARREN: All I can do is be personal here. I can't imagine writing a poem without writing it in my head, talking about it. Or, if you can't talk while you are swimming, composing it in your head—what you're hearing in your head while swim-

ming. You would knock off a long thought during a mile of
swimming, write the poem. You would combine the two
things because the use of the muscles in the regular rhythm
of swimming drains away distractions. The mind floats, as it
were, feels its own way, leads its own life for a change. The
words are coming as heard. Running is another thing you
can do, long-distance running, or just sitting in a chair and
staring at nothing. You have to somehow detach yourself
from the distractions of the physical world. And physical activity can do that; it's rhythmical, even a kind of hypnosis.

FORREST: You have said that literature is a knowledge by enactment.

WARREN: I think it is. It's the taking of roles. It's enactment,
and part of it is the unconscious. It's natural. It's so natural
for you it's unconscious.

Let's compare two lines of poetry in the same meter:
Pope's line "And wretches hang that jurymen may dine";
and Shakespeare's line when Antony is coming back from
the Battle of Actium, deserted in the battle by Cleopatra, and
asks his sword-bearer Eros to kill him: "Unarm, Eros, the
long day's task is done." Pope's satiric line is in the front of
the mouth; it's a contemptuous act of spitting. It's physically
in the mouth. You're enacting this contemptible world; you're
spitting on it.

FORREST: And Pope shaped his language in such a way that as
you utter it, the language imitates the idea.

WARREN: You can't say it any other way: "And wretches hang
that jurymen may dine." It's spitting. But in Antony's line
there is a total heavy relaxation; it's all played well back in
the throat. It's the placement that makes the difference there:
"Unarm, Eros, the long day's task is done." It's open-mouthed,
not the tight spitting effect in Pope's line. Now in these lines
the body is enacting a basic role in the speech. And when
you have added this to the whole context of *Antony and
Cleopatra* it takes on a massive meaning. The same is true of
Pope's line: the body is enacting meaning: the contempt of
the world's contempt of justice. Constantly language is demanding, is providing (inviting rather) the enactment of

meaning in your physical body. It can be carried farther when a child or a grown man actually has a sense of the drama in poetry. He paces about the room and quotes poetry to himself—a piece of poetry he's trying to write or poetry he is reading. He's a real ham. Language invites it; all language invites it.

NOVELLI: What has happened, though, is that teachers have somehow found a way to teach poetry without ever getting into the dimensions of voice and physical enactment.

WARREN: They have; and what that means is that the teaching of poetry is on the skids. Along with a lot else.

FORREST: How did you become aware, by the time you were doing the fourth edition of *Understanding Poetry*, that it was necessary to recommend the oral reading of poetry?

WARREN: I began to be aware that fewer and fewer of my literary students—Yale seniors, say—could quote anything. After long and fancy and expensive educations.

And we had begun to be more and more aware that, in the whole world around us, the notion of language as pure, as a set of mere signs or equivalences, was dominant. Rapid reading, for instance. Rapid reading is the death of literature. It's a useful accomplishment if you can turn it on or off when you want it on or off. But it's the death of literature.

NOVELLI: Because literature has roots in the spoken word.

WARREN: Because it has roots in the spoken word and the echo from the spoken word is important in literature, it gives life to literature. Even with prose the speed is not really the point. I can be a rather fast reader of prose and still get the effect of a decent prose as opposed to a bad prose. I say "I" because I know about myself. I know many people who can do this. It's a sense of awareness which is instinctively cultivated. It's not something to be measured in terms of a watch. It takes education in rapid reading to make a man only half a man.

FORREST: There is an element in your own poetry which is firmly public. It isn't a private or esoteric poetry but a public poetry. Do you feel there is any connection between this quality and your sense of poetry as spoken?

WARREN: What do you mean by *public*?

FORREST: By public I have in mind a poetry that is working to be fully communicative with its audience. First of all, by way of example, it strikes me that your openings move to achieve immediate attention. In other words, right from the start, you're already communicating. Does that strike a note with you?

WARREN: It does. The great battle of the poem is won or lost in the first line, or the first five lines anyway. If you don't get into motion by then, it's probably going to be dead. You can have a great ending, but you better have a new start.

FORREST: Do you believe, though, that that quality of your openings is connected with your sense of poetry as rooted in speech?

WARREN: I couldn't say yes or no to that. I could say yes and no definitely about the question of poetry itself. That is, I want to catch the eye in the opening; I want something to hook there. It's public in that sense. But not yet fulfilled. It's a start. But the word *public* is tricky. The question is always *public* to whom?

FORREST: So that it entices the reader . . .

WARREN: It entices because it ends where the reader catches the scent of raw meat. It's like playing a fish. I should *hope* a poem would be public in the sense of establishing a need for communication first. Readers should be asking, "What's next?" Now part of this is a sense of unfulfilled rhythm, an unfulfilled sense of language. The language itself carries a sense of unfulfillment.

NOVELLI: Then you really have a strong sense that rhythms are not merely metrical phenomena but are living things that you can feel coming to an end or not coming to an end.

WARREN: Yes. I think that any poem that's competently done is a closed arch. You start an arch and you come to rest with it. Ideally—and there is no ideal poem written—a poem will lead to the closing of the circuit. And one of the participating factors is the question of the verbal drive rather than merely the rhythm, because rhythm is only one aspect of the verbal drive. I'd say you *could* make it a matter of rhythm and discuss that alone. But this should also be related to the kind of drive the subject has too. Now, if we think of the characteristic rhythm of John Donne as opposed to the characteristic rhythm of Robert Frost, you see right away that we're talking about two kinds of people. The holy sonnets of John Donne against the poetry of Robert Frost: well, it's just like night and day. I don't mean good or bad; I'm just saying they're different. The whole personality is in that one factor, if you want to put it that way.

NOVELLI: It's ultimately the sound of a particular person talking. You certainly hear Donne arguing with you or talking to some surrogate listener, someone who's out there.

WARREN: Yes, well he's talking to himself, really. Of course, in one sense he's always talking to himself. He has to play audience too, as well as speaker. He has to play double.

If you take the opening of Donne's ninth holy sonnet, "If poisonous minerals, and if that tree," that first line is not fulfilled rhythmically. We have a syntactic need: the sense is not completed yet; the rhythm is not completed yet unless we are thinking of rhythm as an abstraction. We want more of this; the line is asking us to push on. "Whose fruit threw death"—it's knotted. Instead of being straight iambic, "Whose fruit threw death" is all spondaic, all accented. Then next comes "on else immortal us." We don't know what the "if" is about yet. But we find a contrast that means something: "Whose fruit threw death" (a moment of human damnation in the garden scene); and then suddenly "on else immortal us" (he is sadly, nostalgically, looking back on what could have been but isn't possible). You see how that line is balanced on that contrast: "Whose fruit threw death on else immortal us."

Then "If lecherous goats, if serpents envious / Cannot be damned; alas, why should I be?" It has fulfilled its movement. "Why should I be?" picks up and echoes that second line beginning "Whose fruit threw death"; it's a spondee that answers it. "Why should I be?"—you can't tell how to accent it even: it's spondaic but not *spondees*; it's hovering. And now your poem has set the question. It's finally put the hook into flesh. It has also put it in by playing with two kinds of rhythm that are involved in this, the rhythm of salvation and the rhythm of damnation. The knotted spondaic rhythms become the rhythms of damnation. And the others, the released iambics, are the rhythms of salvation, the backward look, you see.

You feel it as a going concern; at each stage it's going to another stage. Now, you feel, having gotten this far, then what? It isn't just an episode: it's part of a whole. And when you come to the end, you know you're there.

FORREST: The other founders of analytic criticism, for instance John Crowe Ransom and Allen Tate, were they enthusiastic readers aloud?

WARREN: I'm sure they were. Anyone who writes poetry reads it aloud. And having taken classes from Ransom, I know he read a great deal of poetry aloud regularly in class in order to discuss it. He almost never discussed poetry without reading it aloud. His constant effort was to make people hear it, and hear it in relation to the poem as drama, although he didn't use that word, I think.

NOVELLI: When you're writing fiction, do you have a strong sense of the characters' voices?

WARREN: I read it out loud. I always read it out loud; I have to. It's a habit of mine after writing a paragraph silently to read it out loud several times.

NOVELLI: And this leads to improvements?

WARREN: It leads to changes, I hope improvements, but certainly to changes. It's a matter of always reading aloud at some stage. Now in poetry it's usually aloud first. It's talking, or talking in my head—really the same experience if you've sort of sunk yourself into the business as I have. But it has to have its moments of the real voice. I mean the spoken voice.

NOVELLI: At the beginning of *All the King's Men* you describe that moment when the crowd is in front of the courthouse, and Willie Stark begins talking to the farmers. There's an almost mystical strength of personality being carried here by the voice, the voice itself. I don't know if you've reflected much on the way you talk about . . .

WARREN: I don't have reflections on how. If it works I'm glad, but I know such a thing can be *true* because I've seen it work over and over again, on the hustings and in cock-fighting pits and other places. The voice is nothing but a noise in the beginning; bit by bit it *becomes* a voice and is developing in people's ears, in people's beings, as they recognize it as a voice. You can see it happening. Of course the experts at political address and so forth know how to manipulate it.

FORREST: It's been said that the South is an *oral* culture, at least in contrast to the North. Do you believe that the oral nature of southern culture was important in your own development?

WARREN: I don't know, I can't be different from what I am, but I do know this: that when I was a child a party would always wind up with tale-telling. But in the 1930's too—in Tennessee. This might be a very decorous party, or might be some men sitting around with bourbon in their hands. Or it might wind up with people acting parts, or playing old-fashioned charades, or one narrator acting all the parts. This was very common, very common indeed. And all classes of people, mind you. It might be tenant farmers, or it might be the man who owned the farm. Or it might even be an eminent professor. It would be the same thing. It was an oral society, and as somebody said, conversation is cheap. It was a long way to the movies, and it cost two bits to get in. In the 1930's this was a characteristic of many parties in Tennessee, including some of the faculty of Vanderbilt University. People like Andrew Lytle, who was a trained actor, on the one hand, and people like myself, certainly not a trained actor, on the other—but people telling tales, acting or half-acting tales. But now *I* haven't heard people sitting around telling tales in many years. They tell *jokes.*

NOVELLI: It's not the same thing.

WARREN: It's not the same thing at all because a joke doesn't require any characterization. A joke is a switch of some kind, and it's usually something you're outside of.

Now it's certainly also true that the sermon-going and

political rallies and so forth in the South were very common when I was a boy, even a grown man. The political passion was halfway a passion for rhetoric, for speech. And it was not just a matter of opinions. It was a matter of entertainment, of how good is that man at his job, you know. He ought to be worth listening to, whichever side he was on. But that's going out fast. TV is killing that off.

FORREST: Do you have the feeling that this was also important for other writers from the South?

WARREN: I can't say how important it was, but I know it existed. I would say that it was generally important, for the simple reason that the good ones and the bad ones all show some effect of it. I mean of course spoken language that has quotation marks around it but also has sometimes affected general style. It is important, much more important in some cases. There is no reason why it should last any longer because the social habits have disappeared. And we are becoming a more or less homogenized nation. I'm not saying what's good and what's bad; I'm just saying that there was a difference. Of course, poverty makes for conversation. It's cheap.

FORREST: In the whole movement of literary analysis, hasn't there been a fairly widespread sense that the results of literary analysis should be constantly tested at least in the inner voice or in an inner-imaginative process of speech? If analysis suggests the possibility of irony in a passage by reason of connotation or allusion, or the slant of the syntax, isn't the tendency to try to verify the hypothesis about the tone of the passage by reading the passage aloud or to the inner ear to see if everything in the language will fit that ironic tone of voice?

WARREN: I'd say yes right away. I don't think we need worry over it. It's clear as day to me that you can't analyze without knowing what you're analyzing. If you don't know before you start, what *are* you analyzing? You have to know before you can talk about it at all. And if you're communicating to a class or to a friend, then you may dramatize it. But I don't have any theory about that. I do know that you have to have some conviction about the meaning of a passage before you can talk about it. You have to come to grips with it yourself.

And irony is more than verbal: I mean an irony in events. Even when a man says nothing. There is a book on the silences of Shakespeare, what they mean. Or when somebody might speak but doesn't—that's another case. But it still is associated with the same kind of thing. The nonsaid then becomes the said, and has its own tone of silence as it were. It's a part of the same picture.

NOVELLI: My students were doing the scene with the rebels in *Henry IV*, Part One, where they quarrel over the map. And I was assigning the parts and suddenly realized that although Worcester says nothing, his silence is the most important thing in that scene. He's watching the whole thing come apart before him.

WARREN: In *Richard II* it's the same thing. Richard talks, talks, talks, talks; and Bolingbroke says nothing. But you build a kind of silence in there, and you know what that silence means.

FORREST: Would you say that in giving the self to the reading of literature, what's important is to match yourself with what's there in the literature?

WARREN: I think the point is to give yourself to it so you yourself become aware of these things. The matching is in the density of the response, the fullness of the response. The awareness that goes with it is what's important, rather than being able to turn yourself into the perfect performer. You're turning yourself into the perfect *audience*. That's what you really are doing.

FORREST: Do you enjoy reading your poetry to an audience?

WARREN: Yes and no. I've never done it systematically except two or three years ago. I went on the road, some weeks reading every night. An agent would have somebody there to get me to the train or plane on time, and so forth for two weeks. I made a business of it, but it's a very tiring business. I'd like to do it four or five times a year, maybe. If you make it a business, it can kill you.

NOVELLI: Do you find that audience response shapes your own delivery?

WARREN: It does indeed. One thing is really important to me. I'd like to sum it up like this: You know the poem—this is *your* poem—and you can tell what's wrong with the poem, what needs a revision, before you get to the line, because of the response. Very often I've done a lot of little revisions on the spot; once the poem is being read I feel that this movement is wrong or that word is wrong. And then I quickly scoot it down on the margin, and it will be corrected when it gets into book form or in the next edition. The *sense* of an audience is very important to a writer—how the response goes. Not how a friend says, "Oh, isn't that nice!" I don't mean that. I mean a real impersonal audience.

Of course, if you have the friendly reader, if you have a friend that you take things to regularly, who'll take the trouble to sit down and write an analysis for you in a letter back. . . . If Ransom would write me a letter, he'd write a page or two, or Tate would, or some other friends. Or John Hollander now, or Cleanth Brooks, and others. People who take it seriously will take the time, if they can give you that time in friendship, and they can help you rewrite a poem. They can explain to you, audibly explain to you, why something doesn't sound right. There's not enough density in that line, or this is wrong or that's wrong.

I was saying at lunch, when we were talking about I. A. Richards, that I sent him the first draft of a little book of mine called *Audubon*. He didn't answer for several weeks. Then I saw him at a cocktail party in Cambridge, and he took me to one side and said: "I haven't answered because I have too much to say. I like what you have, but it's not complete." He said: "It'll be a little book. Now you need some lyric effects here, played against this and this and this. You've got to find your own *kind* of lyricism for that." And we talked for half an hour or so about this. He would hum something, giving me a kind of movement. This had never crossed my mind, and it started the whole process over again. Three or four days later I began working on it, and the lyrics are now in the poem, and the poem would be dead without them. Now Richards had put his mind on it. That's one kind of criticism, but now I'm talking simply about the spontaneous, even uninstructed, response that you get in an audience, when you sense the awareness they are getting from something, and you know from the way the thing is going that two lines down it's got to be a little different, something's got to be changed.

NOVELLI: This really bears on the poem's integrity, or unity, the way it's going to take shape.

WARREN: Ultimately it will, it should anyway. I think there's no such thing as a poem's existing without a potential audience. . . . You try to know how it would affect you if you weren't you. You play a little game with yourself and read it out loud a lot to yourself. Of course, the real central thing you are trying to do is make an object "right." But the only real test of "rightness" is what your other self can make of it.

FORREST: Do you feel that in the effort to get a piece of writing right, a poem or a piece of fiction, part of what you're doing is building stage-directions for how the reader ought to read it aloud into the language of the poem?

WARREN: To use such a metaphor, the stage-directions are, of course, in the material, the content. But there are other stage-directions too. Now, for instance, "Whose fruit threw death." You can't *say* those words fast; you get a block. The language gives you the rhetorical blockage, the dramatic blockage.

Or you take that wonderful poem of Thomas Hardy's done when he was, I think, twenty-five years old, "Neutral Tones." The two lovers have met, and you know that it was their last meeting, and that something irreparable had happened between them. The sky looked gray, and the sun was fading. The poem ends:

> . . . keen lessons that love deceives,
> And wrings with wrong, have shaped to me
> Your face, and the God-curst sun, and a tree,
> And a pond edged with grayish leaves.

You couldn't possibly say those last words fast. The poem *forces* you to read them dwelling on every item as you would something that was loaded with symbolic meaning. That is, those forced pauses where you can't make an elision will force you to read it right.

Only a rapid reader can read it fast, by not *reading* it, just taking the meanings and not taking the words. "Have shaped to me / Your face, and the God-curst sun, and a tree, / And a pond edged with grayish leaves." You *can't* read it fast: it gets slower and *slower*. You're burning the brake bands, you see, and that delay suddenly makes the visualization stronger.

FORREST: When you read Faulkner surely there is some sense of a voice in your own mind as you read it. Is that a very strong experience for you?

WARREN: Sure, it's quite definitely one. It's *crowding* to be a-saying, to be said.

Literature wants to be spoken. You fulfill that sometimes by actually reading it; you go along where nobody's going to listen. But if you are an experienced reader, you can get a lot of it without ever making a noise. But any good poem wants to be read, out loud, and any good piece of fiction. One thing that is a little different, it seems to me, is that in prose the rhythm is never as assertive, or rarely as assertive. It's more like a conditioning element rather than something more positive. It's an offstage music. It's affecting you as deeply as the other will affect you, but it is spread out over a long period. You don't dwell on it unless you come to certain special moments, when the author will open the spigot, you know. One instance that just happens to pop into mind is the death of George Osborne, Amelia's husband, in *Vanity Fair*. The account of the Battle of Waterloo ends: "No more firing was heard at Brussels—the pursuit rolled miles away. Darkness came down on the field and city: and Amelia was praying for George, who was lying on his face, dead, with a bullet through his heart."

Now there you have a wondrous sense of panorama, pulling in to this single wound. And the rhythm of the passage enforces that; it gives you that. It's a tricky little piece of narrative prose. A fiction writer is going to make his rhythms mean something, even though they are not very aggressive, even though they may be very, very withdrawn. But they are conditioning the whole response.

NOVELLI: Novels at that time would often be read aloud.

WARREN: That's right, with the family reading.

FORREST: In the present condition in which there *is* a problem about getting a sense of literature as speech, the problem that you addressed in the more recent editions of *Understanding Poetry* with Mr. Brooks, would it be worthwhile to give active training to students in how to read aloud, not with the idea of making them professional readers, of course, but just to give them the sense of how to get their own voices into literature?

WARREN: I figure that it should be done not as a thing in itself but as a constant accompaniment. I don't say this as something to be emulated, but, for instance, you can take this passage as opposed to that passage, contrasting them, making students actually say the words and find the experience—usually it's for the first time—of what's happening to the muscles in the vocal cords and the whole muscular feel of the throat and head. That's a great eye-opener sometimes, just a little bit of that. It is combined; it is not a thing by itself, it's a thing that grows out of the simple study of the technical side of poetry. The technical side is not only a technical side; it is an expressive side too; it isn't just a box that you put something into. Make them say something and make them introspect what's happening to them *physically*. Then they know that "technique" and "poem" are identical.

You may not get more than two or three out of a dozen, but you get somebody. . . . Once they are aware of it, those aware of it can pursue it. It isn't something you do just one day in the beginning; but every time something of special interest appears then try it again, keep it alive, taking one thing at a time to get that *felt*. And I think in an informal way; it has to be almost stumbled on at the moment, rather than given as, say, two weeks of this, you know; it has to be a natural part of the experience.

FORREST: Along with other types of analysis.

WARREN: Along with other things that you are doing more officially. That is my impulse, the way I've done it, so far as I've done it at all.

Unless we some way recapture in the classroom the physical feel of literature as something spoken, and get beyond the endless abstractions *about* literature and I know not what else, the teaching of literature is just on the skids.

Interview with Eleanor Clark and Robert Penn Warren

The New England Review *published this conversation with Warren and his wife, Eleanor Clark, in its first issue, in the fall of 1978. The Warrens were interviewed at their summer home in West Wardsboro, Vermont.*

INTERVIEWER: What is the degree to which you influence one another? When you're working on a piece of writing, is it something that you like to do, so to speak, in a private space, or is it something that you take to your husband from time to time for criticism, and vice versa?

ELEANOR CLARK: I'm sure that we agree on that: we don't influence each other at all.

WARREN: Never. I don't even know what's she's doing now. I hear a remote rumor that she's in the middle of a novel. I have to get my information from other people, or overhear what she says on the telephone. That's about the extent of our cooperation.

INTERVIEWER: Is that true with respect to your own work?

WARREN: Almost always.

INTERVIEWER: How about in the penultimate phase . . . ?

WARREN: She likes to tell me what she does and does not like when it's finished. I hardly ever show her anything beforehand.

INTERVIEWER: You would see a draft before it went off to the publisher, or not?

CLARK: He usually has seen drafts of my things, more than the other way around, because, as you know, he's an extremely prolific fellow, and if I read everything he does in drafts, well, to begin with, I'd get much too involved in it, and get upset and agitated as if it were my own, and secondly, there's such a lot of it that I never would do anything of my own if I . . .

WARREN: . . . started to improve things.

INTERVIEWER: So you do need private space?

CLARK: Oh, absolutely, we don't work in the house at all, either here or in Connecticut. You just passed his little coop down there by the swimming pond, and my work cabin is way across the road over there, in an old hunters' camp.

INTERVIEWER: So when a book is just beginning, you also need psychological space, because to talk about it would be to ruin the spell.

CLARK: We're the opposite that way. Red has always liked to talk about his ideas. To me, that's really appalling. If I talk anything out, I feel it's gone, and I think I'm usually right.

WARREN: I wouldn't dare start telling a novel to you, though, darling . . .

CLARK: Oh, Red, that sounds so unfriendly.

WARREN: Oh no, it's not unfriendly at all. It's just not in the cards. We could talk about *Oedipus Rex* or Shakespeare, but not about each other's work—at least, not in that way.

INTERVIEWER: Won't you ever talk, say, about a novel you're writing on?

WARREN: To taxi drivers, and anybody else, I'll tell stories over and over again. It's a way of developing an idea. But never discuss them with my wife. And in late years I find myself talking less and less to anybody, or showing things.

That belongs to youth. Eleanor and I have too much to talk about outside of literature, anyway.

CLARK: Outside of our *own* literature. Other people's we talk about quite a lot; we talk shop in that sense.

INTERVIEWER: Still, no matter how divergent your individual writings may be from one another, there do seem to be common concerns. One thing that seems to me directly shown in Mr. Warren's work, and implied, at least obliquely, in your work, is a concern—sometimes a dismay—that *historical* awareness seems to be fading from current culture, perhaps especially among young people, even well-educated ones.

CLARK: That's a concern, yes, but one, I would say, that is shared by a lot of people, *including* young people. People talk about these jaded times, as opposed to the active sixties, but we see a lot of young people, our children's friends, ex-students of Red's that we're very close to—we see loads of young people all the time, and most seem extraordinarily concerned with social developments, and so, with what could be called historical development. Not perhaps in sixties fashion, but the concern still goes very deep.

There is one odd similarity between us. Red is, as you know, a Southerner, and I am absolutely a Yankee, but both of us come from backgrounds with a very strong sense of community, he in the rural South and I in a village in Connecticut, a place of small farms at that time. This gives us a highly similar view of a world of non-community, to put it grossly.

INTERVIEWER: I guess that may be what I was getting at. At one point in *Eyes, Etc.*, you write: "Poor doped-up wandering young, who must spit on pity, else would give up altogether, for the first time I think I begin to feel for you in your stinking jeans and sleeping bags. Wild animals have their lairs and rigorous routes to travel. You don't even care if it was Denmark or Afghanistan or the Long Trail you slept on last night. You don't read, so it makes no difference; anywhere is nowhere." And your husband's latest novel is, of course, *A Place to Come To*. You seem to see connections among place, self, and society that those in an a-communal context may miss.

WARREN: I think that's just as Eleanor said—that's based on a quest for an old-fashioned American community and a sense of firmly fixed family. By firmly fixed, I mean families that are real families. That makes a vast difference.

CLARK: Also, we both came from families with an extraordinarily perceptive sense of the American past. His grandfathers and my grandfathers—for all their great differences of place—had a similar sense of what the whole American experience was, and would talk about in similar ways, as we have found out from each other over the years. His were involved in the Civil War, of course, in a way that mine weren't . . .

WARREN: They were bounty-jumpers!

CLARK: They were *not!* That's so unfair! They were too young to be involved. Isn't he mean? This is what we call healing the wounds of fratricidal strife . . .

INTERVIEWER: Does that make you have a certain distaste for mass migrations to the cities here in the last fifty years?

CLARK: I'd say that whatever distaste *I* have is very mild compared to that of people like Henry Adams and his brother in their time.

WARREN: But their time was what it had to be. You don't keep people starving on the farm when factory jobs are waiting somewhere else. In their time, for economic and technological reasons, the growth of the great city was inevitable. Read Hamlin Garland, read Dreiser. . . .

Jacques Ellul, the French philosopher and sociologist, has said what many people—from Kierkegaard at least on—have been saying for a long time, that you find more and more a death of *responsible personality.* Ellul says that it's not a matter of a single massive thing, in a world of technology; if you go to a dentist, you're a tooth; if you work in a factory, you are number so-and-so; and in all your relations you are taken out of human context and put into a mechanical one. . . .

INTERVIEWER: Is there a way in which art—we're talking

mostly about literature—can mute this development or forestall it without becoming merely wistful? Isn't that a danger?

CLARK: Nostalgia *is* a great sickness now.

INTERVIEWER: Or is art drifting, alternatively, off in the direction of being the possession of a small adversary clique which merely decries dehumanization and technology?

CLARK: That would be more or less the end of art, wouldn't it? I mean, art just can't be in that negative a position and continue to be art. I had to make a speech at my old school recently, and I said that we should be optimistic about American education because it's become so absurdly terrible there's no way to go but up. When you raise a couple of generations of ignoramuses by-and-by you're going to get one or two people who want something better, and the same is true in the arts: art cannot get mechanized and contentless beyond a certain point without a reaction setting in. This is partly an interruption of what you're asking, but one of the things that we love about this part of the world, here in Vermont, is that there are still *characters* who are very much that, and we're very devoted to them, to their strong sense of personality.

. . . .

INTERVIEWER: I'd like to go back to Mrs. Warren's comment that art couldn't continue to be in a merely adversary posture toward the dominant culture.

CLARK: Adversary it always is; I mean it couldn't continue to be merely negative. And I can't see it, either, as merely an exploration of the artist's own innards. There has got to be some interplay with all the rest of the show.

INTERVIEWER: Is this in any way at odds with Mr. Warren's thesis in *Democracy and Poetry?*

CLARK: Red, would you say that it was?

WARREN: My point was that there was a real danger that the "public" could become a great Black Hole, a Nothing which is Everything, the individual dying out. What I would like to see, what I hope for, is enough resistance in the human spirit to maintain the world of personality and the world of art: I equate these two things. But that doesn't mean that I advocate an art of pure self-involvement, any more than I advocate fixity of place or subject matter. You have to try to remain human—that's all—and try to carry your humanity with you. No place has a mystical virtue.

INTERVIEWER: And yet the antidote to dehumanization is not, as Mrs. Warren makes clear, a kind of constant inward exploration. As she says in *Eyes, Etc.*: "Verbally we're allowed two forms of discourse, reporting and arguing. In written fiction the rules are narrowing down to plain and fancy—no brains or nothing but. In the latter it's a point of honor for the reader to pretend to be all agog over the author's next cerebral pinwheel or sparkler: for sustaining interest it's that or nothing."

CLARK: One can think of examples. But let's not.

INTERVIEWER: What, then, will return a *healthy* sense of self to us? When I asked whether or not there was conflict between you two on the question of self, I had in mind the phrase from *Democracy and Poetry*: "What poetry most significantly celebrates is the capacity of man to face the deep, dark inwardness of his nature and his fate." How is that capacity to face a dark inwardness to be distinguished from "mere" inwardness and the attendant intellectual pyrotechnics you both may find distasteful?

WARREN: Well, I'm talking about *tragic* sense, the sense of human complication and paradox. And a sense not only that the individual faces tragedy but also that the public does. Take the Iphigenia story, which is a tragedy both personal and social; or in English literature, isn't it odd that the age at which England became a world power is also the age of its greatest tragic sense? So Shakespeare lived in a world of mass power, but he didn't retreat into mere solipsism, didn't forget that there were other people in England, too.

INTERVIEWER: So that, as you both imply, the self depends on a sense of community, and what you object to is the self that is purely decommunalized and becomes self-reflexive to a fault.

CLARK: Yes, and a self that is in flight. It's a very curious historical fact that the great Greek plays, Euripides, Sophocles, and so on, came at a moment of tragic ending of power in Athens—there couldn't have been a worse time, defeat, plague, the navy at Syracuse, and all that; but drama was at its great height.

WARREN: Yes, but Aeschylus was also great, and was a man of the period of the great stand against Persia, and the great *rise* of Athenian power, and Greek power in general.

. . . .

INTERVIEWER: You never found teaching incompatible with writing?

WARREN: I had quite a lot of self-discipline. I shut my door on Friday at noon, fixed a gallon of iced tea, and went to work.

CLARK: And all along at Yale, he was only teaching one semester a year.

INTERVIEWER: Teaching full time was pretty demanding?

WARREN: Yes, but you were younger then.

INTERVIEWER: Yet you still wrote those novels. You wrote *Night Rider* and *All the King's Men.*

WARREN: Yes, and I wrote two novels that were never published when I was teaching. But in '46 I quit full-time academic work.

INTERVIEWER: Were you able by then to be self-sufficient as a writer?

WARREN: Well, yes, I guess so. I *always* thought of myself, though, as a writer and not a teacher. I was supposed to leave Oxford and come back to Yale to finish my doctorate on a fellowship there, and I couldn't make up my mind. But in the end it was clear I wanted to write, so I took a vow never to write an article for one of the professional journals. I sent a telegram to New Haven saying I couldn't come back. But I did get to teaching. In those days I was teaching

Elizabethan literature, and I could happily have kept on with that. When I got to Minnesota, the Shakespeare spot was filled, though.

INTERVIEWER: Had you done your Oxford B. Litt. on an Elizabethan topic?

WARREN: Yes. Elizabethan verse satire. But I spent most of my time reading poetry of that period and the seventeenth century in general.

.   .   .   .

WARREN: I don't know if it's relevant, but I know that I never had any interest in teaching writing as such. The most satisfying courses—for me to give, I mean—were a graduate course in non-dramatic Elizabethan literature, Renaissance, and Shakespeare. I always taught one writing course, but that was not the main thing, that side of it.

CLARK: Certainly none of us ever *took* a course in writing.

WARREN: Except for the fact that the best writing course is a good one in Shakespeare.

INTERVIEWER: It's interesting that while the Humanities seem to be facing problems of underenrollment and of morale, the so-called Creative Writing programs are growing.

CLARK: Yes, but there are so many peculiar courses now. No one would ever, a while back, have taken a course in business administration. Why would they? I just don't get it. Or a course in journalism, getting a degree in it, before going out to work on a small-town newspaper. I find that perfectly ludicrous.

WARREN: Yes, I've known stacks of journalists. By and large they wouldn't hire a man from journalism school.

CLARK: There are, after all, only two requirements for being a decent writer: one is to have a total passion—meaning a readiness to give up anything for it, rather than expecting to get anything out of it; the other is to spend your life at it, working like hell. I don't know any other way. Of course, behind the passion I'm assuming some native talent, and that's not always so.

INTERVIEWER: How did you manage to write books and raise children, and do all the other things you've done? Did you keep a certain time and place sacrosanct?

CLARK: Nothing is "sacrosanct" around small children. You try, but . . .

WARREN: You said to me a long while back, "I'm going to enjoy my children; that's what we've got them for. I won't fight them to write."

CLARK: We always had a great time with them, never had any inclination, say, to travel to Europe without them. We don't really "travel," anyway. We go to one spot for six months or a year, and stay.

INTERVIEWER: You said that it was becoming fashionable to complain about children and husband. How do you regard yourself with respect to the Women's Movement?

CLARK: I suppose that all these things are necessary up to a point, Susan B. Anthony and all the rest. And there have been a lot of situations when women were not getting equal pay for equal work, for instance. If I worked in a factory, or a university, where some male was getting more than I was for the same job with the same or less capacity, I'd be sore as hell. But all this business of just, in principle, wanting to get out of the home, I find "parlous," to use a nice old-fashioned word. I wouldn't have wanted to be out of the home. You can, of course, say that I was lucky: I was a fairly established writer when I began to have children; I had work that didn't require me to be off the premises. However, I do know plenty of younger people who have managed without all the squawks and wails and recriminations. We know a lot of them, young women who've gotten their Ph.D.'s, had children, done their work whatever it was, all at the same time. Sure, it takes character. . . . There's a whole side to this Women's Movement that's neurotic (I don't see why we can't call things what they are). There are certain kinds of suburbs where you'll find droves of women who haven't had the character to do anything, and they are of course delighted to have someone to blame it on.

Unfortunately, any time you get a big movement going, you'll get the lousy with the respectable, and the terms will get confused. God knows they are now. Several of my good friends are women who are real artists; they simply haven't time to be squawking about rights. One's a well-known musician, another's a painter, and so on. If you're really busy doing something, you don't have time to go around complaining about who prevented you from doing it.

INTERVIEWER: I guess it gets back to that business that Mr. Warren mentions in *Democracy and Poetry*, that cant phrase he objects to: "taking time out to find yourself."

WARREN: Oh, my God!

INTERVIEWER: A self is not something that you go out and find?

WARREN: Of course not.

INTERVIEWER: In order to be a writer, you have to have a self, but that's something, you say, that is made, not found?

CLARK: It's not something you have time to worry about. If you're a writer and people come ask you—if you're a woman they do, especially living with someone like Red . . . "How's your self-image?" It's like a question in the loony-bin. As if you spent hours in front of the mirror, trying to see what developments were taking place. Self is a valid notion, as Red discussed it in *Democracy and Poetry*, but the way it's thrown around in the Women's Movement, it seems more like a term of belligerence.

INTERVIEWER: It's not something that's simply determined for you.

CLARK: It's unmeaningful matter for discussion.

WARREN: It's not something you go find under a leaf. The self is what you *do*. What you want to do, and what you do do.

INTERVIEWER: I think of the Great Twitch view of history in *All the King's Men*. Are we to dismiss Jack's reverie about history as something that just leaps up at you? Or, say, Dr. Stahlmann in *A Place to Come To*, other figures for whom so much of history—both personal and cultural—seems to be something that comes from without, and that you can't foresee or prevent . . . seems to be a Great Twitch, something determined for you. How does that tally with your sense of self as being what you do, and hence of history as something in which the individual has a hand? Stahlmann, to use a word that has come up a lot, is a man dealing with, or trying to deal with, placelessness. He ends by saying that the *imperium intellectūs*, the sum total of all he has accomplished, is bunk. Are we to take him seriously, or is he merely suffering from the placelessness?

WARREN: To speak of Stahlmann is one thing. . . . To speak of that book alone, all the people in it, who are concerned with their relation (or non-relation) to a place—or community—and their relation to self—the book is built around them. The germ is an incident from years ago. I usually carry a book around for eight or ten years before I start it. I know many Southerners who, from babyhood on, hated the South, or felt inferior because of it, and so wanted out. Some are my contemporaries. I know some who have made great successes—heads of corporations, bankers, and so on. And at the same time, they never found a world to live in; they're people without place. They're cut off from one world and never really entered another one. I don't mean a man like Tucker Brook, who was head of the English department when I was at graduate school at Yale. He said, "You know what I'm doing here? I'm spoiling the Egyptians!" He wasn't suffering a bit from inferiority. But what I'm getting at is this: the people who have no sense of human continuity, or community. For example, a man who had been in my freshman class at Vanderbilt—older, or rather, much more mature than the rest of us—didn't come back the next year. He said, "I want to get out of this place. I want to go where the big things are happening." And he went to Chicago. And next thing—more than twenty-five years later—he was on the telephone to me in my hotel, saying "Can I come up?"

I was there alone, and in comes a big wreck of a man. A big powerful fellow, but all bloated with too much food and drink. Richly dressed, a briefcase in his hand. I got him a drink, and we sat down and started old-timing. He said, "I was right to leave college and come up here." Let it be clear that he had made a fortune. Very soon. Then he said, "I want to show you my house." There in his briefcase were photographs of his house, a great rich mansion. "And there's my country place." He showed a sloop moored at a slip, a seventy-footer or so. And "These are my daughters," he said, and showed me his beautiful daughters. "And look at their debutante parties." He had photographs. He wanted to prove his success. He said, "I was right to leave, I knew what I was up to." And then—in the middle of this self-congratulation—he suddenly said, "I'm lonelier than God." People like that were the seed of *A Place to Come To*. But neither in that book nor anywhere else do I attach a mystical significance to a particular place. But I do attach a significance to the way a man deals with the place God drops him in. His reasons for going or staying. And his piety or impiety.

CLARK: I think we can get a little too self-congratulatory, though, if we're not careful. We can't help remembering that masses and masses of the world's population don't have the luxury of a place in that sense . . . not only Vietnamese refugees right now; there have been swarms of refugees. People our age knew many, many from Hitler's Germany and Franco's Spain, for example. The world's politics are not always so peaceful. . . .

WARREN: I'm being perfectly provincial about this. It's all I can be. I just record what I saw and what I knew. I'm not trying to generalize.

CLARK: We can't simply say that a man ripped away from homeland . . .

WARREN: I'm not saying that.

CLARK: I know *you* aren't, Red. I'm just saying that we are perfectly aware that great things can be done, great thoughts thought, and great art made by people who can't live in their own native place.

WARREN: I'm not arguing for regional literature. Not that literature, and fine literature, isn't often provincial; but it's not self-consciously that way. Not *deliberately*—theoretically—provincial.

CLARK: Literature suffers more than any other art from displacement; there's no doubt about that. The painters in Paris in the great Fauve and Cubist and Surrealist years, for instance—they were hardly any of them French. They were Spaniards and Germans and everything else.

WARREN: But they're not painting in traditional ways. They weren't painting out of nature. Picasso is not so much painting a land as an idea, finally. Modern painting had been moving toward abstraction—denial of nature and place.

CLARK: The time and the fact of their immigration coincided happily for that moment. Literature doesn't usually fare that well in displacement. I knew Richard Wright somewhat in Paris in the forties, and it was sad to see him away from his place, because really, France was not material that he could use. He'd been taken up by Sartre and company, and was walking around with great volumes of Heidegger under his arm. Well, I don't think that nourished him in the way that he most needed to be nourished as a writer.

INTERVIEWER: And yet we have the self-conscious exiles of the twenties.

CLARK: Well, if you mean the Americans, they weren't, in many cases, exiles for all that long. For some, it was a fling. It wasn't imposed, and they could come back whenever they liked. Of course, the fabulous *Irish* literary picture in the last century, those who stayed home and those who didn't—Shaw, Joyce, Beckett, and so forth—would upset all generalizations. The Irish are like that.

WARREN: Let's take Faulkner, with his "postage stamp-sized county." He had a look at Paris and said, "Nothing here for me," and came on back to the U.S. and worked in a bookstore in New York, and Stark Young, who was a very good friend of his, a fellow Mississippian, told me, "You know why Bill came back to Mississippi?" I said, "No." "They charged too much for tail in New York," he said. The point is simple. He was *himself*, carried his world in his being, and knew who he was.

CLARK: You know, we all four—our children, of course they're grown—went down to Kentucky recently. We visited Red's brother and his family; they're still there. The children had never been to Papa's home state—a terrific lapse. It had more of an effect on them than many other trips, to Greece or France or whatever. And on me. This relates in perhaps an oblique way to the sense of place, but it also relates to the writer's thoughts—"images" is perhaps a better word—and how they're formed. The three of us got a great wallop out of it, partly from the association with Red: that is, a lot became clear to us about his early life that was crucial and dramatic. But along with that, it was quite a chunk of history, because we stopped a lot along the way, at Harrodsburg and Cassius M. Clay's house, and so on (not Muhammad Ali, but the great abolitionist, a friend of Lincoln's, and a very dashing figure). It was exciting to get under the earth, too, as our daughter Rosanna said: part of the excitement to her (of course, it was exciting to be in the place of many of her father's stories and poems) was to go down into Mammoth Cave or a deep coal mine, to feel the earth that exists under this country. Not to mention the insides of the planet we happen to be on. But there's a matter of what density—and accuracy—of intimate association one brings to this or that piece of it. The same with religion: all these little lightweight, skin-deep Buddhists mouthing around these days—what will they ever know of it? To know a god, you need a thousand years of nursery rhymes that went with it. I'm only talking about where one's images and excitements come from, and why I'd rather not have to be an expatriate.

WARREN: It seems to me that all your vital images are ones you get before you're seven, eight, nine years old. That's true for my life, anyway. What you learn to look at. I've lived in cities a lot, but I can't work very long in cities. Oh, perhaps in city libraries. I just have to be able to walk in the woods, to be outdoors, to be alone.

INTERVIEWER: Is the landscape, then, in the poems and elsewhere, the landscape of the South?

CLARK: A lot of his finest poems are set in the Mediterranean . . . and here—Vermont.

WARREN: The things I look for even there, though, are conditioned very early. You carry some place with you in your head. For example, even a lot of those late poems are really autobiographical—things that really happened. That one about the old black man on the mule cart on the wrong side of the road [39]—well, that happened to me in Louisiana, when I was driving back from a party, kind of boozy. That belongs to a world I knew very well. I lived there. A great deal of . . . well, poetry is different from fiction. It's much more inside: you're reliving your life. For me, anyway. . . . You can absorb a piece of the Mediterranean, or a piece of Vermont, and *combine* them. My book—*Promises*—primarily about the Mediterranean is really half about the Mediterranean and half about the South. Our small children—babies then—were living with us in a ruined sixteenth-century fortress in Italy. This tied up in my mind quite specifically with a recollected Kentucky . . . and my grandfather. They're all one package—contrast and identity in one package—change and continuity—the human story.

INTERVIEWER: You've recently written, though, a novel. I've often wondered what the effect of being a novelist has been on your poetry, and vice versa.

WARREN: I've often stopped novels and written poems in between. I may never start another novel. I had one around for about ten years, and when lately I sat down to write it, this year, I couldn't get off the ground. I ended up writing a poem every time. I'd write a new poem before the day was over. A poem's a different thing: it's shorter, after all. And it's a closer thing, a more intimate thing.

INTERVIEWER: There is a kind of speculative language, which I would associate rightly or wrongly with the novel, in much of your poetry—and there seems more of it as you go along in your poetic career. I'm thinking of lines like "That is a way to love God," or whatever. Some might be construed as prosy—although I think they work marvelously,

as poetry. Is that a borrowing from your training as a novelist, or something independent?

WARREN: There's been some kind of cross-fertilization. And
more and more since I quit writing stories. Even in poems as
old as those in *Promises*, the germ is mostly anecdotal. The
other way around, the influence of poetry on prose, is less
available . . .

CLARK: Nobody wants to write poetic prose.

WARREN: The construction of a novel, though, and the construction of a poem are very close. Even behind a realistic
narrative, there is—for me—a shadow poem. Every novel is
probably one big metaphor. Not just mine; anybody's.

INTERVIEWER: Do you like to read novels?

WARREN: I read fiction. I'm reading *Dombey and Son* right
now. Haven't looked at it for twenty years. But I just
finished one of the worst novels ever written . . .

CLARK: Oh, don't mention that!

WARREN: I won't mention it.

CLARK: They come in here, you know. In the mail.

.   .   .   .

WARREN: . . . When I was a young poet it was hard for me to
tell when an impulse was over. That is, when a book was
over. Now I know just when a volume of poems should
end—because I've lost the impulse that binds it together. It's
time to turn to something else. A thing like *Audubon* was
easy. That started in the forties—it took twenty years. It
started because in that period I was reading a whole range
of subliterary genres—journals, memoirs, and things like
that. And it led actually to two other things. One was
World Enough and Time, a novel, and the other was
Brother to Dragons. But there was a lot of stuff behind all
that besides formal history.

I started a poem on Audubon, but I got stuck in a trap,
a narrative trap. There's no narrative there, as such, to work
from. You can't carry him that way, because the narrative
doesn't have enough bite to it. I wrote a lot about him. I

always have a lot of stuff I put in a folder and let lie, then come back to it. I knew when I came back to the Audubon thing that there was something there, a germ. In the sixties I was writing a history of American literature with R. W. B. Lewis and Cleanth Brooks, and I again read a lot of that stuff, not only my own notes, but the texts themselves, and Audubon was included. One morning I was helping to make the bed—which was a moment very rare, something I don't usually do, because I'm not housebroken very well—and one line of that poem came to me. "Was not the lost Dauphin." [40] That line came into my head from twenty years back. It was not a first line of anything, but it stuck. That's when I started composing, by writing at night, going to sleep, and waking up in the morning early— revising by shouting it all out loud in a Land Rover going to Yale. I saw a new way in. Each element in the poem would be a "shot" on Audubon rather than a narrative. It took about six or eight months, but you can see it as a unit. But any poem or book of poems—you can learn to see where a certain kind of emotional motivation is winding up, its curve is coming back.

CLARK: I often think of André Gide's phrase, *la part de Dieu*, in this process.

INTERVIEWER: Did that reading in subliterary genres account for the Cass Mastern story in *All the King's Men?*

WARREN: Cass Mastern's story had a germ. A lot of the details are historical—it's based on the Jefferson Davis story. His father, Sam, came to Kentucky, to our county, where Jeff was born. Old Sam Davis was so feckless! In our county there's a river valley and rich land to raise horses in. But Sam went up to the northern part of the county, to the Knob section, and tried to raise race horses where the soil is two inches thick over the limestone cap! Instead of five feet thick down our way.

INTERVIEWER: A last question. Time is the great anthologist. When you're a young writer, you may look around and wonder at the shape of things to come. Have you had any surprises?

CLARK: There's a fallacy in your question. I don't think, personally, that when you're a young writer you really look ahead in that way. I was looking ahead to see if I had enough in my purse for that night's dinner. Somebody once asked me what I thought about when I was skiing. I told the simple truth: I think about the next turn. And that's what a young writer does. I wasn't thinking about the shape of things to come when I was a young writer . . .

WARREN: You were a young skier then, too!

CLARK: I was thinking whether this review was going to get me the seven dollars and fifty cents from the *New Republic* that was absolutely necessary to me. I wasn't worried about whether, say, the *New Republic* itself would survive. You don't worry about the shape of things to come; you worry about the shape of *things,* in the sense that you're functioning, and you have to have some sort of outlet, and so on. One does not live in a vague, amorphous, questioning, puzzling Future. There are plenty of questions right now. Of course, one has social convictions too, and they may be passionate ones. I was in the Trotskyite periphery in the late thirties, and I suppose that's reflected in my first novel. In some residual way, it still figures. But I believe that's outside the sense of your question, about the "young writer."

WARREN: I'll tell you one thing right now. The people who talked about the future of the world all the time never became writers.

.   .   .   .

A Dialogue with Robert Penn Warren on *Brother to Dragons*

Warren's new version of Brother to Dragons *was published in the fall of 1979. He and Floyd C. Watkins talked about the published and unpublished versions when they got together at Warren's home in Fairfield, Connecticut, earlier that year. The Watkins interview was first published in the* Southern Review *in 1980.*

FLOYD WATKINS: Was the 1953 version of *Brother to Dragons* what you wanted it to be at the time when you published it?

WARREN: Well, here Albert Erskine [Warren's editor] and I have a difference in memory. Now at the time when the book was in its last stages, he was coming and spending the weekend with me, the last editorial go-over, the last of the editorial revisions and discussions. My wife and I—my wife was then pregnant with Rosanna—were living on a farm called Paradise Farm, outside of Newport. I guess I felt that, well, I was in a rather excited state of mind anyway. It was about the time of my first child. I had a very happy marriage in process after a period of an unhappy one and the stopgaps between. I probably wasn't as critical of what I had done as I might have been. In style I had wandered into a trap—too often caught in the trap of blank verse—and that had meant some padding. And I published it without enough of the cooling off process—the last hard look.

WATKINS: And you think the padding is in the '53 version as it was published?

WARREN: Yes, some of the revisions didn't get in. Albert was called back to New York by a telephone call from Bennett Cerf in the middle of Sunday afternoon. Bennett said, "I've got a problem, and I want your help right now. Get the next train out." So we didn't finish the job, you see. Just assumed we had. Albert put the manuscript in his briefcase, and I swept the other stuff into a suitcase and didn't look at it again. And he headed out. When I saw it, it wasn't the text I had thought it was going to be.

WATKINS: It was different?

WARREN: Quite some severe differences. Now, of people who have gone through the manuscripts at Yale, one of them said, yes, he found the other version. The one I saw. Another said he didn't find it. I've never hunted for it myself. Well, it wasn't worth my time to hunt it. I don't care much about it. At the time Albert said, "Well, when you get the one you want done we'll publish that one." Then it became a matter of trying to make a play. Broadway took it first. There was a whole year they were paying me for it and then with numerous tryouts for actors and things like that. On opening day, the lead actor sent a telegram (I think), withdrawing. It was finally done many times, including New York at the American Palace Theater and then in Providence. The director, Adrian Hall (who was starting out his career then in an adapted church), did a good early production that ran some little time. A year or so later he got hold of a big old Keith theater, remodeled it, and set up the "Trinity Players" in rather splendid surroundings. Meanwhile he had been reworking his *Brother to Dragons* and used that to open his arena theater (there was a proscenium, too). Later he did more work on production and by the time I saw it in Boston after a little tour, a couple of years later, he had it stunningly, imaginatively done. This work on the play also changed my notion of the poem. It still remains a verse play. But when it got on the stage, it changed my sense of the versification and led to a tremendous lot of rewriting and reorganization. There were many changes (bit by bit, mind you) for the twenty-odd years of several versions. But in later years I have taken months of time consecutively and tried to start clean—to leave no old section in if I didn't want it. It must be remembered too that the change of one syllable will sometimes change the rhythm of a whole passage.

WATKINS: So it's a basic difference in technique rather than a philosophical difference. But also a difference in organization.

WARREN: It is no different philosophically. But it is very different technically—in rhythm (the important thing) and in organization. Also a lot of cutting. The original version had certain sections that were repetitious and wordy. I got rid of those, I think.

WATKINS: Do you think it may be less explicit than the first one was? To some extent I thought you interpreted your 1953 version yourself for the critics. Is there less of that?

WARREN: Well, I couldn't answer that. I think there's less commentary, yes. Now how much less, I don't know. And also it's vastly improved in general poetic quality. Now some passages naturally remain the same. Other passages are quite different, and there are many cuts, sometimes very small— but significant.

WATKINS: There are already a good many people who say, and I would not contradict them, that *Brother to Dragons* may already be your greatest work, the 1953 version.

WARREN: That is wrong.

WATKINS: Would it disappoint you greatly if they find the new version not as likable as the 1953 version?

WARREN: Oh, I think they'd be wrong.

WATKINS: I hope they are.

WARREN: I hope they are too. Everybody can be wrong. But I would say they are dead wrong. It is a much more fluid and natural verse movement now than it was before. Of course, I hope I'm not wrong.

WATKINS: Is it a matter of technique, or is it something in the meaning of the work that's kept you working at this single thing twenty-five years and more?

WARREN: It's not just the idea as bare idea, no, but I wanted . . . I didn't feel right about it. Put it that way. It's as simple as that. I can get more out of it than I got out of it.

WATKINS: You can get more out of the same idea with a different technique?

WARREN: With a different technique—or even small differences. The change of the weight of one syllable in a line can make a vast difference. I wanted a more natural and fluid thing. I also changed the organization somewhat. Now in the original version Meriwether Lewis doesn't appear until the very end. Now, he appears early in the poem, you see. He is grounded in the poem. And there's a new scene, a scene in the parting of Jefferson when he sends him out. And a lot of reworking toward the "touch" scene toward the end—touching Lilburn.

WATKINS: Do you know Caroline Gordon is writing a novel on Meriwether Lewis?

WARREN: She is?

WATKINS: She is. She is related to him.

WARREN: So was John Crowe Ransom. Ransom's mother was the descendant of Meriwether Lewis. When the Meriwether Lewis National Monument was dedicated, she was on the platform. Later, I've had twenty-five letters, at least, from people who are related to the Lewis family and discovered that a close friend of mine at the University of California was a member of the family.

WATKINS: When and how did the idea of *Brother to Dragons* first come to you?

WARREN: It was back in the forties. I read a great deal of sub-historical material, like letters and journals and things like that, Audubon's journals. I was soaking myself in the period, and Lilburn Lewis and his story were practically unknown. I had known the folk-tale, garbled version in childhood. Then I began serious investigation of the court records and found that specialists knew little about him. I talked to many famous specialists before I wrote the book, the first version. Dumas Malone wrote me. He said, "I know it happened, but that's all I know. I haven't got that far in my researches yet." And various other people. One man finally gave me the records that I wanted. Francis L. Berkeley, Jr.—anyway, the curator of the Lewis-Jefferson Papers at the University of Virginia. And he wrote me something to this effect: that not only did Jefferson have a philosophical shock, he doubted that Jefferson could ever mention the fact. At least, there was no record. Jefferson had sustained a wound too deep to mention. Of course, that is the assumption of my poem. And it doesn't really matter, in one sense, whether it is true or not. Perhaps he did mention it, but I could find no record. But anyway the assumption is that the shock ultimately changed Jefferson's view of the whole nature of man. He who had esteemed man as perfectible, but finds in his own blood the basic horror that raises the question of perfectibility, you see, in a very special kind of way. Of course there is a great deal of unbalance there. Nuttiness lies in the Lewises, in the whole collection of Randolphs. Jefferson's mother was a Randolph, and he had defective siblings and so forth. But my poem is not about pathology as such—only as symbol.

WATKINS: You know there is a relatively new book out by the Princeton University Press . . .

WARREN: I've read it.

WATKINS: I was going to ask you . . .

WARREN: I know the man—Boynton Merrill, a delightful man— and a fascinating book.[41]

WATKINS: Did that affect your second version?

WARREN: No. I had finished mine.

WATKINS: You had finished it?

WARREN: Before it came out. It wouldn't have affected me anyway. All it did was document the certain divergencies in the family and the intermarriages in the family more than I knew had happened; and also it made old Charles Lewis not a physician, as he was in certain early versions, but a planter. Also it made him a crook.

WATKINS: Oh, really?

WARREN: A crook. He crooked Jefferson. And Merrill does explain something I hadn't known, the reasons for the Lewis family going west. There were many explanations when I was reading the material. But he was failing, a financial failure. The Lewises were going bust. They had sold what land they could next to them, and bought lots of new land in Kentucky but without enough slaves to exploit the new land when they got there.

WATKINS: A lot of people have worried themselves by trying to name the genre of the book. I believe it was Robert Lowell who called it something like this peculiar verse-drama-novel. Do you think of it as having a name?

WARREN: I think it's a poem. I don't worry about definitions. A narrative poem—but in dramatic structure.

WATKINS: A narrative poem?

WARREN: Insofar as it is anything, that is what it is. It is very much to be distinguished from a play. It's not a play.

WATKINS: It is the same genre, the same kind of work, in both versions?

WARREN: It is the same kind of work. Now Random House is going to publish, they tell me, the play version later on. There is a play version.

WATKINS: Is that the one that appeared in *The Georgia Review* or was that . . .

WARREN: It appeared in *The Georgia Review*. That is the one that was done by—the last version—it was done by Adrian Hall with the Provincetown Theater, the Trinity Square Theater, and ended up in a fine production in Boston.

WATKINS: It seems to me that the idea or the fallacy of perfectibility has run throughout most of your work and that this is one of the best embodiments of that constant concern that you have. Is that a fair statement?

WARREN: I think that is probably a fair statement. I wasn't aware of this until quite late, you see. The first time I became aware of it as a central question for me was when I was writing the little book on Coleridge. Now Coleridge takes that view of perfectibility. I discovered it in "The Ancient Mariner" itself—that this appeared in the poem. Preceding the book on "The Ancient Mariner," I had written a poem called "Billie Potts," which was my version of the same idea. But not derived from Coleridge, God knows. I wrote that poem in Minnesota, in 1943, before I began my Coleridge piece—which I worked on at the Library of Congress, in 1944–45, as a lecture for Yale.

WATKINS: Oh, yes.

WARREN: Where the man comes back to claim his patrimony of the evil father. And the evil father killed him, you see. He gives him his patrimony, in other words.

WATKINS: Right. Do you think . . .

WARREN: That's, I guess, where the puritanism comes in.

WATKINS: I see. It seems to me that there is a close tie between what you are working with here and your theme also in the poem "Homage to Emerson."

WARREN: Though I hasten to add I'm not an Emerson man, that could be.

WATKINS: In fact, those are so similar it would be harder for me to state the differences than it would be to state the comparisons.

WARREN: Well, it hadn't occurred to me that they were similar until you mentioned it. But that doesn't prove anything now. Things exist in you without your knowing it. You don't know what comes out of yourself, but it comes. It is you. But you can't predict always. Sometimes you can plan and predict. Sometimes you can't. The Emerson poem and "The Ballad of Billie Potts" and *Brother to Dragons*—they are all of the same cloth, quite clearly—but Emerson is the contrary to the others.

WATKINS: Now I can see the connection better between the other two than I can to "Billie Potts."

WARREN: Well, "Billie Potts," let me run an exegesis of "Billie Potts" as if you hadn't read the poem. The story is about an outlaw, a wicked old man who runs an inn as an outlaw and spots prey at the inn and then informs some members of his gang to pick up the prospects after they leave the inn. Now his son grows up in this world, and his son is sent out to carry a message ahead about a certain traveler, but decides to prove his manhood by doing it himself. He's nearly a grown man. His family would be proud of him. But he miscarries. The other guy spots him and beats him to the gun and shoots him before he gets a shot off. The traveler has a little derringer in his sleeve and he gives him the derringer. Billie howls, and cries, and runs home. But then his pappy says, "Take this saddle and horse and this fifty dollars in gold and head West, get out of here fast before they are after you." And so the boy goes away. He succeeds out West, and the poem says that in the West every man is a new man, reborn. He is redeemed. Secularly, shall we say. Every man gets a new name in Texas, as the old saying goes.

WATKINS: That is the perfectibility.

WARREN: The perfectibility. He comes back rich and, to tease his parents, puts up at the inn. Night comes on. And they think now they've got them a fat one. And the father carries him down to the spring to get some fresh water and sets a hatchet in his head. Kills his own son, and they rob and bury him. The wife, the old wicked wife, and the father bury him. But a friend who has met him on the road and recognized him comes to the house and says, "I've come to see Billie tonight. Where's Billie?" And they say, "Billie hasn't been here." He says, "Oh, you wouldn't know him. He was wearing a big black beard and riding a big bay horse and looking fine." The husband and wife look at each other and realize the truth, they exhume the body and they find the mark under his heart, in the shape of a little mole shaped for luck . . .

WATKINS: Under his left tit.

WARREN: Yeah, under his left tit. And they have killed their son. Well now, this is the question of the man who goes to the West to become a different man—redeemed—prospers and comes back. He must come back. Something calls him back. He doesn't know why he wants to come back. He comes back to his true "human" father—he dies by his own blood—and name. Now when they kill him he accepts from his father's hand the natural gift. He's a sacrifice this time. But he's returned. He's performed the human cycle. He has had the human gift. He receives it from his father's hand.

WATKINS: Your aunt told you that story, I believe, in Cerulean.

WARREN: She told me that story.

WATKINS: Which aunt was that?

WARREN: That was my grandfather's sister-in-law, Aunt Anna Mitchell. I knew my grandfather on the Penn side. He was a descendant of Abram Penn, a Revolutionary colonel, etc.— the highway near Roanoke, Virginia, is named for him in the region where he held a Revolutionary grant.

WATKINS: Do you remember that there is a very long article in German about the innumerable analogues to "The Ballad of Billie Potts" in European folklore?

WARREN: Yes. There are many.

WATKINS: Have you read any of those?

WARREN: I haven't read any of those. No. I didn't even know about them when I started the poem. The poem had its origin originally in hearsay. The old lady was chatting along, telling about things that happened, that she had heard about when she was a young girl. Then I read about it. I read the story in some publication, I think, of the historical society of Louisville.

WATKINS: Filson. The Filson Club.

WARREN: It was primarily the tale she told me that I was telling. The outlaws lived up in the cave-in rock section, I think. I put it down between the rivers in Kentucky, a very wild country at one time.

WATKINS: Don't you think that the perfectibility of *Brother to Dragons,* though it came from the eighteenth century, may have attached itself peculiarly to America?

WARREN: It came out of the Enlightenment. It started in the Enlightenment. Man can be made a different creature—by rediscovering his "natural" innocence, Rousseauism.

WATKINS: Don't you think even our thinking about penal institutions and the correctibility or perfectibility or sinlessness

of man still shows the influence of that kind of Jeffersonian
thinking?

WARREN: Absolutely. Sure it does. The whole notion of America, we find in the penitentiary. The penitentiary is an
American institution, and was based on the idea that a man
could be reformed, and of course the penitentiary backfired
on us. It didn't reform anybody. Of course, this isn't final
evidence on the point. But go look at a penitentiary.

WATKINS: And still is backfiring?

WARREN: Still is backfiring. But it is a product of the Enlightenment and was based on the notion that man can be remade.

WATKINS: Is Jefferson's thinking almost the opposite of the
thinking of writers like you and Herman Melville?

WARREN: Melville was absolutely opposite. He says the eternal
No. Life is basically that, and he capitalized the *No*'s. Face
the eternal *No*. That is the essence of life. He is exactly the
opposite. Also, Melville was obsessed, you might almost say,
with the notion of the difficulty of finding good and evil.
The paradox of life was what Melville saw primarily, the
paradox of life. He would say, the Civil War is where it
comes out most vividly; he was swept off his feet by the
heroic figure of Ahab, you see, and that sort of thing. And
the Civil War comes along and becomes personal. Your own
country is involved in it. He was an emancipationist, but he
also saw the war as a crime against humanity. Now in a
poem of his on Charleston—"The Swamp Angel"—with
Charleston being bombarded, he sees this as a crime, too,
and in another poem, earlier, he had said, however the war
comes out, it will show the "slimed foundations" of the world.
That's his phrase, the "slimed foundations" of the world.
And the war, being fought for good, will show the "slimed
foundations" of the world, as the good cause does not change
the nature of the face of the world. Many things may nest
under the shelter of a good cause.

WATKINS: So you could see yourself not in Melville's position,
but somewhere between Melville and Jefferson.

WARREN: Well, I believe we are stuck with trying to improve
the world. Put it that way. We are stuck with it; we have to

live with nature, so we have to try to improve it. But I have
no romantic dreams about quick improvements, no romantic
dreams about quick improvements of human nature or of
human society.

WATKINS: Jefferson's idea, was that Lilburn's idea also?

WARREN: Lilburn was a madman, really; what his idea was
doesn't really matter. It simply is not relevant to Lilburn.
Now what I put in the story and what is in the history of
the thing—I use things there, but I'm using them for my own
purposes. That is, after all, the mother was not buried on Lilburn's place. She was buried on the estate of the older
brother. I put the grave on Lilburn's place so that the brothers could shoot themselves, each other, across the mother's
grave, and I put the mother there to give her significance in
the story, not in history. Lilburn hates the father because the
mother—he brought his mother to Kentucky—the mother,
who presumably loved Virginia, the old ties, the blood ties.
The mother couldn't see her youngest son becoming a frontiersman, a ruffian, you see. Isham, he was a bum; the real
Isham was a bum. The beautiful aspect is not in the historical
records; I put that in. I did certain things to the story, a lot
of changes. The wife was pregnant, historically speaking, the
new wife. Lilburn had been married before and had children
in the house. Well, you can't clutter a house up in a poem
with children. I changed this with materials for a poem. I'm
not trying to write a history. I stay as close to history as
humanly possible, but there are certain irrelevant things like
children. I put Aunt Cat in. She isn't even mentioned in the
record—and the name was the name of my grandfather's
nurse, whom I knew, and he was born in 1838. But I needed
Aunt Cat, and certainly there was an Aunt Cat around of
some kind, you know. I made changes, historical changes,
but none that are important.

WATKINS: You also changed the moral stature of Isham, if he
was a bum, didn't you?

WARREN: I put Isham not as a bum but as a pawn for Lilburn;
the younger brother, rather dumb, a dumb younger brother,
you see, worshipping him, and deprived (as the historical

Isham was) of education. He crossed the line, to become an almost illiterate frontiersman, you see. The wilderness calls him, you see. These men—the Lewises—are men who are supposed to bring light to the dark wilderness, even civilize it. And as a parenthesis, I'll say that Meriwether Lewis is a true "lightbringer," in contrast. The wilderness, however, gets the other Lewises; they become brutes. But Lilburn keeps the surface of a gentleman. Isham does not. Isham is rather thin-witted anyway. He is younger; he is made more childish in my treatment of him. Actually Jefferson took Isham for a time and tried to teach him surveying. And he got him a job with the government down in Mississippi. But then nobody knows what happened to Isham during this period. He was only periodically at Rocky Hill. But he was present when the Negro was murdered.

WATKINS: And Lilburn was the mutilator?

WARREN: He was the mutilator. Isham was much less intelligent, and he had also lost much of his sense of gentility, you see. The frontier was absorbing the brothers. Now in the present poem I have Madeira in the beginning of the poem and corn whiskey in the end. Now the gentlemen in Virginia didn't drink corn whiskey. They drank Madeira. They drank port, as a great eighteenth-century gentleman would. Now it is said in the poem that the decanter of Madeira has long since been replaced by the jug. And I made that change and tried to indicate other small things like that, and the speech of Isham as contrasted with Lilburn's. But, of course, the frontier brutality entered the soul of Lilburn too, even though he, at one level, hated it and looked back to Virginia. He blamed his father for killing his mother by bringing her to the wilderness.

WATKINS: Now in the '53 version you describe two trips that you made to Smithland.

WARREN: Yes, I did make two trips to Smithland. I may have made another one, I've forgotten.

WATKINS: You make those trips in the '79 version too?

WARREN: I keep them.

WATKINS: And your father went with you?

WARREN: Both trips. Or three trips, I forget which it was.

WATKINS: Is it a fair question to ask you what the purpose of the father is in the poem?

WARREN: Yes, it is a fair question. I want to set the poem in the modern world. I don't want to set it as a historical poem, put it that way. I want a modern man, myself, you see, and my father. I want such a relation too, myself, in time, with my old father there, and older than he are these other people, back there. I want a sense of a historical sweep, you see. And one of these is a modern man, RPW, who talks back to these other people. He has things to say about them that are more modern than they have ever thought of. I want RPW to make some commentary; he's supposed to make commentary to these people. And this is all a fantasy, you see, a kind of dream situation. And my father, I don't know, the special relation with my father that I had is also tied in the poem. He had some relation in his boyhood with that world, some tie to that world. I don't want to get you off on autobiography at this point. I am perfectly willing to discuss it now or later, but I have it in there my father telling of his boyhood and of his own father, who died when he was quite young, when he was about sixteen. The burden of the family on him. And his older brother ran away to Mexico and made a success as a mining engineer. But Father took the responsibility, even as little more than a boy, to raise the family (and take care of a stepmother little older than he and his half brothers and a sister), and struggle for his education and at his writing. In my study there're two or three of my father's old Greek books I want to show you.

WATKINS: I want to see those. You mention them in your poems.

WARREN: He was studying; he hired a tutor at the university to tutor him in Greek, and he learned French from an Alsatian clerk in a boot or shoe store. He was French Alsatian. My father took me to see this old man once. He had given my father lessons for a long time. The other day I found another of the Greek books. There was a dictionary with his name on it and a date on it. Battered. The backs torn off. His books had been thrown around by his stepmother, who was a woman of very little education. And I found the books when I was a boy—in a closet or an attic, a lumber room of some sort. When I was a little boy, I had to spend my yearly, annual day with her, you see, because my father said, "She is a good woman, and she has done the best she could. Because you find her dull and stupid is no reason why you shouldn't spend a day there as a matter of decency, you see."

WATKINS: And that's where you found Dante?

WARREN: That's where I found the Dante and other books like that. I don't understand; it is a mystery to me here. I don't understand how this farmer—my father's father—in the 1850's or '60's. . . . He was rather a young man so he probably got married at twenty or twenty-one, as they did in those days. Where he got all these books now, where would he come in contact with the sources of the books? Of course these small sorts of log colleges, they called them, usually Presbyterian ministers, from, say, Princeton, wandering around and setting up a little school. It must have been that. By the way, it's easy to misunderstand that semifrontier world. When I worked with the Melville papers at Yale and Harvard, I found a letter to Melville from the Clarksville, Tennessee, Literary Society; in 1857, I think it was dated. After Melville had come back from the Holy Land and his trip to Europe, which was (he said) for curative purposes (he was about to lose his mind). This was a very formal letter, signed by so and so, secretary of the Clarksville Literary Society and signed by the president, other officials, saying, "Dear Mr. Melville, The members of our society have read all of your works and discussed them in great detail."[42] Now this was in a town of about three or four hundred people—maybe more—in Tennessee, you see, in the 1850's. I recognized the names as old settlers—names still carried on in the neighborhood. Now, 150 years later, I'm sure you wouldn't find four leading citizens of a thriving city like Clarksville who read Melville.

WATKINS: That's unusual.

WARREN: "We have read all of your works as part of our general interest in literature. We are great admirers. We hear that you are going to give a series of lectures this coming fall, and we have no concern with your fee. We have no concern with your fee if we can have your presence, can see the man, and shake the hand of the man whose work we admire so much; we would consider it an inestimable privilege. If you would let us know on what terms we could persuade you to come to Clarksville."

WATKINS: Did he ever come?

WARREN: So far as I know, he never came—in fact, no biography ever says he did—and there is nothing else in the file in the library. It is strange, these backwoods contacts, you see. Things like that. It is a strange floating culture that was mixed up with all of the frontier. Brutality and ignorance. This grasping for something else going on in many places. And on the frontier, you could usually find adventurers or pioneers of culture, or cultural yearnings.

WATKINS: I believe that probably happened more around Guthrie than it would have in my hill country. No one where my father grew up and his family in South Carolina did that.

WARREN: But Guthrie had not then been founded. It was a railroad town, not like the native settlements. Guthrie was founded as a railroad junction, in '79, after the Civil War. It has no relation and very little to do with the ordinary Southern settlement. It is a different kind of town, a real-estate venture where two railroads make a crossing.

WATKINS: I meant that general area of Clarksville. When you went to Smithland, what did you hope to find in the place that would have a connection to your poem?

WARREN: I just wanted to see it and see what it's like. Concreteness.

WATKINS: Well, I've been there myself.

WARREN: You've been to Smithland?

WATKINS: I have.

WARREN: And did you go up to the top of the hill?

WATKINS: I was older than you were when you went, and it was the hottest day of the hottest summer; so the man who was there told me he didn't have much sense but he had too much sense to try to climb it.

WARREN: He had been up it.

WATKINS: Yes. But today I didn't climb.

WARREN: Uh huh.

WATKINS: Do you think there is, well, we both went for curiosity, but I have a feeling—I don't know whether it came from your poem or from history—but I still feel that there is something there between the crime and the place. Is that absurd?

WARREN: I wouldn't want it absurd. Of course it's gone back to wilderness and the carriage road built up there to the place is in ruins and rubble now. You can see the old stone work bracing the road—the retaining walls up to the big house.

WATKINS: It is overgrown in trees entirely now.

WARREN: It's all gone?

WATKINS: Overgrown entirely in trees.

WARREN: But on the top, as I remember it, there was a kind of a tree-grown meadow. There were grazing cattle back in there and big trees with open grazing space between them, but the snake is true.

WATKINS: You saw the snake?

WARREN: I saw the snake. It was staring at me on a pile of stone work of a ruined chimney, a big old central chimney. And this snake, an *elaphe obsoleta obsoleta*, is big, you know. That is, it wasn't a black racer, but the other kind, bigger. I've checked on this. They grow as long as eight feet, but five and a half to six is the usual length. This thing rolls up [*Gesture; laughter*] about three feet and a half from my face, looking down at me like that. And this was a find, the very spirit of the demon of the place. And that the thing happened, actually happened, was too good to be true because you would have to put it in if it didn't happen.

WATKINS: Yes.

WARREN: You would have to put it in there anyway. And the little town was just about like Hannibal, Missouri, in Mark Twain's time, a little river town, defunct. And a little brick jail on the green, and a man in jail hanging on the bars, and a little girl.

WATKINS: You saw the man and the girl?

WARREN: And the girl and a tin cup, and she'd play with acorns or dolls or something under the window of the jail. Then the man would yell, "Daughter!" And the daughter'd go and she'd get the cup and go pump him some fresh water, and he'd take a drink. The town drunk, you know, sobering up, no harm in him, just a drunkard. And the little girl, six or seven, five maybe, taking care of her drunk Pappy in jail. When I first went there in those days, there was little paved road, gravel, and it was wild. The last time I was there they had good signs, traffic lights, and they had some pavement, and the Korean War had made them prosperous.

WATKINS: They have rebuilt two or three of those old homes now.

WARREN: They have?

WATKINS: So that they look beautiful. Did you see the inn there where Lafayette and Charles Dickens stopped on their journeys . . . ?

WARREN: In Smithland?

WATKINS: Yes.

WARREN: I saw it, but it didn't mean anything to me at the time.

WATKINS: It is still very much falling down.

WARREN: It is?

WATKINS: Yes.

WARREN: The oldest inn in Kentucky in continuous use is in Bardstown, which used to be beautiful and had marvelous food. It had a clock, about four feet square in the face, on a short stubby bottom, keeping time. I was interested in it, and I began to inquire about it, and the proprietor (this was Nelson County, in the thirties, in Bardstown) told me that a pioneer (way in the backwoods) family had taken a wandering preacher for some days, and the preacher had a watch. The fourteen- or fifteen-year-old boy had never seen a watch. He would look at it and look at it and try to see what made it work, and the preacher would try to explain it to him, and the boy would draw pictures of it as best he could, and after about a year or two of struggle, he made a clock that would keep time. All carved with a hunting knife from hardwood. Now that boy had the mind of an Einstein.

WATKINS: He did.

WARREN: With that much of a start, to build a timepiece which was there in the inn, I'm trying to trace the thing now. I've got a man trying to trace the thing in Kentucky—who's got it. Of course, the old inn folded. They've got a little junk eatery, you know, in that beautiful building. But I'm trying to trace that pioneer boy's clock.

WATKINS: This is old territory that we don't need to rehash, but what right does the artist have to make a change in, say, the character of Jefferson? Jefferson in your poem I believe has already at the beginning of the poem completely changed his idea about perfectibility . . .

WARREN: He's dead. He's dead. He now wants no part of . . .

WATKINS: So you're not changing the living Jefferson?

WARREN: No, not changing the living Jefferson. He's dead. He's a spook. He speaks of much later events in American history. They're all spooks. It's said in the poem. This is no place and no time—this dialogue has no place and no time—a meeting of spooks, as it were. A real person like myself may step in and talk too. But I'll add this: nobody knows what effect the terrible crime in his own blood had on Jefferson.

WATKINS: I see.

WARREN: But the poem is a fantasy. It is all one large metaphor. Put it that way. It is thought of as one large metaphor. I see no obligation when you put a historical character into a poem or a novel to be bound by any fact. You say, I'm doing this my way. Now there's a bargain that goes on from very close to the reality or to the actuality or as close as you want to get it, to a pure fantasy. But I see no principle involved there. If the reader knows what you're doing. If I put Lucy's grave on Lilburn's farm or Lilburn's plantation, instead of on his brother's plantation up the river, I don't feel bad about it. I don't feel I'm lying. I want the relation to the mother, because the mother's pitcher is the cause of the killing of the Negro, you see. The mother's pitcher, a gift from Jefferson.

WATKINS: Yes.

WARREN: And I want Lilburn to go out and look at the mother's grave and to hate the grass because the grass will grow back and cover it up. Robbing him again of his mother by covering up the grave. And I want those things more than I want accuracy with where she's buried. His first wife was actually buried out there. I just transferred the graves.

WATKINS: I taught this work especially in the sixties to my classes in Southern literature, and once I asked the class after I had taught it, "What would you think about my leaving out *Brother to Dragons?*" I was met with a howl of protest because they felt, surprisingly to me, a very strange and strong affinity with the work's definition of the possibility of the evil of man. I found that rather surprising in college students. And maybe this is too much outside the work, but I believe the current generation may be renouncing perfectibility more than my generation did. Or perhaps yours.

WARREN: I think that is probably true, though you have in modern education the great drift toward "let's improve it," you know. "Let's improve man. Let's make man different." I say "improve" too, but I know that it's slow and hard. And you have the other old-fashioned view that man could make himself better with institutions and so forth, with some organized approaches very different from the old-fashioned notion of facing the self (a conscience, or God).

WATKINS: You read Meriwether Lewis's speech at the Fugitives' Reunion.

WARREN: I had forgotten that.

WATKINS: Is that speech preserved pretty much intact in the new version?

WARREN: Yes. That's preserved. I've done some changing in versification and I've done some cutting in that, the Meriwether Lewis speech. It is substantially the same. I have done some cutting and some changes in rhythm and some other things.

WATKINS: The work must exist in dozens of versions by this time.

WARREN: It does indeed. There's some samples. Just opening at random, some sample pages. I tried to cut. I tried to change rhythms, and I tried to cut. Those are very slight cuts. There's sometimes one little thing, one little thing like that will change the rhythm of a passage, you see [*Turning the thick manuscript*]. Those are—every—page—those are—there's nothing on those pages. There's a whole section cut there, you see. These are additional pages that have had to be added. And whole sections like that. It's a reworking; it's a thorough reworking over many years. Sometimes one word gets changed. Sometimes a whole page.

WATKINS: Have you thought of the similarities in technique between *Brother to Dragons* and Faulkner's *Absalom, Absalom!*?

WARREN: It never crossed my mind.

WATKINS: That wouldn't negate the similarities.

WARREN: It wouldn't negate the similarities. It never crossed my mind, is what I'm saying. That's not saying it is not true.

WATKINS: It seems to me that it's an unusual likeness in Quentin's and Shreve's and the other narrators' of *Absalom, Absalom!* searching for the truth of the past and their knowledge of their region and man in those long discussions in a way that is certainly not unlike the search for the truth in *Brother to Dragons*.

WARREN: What you are saying makes sense to me, but I would also say that these are not the only two examples of this in literature. You see, it isn't just A and B only; it's A to Z. In any case, it never crossed my mind. Not that I'd care if it had.

WATKINS: Well, I think it is a mark of the greatness of the two works—they may be two of the best examples of their . . .

WARREN: Of their time? But I'm saying it didn't cross my mind. Let me say one more thing. There can be all sorts of influences, all sorts of suggestions from other works that you are never aware of.

WATKINS: Oh, surely.

WARREN: And then life itself. Life itself.

WATKINS: Even a spirit like mine which is not creative like yours can certainly see that.

WARREN: You can't say yea or no to certain questions because you don't know. What I do know is that it never crossed my mind.

Poetry as a Way of Life: An Interview with Robert Penn Warren

The following interview first appeared in The Georgia Review *in 1982 and is a composite of conversations David Farrell and Warren had in Connecticut and Kentucky during 1980 and 1981. "At least one of our talks was brief," Farrell remembers, "—just a few questions and answers after breakfast in his Fairfield home—but other conversations lasted for hours and ranged widely in their subjects and moods."*

DAVID FARRELL: Did your parents or family encourage any artistic interests in you?

WARREN: I started out to be a painter as a twelve-year-old. One summer my father tried to get me a teacher, and the only teacher he could locate (though she wasn't very good) was Sister Mary Luke, a nun at St. Cecilia's Academy in Nashville. So I stayed with a family who knew my mother, and I went out to St. Cecilia's every morning on the 8 o'clock bus and painted all day with Sister Mary Luke. I was mad to paint animals; this is what coincided with my interest in the woods—the boy naturalist, you see. You know, many boys have that phase.

FARRELL: Were you particularly fond of birds?

WARREN: Well, I was very keen about birds, but animals even more so, even snakes which I captured and kept around.

FARRELL: A sort of boy Audubon? Did you capture animals to paint from life?

WARREN: Sometimes I did, but most of the animals I did that summer with Sister Mary Luke (when I began to get a little technique—God knows I was no good, as I quickly discovered) were animals in Glendale Park Zoo. She would go with me and, poor old lady, she'd lie on her back and snore like an elephant in her robes—you know, with her little black kid shoes pointed skyward—while I would paint a lion or something. I painted the whole damned zoo, practically. And she'd snore and then wake up, then we'd eat all this great delicious feast that the nuns had sent out with us. They all took an interest in me: I was the only male in the whole academy. I came only in the morning and went back out at night. I painted in the studio with her sometimes, too. Sweet old thing; I called on her years later when she was a very old lady still in the nunnery, and we talked over old times.

FARRELL: Was she a trained artist?

WARREN: She had taken first prize in watercolor at the Chicago World's Fair. She had that much of a reputation, whatever that means; I don't know. She had some talent; she knew a lot of technical things.

FARRELL: You worked primarily in watercolor?

WARREN: Yes. And she knew a lot about watercolor, about the application of watercolor. I didn't. That's the last I ever painted except when I went to California. Every time I got to California I'd want to paint.

FARRELL: Why?

WARREN: It's such a paintable land out there. I was there in graduate school and during the summers in the thirties. And one summer I spent painting, partly with the wife of a couple who were visiting us up in deep, wild country. She was a rather good painter, in fact, but somehow it didn't seem quite appropriate to my then-wife when I'd go off to the mountains with another painter, so it sort of broke down.

FARRELL: This was in northern California?

WARREN: Yes, where there are the great yellow hills and mountains, wonderful yellow hills and live oak, and the sky—all full of colors. But I never pursued painting elsewhere. I haven't touched a brush in years and I never will again. I know I'm no painter, but I had the impulse to get the images of landscape down whenever I was in California. I can understand what's behind the landscape painter's impulse—the link with nature, I mean.

FARRELL: I heard that you made some paintings inspired by *The Waste Land* when you were an undergraduate at Vanderbilt.

WARREN: Well, "paintings" is not the word for it.

FARRELL: What were they?

WARREN: Well, this goes back to the little room in Wesley Hall, the Divinity School at Vanderbilt, which I shared my sophomore year with Allen Tate, William Cobb (a graduate student who later became a textbook editor at Houghton Mifflin), and Ridley Wills. Wills had fought in World War I and published a novel before I knew him.[43] Now, while finishing college, he was also an editorial writer on a local paper. Wills asked me to come room with him, and I was greatly flattered; he was a most amusing man, wonderfully witty and friendly, and he knew a lot and read a lot.

So there were four of us in two double-deckers in a tiny room. The room was filled with dirty shirts, cigarette butts, filth to the waist, and empty bottles. Gangs of people would come there to argue poetry and read aloud. Tate would hold forth and Wills would hold forth on some poet, and so I contributed by decorating the walls with episodes from *The Waste Land* and *The Triumph of an Egg*[44] and God knows what else.

FARRELL: What did you draw with?

WARREN: Well, the walls were so dirty I simply drew on them with art gum. They were comic representations. I discovered that by using an eraser you'd get back to a pale yellow, a perfect line. Then the University wanted to make me pay for the damage, and I said, "Well, if you'd clean the walls properly you wouldn't have any damage. I was simply getting part of the dirt from your walls; it's your job to do the rest." And I got by with that.

. . . .

The only thing approaching "creative writing" was this three months, one term, course in advanced writing; thank God there was no other creative writing course. I studied literature the rest of my time there, and philosophy.

. . . There was the miracle of people like Donald Davidson, who in sophomore English would allow you to write imitations instead of the biweekly critique. You could write a new episode for *Beowulf*, keeping all the form—not in Old English, of course, but keeping all the alliterative form. Or Chaucer: we could write a new Chaucerian episode. Every two weeks I always chose, or nearly always chose, to do an imitation, unless it was somebody like Lamb whom I wouldn't be caught dead imitating.

. . . .

FARRELL: So you began by writing imitations.

WARREN: Well, it was not a deliberate intention, but the thing was there, I can see now, looking back on it. And there were poetry societies; there were formal ones and there was an informal one. And one friend somewhat older, who was expert in French, gave what amounted to a seminar many a night from about 9 o'clock until 4 in the morning on Baudelaire or Rimbaud; he had a big collection already of such things and later had one of the great Baudelaire collections, which is now in the Vanderbilt library.

FARRELL: How did this influence your writing at the time?

WARREN: Well, I just know it did. Rimbaud—how much? I don't know. It was, you know, some booze (in reasonable quantities) and Baudelaire; this fellow, W. T. Bandy, started

Tate on Baudelaire translations. Bandy created a one-man Left Bank on West Side Row. And then there was the new type of poetry. Ransom was never very hot on Hart Crane or on T. S. Eliot, but I was deeply impressed by them both and by Ezra Pound.

Then in junior year I had a brilliant teacher of Shakespeare, Walter Clyde Curry, and then I salted away the Elizabethans as well as I could to go with the Shakespeare—here Tate and other friends being guides. . . . And the imitations of the poetry later wound up in poems of mine like "Bearded Oaks," which has a touch of the Marvellian, or "The Garden," which is definitely a Marvell imitation.

Under a maple tree on a blanket, on a weekend visit to Guthrie, John Ransom read some Hardy to some other guests and me one afternoon, and I was never the same. I thought, this is the real thing, and I still think it is. He's the greatest poet after Wordsworth up to . . . I don't know who or where you should stop. I used to say, to Eliot, and I still think Eliot's a very great poet. But somehow I like Hardy more; he was somehow a writer I felt closer to. And I first saw in Ransom's poetry—the first book, *Poems About God*—a world I could feel some recognition of. You see, I could feel *his* experience, not mine; I could feel experience, human experience, through his work. Ransom made me see poetry in the common light I saw around me every day, in the country. Hardy did the same thing for me. Of course, he's a very massive, much more massive, poet than Ransom; a much bigger poet. Ransom was more polished, more classical and literary, less ambitious, a more nearly "perfect" poet. Ransom was mad for Hardy, as a matter of fact.

FARRELL: Was Whitman in Ransom's pantheon?

WARREN: No, I don't think he ever mentioned Whitman. But, mentioning pantheons, don't let's make Ransom's taste the point here. "Ransom and his disciples"—that phrase would have appalled him. There were people with violent divisions in the Fugitive Group; I mean, Tate and Ransom almost had a breaking of friendship over *The Waste Land*. And there was no church, as it were, of principle. They had a common

passion in poetry and a common background in the world
and a mutual respect; but there was usually a finger-shaking
quality as much as a *bruderschaft.*

FARRELL: Like many families, a range of tastes?

WARREN: Yes, like a family. You can't make any school out of
their poetry, you see; many had totally different views, violently different views. They hung together because they were
all crazy about poetry.

FARRELL: Whom did you know at Vanderbilt besides members
of the Fugitives?

WARREN: Well, I had another set of friends who were different
people entirely.

FARRELL: At the same time you were learning about literature?

WARREN: At the same time. They didn't even know each other.
The last three years at Vanderbilt I was rooming with poets
but I had other friends, too. Some were journalists; some
were ruffians.

FARRELL: Students?

WARREN: Graduate students, mostly.

FARRELL: Were they of a more scholarly bent than the creative
ones you knew?

WARREN: They weren't scholarly at all; they were able to do
their work, but none too seriously. Most of them never
amounted to anything as far as I know. The ones I was
closest to who *did* amount to something were Charles Moss
(a young poet who later, however, was editor of the *Nashville Banner*); Ralph McGill, who started out as a sports-
writer (out of Vanderbilt) for the *Atlanta Constitution* and
wound up as an editor and then publisher with a national
column; and Brainard Cheney, who knows more about Tennessee politics than any living man, still a close friend, wonderful company. He helped me a great deal when I was writing *All the King's Men.* These three were a constant source
of information, pornography, and friendship. We remained
friends all our lives. Only Cheney still lives. Ralph was a man
of great wit and courage who helped me when I was writing
Who Speaks for the Negro?

You know, it almost dropped out of my mind until now,

the memory of that first period of poetry. It was so different from what I had set my life up to be; I mean, being a naval officer and all of that. But the poetry became so extraordinarily important to me. The reading of it and the trying to write it became simply matters of life and death to me.

FARRELL: During the Vanderbilt years?

WARREN: Yes. And part of it was the influence of the people I knew and the Fugitive group. I absorbed so much from them. But there was something else, too, involved in it, I think—now that I look back on it. This real sort of passion I got for poetry may have been due in large part to my fear of going blind at that time. I had been told that the injury to the first eye somehow would affect the other eye, you see; nobody understood why, so far as I know.

FARRELL: Your physicians thought that the injury to the first eye might transfer to the second eye?

WARREN: That's right; you could get sympathetic blindness. So I was watching for this and for a while using glasses on the other eye to protect it. And I got fits of depression during that period. I felt myself going blind. I was sort of, you know, watching, watching, watching . . . always aware of it. And my refuge became in a way the study of poetry and the writing of poetry.

FARRELL: So you had all the pleasure and excitement of new friends and the discovery of poetry, but at the same time you were terribly anxious about your physical handicap?

WARREN: That's right. I was sometimes—God knows, not always—in a state of depression, and I'd fight it by work and by the passion I had for poetry and by the natural pursuits of youth. I don't mean anything ever was said, but the fact is that certain friends, a few of them, took a real interest in helping me.[45] I didn't realize it at the time, no, but I must have sensed it.

And this was a great support to me, though I loathe the word "support." I had these fits of depression, one of which actually led to a suicide attempt. I would never do that again; I would never *have* done it because it was so wicked, as the results would have been for other people.

FARRELL: Did your friends know about your depression or your suicide attempt?

WARREN: I never talked about it. They were bound to know about the attempt, yes. That was bound to be known, and for a while it was misinterpreted by various people. I never tried to explain it to anyone.

FARRELL: How could it have been misinterpreted?

WARREN: I mean the reason for it, which was that I was quite sure at that time—I had talked myself into the notion—that I really was going blind. I was watching every day, you see, and it was a constant obsession.

FARRELL: Did you consult doctors to get a medical opinion?

WARREN: No, I didn't. I was afraid to face it. I just worried about it; I never discussed it with anybody.

FARRELL: When did the fear finally leave you?

WARREN: Well, it remained a long time, but I never got that down again with it, you see. Later on, the doctors began to get certain of the effect on the other eye, so they removed the bad eye (which by then was completely blind). This was in 1932 or 1933 when I was teaching at Vanderbilt.

FARRELL: What were your feelings about the handicap itself?

WARREN: Well, I felt maimed. One thing was the purely psychological effect of *feeling* maimed.

FARRELL: Even though it wasn't apparent?

WARREN: Even though it wasn't; still, it gave a sense of somehow feeling disqualified . . . or maimed, you know. It's something that one sensible talk with one sensible person might have changed; but I never had a sensible talk with a sensible person about it.

FARRELL: You had sensible people around you.

WARREN: But we never discussed it. It was never mentioned.

FARRELL: Not even to your parents? Or to Ransom?

WARREN: No, I never talked about anything with my parents, not seriously. I mean, I was totally aware of their affection and concern for me, but we never had any talks. Meanwhile I was leading a perfectly normal college-boy life; I mean, going to parties and dances, and had girl friends and all the rest of it, you know. And in the summers I'd get jobs of hard physical work. When seventeen I toted a Springfield rifle around Fort Knox in the ROTC camp. The next summer, to stay in Nashville where I had friends and a girl, I drove a truck for American Express. And I once worked on the highway; pick and shovel work. I liked that. But it was all a façade.

FARRELL: Consciously a façade?

WARREN: Yes. Well, no—only at times. This life had its real interest. But it was a way of trying to distract myself, you see, and the poetry was the thing that was a real, passionate concern with me. It was a way of talking to somebody or of talking to yourself; it was kind of like taking dope.

FARRELL: Do you think this anxiety came out in those early poems?

WARREN: I don't know; I never thought of that. That's the natural thing to think about but I never did. Now I see that wanting to be a poet gave some direction to my life which was lacking in the first year or so in college.

FARRELL: Did it make you feel special; I mean, other than feeling maimed? Did you feel your injury gave you a special outlook?

WARREN: No, I've never had that sense about it at all. I don't have any sense of the poet as a special person in any sense at all. He's a man who has a special interest in life, yes—but no more than a lot of other people do, no more than a man in the Pacific fleet might have.

FARRELL: But there are, obviously, differences between the poet's outlook and the sailor's.

WARREN: Obvious differences yes, but none that mattered for me at that point. Poetry then was a refuge, it was something to do, it was (and is) simply something I got a great emotional bang out of. And fear of blindness was a chief factor in those years, but it's so far away I had almost forgotten it. I think of those times now without even thinking of that.

FARRELL: Since Vanderbilt, your professions have been writing and teaching, and you've seen a lot of the world. I wonder about your life in Italy—just to pick more or less randomly among experiences that have greatly influenced you. Why did you go to Italy?

. . . .

WARREN: Well, I've always been interested in the Elizabethans; I took my graduate work chiefly in Elizabethan literature. And I had an interest in Italian history from that; a lot of things take one back to Italy. For instance, you can't understand Thomas Wyatt without knowing what he did with Petrarch. I once did a complete comparison of Wyatt and Petrarch—line by line—but got no impulse to publish it. And of Aretino, too.

So I got to reading Italian, and later all those things flowed into the novel *All the King's Men.* Machiavelli and Italian history flowed into that, too; the whole case of the man of power, the man of virtue and the world about him, flowed into the novel (along with William James and American history). They all tied back to my learning to read Italian and then coming to Italy as some sort of vague . . . what? You can't explain these things.

FARRELL: You taught Elizabethan literature, didn't you?

WARREN: I taught Shakespeare, and for years I taught a graduate course in nondramatic Elizabethan literature. I was soaked in Shakespeare from the years I'd taught it. In fact, I had always planned in old age to write a book on Shakespeare as poet, a very special kind of book. There isn't one like it even yet. I don't mean just the sonnets and lyrics; I mean the plays, too.

FARRELL: When did you first go to Italy?

WARREN: I was there in Perugia and Umbria in the summer of '38. Then at Sirmione. In fact, I began writing the verse play *All the King's Men* there, in a wheat field near Perugia, sitting under an olive tree. And I wound up towards Christmas in Rome, in '39, hearing the boot heels of the Fascist troops on the cobblestones.

FARRELL: Did you see Mussolini?

WARREN: Oh, yes, speaking in front of the Palazzo Venezia.

FARRELL: Did you meet Pound in Rome?

WARREN: No; I had known Pound slightly in Paris in 1928 or 1929 when I was an Oxford graduate student. But I didn't look him up in Italy. By that time I was thinking he was a crazy man—though a great poet, which I still think.

That same year I was writing a great deal of poetry, and I finished the basic version of *All the King's Men* at Christmas. Then I went back to *At Heaven's Gate* during the winter of 1939–1940. At one point I became stuck. Then I had typhus with a good deal of fever. In a delirium one night my problem was suddenly solved. I had the most vivid dreams during this fever and went through the whole story of the mountaineer coming down the river and into Nashville and his torch blowing the thing up. That all began with a dream.

FARRELL: A dream, or a series of dreams?

WARREN: I'm not sure; it seemed continuous. The fever had breaks and would begin again and break and begin again, you see. The fever was up to a hundred and four or five.

FARRELL: Were you in a hospital?

WARREN: I was at home with a nurse, and the nurse would put her feet on the pillow by my face at night and she would snore. God, what a nurse! She knew nothing about nursing, for sure, but those feet and that snoring! Anyway, that was a dream; but the typhus and the feet weren't dreams. And, God, the fool Fascist doctor! He didn't even know it was typhus. I got that diagnosis back home from a record of the symptoms. And when I got well enough to write I had the novel practically written.

FARRELL: Dreams come up a lot in your work, especially in recent poems.

WARREN: Well, I dream a lot. I love dreams, especially funny dreams, funny, elaborate dreams. I'll tell you one. I'm in a barroom that somehow is like a fake barroom scene in the Far West; but clearly fake—as if it had canvas walls or something. There's a big bar, a lot of high-heeled gunmen around with Stetsons—ranchers and cowhands and so forth—and everybody's drinking. A man leaps on the bar. He's a man of some importance, a rancher, and he has a gun in each hand, and he says, "Everybody knows I know how to use a pistol." He waves them around and he says, "Somebody here's betrayed my daughter. Now, I never shot a man down without warning. I'm going to give him the count of ten to declare himself." And he begins, "One . . ." and he shoots out a light. But it doesn't make a boom; it makes a "ping"! Then, "Two . . . three . . ." He got to nine and then, "Ha, ha, ha!"—a burst of laughter comes in sudden blackness and a big explosion, and offstage a voice says, "And he fell with sixty bullet holes in his body!"

FARRELL: What was your role in this dream?

WARREN: I'm an observer.

FARRELL: Not the man who's betrayed the daughter?

WARREN: No. I wish I had been, but I can't say that I was.

FARRELL: Is this a recurring dream?

WARREN: No; it just happened once. And I often dream poems.

FARRELL: Whole poems? And you wake up and write them down?

WARREN: No, I've never done that in my life except once: a short poem. The dream may come back when I'm writing later, or it may not. But mostly my dreams are comic; I often awaken laughing. But I have to say, I've sort of had my quota of vague anxiety dreams, too—nagging anxiety dreams. I don't remember those very well. I'm a pretty heavy sleeper, and I don't awaken much unless my wife kicks me for snoring. Then I go in the next room and sulk.

FARRELL: What took you both back to Italy in the 1950's when you were writing *Promises*?

WARREN: I had spent a year there just after the war, on a second Guggenheim. But in 1954, when I went back, the summer I began *Promises*, I had recently married Eleanor, and we had a baby. Italy meant a lot to my wife and to me. She had spent a lot of time there in childhood. Several years before, one Sunday, we had once gone to Cosa on the Tuscan coast, where Frank Brown, who was a Yale professor, was supervising a dig. Eleanor pointed to a castle on a hill across the bay and said, "I'm going over there tomorrow, and I'm going to live there." And she worked it out. She found the old lady who owned the fortress, and she got a big section of it.

FARRELL: Did you move in then?

WARREN: No, *she* moved in; we weren't married yet. Much later we got better acquainted. Anyway, that's the reason we were there in Italy; but there were so many factors. . . . It was a new life with wonderful swimming, and so forth. And Italian friends. . . . In this great fortress by the sea— in Argentario, which had been the Borgias' hunting ground at one time. But the fortress was not begun until 1559, by Philip II of Spain. It's a blood-drenched place and an incredible, beautiful place as well. And we had a pretty, yellow-haired baby girl, a baby of a year, and next door was an idiot child and a saintly older sister of twelve or so who kept trying to teach the child to say one thing, to say "Ciao," the Italian greeting.

FARRELL: What was your apartment like?

WARREN: Well, we rented a big quadrangle of the fortress. The apartment had a tremendous living room about seventy feet long—it had been a stable when the Spanish were there—a big stone room with a stone floor and beamed ceiling and a built-in stove at one end. We had a marvelous cook and oleanders blooming around and dust and storms and sea in every direction. Across the quadrangle there were some regular rooms which we used as bedrooms, and we had a sort of reception room close to the big room where we occasionally entertained guests while the cooking was going on.

Then we had, way high up, the *vedetta*, a lookout house. It had two rooms and a hall between and a toilet to share; so Eleanor had one room for her study and I had the other for my study. But I worked outdoors chiefly. And there were moats seventy feet deep on each side of the castle—all a most elaborate piece of Renaissance military architecture, extraordinarily elaborate. And beautiful. . . . So, every time Eleanor and I went to Italy, it was poems, poems, poems. It's a magic country; crazy, crazy, crazy. It was magic.

And the poems that resulted were a combination of my childhood and my early world and the country and the European world. They played back and forth, intermingled. Not autobiography—that would have been too easy—but a psychological penetration. From that time on, poetry never ceased again. That book, *Promises,* came out; it took all the prizes; was a fresh start.

FARRELL: While we're on the subject of writing a successful collection of poems, what would you say the profession of poet means to you?

WARREN: Well, there's something I can say about it. I would say poetry is a way of life, ultimately—not a kind of performance, not something you do on Saturday or Easter morning or Christmas morning or something like that. It's a way of being open to the world, a way of being open to experience. I would say, open to *your* experience, insofar as you can see it or at least feel it as a unit with all its contradictions and confusions. Poetry, for me, is not something you do after you get it fixed in your mind. Poetry is a way of thinking or a way of feeling; a way of exploring.

FARRELL: Can it be summed up in your phrase, one that goes something like "[It's] a way to love God"?

WARREN: Well, yes, I think so. It's a way to accept, to deal with the world. A way to love God?—yes, I think it is. If you want to put it that way. The only way some people can live is by assuming that life is worth being interested in. It's worth giving yourself to; and giving the best you can. I would also say that poetry is not like a profession, but a way of life. These are two quite different things.

FARRELL: A profession isn't a way of life?

WARREN: Not often; not usually; not necessarily. Very infrequently you find a devoted family doctor or somebody to whom his profession is a way of life. It can be a way of life, but I'm saying that poetry damn well *better* be a way of life, because it's something quite different. It's a way of existing meaningfully as much of your time as possible. And that's never much.

FARRELL: Are you distinguishing between poetry and prose?

WARREN: No. I wouldn't set poetry apart from prose here. I think this would be perfectly true of a novelist or a dramatist. I'm really talking about literary art—or any art. But since we were talking about poetry I kept it to poetry.

FARRELL: Are you still writing prose?

WARREN: I've sworn off all expository prose. I'm not going to write any more lectures and I'm not going to write explanations or criticism.

FARRELL: Short stories?

WARREN: Short stories kill poems.

FARRELL: How about novels?

WARREN: I started to write a novel a summer or two ago; I owe Random House a novel. And for a week or ten days—or more, a month—I started every morning at 9:30 and put a pad on my knees and picked up my pen and started to write a novel. And after an hour or so, I had not written a line of a novel, but way down in the corner I had started a poem. So, despite my good intentions, I gave it up. I felt very good about the novel, and I wanted to write it, but the poetry was just too demanding.

FARRELL: It seems like you feel almost in harness, almost gripped, by the poetic urge.

WARREN: For now, yes. The future will take care of itself, and I'll write the novel if I can. I just don't believe in making something a job that doesn't have to be a job.

FARRELL: You're enjoying good fortune with poetry now; you're writing more than ever.

WARREN: Well, I've got more time than ever before. I do a lot of gardening, and I do a lot of extra things, but I stay home a lot.

FARRELL: Would you have written much more in the past if you'd had more free time?

WARREN: I would have put time into poetry, if I'd been freer; but, you see, I enjoyed teaching so much. . . . I liked it, knowing the young. They're stimulating; they have ideas; they are a different world, and your own children don't make up for it. In one way you know more about other people's children than you know about your own. My own I know in a different and deeper way.

FARRELL: Some readers of your work have remarked that you're drawing more, and more consciously, on memory now, late in life.

WARREN: Yes; I'm drawing more and more on memory. Memory reinterpreted, of course; not memory taken literally. It has a strange liability; I feel like I'm using up stock, capital. You know, there are so many things that happen that you don't know the meaning of at the time; they acquire meaning only after a long time. They *may* acquire meaning after a time. I'd have to say there's an apprehension, too, at this late stage. One thinks about the day when it won't come.

FARRELL: Of course, that's always been true. One day it won't come.

WARREN: Sure, it's always been true, but nobody ever liked it!

FARRELL: You feel a lot closer, then? It's around the corner . . .

WARREN: Right; not ten miles down the pike, you see.

FARRELL: Do you feel pressure about that, a sense of urgency?

WARREN: No, I don't feel that way at all. I feel more leisurely, in fact; I can take all day with a line, then throw it away. That's how I live—with that limitation. And one thing one has to realize is that there's no virtue in writing a poem if it isn't good. Just writing a poem doesn't mean a goddam thing. Anybody can write a sort of poem.

FARRELL: Well, your poems are finding publication readily in a variety of journals; critics like them; people think they're very good.

WARREN: That's something you can't know, really. Let's hope so . . . but, you know the breaking point's approaching—you're bound to know that. The thing to know is to know when you've hit that line and try not to force it.

FARRELL: How are you going to know?

WARREN: God's got to tell you. Just trust God—whatever God is.

FARRELL: So, for the present, you're writing and you're pleased enough with what you're writing. Do you think your writing is as good as it's ever been?

WARREN: I've done some of my best poems in the last few years, and I've thrown away a lot of poems I didn't think were. Quite a few I've thrown away. I'll just say that it's the best I can do. Ultimate judgments are just not to be had, you know. The whole history of literature or art shows us that painting something to one generation means nothing to another generation.

FARRELL: Are you working every day?

WARREN: Not every day. I've been doing a lot of hot, physical work for the past month. I haven't written a poem in a month. I've been using a pick and shovel in the yard!

FARRELL: That's another kind of vigor remarkable for a seventy-five-year-old . . .

WARREN: Yes, six hours a day of it. If you don't believe it, look around the place.

Of Bookish Men and the Fugitives

Warren was the focus of an Institute for Southern Studies program at the University of South Carolina in 1982. When he was unable to attend, Thomas L. Connelly went to New Haven and interviewed him on camera. The following is an edited transcription of the videotaped interview made February 10, 1982, and first published in A Southern Renascence Man: Views of Robert Penn Warren *(1984).*

CONNELLY: Mr. Warren, we're sorry you can't be with us at the Southern Studies Institute program in South Carolina.

WARREN: I'm very sorry for more reasons than that of climate—humanly sorry but I must say that our luncheon conversation was some compensation for the fact that I couldn't come.

CONNELLY: Well, we'll miss having you there. I would like to ask you first some things about your background as a writer. We're both from the same area of the country; I grew up in middle Tennessee and you grew up in Todd County, Kentucky, which is really a cultural satellite, I suppose, of Nashville.

WARREN: Well, a hundred yards from the state line, whatever you want to call that.

CONNELLY: As a matter of fact, you went to high school in Montgomery County, Tennessee, in Clarksville.

WARREN: Well, one year. I went the first three years in Guthrie, and being young to graduate from Guthrie was no great feat, I must say. And I couldn't get in Vanderbilt because I was not old enough, so I had the good sense—or the good luck—to go to a very good high school in Clarksville the next year while waiting for my sixteenth year to go to Vanderbilt. Autobiographically, my family was so bookish. My father read to the children before dinner, or after dinner, poems or history before we had to do our lessons. . . .

CONNELLY: You said you had to memorize a lot.

WARREN: That was in school; but of course we know education is in terrible condition. Don't deny that! One thing to be said for the schools in Guthrie, Kentucky, is that you had to memorize poems, good or bad. It's hard to believe it, but in a school of six rooms, twelve grades, and six teachers, I . . . and others . . . read *The White Devil* by John Webster. There was still some contact with literature. It was possible there, in a town like that. And men, the older men, you might say, the better farmers, many of them were men of bookishness.

CONNELLY: Do you think being a Kentuckian has had something to do with your approach to the difference between reality and myth? Louis Rubin said something in an essay about you, that more than most writers in Vanderbilt's group in the twenties you had more of a double vision, that you had more of a border-state way of thinking than Faulkner or Eudora Welty, that you never as much subscribed to the myths of the lower South as they did.

WARREN: I just don't know . . . I haven't thought about that. I always felt myself more of a Tennessean than a Kentuckian because . . . only a hundred yards from the state line. . . . And then I lived in Tennessee a lot. I went to col-

lege in Tennessee and taught there later on. So I always felt
Tennessee . . . I knew it better as a state. I felt it much
more my own country than Kentucky. I began to systematically investigate Kentucky later on.

CONNELLY: A lot of your work is Kentucky-oriented.

WARREN: Yes, but that was just my wanderings in Kentucky. . . . The time I've been wandering in Kentucky,
learned Kentucky.

CONNELLY: I think another part of that strikes me, another part
of that Kentucky or Tennessee influence on you . . . that
border-state influence is that you were really in the last Confederate generation, weren't you, the last generation of Confederate veterans, people who knew veterans, who heard their
tales?

WARREN: Well, I spent every summer from age six to fourteen
with a grandfather who had fought in the war. He was also
a very intelligent man, and a bookish man; and he, like my
father, quoted a lot of poetry at the drop of a hat. And he
had me read to him from an old book called *Napoleon and
His Marshals*—or he, on the ground, scratched the Battle of
Fort Pillow or Brice's Crossroads or other adventures and
explained the tactics thereof. So I felt quite Confederate in
that sense. It was purely a literary sense; I felt that that was
the way God had made it.

CONNELLY: My great-grandfather rode with Forrest, too; he's
the one I told you deserted after the Battle of Chickamauga.
One thing that strikes me again about that border-state area,
Tennessee and Kentucky, and growing up there, is that even
the Confederate army there never indulged in that mythol-
ogy of the army of planters' sons, such as the Army of
Northern Virginia has for an image today. It was the rather
hard-core western approach, people very much into evangelical religion—quite a different image from that of Robert E. Lee's army, wouldn't you say?

WARREN: That picture in general, I think, is right. But also,
let's not forget what was made of the Confederacy by the
Civil War writers who created a mythological Confederacy
which has gained much popularity in the North.

CONNELLY: Sometimes it was more popular in the North than in the South. You went to Vanderbilt when you were sixteen. You left Guthrie and Clarksville. Was it purely by accident that Vanderbilt flourished at this time as a cultural center? Wasn't 1914 the big date when the university won control of the school from the Methodist bishops?

WARREN: Sometime along there, before I can remember, anyway.

CONNELLY: Then right after that the Fugitive movement started, right before World War I. . . .

WARREN: Well, the Fugitive movement had so little to do with Vanderbilt. Certain members of the faculty thought it was rather a shame to be associated with the Fugitive group. It didn't seem good enough academically or something . . . but it started long before my days there. . . . It was before the war, before America got into the war anyway. Some were young businessmen: one was a young banker, one was a merchant . . . young men who were interested in philosophy rather than in poetry who met together because they liked each other, because they all had common interests. That's long before my time. They had all been fighting in the war and then going off to places like Oxford and the Sorbonne . . . as some of these young men did in that period. They got more interested in poetry and Ransom published his first book of poems, just after the war was over. I ran into a man in California, an editor out there, who said: "I know a friend of yours, I have a book of his. . . . He gave it to me the day the first two copies reached him in France." And he had the second copy. So this book came out during or just after the war when Ransom was still in uniform.

CONNELLY: Was that *Poems About God?*

WARREN: That's right. Ransom, as I remember, was an officer of regulars—Davidson of volunteers. They had very different attitudes toward the war. Ransom rarely mentioned it and certainly had no romantic view of war. He was the old twenty-year man, you know. He was in artillery. But there was something of a romantic spirit of war about Davidson. I once started out to be a naval officer. I had an appointment to Annapolis and couldn't go because of an accident. But my desire was to be admiral of the Pacific Fleet of course. . . . Who wouldn't want to be admiral of the Pacific Fleet? I could clearly tell there was going to be a war with Japan— but I was saved from the burning.

CONNELLY: After World War I, you were sixteen when you entered Vanderbilt in 1921 and became a member of the Fugitive group.

WARREN: I entered college in '21 so it must have been '23. I'm guessing now. I can't be sure. . . .

CONNELLY: My impression is the Fugitives had really kind of divided into two groups: those who took it seriously as a poetic exercise, like yourself and Ransom or Allen Tate, and some local businessmen whom you could almost call dilettantes.

WARREN: Well, they were serious in their thinking about it. Some of those men were clearly not poets . . . were not talented the way Ransom was, but they were serious about their interest and they would talk seriously. They could understand what was going on; they had opinions that were argued. I remember that quite well.

CONNELLY: You roomed with Allen Tate at the old Theological School.

WARREN: Well, when I was a freshman, the only undergraduate was a man named Ridley Wills who had been in the army in the Tennessee regiment that Luke Lea commanded.[46]

CONNELLY: The one that tried to capture the Kaiser.

WARREN: Tried to capture the Kaiser. Ridley had come back to finish his degree . . . and I was seeing a young man, an undergraduate who had written a real book published by a real New York publishing house. I thought that was quite wonderful, and it *is* quite wonderful when you are sixteen to have a friend like that. And he asked me to come room with him and he was rather a wag . . . a very funny man . . . a very great wit and so he said: "I'm getting a room over in the Theological Dormitory," which was a piece of early Methodist Gothic, about five stories high. And so we got a room over there among the theologs, as a kind of joke we were playing on ourselves. And then, the next thing he brought in Allen. It was a little bitty room and two double-decker beds. Allen took one of the double-decker beds. And then another came in and there were four of us. In the evenings among the dirty sheets and cigarette butts and not-quite-dry bottles in the corners, poetry was discussed and argued and so was modern philosophy. Tate and Wills were much older than the others and dominated. This became a kind of nameless club. Most people were undergraduates, but they led a very active undergraduate literary life . . . had the last of an old-fashioned kind of teaching in some of the classes. In freshman English you had to memorize at least nine hundred lines of Tennyson before Christmas and be tested on it. You had to memorize things.

CONNELLY: Did you memorize Coleridge?

WARREN: Not then, no. I found I could memorize poetry very easily because I had been living with it all my life with my father and my grandfather and so I enjoyed doing it. Many students would line up just to buy the latest *New Republic* to see the latest poem by Yeats or Frost that might be in there. There was a large, a big interest among the undergraduates. It is very hard to understand now in my later years of teaching, the lack of that, by and large, in the undergraduate body.

CONNELLY: So you say, Mr. Warren, that there were really two poetry groups at Vanderbilt?

WARREN: Two, quite different. One was undergraduate and this poetry club met regularly, wrote a great deal, published a book, a hard cover book of their own, before *The Fugitive—* or just after *The Fugitive* began to come out. Just after, I guess. The poetry of Eliot, particularly *The Waste Land*, had a tremendous impact. You could probably find twenty people who could quote it in the freshman and sophomore classes. This sounds romantic but it wasn't. There was a sense that this was new; something was happening or was felt to be happening. And there was! An interpenetration of the young students and people like Wills and Tate who were older, who were members of the Fugitive group through this room that I mentioned where Tate and I lived. You see, it was kind of an interrelationship and this was something I haven't seen duplicated—this passionate interest in an art or in certain ideas that occurred then. And later on, being personal: when I was struggling with my poems, Wills and Tate would come in; and I might be asleep; and they would sit down and start revising them or talk to me the next day about them . . . or criticize. So I was getting a kind of tutorial free during that period. But I was not alone. There were a lot of young men in the same situation, only I was more privileged by having these guardians, as it were, at hand.

CONNELLY: A lot of people who have written on you—as you well know there's a book of 275 pages which is nothing more than a bibliography of writing that you have done and a bibliography of things people have written about you. And a lot of people have commented on John Crowe Ransom's influence on you at this time—that there was a tremendous influence in two respects: one was in the nature of a poem. . . . Did he teach you something about what a poem was supposed to be?

WARREN: He taught it to everybody who would listen! In his class he always brought a new angle, a new view to the question of a poem and explained its especial qualities. Never, ever as a job, but always as a kind of running comment. And his influence on a lot of people—and many people have said this—was highly personal. That is, it was not the question of what he had to say or what he had in his head, but a kind of personal dignity and personal self-control that was felt by almost everybody around him; and he was a man who was greatly full of fun and loved poker and loved athletic activity.

CONNELLY: He almost believed that a poem was a miniature world, didn't he, an entity of interplay complete with a backdrop and landscape?

WARREN: I remember one thing when I saw his first book when I was a freshman. There's a man who's written a book. That was a great shock. There stands that little man who has written that book. And I read the book; and the book was mostly about the background that I knew. It was about the background of Tennessee, Kentucky, and north Mississippi, you see. And he somehow brought poetry into your world, my world. You felt it was a world that you inhabited. Now that book is not anything like his real books that came later, but it did bring the sense of poetry belonging to life, poetry being connected with life—with your life, your place. I remember that very strongly and the effect it had on me. . . . Later on I heard him say, "I want to be a domestic poet. I want to write about the small things of life as I live it." And you can see that in his poetry. Well, I must say that wasn't exactly my ambition . . . or the ambition of say, Allen Tate, but the perfection of Ransom, he was a perfectionist. His small poems are perfectly done . . . perfectly done, and of deep feeling. . . .

CONNELLY: Did he influence you a lot in your later approach to the New Criticism, and attention to text, to images?

WARREN: He always did. Later on it became more formalized. But he was constantly, from the time of the freshman class on. Mimms taught the poetry one day a week. Two days a week Ransom taught the writing; and the writing meant all sort of stylistic problems brought to the level that a freshman could understand. After the first term (I boast now a little bit), he said, "I'm taking you out of my class, I'm taking you to another class I have which is more concerned with the problems I'm now dealing with." And this was the greatest day of my life. That he would then give *me* some personal attention in another class of older people.

CONNELLY: I believe, in 1930, came *God Without Thunder* in which Ransom defended belief in religion; and he said in effect that religion was almost a metaphysical myth established in order to understand nature. One thing I've noticed about those of you gathered at Vanderbilt in that day is that most of you came out of that common heritage of middle Tennessee, southern Kentucky evangelical religion: Methodist/Baptist. . . .

WARREN: I came out of it with no religion at all. My father was called an old-fashioned free thinker who gave me Darwin to read when I was fourteen. He also made me read the Bible. . . . He played fair.

CONNELLY: But, don't you think as a group that religion, that Southern religion in the upper South did affect their whole view of being somewhere between the Old South, the agrarian South that had passed and the industrial New South?

WARREN: I think it may have had. Now let me tell you one thing about Ransom in *God Without Thunder*. In the end, that book is not a book about religion at all. It is a philosophical work. Because, really, it just dawned on me that that's what the book's about, not a theological book at all. Way back in 1931, standing in a kitchen, with a bottle of bourbon in hand, pouring me a drink, he said: "I find it very odd that I who am not a religious man, should write such a book; but I had to write it for the truth that's in it." Now he said that to me in '31 and it clarified something in my mind about it, myself being a very nonreligious man . . . not antireligious; that is, I have the deepest awareness of its importance. But I'm a yearner. I mean I wish I were religious. Ransom certainly said that religion is a necessary myth; a necessary myth is what he was saying—to paraphrase him. You see what I'm trying to say? I'm bumbling it I'm sure.

CONNELLY: In one form or another did not a lot of people in the Vanderbilt group in the twenties, some of whom were later in the Agrarian group, cope with religion? Allen Tate, for example, coped with religion in a different way.

WARREN: He was deeply concerned. He was a Catholic twice! And buried a Catholic.

CONNELLY: Your own approach wasn't a total rejection was it? You talked sometimes of what you said was a "religious sense" in your work. You've mentioned that several times.

WARREN: I think it is. It's about the quest for religion.

CONNELLY: After graduating you went to California and then went to graduate school and became in a sense, a non-Southerner. How important do you think it is in your own writing that you had a quality of what you would call alienation, being out of the South?

WARREN: May I interrupt just a second? I think I became a Southerner by going to California and to Connecticut and New England. When I was at Vanderbilt, I couldn't have been paid to go to the Scopes trial. I was right there by it. I was not concerned with it, at all. My Civil War was primarily anecdotal from my acquaintance with old soldiers. They were my old soldiers all right. When I went west I began to read, much more than in some of the graduate courses I had, Southern history and American history. That continued. I really became a Southerner by not being there.

CONNELLY: Do you think Southerners sometimes have a love/hate relationship with the South?

WARREN: Well, I think that is necessary, there's so much wrong with it and there's so much right with it. You have to have it divided. I was always not at ease with the whole race question and I wrote two books about it.

CONNELLY: *Segregation.* . . .

WARREN: . . . and then the other one [*Who Speaks for the Negro?*] Previously, the Agrarian thing was an essay about it. . . . It was a constant nag to me.

CONNELLY: In your book *Segregation,* which is subtitled *The Inner Conflict in the South,* you talk about the race problem as being one you called "self-division," not just division of a society between a Southerner and society but the self-division within a man.

WARREN: One woman, an extremely intelligent woman and a thoughtful woman, a well-educated woman, talking about this to me during the period that I was writing that book, said (she was a religious woman, too, in a very intelligent way, not just automatically so), "I pray to God to change some of my feelings about this question." Now she was really divided.

CONNELLY: As long as we're on this subject, may I ask you this? When the Agrarian movement came along—and I know that your relationship to the Vanderbilt Agrarians is quite different from many of them—that you were far less into the economic and political interests. But you received some criticism for your essay "The Briar Patch."

WARREN: Are you referring to criticism from my friends or others? I got both kinds!

CONNELLY: I was referring to criticism from others, that from a position standpoint they felt that your essay was attempting to defend a racial status quo.

WARREN: I was just very uncomfortable with the piece, but it was this. My position was exactly that of the Supreme Court. Equal, you see; "different but equal" was the view of the Supreme Court and of 99 percent of the white people in the country.

CONNELLY: You feel very strongly about that criticism of the thirties.

WARREN: Well, I think that point is quite clear. Unless I misremember the book entirely—and I haven't read it in a thousand years and don't intend to read it again—that was the basic legal view of the world and that was the one I took. Now that doesn't cover the whole case. There are all sorts of things gone and done and there was unevenness of all kinds. But I remember this quite distinctly that my father, who was a very remarkable man in many ways, saying to me when I made some slurring remark about a Negro, he said: "I have never found a man whom I have treated like a decent human being that has not treated me like one." Another time, using the word "nigger" in his presence. . . . "Never let me hear that word come out of your lips again!" These things I just told you occurred when I was ten or twelve, something like that. But the other part . . . equal pay/equal work, that's clear enough in there. And the Supreme Court view of equal schools and equality . . . but a social difference . . . a social distinction between them . . . a separation. And that's about all of that! Now the way I came back after many years away from the South . . . to live in the South in 1930. . . .

CONNELLY: When you came back to Vanderbilt?

WARREN: I came back to Memphis first, to Southwestern College. I was then struck by the quite undefinable pressures that were there. It didn't come under the picture I had remembered. I felt quite differently and bit by bit it crept into my poetry. Vinegar Hill was the name of a Negro graveyard in Todd County. And some others. There's something about a lynching in "Pondy Woods." It is something that has always been on my mind in some way or another. There was some sort of confusion of mind about it. Then in novels later on, it began to enter in. *Band of Angels* is such a book, a novel about that question primarily and what it means to be free. You can be enslaved in many ways, the book says. What does it mean to be free . . . the book's about that. Then there are the two books directly on the subject which I did first for *Life* magazine and the second for *Look* magazine. *Segregation* was done originally for *Life*. The other was done originally as an option for parts of it for *Look*. I had to have somebody to pay the bills. I was taking two years off, you see, to make a living. They would pick up the bills.

CONNELLY: I think one of the ironies of the criticism you received for "The Briar Patch" is that it was almost your only effort for the Agrarians. And yet, so many times people have identified you with the Vanderbilt Agrarians, but weren't you really a lot different?

WARREN: "Agrarianism" is just a word. It did not describe in any basic fashion to my mind what the thing was about. It was like a tent with a menagerie, with fifty kinds of animals under it. Disagreement was more important than agreement. Now for instance, in the industrialized, mechanized world, a man like Ransom would feel, I think, primarily that other things, too, are involved here, not only economic problems, but would also feel that this is a misunderstanding of man's relationship to nature . . . using nature as a thing to be exploited, as a tool of man and not as man having a relationship to nature which is both aesthetic and spiritual. See what I'm driving at? I think his emphasis was going somewhere in that direction and mine would have gone somewhere in that direction, too.

CONNELLY: But not Donald Davidson?

WARREN: Not Donald Davidson! In many ways, he was like those people who see the violation of nature as a way to commit suicide, for society to commit suicide. Then there are the people who really took it as a way to go live, like Andrew Lytle's buying a farm, and running a farm and trying to be a writer at the same time! Well, you can be a writer at the same time if you don't write very much! I know enough about farming to know it takes time. I would never have tried . . . I like to live in the country. I do live in the country. I have a place in the country in Vermont and I have a place in the country in Connecticut.

CONNELLY: The land was more of a metaphor for you wasn't it?

WARREN: That was the place to be alone. A year's time in the city is enough for me. I have been in many cities but that's enough. I want to see myself in relation to the natural objects. That is an important point in my life and I basically live in the country. I go to the city and I've lived in many cities. I've lived in San Francisco a long time and then New York and Rome and other cities . . . Paris, and London . . . but I don't stay there.

CONNELLY: One thing I've noticed . . . one difference between you and the other Agrarians is the way you deal with history. That you were never that concerned with the events, rather what you called the historical sense, the meaning of the event, the philosophy of the event. I've seen that even in your poetry. I brought one of your poems which I wish you would read for the audience. It's from "Kentucky Mountain Farm." It's "History Among the Rocks."

WARREN: This is so long ago. I'm turning now back to my twenties. I'm glad it's not a mirror. This is also a poem that involves, you might say, the divided world of the Confederacy, of the Civil War. And I was thinking specifically here of a division of the hill sections of Kentucky—which these sections of Kentucky were, then completely unknown to me firsthand. This was purely just fact I knew from other sources. I had never been in the Kentucky mountains until I was a grown man, quite grown.

History Among the Rocks

There are many ways to die
Here among the rocks in any weather;
Wind down the eastern gap, will lie
Level along the snow, beating the cedar,
And lull the drowsy head that it blows over
To startle a cold and crystalline dream forever.

The hound's black paw will print the grass in May,
And sycamores rise down a dark ravine,
Where a creek in flood, sucking the rock and clay,
Will tumble the laurel, the sycamore away.
Think how a body, naked and lean
And white as the splintered sycamore, would go
Tumbling and turning, hushed in the end,
With hair afloat in waters that gently bend
To ocean where the blind tides flow.

Under the shadow of ripe wheat,
By flat limestone, will coil the copperhead,
Fanged as the sunlight, hearing the reaper's feet.
But there are other ways, the lean men said:
In these autumn orchards once young men lay dead—
Gray coats, blue coats. Young men on the mountainside
Clambered, fought. Heels muddied the rocky spring.
Their reason is hard to guess, remembering
Blood on their black mustaches in moonlight.
Their reason is hard to guess and a long time past:
The apple falls, falling in the quiet night.

CONNELLY: Someone said about you that you are not a historical poet, historical novelist, but that you are a philosophical
poet and novelist who uses history for understanding. History permeates so much of your poetry . . . and your fiction, of course.

WARREN: I don't see a sharp division between the use of history in the two things. I can see what they meant by saying
that. Looking back on the origins of one thing, a poem,

another thing a novel, I see something very similar, not basically different. Now the poetry tends to be more philosophical because it's less narrative. It has only an echo of narrative in it. Most poetry does.

CONNELLY: Your use of history is not just facts; it's symbols, really.

WARREN: It is the significance of those facts.

CONNELLY: Do you think a poet or a novelist, I always thought so, in some ways can be a better historian than a historian? That he can generalize about. . . .

WARREN: Well, he might be. . . . Which historian?

CONNELLY: This idea of tension in history, of tension between the past and the present certainly permeates at least the first five of your novels.

WARREN: Novel after novel that I have written, and poem after poem, have had some germ in historical reality. I mean it had some germ in it. It's interpreting that not as mere history, but as history moralized, to use a more obvious word.

CONNELLY: I know in your first five novels you had this common theme of a search for understanding and this kind of tension between the ideal and the practical—of a self-division within a person as he gropes for understanding in reaching back to the past. I got the impression when I read *The Legacy of the Civil War* that you were taking the same structure and applying it to the nation as a whole.

WARREN: Well, I wouldn't deny that. I wouldn't know how to deny that, really. I think I see what you mean more clearly now.

CONNELLY: Do you think the Civil War was the great Southern experience, the great catalyst?

WARREN: Well, it's the thing that we most violently lived through as a nation. It also produced our power. And I'm glad of our power, but I think there is also a great danger in the kind of victory that was had. We have been lulled into the assumption that the mechanical expert and the advertising man can control all the values of life. I can't quite bring myself to believe that.

CONNELLY: And I think in sixty years of writing, in your poems and your criticism and your fiction, that you never have believed that.

WARREN: I never have.

CONNELLY: Mr. Warren, I want to thank you for giving us this interview and again we regret that you can't be with us at the Institute for Southern Studies at the University of South Carolina.

WARREN: I regret it deeply for personal reasons, not that I regret I can't bring the wisdom fresh off the griddle, but I regret not seeing your human presences before me.

A Conversation with Robert Penn Warren

███

On April 15, 1985, Tom Vitale interviewed Warren, honoring him for his eightieth birthday (April 24) and for the publication of New and Selected Poems, 1923–1985. *Vitale aired parts of the interview on his radio program "A Moveable Feast," and later published the complete version in the* Ontario Review.

TOM VITALE: Many of your poems are filled with images of memory and mortality and references to time. Do you think it's fair to say that you're obsessed with time?

WARREN: I can only answer by saying that I was born of human flesh.

VITALE: But after you say that, what can you say about time? You have a reference to knowing time, but we can't really know time, can we?

WARREN: An old question I encountered first in conversation with a professor of medieval literature. He said, "What is 'now'? What does 'now' mean? 'Now' is all that is passing. Have you felt a 'now'? He was quoting a passage from St.

Augustine, from *The Confessions*. The question of how man
lives in time: he's constantly aware of it, or should be. He's
always dating himself in one way or another—tomorrow,
yesterday. He's trying to find a place in time. And I don't
think it's morbid at all—it's only natural. We're consigned to
that. And you think of the past, you think of parents and
grandparents and you feel your way back, back to what?
You have children: you think forward. To what? You're in
a flow, and it's only natural to swim, if you can.

VITALE: Many images in your poetry show careful observation
of nature. Would you consider your work to be in the
Romantic tradition?

WARREN: I don't think that way. I know perfectly well how it
began, because a boy a couple of years older than I was,
when I was seven, was a real woodsman. . . . He'd go to
the woods, and take me with him. He was two years older
than I, and a hundred years older in experience. Going to the
woods was a great escape, because I spent all my summers at
my grandfather's farm. Nobody ever came there; he didn't
want to see people. He said, "Any man here who opens his
mouth, I know every word he's going to say. Why talk to
him?" And he lived with his books and so forth, and talked
about his adventures in life. I'd go to the woods, or the cane
brakes, or swimming holes all summer, and I got the habit of
observation. And I continue with my wife. We'll go to the
mountains of Vermont, at every opportunity, where we have
a place.

VITALE: You were born in Kentucky. Your roots are in the
South, in the rural South. As a young man, you were asso-
ciated with Southern intellectuals, the Fugitives and the
Agrarians.

WARREN: Well, the Fugitive group, . . . that was my university, . . . grown men with books and things like that, discussing high matters—it was wonderful! That's what a real
university should be like. That was my "Classics."

VITALE: And those groups took a stand against industrialization
and urbanization?

WARREN: Well, the poets weren't much concerned about that.

Some of the people there got involved in something else later on, of their own manufacture. They were opposed, I think quite justly, to the excesses and confusions of the modern, mechanized world. Now people who were born into that world and don't know anything else, don't understand that.

VITALE: And how did you feel at that time?

WARREN: I was a boy. I wasn't even there at the time that was going on. But they asked me to write an essay on the race question. I was in England then, doing graduate work at Oxford. And I tried to say what I thought. And my view was simply this: that (this was in 1928 or '9, a long time ago)—and this was perfectly legalistic, mind you—that as far as prejudice, the Supreme Court's decision on race at that time, follow it honestly. Separate but equal: I wanted equal, that's all.

VITALE: What was the reaction to that?

WARREN: Well, some didn't agree, and some did. Those I was closest to, agreed. The South has always been a very mixed package. When I was a boy, I used the word "nigger" once at home. My father said, "If you go on living under this roof, you're never to use that word again in my presence." And he said, "I don't know a man black or white who, I treated him decently, did not try to treat me decently." My grandfather, who was an officer of the cavalry under Forrest, said, "I didn't join the Army when it was first talked about, because I didn't want to see the country Balkanized." I never heard the word before, or since. He said, "My folks helped found the country," and they did. And he said, "I didn't want it Balkanized." And he said, "Slavery? Anybody could see that slavery was an outmoded mode of labor." "But," he said, "when they put their feet on Virginia soil, I joined, as a private."

VITALE: So you had a real personal sense of American history.

WARREN: Well, I knew something about family, I did, and it was a bookish family. . . . But then I came back to the South in '31, and I was then twenty-five years old. I got the notion that "separate but equal" had proved itself ineffective.

Because nowhere was "equal" taken seriously. Anyway, I was in California; I lived there for a couple of years. Orientals were treated like dogs. The Californians would say, "How are the Negroes treated in the South?" Same thing. Another race. And I lost faith in the "equal" business, bit by bit. And then I got very much concerned with the race question later on. I spent several years over this; I wrote two books about it, one called *Segregation*, which is a trip, just a trip I had taken privately here and there in the South, talking to people. This became an article in *Life* magazine.

It wasn't big enough because I got too interested in the question. So I went, or my agent went, to *Look* and made a contract with them. They would pay all expenses for two years or so of travel, and all the expenses of interviewing, and so forth, if I would devote my time to it and mix in some poems, and I was in Mississippi and all over the place and talked to everybody. You can't call Martin Luther King and say, "Let's talk sometime." You say to his secretary, "Look I'm doing a piece for *Look* and I have a contract for a book to come out thereafter." You know what he thought: "Oh, yes!" You couldn't get anyone who wouldn't fall for it, except Malcolm X. But he I got in the end. He was one of the smartest men I ever knew in my life. He sat there with two of his goons, one on each side of him. And he said, "I'll give you ten minutes. You newspapermen are all liars." I said, "I never worked on a newspaper in my life." We stayed there for three hours. He had a real boxer's mentality. He came out always from his corner. He was powerful, you know. And when it got to be three hours, I said, "I got to go now. I'm sorry." And he said, "Come back tomorrow. I got the day off." I was going to Italy the next day. I couldn't go. Too bad. He was killed five months later, in February.

VITALE: Are you still interested in race relations? How do you feel now?

WARREN: Well, I see it's a different story now. Now, Malcolm X was partly to blame for that, but not entirely. He had changed his mind in the end, definitely. He said to me,

"Muslims"—he was a Black Muslim—"I went to Mecca, as a Muslim you see, and I said, My God, there were people there that had blue eyes and yellow hair!" And so he recanted on the black nationalism. That's why he got killed. Anyway, I just watch things, now. It's just curiosity. It was a sideline; it wasn't my profession. I wanted to be a writer. But meanwhile, poetry had taken over entirely for me. I had been writing mostly fiction, or reading American history. I love American history. But poetry became more and more important.

VITALE: Since the 1950's you've been primarily writing poetry.

WARREN: Yes. I had been writing a lot of poetry before, since I was sixteen or seventeen, and took it seriously, or tried to, and had it published a lot by that time. But that last period in the late forties, most short poems would die on me. . . . But it was in the early sixties when my poems first began again. We were living in Italy, Eleanor and I; I got married sometime in the early fifties, and we went to live at a place where she had lived—a fortress on the Mediterranean, ninety miles north of Rome on a seacliff, the sea on three sides and a mountain beyond, and a tremendous view of a Renaissance fortress. . . . And we had a little baby, and the sight of this little baby—a beautiful little yellow-headed kid—I finally wrote a poem about that baby ["Sirocco"] and started all over again. Poems came, and they kept on coming. The next little boy came along the year after, and then the book *Promises* in '56, a book of those poems, was laid in that place; and recollections of my own childhood, and my own world as a child, were in the same book, *Promises*. And the book had success—a Pulitzer Prize, among other things.

VITALE: For many people, you're best known for *All the King's Men*, your novel.

WARREN: Oh, that was '45, '46.

VITALE: Yes, I know. You've been writing primarily poetry, and you've written a lot of criticism. How would you evaluate those separate facets of your writing?

WARREN: I don't. They're things I wanted to do, that's all. I got interested in them. There was no plan to it. How the interest took hold—how does anyone know? The poetry was always primary for me, from the start, from fifteen, sixteen, seventeen on. There were things I was interested in and went off and pursued.

VITALE: And you've said elsewhere the idea you want to get across is primary and not the form, that you're fluid. If an idea started out as a poem, you could also express it in fiction.

WARREN: Sometimes you start, that's all. *All the King's Men* started out as a verse play. I began under an olive tree, by the side of a wheat field, in Umbria. . . . I finished it by a lake in northern Italy, and in Rome. I sent it to Kenneth Burke and two or three other friends whose opinions I valued, a few days before Christmastime that year, '39. The war had already started by early fall. I got permission to stay in Italy, and I stayed on until they let the refugees out at the end of the war.

But back to *All the King's Men*. . . . Years later (I had discarded it—it didn't succeed), I took it out of a drawer and looked at it again, at the writing. And I thought, "No, this couldn't be a play. That's too cramping." It has to be a novel, because the vague notion in the play was that a man of power isn't a man who has the power to dominate other people, though he has something of that, but he feels some need to have it. They feel in him a frustration to help them. So the play then—the novel then—became something else. You had to populate this whole world to get a sense of him. You couldn't do it in a verse play: that was too tight to read. See what I mean? So, well, Adam: he does things for many people, but what he does for them is always very different. For Jack Burden, a man with no sense of direction—brilliant, but with no sense of direction—he gives him something to *do*. Which he does cynically. It's a form of life for him. He had no ambition, no direction. . . .

Well, it just goes on and, finally, the woman, the other woman, Stark's sister, he seduces her. He gives her something she couldn't have before, some sense, as with her brother, some meaning to life: he brings her that. And all the people around him have the same sense. That's what makes power. It's not being strong; it's knowing instinctively how to use other people, without thinking about it.

VITALE: And how did you get interested in the question of power?

WARREN: Well, I had been interested in that before. I had written one novel about it already; it's just been republished. That novel [*At Heaven's Gate*] was also about politics in another state: Tennessee. But I wasn't writing about Long: I didn't know anything about him. I never saw him in my life—and I never tried to talk to him. I was interested in the myth of Long, not Long himself: I couldn't have cared less.

VITALE: You talked before about nature, about writing what you see. But with politics, that's something else, unless you're observing very carefully.

WARREN: Well, I couldn't have cared less about what any individual politician *did*. I was interested in a notion that seemed to be borne out by history, from Caesar on—before that too, really.

VITALE: Did you find that certain forms are better for certain subjects? You talked about *All the King's Men* starting as a verse play and then becoming a novel, because of the situation. But are novels better for writing about power, and poems better for writing about mortality?

WARREN: Well, it depends upon what kind of form it is. Now, I wouldn't offhand make it general like that. It depends on who's doing it, and what. For me, it had to be that way. Now, I don't think I could have written Shakespeare's *Julius Caesar*, for instance. I don't think I'd have been up to it. But in my little play, that later on became a better play and was published and acted several times, were the seeds of the novel that grew slowly out of an idea that I had long before I saw Louisiana. But Long was an example of it, that was the thing: what he meant to people, not what he was. I had no idea what he was like. I'm sure he was a son-of-a-bitch, in many ways.

VITALE: What about literary influences? You've said that you were steeped in Shakespeare when you were young.

WARREN: I taught the senior Shakespeare course for seven or eight years in the university. If you want to write, immerse yourself as best you can in the best stuff that's been written.

VITALE: What other writers had powerful influences on your ideas and your own writing?

WARREN: Well, it's hard to pick and choose, but I can tell you, all kinds of writers. Folk balladry became very important to me. And at the same time, in the old days, in the country school, some old warhorse of a teacher would make you memorize a poem a week, and stand there and recite it. The poetry wasn't very good, some of it, sure—Longfellow was one of them; some of them were—but you had to memorize the whole poem—you had to, goddammit, to pass! And then in college, in freshman English, one day a week—one class a week was taught by somebody else (not the regular teacher, a Brahmin, you know)—you had to memorize that term nothing but Tennyson. You studied Tennyson all term. You had to soak in one man a term of freshman English year. You had to memorize a minimum of 700 lines and prove it. And they had a very tricky way of finding out, too. They gave a bonus for every fifty lines above that. Having been to a country school, I had no trouble memorizing. You get soaked in the poetry of a poem. And then as you get older, you get interested in it. Blake I got soaked in, and Keats, and Donne, the Elizabethans and the Metaphysical poets of that period. Plus the Shakespeare poems. And so, if you liked it you'd go into it—just as simple as that. So your head is full of it. Whether you know it, you find you've picked it up, things you never even knew you picked up.

And now I've tried in classes in universities, advanced students, every year, "Who can quote a poem?" And only one time has anyone ever said, "I can!" and quoted one—a good one—by William Butler Yeats. And this has just drifted out of the world. Except for the poets, I guess. They naturally do it because they want to.

VITALE: Should teachers today encourage learning poetry through recitation?

WARREN: Well, I think so. If they're going to teach it at all—

go ahead and teach it! You know, a kid doesn't know whether he likes it or not or whether it's interesting or not. My children have been to school in France and every week they had to learn a poem by a good French poet. And I've seen kids catch fire that way. My son did. And I sent him to a French school and he didn't know French—a little bit, maybe. He was only about nine or ten. And he was angry for several months, and then suddenly he loved it; he'd go about and quote poems with me. You get hooked.

VITALE: Is there any particular direction that very recently you find your poetry moving in?

WARREN: I can't say that. For one reason, it hasn't crossed my mind to be curious about it, except in individual cases. There are some poems I'm no longer interested in, that I was once mad for. That's bound to happen. And I certainly wouldn't want to write the same way anymore. I have a new batch of poems—they're too much like the ones here [*New and Selected Poems*]. I'm not going to publish them in a book. You find that self-imitation you've got to guard against all the time, because you've done something that seems to work a little bit, and then you do another just like it. Uh-uh—that's a bad sign. Stop! Start over again! Retool! Give yourself a chance to retool. And you go through that many times. And if you just take a book that's a long time-period collection like this, you can see it. . . . Some poems I have written are in magazines, but I wouldn't put them in a book. They lack a new impulse. You can tell phases. You go through a certain phase and you realize when it's done, as quick as you can. You're just imitating yourself. You can do that trick over and over again, if you want to. Some poets do their whole lives. That's death. Now growth is another thing. You can have the same thing continuing in terms of development; that's one thing. But to repeat yourself in the same old way: that's death. And you have to fight it, all the time.

VITALE: Your work is unique and distinctive. Do you feel allied with any of your contemporaries among the poets?

WARREN: Well, I admire a great many of them. It's been a very rich century. There are many fine poets in it. But, again, you have to try to be yourself in some way, and you can say this of all poetry, probably: any poet's work is a long attempt to define himself.

VITALE: Are you satisfied with the definition you've come to?

WARREN: Satisfied isn't the word. You do the best you can, period.

VITALE: Do you feel you've got it?

WARREN: When you feel you've got it, you're through.

VITALE: You've grown up with the century.

WARREN: Well, I was born in 1905, so my awareness didn't begin until 1920, say.

VITALE: But as you say, there's been a lot of fine literature created in your lifetime.

WARREN: In my lifetime—I remember when *The Waste Land* was first published. I was a sophomore in college. And there must have been twelve boys in my class who could quote the whole damned thing. . . . And it was unbelievable. None of us, I'm sure, could have written an essay, when it came out, or analyzed it. But it hit you. This last summer, I read the whole of Eliot's work again, just to be sure how I felt about it. *The Waste Land* still works. Even with all the nonsense and dissemblance about it, it still works. Even though it's a false picture of the universe we live in, that's not the point. He's writing in his own times.

VITALE: And at this point, in the mid-1980s, are you optimistic about the future of English literature and American letters?

WARREN: Well, I cross my fingers. We'll see. There are certainly some damned good poets around, right now. I had dinner with two of them in Boston last week; they're quite remarkable. They're both non-Americans—Seamus Heaney and Derek Walcott. Our daughter teaches in Boston, and in fact she's a poet, and she's a friend of theirs, and she had a little dinner when we were there and they were among the guests. And I know their works pretty well and they're both fine poets, very fine poets. I got a lot out of them, personally, too. What an evening! And Richard Eberhart is a poet who's never had his due. He's published so much. And you can't tell one poem from another, in a way, but you don't have to.

He's a good poet, marvelous. I hate to say this—on this thing [tape], anyway—because I like him, but I won't take it back—but he is a marvelous poet. I've read his poems since way, way back—my God, fifty-nine years.

VITALE: Well, what do you like in a poem? What's your criteria for what's good in a line when you read it?

WARREN: Well, I don't know. Any word I use would be wrong. If I had a line before me, I could say something about any poem, but not a line. You have to have more of a context. But the line itself must fully be what it means. And I'll give you an example. When Antony comes back from the battle after Cleopatra has fled in her own ship—she's just trying to see if he'll follow her. What a witch! And he does. And the battle's gone. The world is gone from his hands, at that moment. Now, in Shakespeare's play, Antony says, "Unarm, Eros, the long day's task is done and we must sleep." Listen how it goes: the line gives the emotion of what is said, in words: "And we must sleep." See how the line flattens out? It says what it means: it *is* what it means. The isness of meaning is what the purpose of a line of a poem should be.

Notes

1. Gabriel Thomas Penn, who lived in Cerulean Springs (now Cerulean), Kentucky.
2. *Brother to Dragons* (New York: Random House, 1953; New Version, New York: Random House, 1979).
3. Walter Clyde Curry, Professor of English, Vanderbilt University.
4. Filmore Stuart Cuckow Northrop, Professor of Philosophy, Yale University.
5. Herbert Cushing Tolman, Professor of Greek, Vanderbilt University.
6. Herbert Charles Sanborn, Chairman, Department of Philosophy, Vanderbilt University.
7. See Poe, "The Philosophy of Composition."
8. Henry Crabb Robinson, *Blake, Coleridge, Wordsworth, Lamb, etc.*, ed. Edith J. Morley (Manchester: Manchester University Press, 1932), p. 53.
9. The Rockefeller Foundation sponsored the Fugitive Reunion at Vanderbilt University, 1956.
10. The actual title is "How They Brought the Good News from Ghent to Aix."
11. Adam Gurowski, author of *America and Europe* (1857) and *My Diary: Notes on the Civil War* (1866).
12. Warren was quoting from memory. Compare this quotation with *Brother to Dragons* (1953), p. 194.

13. Editor at Harcourt Brace, later director of the University of North Carolina Press.

14. *Renaissance in the South: A Critical History of the Literature, 1920–1940* (Chapel Hill: University of North Carolina Press, 1963).

15. Albert Erskine, Warren's editor at Random House, was a friend of Warren and Cleanth Brooks at Louisiana State University, where he was business manager of the *Southern Review.* Erskine married Katherine Anne Porter in 1938; they separated two years later.

16. American writer John Hersey, author of *A Bell for Adano, Hiroshima,* and other works. He has referred to himself as "a novelist of contemporary history."

17. Rosanna Phelps Warren, now a poet.

18. *Arturo's Island* (New York: Alfred A. Knopf, 1959).

19. Anthony West, *New Yorker,* 12 September 1964, pp. 204–5.

20. *Go Down, Moses* was published in the spring of 1942 and had been out for two years when the novel by Lillian Smith appeared.

21. With some revision, this version was later produced at the University of Minnesota, thanks to the intervention of Eric Bentley. The later prose version was first produced by Irwin Piscator at the President Theatre in New York in 1948.

22. Coleridge actually wrote that he "wrote down the lines" before he was "called out by a person on business."

23. Compare Keats's description of what he called "negative capability."

24. Compare *Brother to Dragons* (1953), pp. 42–43.

25. Charles W. Pipkin, Dean of the LSU Graduate School, was editor of the magazine when it was founded in 1935, and Cleanth Brooks and Warren were managing editors. Later all three held the title of editor.

26. Van Wyck Brooks, *The Flowering of New England* (New York: Dutton, 1936).

27. See Thomas Jefferson to Martha Jefferson, 28 March 1787, *The Papers of Thomas Jefferson,* II, ed. Julian P. Boyd (Princeton: Princeton University Press, 1955), pp. 250–51.

28. See *Who Owns America?: A New Declaration of Independence,* edited by Herbert Agar and Allen Tate (Boston: Houghton Mifflin, 1936). Warren was one of the contributors.

29. See Warren's poem "Flaubert in Egypt," *Selected Poems, 1923–1975* (New York: Random House, 1976), p. 55.

30. See "Court-Martial," *Selected Poems, 1923–1975*, p. 228.

31. The "big book" was *Local and National Poets of America*, edited and compiled by Thomas W. Herringshaw in 1890, not 1895. This book probably was a vanity publication.

32. The quotation from John Crowe Ransom's preface to the first number of *The Fugitive* actually reads: "*The Fugitive* flees from nothing faster than from the high-caste Brahmins of the Old South."

33. The offices of the Louisiana State University Press were across the hall from those of *The Southern Review*. The LSU Press published *An Approach to Literature* in 1936; the revised edition was published by F. S. Crofts & Co. in 1939.

34. Warren apparently means after Prohibition, which began January 17, 1920, and ended December 5, 1933.

35. *Meet Me in the Green Glen* (New York: Random House, 1971) and *A Place to Come To* (New York: Random House, 1976), pp. 13–17.

36. See note 31.

37. Kent Greenfield, K in "American Portrait: Old Style," *New and Selected Poems*, pp. 137–41.

38. Newspaper editor in Greenville, Mississippi, famous for his early stands on civil rights. His son Hodding Carter III later served in the Carter administration.

39. "Old Nigger on One-Mule Cart Encountered Late at Night When Driving Home from Party in the Back Country," *New and Selected Poems*, pp. 170–73.

40. Legend, without any foundation in fact, identified Audubon as the lost Dauphin, son of Louis XVI and Marie Antoinette and heir to the throne of France.

41. *Jefferson's Nephews: A Frontier Tragedy* (Princeton: Princeton University Press, 1976).

42. For a fee of $75 Melville read his lecture "Statuary in Rome" to the Clarksville Literary Association on January 22, 1858, according to Jay Leyda, *The Melville Log: A Documentary Life of Herman Melville* (New York: Harcourt Brace, 1951), II, 590.

43. Ridley Wills published two novels, *Hoax* (New York: Doran, 1922) and *Harvey Landrum* (New York: Simon & Schuster, 1924).

44. Sherwood Anderson, *The Triumph of an Egg: A Book of Impressions from American Life in Tales and Poems* (New York: B. W. Huebsch, 1921).

45. Charles Moss prevented Warren's suicide.

46. Luke Lea became an unscrupulous financier in Tennessee; his career coincided with Warren's tenure as a student at Vanderbilt. Lea is the prototype of Bogan Murdock in *At Heaven's Gate*.

Index